# NATIONALISM, GLOBALIZATION, AND ORTHODOXY

# NATIONALISM, GLOBALIZATION, AND ORTHODOXY

## The Social Origins of Ethnic Conflict in the Balkans

Victor Roudometof
*Foreword by Roland Robertson*

Contributions to the Study of World History, Number 89

GREENWOOD PRESS
Westport, Connecticut • London

**Library of Congress Cataloging-in-Publication Data**

Roudometof, Victor, 1964–
    Nationalism, globalization, and orthodoxy : the social origins of ethnic conflict in the
Balkans / Victor Roudometof ; foreword by Roland Robertson.
        p.  cm.—(Contributions to the study of world history, ISSN 0885–9159 ; no. 89)
    Includes bibliographical references and index.
    ISBN 0–313–31949–9 (alk. paper)
    1. Balkan Peninsula—Ethnic relations—History.  2. Balkan Peninsula—Ethnic
relations—Social aspects.  3. Balkan Peninsula—Ethnic relations—Religious aspects.  4.
Nationalism—Balkan Peninsula.  5. Globalization.  I. Robertson, Roland.  II. Series.
DR24.R682001
320.9496—dc21        00–069154

British Library Cataloguing in Publication Data is available.

Library of Congress Catalog Card Number: 00–069154
ISBN: 0–313–31949–9
ISSN: 0885–9159

First published in 2001

Greenwood Press, 88 Post Road West, Westport, CT 06881
An imprint of Greenwood Publishing Group, Inc.
www.greenwood.com

Printed in the United States of America

The paper used in this book complies with the
Permanent Paper Standard issued by the National
Information Standards Organization (Z39.48–1984).

10 9 8 7 6 5 4 3 2 1

**Copyright Acknowledgments**

Parts of Chapters 1 and 2 are adapted from Victor Roudometof, "From *Rum Millet* to Greek Nation: Enlightenment, Secularization, and National Identity in Ottoman Balkan Society, 1453–1821," *Journal of Modern Greek Studies* 16 (1998): 11–48. © The Johns Hopkins University Press.

Chapter 4 is a slightly revised version of my "Invented Traditions, Symbolic Boundaries, and National Identity in Southeastern Europe: Greece and Serbia in Comparative-Historical Perspective (1830–1880)," *East European Quarterly* 32, no. 4 (January 1999): 429–68.

Chapter 6 is a revised and extended version of my "The Social Origins of Balkan Politics: Nationalism, Underdevelopment, and the Nation-State in Greece, Serbia, and Bulgaria, 1880–1920," *Mediterranean Quarterly* 3, no. 3 (summer 2000): 146–64. © Mediterranean Affairs, Inc.

Parts of the introduction and the conclusions are adapted from my preview article, "Nationalism, Globalization, Eastern Orthodoxy: 'Unthinking' the 'Clash of Civilizations' in Southeastern Europe," *European Journal of Social Theory* 2, no. 2 (1999): 234–47. Reprinted by permission of Sage Publications Ltd.

For my parents

# Contents

# Illustrations

# Foreword

In this book Victor Roudometof applies much of globalization theory to one of the most fateful circumstances of our times, namely, the tragic events in the Balkans since the early 1990s. It should be emphasized that he mainly approaches these recent and continuing conflicts and tensions historically. In other words, his primary concern is with locating the present situation within a sociological history of Southeastern Europe. This history attends in particular to the impact of the Enlightenment of Western and Central Europe on the Balkan area, the rise of nationalism with an ethnic face, and the closely related collision between the Ottoman Empire and predominantly Christian Europe. This collision is one of the least studied of the various substantive issues that have attracted the gaze of globalization theorists. Roudometof performs a great intellectual service in illustrating the relationship between the Ottoman Empire and West-Central Europe in reference to the specificities of the Balkan region.

In applying what he calls a world-historical perspective to this theme, Roudometof successfully pushes this relationship to center stage. In saying this, I mean not only to highlight the importance of the complex relationship between Islamic Ottomanism, Eastern Orthodox Christianity, the Austro-Hungarian Empire, and the contentious Christianity of much of Europe (particularly after the Protestant Reformation of the sixteenth century), but also to indicate its virtually *worldwide* significance. Although Roudometof does not dwell on this aspect, it is also of considerable import that, following the demise of the Ottoman, Hapsburg, and Romanov Empires at the close of the Great War of 1914–1918, the tensions of many centuries were to continue in another form, with what became Yugoslavia in the 1920s, at the center of these tensions. In continuation of Old Russia's imperial ambitions and, specifically, in its seeking to obtain sea access to the Mediterranean, Soviet Communism became a formidable enemy of the West.

This was, of course, short-lived in comparison with the temporal length of the Ottoman Empire, not least because the center of the latter—namely, the Turkish Republic that came into existence in 1923 in the wake of the war of 1914–1918—was later constrained into joining the NATO alliance against Soviet Communism. Nonetheless, the nonaligned status of Tito's Yugoslavia, combined with the charismatic authoritarianism of his polyethnic/multicultural policy, made what had previously been seen as the contentious area of the Balkans a pivotal feature of the Cold War, defined mainly by the hostile relationship between the United States and the USSR. In sum, it seems to have been the destiny of the Balkan and the East Mediterranean area to be at the political center of the world as a whole. The Yugoslavia of Tito involved the precarious coexistence of a number of ethnic groups, which the Communist Party rather successfully succeeded in playing off against each other until Tito's death and then the collapse of Soviet-style Communism, although the sleep of nationalism had ended by the time of this demise at the end of the 1980s. In view of the events of the last few years, it is difficult for many to realize that, for many socialists in Western Europe, Tito's Yugoslavia was often exhibited as a model form of socialism.

Roudometof's deployment of multidimensional globalization theory is striking in his attempt to come to terms, historically and sociologically speaking, with the problems of the Balkans and its contextualization. There is a not infrequent tendency to regard Southeastern Europe as more or less unique as a tinder-box. But it is carefully shown in this book that, insofar as this is the case, it can be accounted for in world-historical terms by an admittedly very complex set of globalizing processes. In using the concept of globalization, Roudometof eschews the very recent and mainly ideological meaning that nowadays is attributed to this term. Instead he invokes and utilizes globalization in a strictly conceptual way, as opposed to a figure of rhetoric of contemporary politics. This means giving economic issues their due, as in his use of world-systems analysis, but relating them to cultural, social, and political developments, as well as conceiving of globalization as a very long process, extending over many centuries.

Well aware of and deeply involved in sophisticated discussions of globalization, world-systems, world society, and yet other frames of reference for the analysis of long-term global change, Roudometof is well placed to consider in detail the growth of nationalism in the Balkan area during the nineteenth century. In a more humanistic vein, however, I certainly do not wish to minimize what may reasonably be called the Balkans tragedy by placing it *in context*. It is one of the moral perils of much of contemporary globalization theory (in its noneconomistic sense) that it involves the ongoing relativization of *everything* and thus runs the risk of rendering every horror as but one among many others. However,

Roudometof does not run into this problem, particularly since the spatial and temporal scope of his book is so extensive.

It is conventional to think of globalization and nationalism as necessarily in tension. However, as Roudometof shows, this is a particularly egregious fallacy of the recent discussion of these two motifs. Nationalism has largely developed as an aspect of globalization rather than as simply a reaction to it. One feature of the connection is that nationalism developed as a cultural idea via its diffusion across what were to become national boundaries, or—to put it another way—much of the growth of nationalism in the crucial period of the nineteenth century rested, in part, on collaboration among nationalists from different regions of Europe. Stated in either of these forms, it begins to become clear that the idea of an historic and continuous clash between globalization in its comprehensive sense and nationalism is implausible. This is not to say that some nationalisms do not derive their force from reaction against the perception of allegedly homogenizing forces of globalization, but for the most part nationalism has, as I have stressed, been a critical aspect of globalization itself. One might summarize the major issue here by making a rough distinction between nationalism within the world and nationalism against the world. There have been relatively few examples of the latter. One of these in fact has been in Southeastern Europe, namely, Albania in the period between its break with Soviet Communism and the overthrow of communism in the conventional sense around the same time as the recent Balkan crisis.

Roudometof rightly emphasizes the ways in which the discourse of nation-statehood was institutionalized in the second half of the nineteenth century within a wider, increasingly global framework, this—again in terms of trans-national norms—being inevitably followed by conformity to the norm of national homogeneity. Without denying completely the significance of primordial ethnicity, Roudometof nonetheless illustrates cogently the historically and inter-civilizationally constructed nature of ethnonationalism. It was the encounter between (largely Western) ideas about national emancipation and Ottoman and Eastern Orthodox conceptions of mainly religious (partly ethnic) domains in an imperial context that set the stage for the various aggressive forms of nationalism in the Balkan region of the last one hundred years or so.

Needless to say, powerful nation-states outside the geographical areas of which I have been speaking have exacerbated the so-called Balkans problem. Indeed, the degree to which these interventions have greatly magnified—indeed, partially caused—the Southeastern European crises remains an important question, one about which quite a lot has already been written, particularly since the early twentieth century. This is a matter that Roudometof has insufficient space to explore. Nonetheless, although he says very little about this issue, the attention he pays to the Ottoman versus European roots of many of the region's problems is, given his self-declared goals, of much greater relevance.

There can be little doubt that in this book Victor Roudometof makes a major contribution to both globalization theory and the history of the Balkan region. In addition, his work enhances our understanding of the recent history of the world as a whole. Readers should appreciate the simultaneity of these two foci; both are of equal significance here.

Roland Robertson

# Preface

This book evolved over six years and benefited from the material and intellectual support of many individuals and organizations. The original manuscript was written between 1994 and 1996. I am intellectually and morally indebted to my advisor and committee chairperson, Professor Roland Robertson, for encouragement, assistance, and inspiration. His support extended far beyond the boundaries of this project. He has been an invaluable contributor to my intellectual development as a scholar. Also, the committee members at the University of Pittsburgh, Dr. Burkart Holzner (sociology), Dr. Seymour Drescher (history), and Dr. Dennison Rusinow (history) deserve special credit for their helpful comments and guidance.

I should give credit to Dr. Irene Livezeanu (history, University of Pittsburgh) and my fellow graduate students at the time, Melissa McGary, Rachelle Schaaf, Mark Harisson, Sara Kortum, and Tony Lack, for their help in editing different chapters of the work. I extend my appreciation to the cultural studies program at the University of Pittsburgh for awarding me the Cultural Studies Fellowship during the 1992–1993 academic year, and to the Gerondelis Foundation for awarding me their predoctoral fellowship during the spring of 1996. I am also indebted to the West European Studies program for offering a teaching position and stipend during the 1995 fall semester. These fellowships significantly aided the timely completion of the work.

On a more personal level, my parents, Nikolaos and Panagiota Roudometof, gave me their invaluable moral and financial support. In addition I thank the following individuals for their emotional support and friendship over the years: Dr. Janet Stocks, Dr. Mike-Frank Epitropoulos, Dr. Anna Karpathakis, Sara Kortum, Dr. William Haller, Dr. Athanasios Taramopoulos, Costas Aliferis, M.D., and Beth Tiedemann. I also thank Dr. Donald McGuire, my former advisor at Bowling Green State University, for his help in my first timid steps in the academic world. A special thanks goes to Dr. Odysseus Macridis, for his help when I first contemplated undertaking graduate work, and for his moral support over the years. Finally, I would like to thank the Pittsburgh sociology department staff (Carol Choma, Nancy Collins, and Jossie Caiazzo) for their professionalism and help.

The Mary Seeger O'Boyle Postdoctoral Fellowship of the program in Hellenic Studies at Princeton University offered me the opportunity to spend the 1996–1997 academic year revising my original 665 pages into a more manageable 500-page manuscript. I extend my appreciation to Dimitris Gondikas, the program's executive director, for his help with a variety of issues during the fellowship year. The manuscript was modified as the result of various conversations and written or oral commentaries by Dr. Antonis Liakos (history, University of Athens), Dr. Molly Greene (history, Princeton University), Dr. Traian Stoianovich (history, Rutgers University), Dr. Elizabeth Prodromou (politics, Woodrow Wilson Center, Princeton University), Dr. Fotis Dimitrakopoulos (history, University of Munich), and historian Dr. Alekos Kyrou.

For her help with further revisions during the 1997–1998 academic year, I wish to express my appreciation to Anne-Marie Wareham, of the United Kingdom Norton Academic Services, for her willingness to make sense of some very confused chapters. I also thank the library staff of the American College of Thessaloniki and the college's academic dean, Dr. Deborah Brown-Kazazis. Also, I extend my appreciation to Dr. Gerard Delanty (sociology, University of Liverpool), editor of the *European Journal of Social Theory*, for his encouraging and thought-provoking comments while I was organizing the manuscript's main thesis into a preview article for the journal; and to professors Heinz Richer (history, University of Mannheim, Germany) and Constantine Danopoulos (Department of Political Science, San Jose State University) for their positive feedback and appraisal of my work.

Financial support for research and writing during the 1999–2000 academic year was provided by the Historical and Literary Archives of Kavala. I thank Dr. Burkart Holzner, director of the Center for International Studies at the University of Pittsburgh, Professor Alberta Sbragia, director of the European Center and the West European Studies program, as well as Dr. Robert Donnorummo, associate director of the Center for Russian and East European Studies, for their intellectual and institutional support during the 1999–2000 academic year. The final copy editing of the manuscript took place during the 2000–2001 academic year, while I was visiting assistant professor of sociology at Washington and Lee University. I am grateful to the faculty and staff of the Department of Sociology and Anthropology for the generous institutional support during the year. Also, I extend my thanks to Carole Bailey (Media Center, Washington and Lee University) for her technical assistance with the maps included in the book.

Some chapters of the book have been published independently as journal articles. I owe a debt of gratitude to Dr. Peter Bien, president of the Modern Greek Studies Association and former editor of the *Journal of Modern Greek Studies*, for his kind words of encouragement over the years. I also extend my thanks to the reviewers of these journals for their helpful remarks in revising the final manuscript. Also, I express my thanks to Dr. Stephan Nikolov (Institute of Sociology, Bulgarian Academy of Sciences) for his help with Chapter Five and for his general feedback on issues relating to Bulgarian affairs. Finally, I thank Dr. James Sabin, executive vice president of the Greenwood Publishing Group, for his patience and cooperation.

# Introduction: Nationalism, Globalization, and Modernity in the Balkans—A World-Historical Perspective

This book places national rivalries within the process of globalization and analyzes this process dynamically in the context of historical developments. In particular, the book seeks to answer the fundamental questions of why and how the Balkans have been immersed to recurrent ethnic and national rivalries. The central thesis of the book is that the production of local national rivalries (or what is referred to as "ethnic conflicts") is a direct consequence of the manner in which the Balkans were integrated into the modern world. In particular, the rise of nationalism among the Eastern Orthodox Christians of the Balkans was a corollary of the world-historical process of globalization. The social origins of ethnic conflict in the Balkans are sought in the export of nationalism in the Balkans—and not in primordial ethnic hatred or the "clash of civilizations" (Huntington 1996).

According to my analysis, the term "nation" is a signifier or "container" of a global form of social organization, the content of which is determined by a combination of global factors and local peculiarities. Consequently, national ideologies can develop in markedly different directions. In contrast to the industrialized democracies of the West, in the twentieth-century Balkans, local national ideologies have led to the marginalization of minorities and aggressive policies of assimilation. The absence of bonds of solidarity between minority and majority populations has contributed to the creation of defensively oriented national minorities who developed as strong pockets of resistance to the political and cultural priorities of the majority nationality. It is against the backdrop of these more long-term processes that the post-1989 crises in the region operate.

In this regard, the Balkans provide an almost paradigmatic case for the argument that globalization has long been involved in the production of national rivalries. Therefore, the production of conflict, heterogeneity, and difference is an integral part of the world-historical process of globalization—and not an opposing tendency (Barber 1995; Huntington 1996; cf. Robertson 1995). The very concepts of nationalism and globalization are among the most difficult and contested in the social sciences. Neither of them has a universally accepted definition. Moreover, their interpretation in social scientific literature has long been influenced by the legacy of Eurocentrism in social theory.

## THE LEGACY OF EUROCENTRISM

One of the most disturbing aspects of many commentaries on ethnic conflict in southeastern Europe is the Orientalist portrayal of these societies as prone to violence because of their cultural features (for example, Kennan 1993; Rezun 1995; Mojzes 1994; Kaplan 1992). Huntington (1996) in particular argues that the ethnic conflict in the Balkans is a civilizational conflict (Islamic versus Orthodox versus Western), an illustration of his broader point, that conflicts among civilizations will be the most significant conflicts of the postcommunist "new world order." Although the conceptual and historical inaccuracies of these perspectives have been pointed out in the literature (see Said 1978; Todorova 1997; Bakic-Hayden and Hayden 1992; Prodromou 1996), such biased views show remarkable persistence in policy making and historical discourse. They persist because they are an extension, indeed an outcome, of the way in which social theory has traditionally conceptualized "society" and the nation-state.

Therefore, in order to "unthink" (e.g., Wallerstein 1991a) the "clash of civilizations," it is necessary to reconsider some key ideas of the sociological tradition. Social theory itself has absorbed into its vocabulary aspects of the philosophy of civil rights, especially with regard to political culture, civil society, and democracy (Somers 1995), and the theoretical biases resulting from this influence are revealed in the treatment of nationalism in scholarly discourse. Although a number of authors (e.g., Kohn 1961; Greenfeld 1991; Bendix 1978; Lipset 1963) have interpreted *citizenship* as the fundamental element of the national idea, a second group (e.g., Kedourie 1985; Berlin 1981; Smith 1986, 1991; Alter 1989) use *nationhood* as their main element and disregard the earlier civic connotation of the "nation." The discourse of citizenship represents the approved, universalistic dimension of "nationality," whereby rights and duties are distributed on an egalitarian basis; to be set against the disapproved, particularistic discourse of nationhood, which excludes those who do not share the defining characteristics of a particular community. However, citizenship and nationhood do not receive equal treatment. Civic-oriented forms of nationalism are considered natural and desirable, whereas other nationalisms are viewed as deviations from this earlier normative standard (e.g., Greenfeld 1991; Kohn 1962, 12). Consequently, in most accounts, nationalism "begins as Sleeping Beauty and ends as Frankenstein's monster" (Minogue 1967, 7).

Western nationalism is seen as civic oriented with a strong emphasis on citizenship, human rights, democratic values, and the so-called territorial nature of the state. Eastern nationalism, by contrast, is seen as collectivistic with a strong emphasis on ethnicity, cultural uniqueness, nationhood, and so on (Smith 1986, 1991; Plamenatz 1976; Kohn 1961; Seton-Watson 1977). This division has grown from Meinecke's (1909/1970) distinction between "political" and "cultural" nations and, as Alter (1989) notes, it has influenced historical work for most of the twentieth century. The spatial link between types of nationalism and geographic regions contributes significantly to the proliferation and popularization of inaccurate stereotypes about the Other. In mass media, for example, peripheral or non-Western nationalisms are routinely discussed in terms of "tribalism" or ethnic unrest, interpretations that confirm assumptions of cultural superiority and inferiority. The concept of ethnonationalism crystallizes this line of interpretation (Connor 1994).[1]

By far the most influential work on nationalism has been that of the late Ernest Gellner (1983). It is difficult to find a single book on the subject that does not engage with Gellner's theory. A considerable part of the social scientific research on nationalism consists of elaboration, critiques, extensions, or modifications of Gellner's theory (for examples, Hobsbawm 1990; Hobsbawm and Ranger 1983; Kellas 1991; Smith 1986). For Gellner, nationalism is a new form of consciousness that emerges out of modernization, a term which Gellner interprets to mean the transformation of agricultural to industrial societies. Nationalism emerges as the outcome of the cultural changes associated with this process. Its key ingredient is literacy, which makes it possible for individuals to become aware of their connections and common bonds with their fellow nationals. This conceptualization draws a strong connection between industrialization and nationalism that makes problematic its application to nonindustrial societies, such as Latin America or the Balkans (Mouzelis, 1998; for critiques, see Schlessinger 1987; Chatterjee 1986; Smith 1984). To cope with this discrepancy, it is necessary to amend this model by including the challenges posed by modernization to non-Western societies (Hall 1993). If amended in such a fashion, it is no longer possible to maintain the link between industrialization and nationalism that lies at the heart of Gellner's argument. However, accepting the broader concept of modernization as an alternative formulation raises another important conceptual issue, namely, the extent to which modernization inevitably involves Westernization. → Gellner's theory

## GLOBALIZATION AND WORLD-SYSTEM ANALYSIS

Since the end of World War II, the rise of world-system analysis (Wallerstein 1974), the revival of world history as a focus of scholarly discussion (Allardyce, 1990; Mazlish and Buultjens, 1993; Hodgson, 1993), and the emergence of historically oriented and postmodernist perspectives have led to the questioning of such Eurocentric narratives. The "historic turn" (McDonald 1996) in human and social sciences has reshaped their orientation and has reconfigured conventional disciplinary boundaries. During the 1990s, these factors coalesced into regional, disciplinary, and ideological discourses on globalization (Robertson and Khondker, 1998), in which the dominant trend has been to concentrate on contemporary aspects, such as the reconfiguration of state sovereignty, the articulation of postnational forms of citizenship, or the floating finance and labor markets. The subsequent neglect of the historical dimension has been duly criticized (Harvey 1995), but this neglect is not inherent in the perspective itself.

In fact, globalization—"a social process in which the constraints of geography on social and cultural arrangements recede and in which people become increasingly aware that they are receding" (Waters 1995, 3) should not be viewed as a twentieth-century phenomenon. At least since the closure of the global *ecumene* in 1500, the world has been moving toward becoming a single place (McNeill 1963; Wallerstein 1974; Wolf 1982). The fundamental historicity of globalization leads to a reconsideration of the linear character of modernity (i.e., *Gemeinschaft* into *Gesellschaft*), whereby, instead of the idea of a transition from a presumed "tradition," into a Western-style "modernity," it becomes possible to consider the existence of different routes to modernity (see Therbon 1995b; Gran 1996; Featherstone, Lash, and Robertson 1995; Spybey 1996). In order to cast modernity in a new light, it is necessary to conceive of modernization projects as inherently reflexive (cf. Beck, Lash, and Giddens 1994; Beck, 2000), that is, as involving comparison with Others and the construction of national "authenticity" out of a process of selective incorporation of organizational models. Such comparisons are political enterprises, shaped as much by internal cultural and institutional configurations as by the availability of external options. Moreover, such comparisons are not recent phenomena, confined to the late twentieth century.

World-historical sociology has not been indifferent to the concerns raised by globalization. In fact, world-system analysis has long championed inquiries that closely resemble the globalization agenda. Therefore, an engagement with the historicity of globalization brings forward the well-known "rift" between world-system analysts and cultural theorists (Forte 1998; for an overview, see Kilminster 1997). On the one hand, cultural theorists criticize world-system analysis as essentially a materialist perspective (Featherstone 1990; Robertson and Lechner 1985; Appadurai 1996). On the other hand, world-system theorists look with great suspicion on the proposition of a "voluntaristic" neo-Parsonian framework for globalization (cf. Robertson 1992; Spybey 1996). Waters's (1995) and Axford's (1995) discussions of globalization, for example, apply a tripartite division of culture, politics, and economics in social life, a division that bears a close resemblance to Parsons's structural functionalism. In addition to the ideological and epistemological disagreement, generational rivalries also play an important role. Voluntarism has long been associated with Parsonian functionalism, the very movement dependency and world-system analysts have consciously sought to delegitimize. But the protagonists of the 1960s "sociological revolt" against

Parsonian functionalism are currently a new orthodoxy sharply criticized by the upcoming cohorts of the post-1960s social scientists and the plethora of cultural studies scholars (Bencomo and Colla 1993).

World-system theorists (Arrighi 1998b; Wallerstein 1998) have responded to cultural theorists by charging that the trends typically subsumed under the rubric of globalization are better explained by employing world-system conceptual tools. Moreover, their counterargument is that culture is indeed a field of considerable attention for world-system analysis (Forte 1998). Of course, there is a difference regarding what the two sides mean by the term: while cultural theorists hail the examination of cultural difference to be a topic of critical importance, world-system analysts speak of a "geoculture" of the world-system (Wallerstein 1991a). This geoculture is viewed as a key mechanism for the reproduction of the hegemonic relationships of global capitalism. For the cultural theorists such a viewpoint is an instrumentalist view of culture and agency, a viewpoint considered to be empirically unsubstantiated (Abercrombie, Hill, and Turner 1980; Robertson 1992).

However, even within the world-system perspective, there is increased awareness of the problems associated with the legacy of Eurocentrism. Specific proposals have been advanced to decenter world-system analysis. First, the extension of world-system analysis to pre-1500 historical systems has sought to reconceptualize the world-system as consisting of intersocietal networks (Hall and Chase-Dunn 1991, 1997). This redefinition aims to solve the problem of excluding trade in luxury goods from the original Wallersteinian analysis. Luxury goods, anthropologists have argued, are of critical importance in precapitalist societies, although, obviously, they are not accessible to the majority of a population. The shift has had unforeseen consequences. It has reinforced skepticism about the definition of the world-system and raised important methodological questions (see Arrighi 1998a). Simply put, world-system studies have insisted on negating the image of the isolated, reified society (Wallerstein 1979) and, consequently, redefinitions of the world-system that shift the focus back into a "society" fail to push the research agenda forward (Bergesen 1995).

Second, the still unresolved issue of the origins of capitalism has resurfaced once again as a corollary of these debates. In the original formulation (Wallerstein 1974), world-system analysis is basically a theory that explains not only the "rise of the West" but also the impossibility of changing the system without a world revolution. Third World intellectuals and policy makers are inevitably put into an impossible position since this approach does not provide concrete alternative strategies for improvement in their countries. This conceptual impossibility leads to an internal critique of the Eurocentric biases of world-system analysis (see Dusserl, 1998).

For example, Arrighi (1994) has sought to resolve the issue of the origins of capitalism by moving the dating of the modern world-system to thirteenth-century Italy. His goal is to provide a bridgehead between Abu-Lughod's (1989) pioneer work in Near Eastern world-systems of the twelfth and thirteenth centuries and the sixteenth century world-system. Indeed, if such a solution is accepted, the inevitable question emerges in a dramatic fashion: What exactly is the significance of the "long sixteenth century"? Did anything really important happen in that century?

Consequently, to convincingly argue his case, Wallerstein (1992, 1995) has maintained that one and only one world-system ever existed. Against this singularity, world-system theorists who have sought to expand their research agenda have called on anthropologists and historians to examine the entire group of social systems known as cultures or civilizations (Sanderson, 1995). Politico-military definitions of civilizations converge with the so-called pre-1500 group of world-system analysts to expand the domain of study into prehistoric periods. Although this group champions the existence of a plurality of world-systems, Frank (1998; see also Frank and Gills 1992, 1993) has proposed the existence of a singular world-system dating 5,000 years. The goal here is to delegitimize the "rise of the West" by suggesting that this phenomenon represented just a minute alteration in world history.

As a result of the debates briefly reviewed here, the existence of pre-1500 world-systems (in its singular or plural versions) is becoming more and more an accepted orthodoxy.[2] But the important unresolved tensions in conceptualizing such systems remain. For example, the suggestion that Islam can be conceived of as a world-system united in the symbolic realm (Voll, 1994) is an outright attack on the materialistic foundations of world-system analysis.

As I have argued elsewhere (Roudometof and Robertson 1995), the answer to the unresolved contradictions of the world-system perspective is provided by the globalization proposal. If we are to understand that globalization is a social process distinct from eighteenth-century European modernity (Robertson 1992, 58–62), then its proper starting date should be sought in the sixteenth century, the first era of world history that witnessed the beginnings of global interconnectedness. Irrespective of whether Eurasia has had commercial, cultural, and politico-military connections in the past centuries, the defining characteristic of the new era is its truly global scale—that is, (1) the inclusion of the Americas and Oceania in Eurasian circuits of circulation; (2) the more systematic contacts between Western Europe and the Indian subcontinent, Africa, the Americas, and Southeast Asia; and (3) the emerging awareness of globality and the concomitant reflexive nature of human action. To conceptualize global–local relations, it is necessary to shift the focus away from the "rise of the West." The uniqueness of this historical phenomenon does not offer the possibility of extrapolating useful sociological knowledge that would be applicable to other countries and regions. On the contrary, globalization itself undermines such an applicability, because other countries and regions can draw on the Western experience in a reflexive manner to construct their own routes to modernity.

Furthermore, there is a conceptual shift in the methodological tools employed. In particular, globalization involves contacts among different networks of human interaction, thereby refusing to absorb human relations into systemic logic. This shift in metaphors is an important one because "system" carries with it the conceptual heritage of social evolutionism and determinism, and "network" implies contact and density (Gilb 1997). Following up this network logic, Held et al. (1999, 16) have proposed an operationalization of globalization as a set of processes "which embodies a transformation in the spatial organization of social relations and transactions—assessed in terms of their extensity, intensity, velocity, and impact—generating transcontinental or interregional flows and networks of activity, interaction, and the exercise of power."

Held et al.'s (1999) valuable analysis of globalization suggests a tripartite periodization into early modern globalization (1500–1840), modern globalization (1840–1945), and post-1945 contemporary globalization—what Albrow (1997) refers to as the Global Age. This periodization offers a broader historical canvas upon which to describe the specifics of the Balkan case. With minor changes in dating the precise cut-off points of the three periods, this broad periodization is also adopted as the organizational guide for this book. However, in sharp contrast to the unitary singular logic of the connections investigated by Held et al., the analysis in this book focuses on local-global interactions and, more specifically, on the manner in which nationalism was absorbed, decoded, reinterpreted, and reshaped in the Balkan context.

## NATIONALISM AND GLOBALIZATION: A DECENTERED VIEW

Since the sixteenth century, the global structuration of the world involved the gradual rise of nation-states as part of the process of globalization itself. In fact, the conceptual presuppositions for the rise of nationalism are closely linked with the new spatial connections inscribed by globalization.

The impetus for the European "Age of Discoveries" was provided by the Ottoman expansion into the Eastern Mediterranean area and North Africa. In response to these advances, the Italian city-states (Genoa in particular) searched for alternative commercial routes to the "Orient" and provided financial support to Spanish expeditions into what became the New World. The Age of Discoveries also put into motion an entire array of cross-cultural interactions between western Europeans and their newly "discovered" peoples of the Americas, India, and Southeast Asia (Mukerjee 1986). Of particular importance was the invention of printing and the concomitant printing revolution (Eisenstein 1979). These two world-historical events signaled the gradual end of the European medieval *"transnational"* worldview (Anderson 1991; Robertson 1992, 58). The new spatial connections made possible imagining commonalties among peoples who were not in physical contact with each other, thereby providing the necessary prerequisite for the construction of "imagined communities." Moreover, the development of a linear perspective on time fostered the construction of continuities, an indispensable component for the justification of the nation as a trans-historical unit.

Although the English are sometimes credited with being the first nation

(Greenfeld, 1991), nationalism was not confined to the Old World but was rapidly exported to the new one by the North American British colonies that later became the "first new nation" (Lipset 1963). Anderson (1991) in fact highlights the processes of creolization that fostered the development of national identity in the Americas. In the 1820s, national movements first appeared in Latin America and the Balkans, providing the major thrust for societal reorganization in both regions. This adaptation of nationalism to contexts that did not share the historical legacy and socioeconomic and cultural features of Western Europe and North America was a first major step toward the reorganization of the globe into a world of nations and, as Kedourie (1971) notes, it paved the way for the postcolonial experience during the second half of the twentieth century. Over the nineteenth and twentieth centuries this process of global nationalization continued and intensified, leading to the construction of a global international society (Mayall, 1990). Thus, nationalism, an ideology of originally Western origin, has served as an organizational principle for the overwhelming majority of states worldwide (Meyer and Hannan 1979).

This similarity in form does not imply similarity in kind. Indeed, the very term "nation" defies definition.[3] Therefore, it is perhaps more appropriate to treat nations and nationalism as a discourse, in which the "nation" stands for a cultural form of worldwide importance, but one whose meaning is determined by different discourses, varying between contexts. The implosion of time and space inherent in the process of globalization (Harvey, 1989), facilitates global cultural flows, which allow local communities to appropriate ideas, practices, and organizational forms developed in other places. Since the nineteenth century, a key epoch for the "take-off" phase of globalization (Robertson 1992, 49–60; Geyer and Bright 1995; Held et al. 1999), citizenship and nationhood have operated as discursive formations shaping the meaning of the term "nation." Their success or failure in specific regional contexts has been crucial to the local routes toward modernity. Focusing the analysis on them provides a decentered view of the rise of nationalism, and counters the strong biases of Western discourse in favor of citizenship. Moreover, this line of inquiry focuses attention on human agency as an important component of social analysis. Discursive formations encompass not only ideas and mentalities but also rules that guide human activity and, therefore, provide the foundations for the mobilization of peoples and resources.

Within the discourse of *citizenship*, membership of a nation is fundamentally political and pertains to the rights and obligations of a citizen vis-à-vis the political community to which he or she belongs. In principle, other forms of distinction should not be relevant in political life. Prominent in the United States and other British postcolonial countries, this discourse pushes particularistic distinctions to the margins, thus generating what is usually referred to as "race and ethnic relations." Historically, citizenship was articulated within the confines of the Western European and Anglo-American political formations (Navari 1975; Bereciatru 1994, 3–16; Grew 1984). The concepts of citizenship and citizen are intimately tied to the historical development of the German, Dutch, French, British, and American political institutions, and their gradual redefinition and expansion over the past two centuries has been influenced by the particular context in each country.

In sharp contrast, *nationhood* implies the employment of particularistic criteria—most often derived from a local culture—as the basic foundations for the construction of a distinct national identity. In the discourse of nationhood, the nation is an entity constructed in terms of the genealogical or cultural ties of a particular ethnic group or ethnic community. In this case, membership of the nation entails participation in a specific culture. Lack of acculturation into the legitimate majority national culture provides a justification for a person's exclusion from the national imagined community. Nationhood implies a complex of ideas and mentalities concerning the politicization of cultural life. In the discourse of citizenship, membership of a nation becomes a political issue of rights and duties, thus creating room for the concept of ethnicity, which designates distinctions of race, class, religion, or skin color in the industrialized democracies of the West (Gran 1996; Hobsbawm 1996, 256–8). However, although ethnicity serves in that case as a complementary category, in the discourse of nationhood it provides the very foundation of national identity, in which cultural markers (religion, language, folk culture) are elevated to determinants of the legitimate membership of a nation. When such a process creates social bonds, a different kind of national identity is born, as membership of existing *ethnies* or an ethnic community is politicized (Smith 1986; Rothschild 1981), thus transforming them into nations.[4]

The articulation of nationhood found fertile ground in nineteenth-century romanticism, which exerted considerable influence on the expression and the reception of French, Italian, and German nationalisms (Bereciatru 1994, 42–6). The "nationalities" principle emerged after the 1789 French revolution and after the 1830 revolution it gained considerable popularity. Throughout Europe, movements such as Young Italy, Young Germany, Young Turkey, Young Ireland and Young Switzerland proceeded to utilize the romantic spirit to create social and cultural cohesion. Its ultimate codification was in the 1917 principle of self-determination, which paved the way for the reconstruction of the political map of Eastern Europe. Indeed, the considerable difficulties surrounding the applicability of this principle are precisely due to the simultaneous existence of the discourses of citizenship and nationhood; self-determination can be appropriated in distinctively different ways within them. In interwar east-central and southeastern Europe, where nationhood provided the very foundation of national identity, national self-determination was used for the purposes of political revisionism, territorial expansion, and national rivalry (Musgrave 1997; Pearson 1983).

As this book aims to show, over the nineteenth century, the Balkan peoples struggled between the options of nationhood and citizenship. The conclusion of this struggle was neither inevitable nor predetermined. The analytical differentiation between citizenship and nationhood cannot be transferred to an empirical differentiation between Western and Eastern nationalisms (cf. Plamenatz 1976). This not only confuses the analytical and empirical levels of scholarship but also disregards historical contingency. For example, even in Western Europe, the second half of the twentieth century has witnessed the rise of peripheral "ethnic" nationalisms in northern Italy, Spain, France, and Britain. Citizenship and nationhood are not necessarily antithetical to each other; it is likely that they are present in every national culture. Their place in a specific social formation is a matter of cultural ordering, a hierarchy that allows one or the other to become the foundational principle of a specific understanding of a nation (Brubaker 1992).

Although for southeastern Europe (or any other historical setting), nationhood and citizenship should be taken as a priori considerations, their success or failure should be examined in concrete historical terms. In this regard, the analysis in this book is similar to what Sewell (1996) has referred to as "eventful" sociology: the series of historical events discussed, while each leading into another, do not imply historical inevitability. This relational mode of analysis offers particular advantages. First, it avoids the overdetermination of social processes by external or internal factors. Second, it allows for interactive and relational factors to be incorporated into the analysis; more importantly, it uses a common set of variables for explanatory purposes in varied social contexts and different historical cases. Third, it illustrates how the global discursive formations of citizenship and nationhood interact with local internal factors. Instead of trying to discover the primordial element that determines the nature of nationalism per se, a more fruitful approach is to ask how citizenship and nationhood are adapted in different contexts around the globe.

## THE STRUCTURE OF THE BOOK

The organization of the book follows closely the periodization of globalization suggested by Held et al. (1999). The first two chapters explore the early modern period of globalization in the Balkans (1500–1830). Chapters 3 through 7 examine the modern period of globalization (1830–1945), up to the internal pacification of the region after World War II (1949). Finally, Chapter 8 discusses regional development in the post–World War II era of contemporary globalization. In each historical period, there are different sets of issues that played an important role both globally and locally, and these differences are reflected in the substantive issues addressed in each chapter.

The first two chapters analyze the impact of early modern globalization on the region. During this period the "Balkans" did not truly exist as an object of inquiry. The standard classification of geopolitical entities until the twentieth century classified the territory of the Ottoman Empire as "Near East" (Arnakis 1969). The term included the contemporary states of Yemen, Saudi Arabia, the principalities of the Persian Gulf, Iraq, Turkey, Jordan, Syria, Israel, Egypt,

Greece, Albania, Bulgaria, Romania, and most of former Yugoslavia (Slovenia and Croatia excluded).

According to the Ottoman geographers the term "Balkan" denoted the Stara-Planina mountain in Bulgaria, whereas the term "Rumeli" (*Rum-ili*) was employed to characterize the European part of the empire (Orhonlu 1977, 280–1; Romanides 1975, 22). In order to examine the impact of globalization on this region, it is necessary to take into account the political, economic, and cultural relationships between Southeastern and Western Europe. These relationships are conceived of as multidimensional and open-ended. That is, the analysis does not single out any of the three factors as the most important or crucial. Moreover, in accordance with the general focus of the book, the analysis focuses on the role of these relationships in determining the occurrence, shape, and success of the Balkan national revolutions (Greece, 1821; Serbia, 1804; Wallachia, 1821). According to local historiographic traditions, these revolutions were the first open manifestation of nationalism in these countries, indeed, in the Ottoman Empire itself.

Therefore, the first two chapters form a single argument aiming at a multi-dimensional analysis of these revolutions. The analysis focuses on two key questions: What was the significance of interactions with Western Europe in fostering these revolutions? and Were these revolutions genuinely national movements? In order to answer these questions, I begin with a brief overview of key features of the Ottoman socioeconomic organization, followed by a brief narrative of the three movements. This narrative informs the reader about the events in question and also reveals the key issues under consideration in the literature.

For an effective operationalization of the notion of multidimensionality, I turn to Michael Mann's (1986) image of societies as organized power networks and inquire into the socioeconomic, politico-military, and cultural-ideological power networks of the Ottoman Empire over the 1500–1830 period. The analysis aims to illuminate the manner in which shifts within these networks provided the indispensable preconditions for the Balkan movements and to determine whether these shifts may be due to interactions with the Western European world system. Chapter 1 analyzes the economic and politico-military networks; Chapter 2 addresses the transformations of the cultural-ideological network.

With regard to the influence socioeconomic ties with Western Europe had in fostering these movements, the standard argument has been that the Ottoman Empire was "incorporated" into the modern world-economy during the second half of the eighteenth century. However, I argue that this thesis is not fully substantiated by the historical evidence. Although commercial ties did exist between the two regions, the incorporation thesis seriously underestimates the commercial contacts of earlier periods. The perceived decline of the Ottoman Empire over the post-1600 period is closely tied with the administrative reorganization of the empire, the gradual loss of effective control over the provinces, and the rise of local Muslim overlords who, during the eighteenth century, became so powerful as to threaten the existence of the empire itself.

The Balkan movements are located in the context of these rivalries. In turn, the development of the Ottoman pattern of decentralization must be compared with the experience of the Western European system of states, in which strong states emerged out of a policy of centralization.

Chapter 2 examines shifts within the cultural-ideological network of the Ottoman Balkans as well as the issue of nationalism as an ideology present in the three movements. Important shifts did occur within the cultural-ideological network in the course of the eighteenth century: Western intellectual currents, such as the Enlightenment, gradually influenced the theocratic Orthodox millenarianism and its Greek Orthodox ecclesiastical culture. Yet, nationalism as an ideology was largely absent from the Romanian and Serb revolts, although it can be detected among Greek-speaking intellectuals prior to 1821. However, there is considerable conceptual ambiguity with regard to the definition of the "nation." Simply put, pre-1821 intellectuals use the Ottoman confessional model of association (the *millet* system) as their frame of reference. For the most radical intellectuals, the "nation" is understood in secular terms—heavily influenced by the Enlightenment and the French revolution. In other words, the dominant influence over this period is what I have referred to as the discourse of citizenship. Citizenship frequently entails an interethnic dimension, whereby people of various ethnic origins are considered members of the same nation. Still, the "nation" is almost synonymous with the Ottoman Greek Orthodox *millet* (the *Rum millet*). Consequently, there is insufficient evidence to suggest a cultural-political differentiation among the Balkan Orthodox Christians prior to the late eighteenth or early nineteenth centuries. During the eighteenth century, cross-cultural contacts with Western European intellectual currents led to a secular trend delegitimizing the Ottoman *Rum millet* system—the confessional model of social organization, dominant in the Ottoman Empire for almost four centuries.

In Chapters 3 through 7 the focus shifts from a power-based analysis to an analysis of the global cultural flows that proliferated in the region during the modern era of globalization (1840–1945). The goal of this conceptual shift is to capture the ideas, projects, and organizational models that proliferated in the region over this period, as well as to deal effectively with the continuous territorial changes during the nineteenth and early twentieth centuries (see Map 1). As just discussed, the discursive formations of citizenship and nationhood provided quite distinct routes for the political reorganization of the Balkan peninsula.

Although prior to 1820, nationalism emerged as an ideology strongly colored by the discourse of citizenship, it was later developed on the basis of nationhood. Contrary to interpretations that emphasize historical continuity between premodern and modern forms of national identity (Smith 1986; Armstrong 1982), I suggest that this development was the outcome of the historical process of nation building in the region over the past 150 years. This was a contested process, closely connected to the manner in which the local peoples experienced their transition into the modern world. The search for new models, largely

**Map 1**
**The Territorial Expansion of the Balkan Nation-States, 1830–1913**

**Table 1**
**Male Population of the Balkans According to the Ottoman Censuses of 1831 and 1851[a]**

| Vilaets | Christians | Muslims | Gypsies | Jews | Armenians | Others | Total |
|---------|-----------|---------|---------|------|-----------|--------|-------|
| Danube | 306,534 | 159,308 | 11,603 | 417 | -- | -- | 477,862 |
| Edrine | 247,666 | 158,249 | 11,298 | 2,128 | 1,787 | 593 | 421,721 |
| Saloniki | 127,200 | 100,249 | 7,047 | 5,915 | -- | -- | 240,411 |
| Monastir | 120,582 | 81,736 | 4,682 | 1,163 | 24 | 35 | 208,222 |
| Bosnia | 263,587 | 175,177 | 4,640 | 1,074 | -- | -- | 444,478 |
| Total | 1,065,569 | 674,719 | 39,270 | 10,697 | 1,811 | 628 | 1,792,694 |

[a]Information is based on the Ottoman census of 1831 except for the vilaet of Bosnia, where it is based on the 1851 census. Using the 1831 census, Shaw (1978, 326) estimates 513,448 Muslims and 811,546 Greek Orthodox Christians in Rumeli (European provinces) and 1,988,027 Muslims and 366,625 Greek Orthodox Christians in Anatolia. Because the table includes Bosnia, the population estimates appear to diverge; however, they are remarkably close.

*Source:* Todorov (1986 II, 429).

adapted from the Western European and American experience, was a pervasive characteristic of nineteenth-century Balkan social life, particularly after the 1820s, as a series of mostly international events transformed the region. These include the recognition of Serb autonomy (1830), the Organic Statute of the Danubian principalities (1831), the creation of the Greek kingdom (1832), the initial stirrings of the Bulgarian national movement (1838), the two Egyptian Crises (1839–1842), and the gradual emergence of an Ottoman bureaucracy following the 1821 Greek revolution.

In order to understand the discourse of citizenship as it was manifested in Southeastern Europe, it is necessary to break with historiographic interpretations that assume an "essential" quality to national identity. Balkan national histories offer a reified view of national identity and fail to address the problem of clearly defining the boundaries of various ethnic groups (cf. Barth 1969). This difficulty was one of the basic issues that fueled Balkan nationalisms in the second half of the nineteenth century. Even after Serbia and Greece ceased to be parts of the empire, the picture remained quite complex.

Table 1 provides an account of the Ottoman Balkan population in the first half of the nineteenth century. Ethnic intermixing and geographical dispersion rendered the situation complex, and the Ottoman cultural influence was evident in folk songs, traditions, legends, costumes, and other customs. The compact Muslim communities in Bulgaria, Macedonia, Albania, and Bosnia contributed to cultural syncretism between the Christian and Muslim traditions (Norris

1993). In fact, most of the Muslim converts in Bosnia and Albania did not follow strict Islamic rules of conduct and maintained many of their traditional customs. Others converted in theory but retained their Christian faith in secret and are known as Crypto-Christians (Skendi 1980, 233–58; Bartl 1984; Malcolm 1998). Especially among the Albanians, mass conversions occurred as a means of escaping the poll tax that was applicable only to Christians. These processes suggest the instrumental use of religious affiliation. Religion was often the basis for power inequality and did not imply broader cultural differences.

Despite these situations, national histories treat Serbs, Greeks, Bulgarians, Albanians, and Romanians as nations in a "pre-awakening" state. This tends to reify their existence and make their presence and contemporary form a reality projected back in time. By far the most common approach is to present the narratives of particular national histories in parallel form (Pasic 1971; Kondis 1976; Jelavich and Jelavich 1977). Objectively, "ethnic categories" are groups classified as such by the researcher. In such classification, the researcher replicates in the analysis his or her own relationship with the object of inquiry (cf. Bourdieu 1977). In the case of a nation or an ethnic group, the researcher, by attributing transcendental existence to it, fabricates its very existence. By transforming ethnic categories from "categories on paper" into real groups, the researcher "takes a conception inherent in the practice of nationalism and in the workings of the modern state and state-system—namely the realist, reifying conception of nations as real communities—and . . . makes this conception central to the *theory* of nationalism" (Brubaker 1996, 15; see also Brass 1985, 24). In reality, even as late as the nineteenth century, the vast majority of peoples in Bosnia, Macedonia, Greece, Albania, and other parts of the peninsula still used religious and not secular cultural markers for their identity (Malcolm 1994, 1998; Karakasidou 1997; Vermulen 1984; Skendi 1980).

Therefore, the development of national identity was the product of a deliberate social construction and not the realization of a natural quality inscribed in the people themselves. During the nineteenth century, various ideas and projects of transnational and interethnic citizenship were articulated and pursued unsuccessfully by a number of Balkan activists and policy makers. Developing an institutional arrangement that would include peoples of different faiths and ethnicities in national communities constituted the basic goal of the Balkan federalists and the Ottoman (and Greco-Ottoman) reformers. A review of the efforts undertaken by advocates of these political plans is undertaken in Chapter 3. This review reveals the factors responsible for their failure. Geopolitical rivalries prevented the implementation of the federal idea. In the case of Ottomanism, the growing economic gap between Orthodox commercial and urban communities, and the Muslim rural and impoverished population, did not allow for a common identity of interests to develop between the two groups.[5] The specific factors outlined previously (and discussed at length in Chapter 3) contributed to the failure of citizenship to become the dominant political feature in the emerging national societies of the region. While these options were being pursued, the discourse of nationhood was also being articulated within the confines of the new Balkan nation-states. Indeed, its promotion by the local states was one of the factors that inhibited the success of Ottomanism.

With the failure of citizenship to provide a normative standard in the emerging Balkan national societies, the discourse of nationhood gradually became dominant. The new state-sponsored national churches (Greece in 1832, Serbia in 1832, and the Bulgarian Exarchate in 1870) provided a medium through which the traditional ties of Orthodox Balkan peoples could be severed and new national ties constructed. Although church affiliation became the domain of nationalists, religious symbolism was also redeployed as national symbolism, thus facilitating the *redeployment of Orthodoxy* as part of the Balkan peoples' national identity. St. Vitus's Day, Annunciation Day, St. Cyril's and St. Methodius's Day—all of which had initially religious connotations—were reinterpreted as national symbols of the emerging Greek, Serb, and Bulgarian nations. The political cleavage between Christians and Muslims was reinterpreted as a national cleavage between "oppressed" Balkan peoples and Ottoman "oppressors." The use of poetry, prose, and journalism for nation building further contributed to this process. Education provided the means through which the Orthodox Balkan peasantry was socialized into the emerging Serb, Greek, and Bulgarian "imagined communities."

This process is described in rich historical detail in Chapters 4 and 5. Chapter 4 describes this process with regard to Greece and Serbia, the two states originally carved out of Ottoman territory in the 1830s. Chapter 5 discusses the structurally different position of the latecomers to this process—Bulgaria, Macedonia, and Albania. In sharp contrast to Greece and Serbia, the latecomers lacked their own state for a longer period of time, and their respective national homelands were targets of territorial expansion for the Greek and Serb nation-states.

Chapter 6 addresses the transformation of these initially cultural-political projects and plans into state policy in Greece, Serbia, and Bulgaria over the 1880–1920 period. In all three states, the proliferation of nationalism is closely linked to their underdevelopment and the local statist tradition. The consolidation of a free-holding peasantry led the Balkan elites to use the state as a mechanism of fiscal extraction and income redistribution in favor of the state-dependent urban strata. Moreover, support for irredentism came mainly from groups associated with the state. Over the 1880–1920 period, such elite groups championed the nationalist agenda, with the military corps on the forefront. By contrast, the peasantry and the parties it supported adopted a passive or even openly hostile attitude toward this agenda.

The 1912–1913 Balkan wars and World War I (1914–1918) offered the opportunity to turn these irredentist visions into reality by conquering almost the entire territory of the Ottoman state. Chapter 7 analyzes the impact of this territorial expansion with regard to the policies of national homogenization and the status of the various minorities. During the 1912–1949 period, *nationhood* was widely used for determining legitimate membership of the nation and for dealing with the question of cultural heterogeneity. Consequently, state policy led to the marginalization of those minorities considered to belong to a rival nation-state. The outcome of these policies of assimilation was increased tension both within and across state boundaries. Macedonia and Anatolia were the sites of extensive population transfers; similar transfers were carried out in Yugoslavia, Bulgaria, and Greece. These population transfers did not resolve the "minority issue." The formation of the first Yugoslavia was an effort to develop an alternative path, avoiding policies of ethnic cleansing. However, the new state was plagued almost from its very conception by the "national question." The absence of Croat–Serb cooperation in the 1920s and 1930s was a manifestation of the regional failure to institutionalize the discourse of citizenship. Gradually, the national question became dominant in regional politics. The engulfment of the region by World War II further spurred political revisionism, leading to the tumultuous 1941–1949 period.

Finally, Chapter 8 addresses the evolution of the Balkan nation-states in the era of contemporary globalization. After World War II, the region experienced a marked decline in national conflict, mainly due to the strong bipolarism of the Cold War. As the world entered into the Global Age (Albrow 1997), important developments further marginalized the region. First, there was a marked increase in the socioeconomic gap separating the Balkans from Western Europe. Important socioeconomic problems appeared as a result of this increasing gap. Second, there was a proliferation of international agreements leading to a new and still evolving standard for human rights. The post-1945 gradual reconfiguration of state sovereignty implied loss of autonomy for individual states (Sassen 1996). Nongovernmental organizations proliferated, claiming an important role in international affairs. The discrepancy between global and local trends put the Balkan states in a defensive mode because their infrastructure is unable to handle the demands of the new environment. The result is a growing regional imbalance between Western Europe and the Balkans. This imbalance will be the defining characteristic of East–West (or North–South) relations in European politics during the twenty-first century.

## NOTES

1. In particular, Connor (1993, 374–6) claims that nationalism is an irrational primordial force that arises in ethnic groups that claim common origins of blood. Nationalism, he claims, is absent from immigrant states such as the United States, Australia, or non-Quebec Canada. Connor differentiates between "patriotism" and "nationalism"—the former is a property of the United States, the latter a property of other peoples. This differentiation allows Western authors to situate "nationalism" in other societies and to be willfully blind to the nationalism of their own societies (cf. Billig 1995, 56).

2. The periodization of world history and of globalization remains the subject of an ongoing debate. Bentley (1996), for example, using cross-cultural connections as the

main criterion, proposes a periodization going back to prehistoric times. For other similar viewpoints, see Clark (1997) and Frank (1998).

3. While in English, the word indicates membership of a sovereign state (note the use of the adjective "national" instead of "interstate" in organizations such as the United Nations), in German a sharp distinction is drawn between *Nation* and *Staat* (Alter 1989, 4–22; Krejci and Velimski 1981, 32–41). The term *narod* is used in a number of Eastern European languages, but this lacks the connotations of the English "nation" since it refers to culturally integrated units displaying strong sentiments of collective solidarity.

4. The postulate of nationhood as a discursive formation resulting from the politicization of ethnicity solves the theoretical problem of clearly differentiating *ethnie* from nation. Smith's (1991, 40) definition of the nation is a circular one, making it difficult to analytically differentiate between *ethnie* and nation.

5. The traditional interpretation of Turkish historiography considers Balkan nationalism an offshoot of Balkan economic incorporation into the modern world-economy (Keyer 1997). The evidence does not in fact substantiate the argument: Nationalism was promoted by the state elites of the Balkan states, but the Ottoman Christian middle strata supported Ottomanism. These strata were the economic beneficiaries of the empire's incorporation into the modern world-economy. Consequently, Keyer (1997) is forced to question the inevitability of the transition to the nation-state model.

# 1

# A Multidimensional Analysis of the Balkan National Revolutions (Part I)

Although the Ottoman Empire occupied a considerable part of the European continent, its historical trajectory does not mirror that of the Western European part. Traditionally, the Ottoman Empire is said to have entered into a long-lasting decline after the reign of Suleiman the Magnificent (1520–1566). This decline persisted and intensified over the next three centuries, eventually enabling the Serbs, Greeks, and other Balkan Orthodox Christians to shake off Ottoman control over parts of the Balkan peninsula. With this perspective, the three Balkan national revolutions of the pre-1830 period (Serbia, 1804; Greece, 1821; Wallachia, 1821) have traditionally been explained as national liberation movements. Although popular in the Balkan countries, this thesis is viewed with skepticism by outsiders, who point to obvious gaps and inaccuracies, or simply suggest that the modern Western concept of nationality did not really apply to the region.

Therefore, the decline of the Ottoman Empire during the era of early modern globalization (1500–1840) is directly linked with the Balkan national revolutions. In order to further illustrate the multiplicity of factors involved in these revolutions, my analysis begins with a review in some detail of the historical events in Greece, Serbia, and Wallachia. The brief narrative helps clarify the issues at hand and the manner in which particular interpretive models are connected with the analysis of the historical record. Then, I proceed with a review of the two major interpretive models, the decentralization thesis and the incorporation thesis. These models are valid to a degree, but neither explanation is complete.

My discussion in this and the following chapter aims at developing a multidimensional analysis of the Balkan revolutions. These revolutions are viewed as particular combinations of factors present in the empire's socioeconomic, politico-military, and cultural-ideological networks. The analysis aims to determine the impact of each factor in them and the degree to which shifts within each network were connected to the historical process of globalization.

## THE BALKAN REVOLUTIONS: A BRIEF OVERVIEW

To guide the reader in the complexities of the Ottoman social context, it is necessary to briefly review the system of land ownership and the politico-military power relations within the Ottoman Empire. Then, the narrative of the three revolutions can be understood in the context of the local society.

In the early stages of Ottoman expansion, the major social division was between the *askeri* (military ruling class) and the *reaya* (subjects). With the growth of the empire, the *askeri* became differentiated among the bureaucrats, the clergy (*ulema*), and the military. Initially, Christian overlords were integrated into the *askeri* without converting to Islam. Later on, they were converted to Islam on a voluntary basis. The central bureaucracy and the imperial house were staffed with Muslims and access for Christians or Jews was possible only via conversion. On the other hand, the *reaya* could be Christian or Muslim. The *askeri* members were recorded in separate registers by a special official, the *askeri kassan* (Faroghi 1994, 550; see also Sarres 1990, I:344–55). Although the *askeri* estates were liable to confiscation by the Sultan, *reaya* property devolved upon the heirs of the deceased. According to the Ottoman view, the state rested upon the fundamental divisions between the *askeri* and the *reaya* (Kunt 1982; Sarres 1990, I:240–50; see Sugar 1977, for an overview). The *reaya* produced the wealth that supported the *askeri* and their prosperity depended on justice; the function of the Sultan was to see that justice reigned.[1] This political philosophy provided the basic principles of Ottoman administration until the reforms of the Tanzimat period (1856).

The elite group advocating this philosophy was the imperial bureaucratic service. During the Ottoman "Golden Age" (1300–1600), the central bureaucracy posts were reserved for the janissary or "child-levy" (*devshirme*) recruits from all over the empire. These were Christian children taken from their parents and educated to become Muslim "slaves" to the Sultan (Lewis, 1971, 25–7; Sarres 1990, I:226–40). The Muslim population resented this practice and eventually they were successful in monopolizing the administrative positions for themselves. By the seventeenth century, the child-levy came to a halt and Muslims entered the janissary ranks. Although 83 percent of the Grand Viziers in the 1453–1579 period were converts from various ethnic groups, the number dropped to 38 percent in the 1579–1800 period (Sarres 1990, I:233, 262–3). The janissary corps degenerated as their position became hereditary. They were allowed to marry and engage in commercial activities (Shaw 1963; Faroghi 1994, 565–72). The janissary became champions of conservativism and fought passionately against any modernizing reforms until the elimination of the system in 1826. After the abolition of the child-levy, entrance to this elite became associated with the large households of prominent families. The patrimonialism of the Royal House of Osman was duplicated among the bureaucratic and provincial elites.[2]

This imperial elite and the urban strata referred to themselves as Ottoman. The emergence of an official elite language, created from a fusion of Turkish with Arabic and Persian elements, accelerated the symbolic distinction between the elite group and the ethnic Turks who lived within the empire's boundaries. For the Ottomans, a Turk was a peasant or yokel and the word was used to refer to the Turkish-speaking peasants of Anatolia (Berkes 1964, 9; Kushner 1977, 20; Lewis 1971, 19). Therefore, the employment of the word "Turkish" to refer to the Ottomans is in many respects misleading and does not reflect accurately the orientation of the Ottomans themselves.

According to the theocratic view of society, religious identification was the key to an individual's position. The relationship between religion and estate position was not a linear one. The Ottoman system united religion and estate position in the higher strata, but did not imply a complete subordination of state functions to religious criteria. Of the Ottoman estates, the *askeri* were exempt from taxes while the merchants, artisans, and peasants who constituted the *reaya* (producers) were subject to taxes. The *askeri* and *reaya* groups and their subdivisions constituted social estates separated by their different rights and obligations (clothes, style of life, right to arms bearing, etc.) (Gocek 1996, 33–6): Table 2 provides an overview of the Ottoman social structure during the empire's Classical Age (1300–1600). This type of social organization, although not new in Europe, opened a social gap between (Orthodox and Catholic) Christian and Muslim communities. The employment of religion as a social barrier and the marginalization of direct contact with the state led to a withdrawal of the Christian religious communities from the public domain (Castellan 1988, 9; Berkes 1964, 10).

Under the reign of the Sultan, all conquered land belonged—at least in theory—to the Sultan himself. In the 1528 census, 87 percent of the Ottoman territory was state land (*miri*) (Lampe and Jackson 1982, 24; for a detailed description, see Inalcik 1994, 103–54). The Sultan also distributed land among the military cavalry in exchange for their continuing service to the army. Initially, the Ottoman military rested on a formidable *sipahi* cavalry that was supported partly by income derived from estates (*timars*) and partly by booty from military expeditions. For the large majority of soldiers the *timars* did not yield enough revenue and this provided an incentive for them to continue their participation in the army.

The *sipahilik* system was not unique to the Ottomans; similar arrangements existed in the Western feudal world, in the Byzantine Empire, and in a number of Asian countries (Cvetkova 1979a, 132–3). In contrast to European feudalism, however, the Ottoman system was characterized by the direct appointment of

**Table 2**
**Ottoman Social Structure During the Classical Age, 1300–1600**

| Askeri | Muslims | Christians and Jews |
|---|---|---|
| Men of the Sword | Sultan, *sipahis*, central government elites, army and bureaucracy | Some *sipahis* |
| Men of the Pen | *Seyhulislam* (Muslim religious leader) The *ulema* (Muslim clergy) Intellectuals, *sufi* religious leaders | The four Patriarchs Chief Rabbi and other religious leaders Intellectuals and lower clergy |
| **Reaya** | | |
| Merchants and Craftsmen | Manufacturers, wholesale and retail buyers and sellers of food products, craftsmen organized in guilds, apprentices and journeymen, workers (to varied degrees, these occupational categories included both Muslims and non-Muslims) | |
| Peasantry | Tenants of *timar* and *wakf* lands, small freeholding peasantry, sharecroppers and landless peasants, nomads and pastoralists. (These categories included both Muslims and non-Muslims.) | |

the overlord by the Sultan and the nonhereditary status of the estate.[3] This feature resulted in the absence of a landed hereditary aristocracy and the presence of relative social mobility. The state never lost completely its grip over local lords; hence, its major difference from Western European feudalism, where the elaborate rituals of fraternization served to conceal the inability of the king to exercise effective control over his vassals (cf. Bloch 1961). The central role of the state in public life and the direct relationship established between peasantry and central authority further distinguished the Ottoman world-empire from the decentralized system of the European small feudal states.[4] It also greatly influenced the people's mentality regarding the relationship between state and society; the state was conceived of as an organic part of the society and not as an independent agent.

In addition, there were the Christian or Moslem ecclesiastical estates (*wakf*), which consisted of religious endowments. Under Islamic law, these endowments were not liable to confiscation. During the period of Ottoman conquest and consolidation, the central authority had created a type of seignorial holding (*mulk*) which enjoyed full ownership and broad immunity from confiscation. Some of them went to members of the imperial family, others to outstanding Ottoman generals and dignitaries, and still others were assigned to Muslim religious missionaries who used part of the income to maintain religious institutions. Since the *mulk*s, although privileged, were still subject to royal interference, their holders tried to convert them into *wakf*s. By turning the *mulks* into inalienable *wakf* property, the *mulk* masters protected their possessions from encroachment by the Sultan. As early as 1478 Sultan Mehmed II ordered all *wakf* lands to be investigated and those not meeting the proper criteria to be reassigned into state ownership. Not surprisingly, the announcement triggered extensive social and political upheaval. The problem was not too acute yet: In 1528 the total revenues of all *wakf* and free-holding lands constituted only 12 percent of all imperial revenues (Inalcik 1994, 126–9). However, the trend was unstoppable. By the second half of the sixteenth century "one could claim that the number of people who could transmit wealth and power to their sons increased" (Faroghi 1994, 550).

During the fifteenth and sixteenth centuries the hereditary possession of these *mulk*s and *wakf*s led to the formation of a Muslim aristocracy in the European part of the Empire (Rumeli) (Cvetkova 1979a, 137; see also Cvetkova 1979b for a sixteenth- to eighteenth-century overview). In contrast to the Western European estates, this aristocracy received no legal codification. By the early nineteenth century, some foreign observers believed that one-half to two-thirds of Ottoman land was turned into *wakf*s, though this is open to question (McGowan 1994, 660). Tax farming and usury further facilitated the formation of large estates known as *cifliks*.[5]

In the meantime, chronic deficits led the government to entrust local governors with raising their own troops. These mercenary troops, however, were paid irregularly and frequently proceeded to extract money from the peasantry (Faroghi 1994, 434). By the eighteenth century, members of the Ottoman elite—especially tax farmers with life leases and military status—were able to appropriate even state-owned lands (*miri*).[6] During the eighteenth century, these local Muslim provincial leaders—referred to as *ayans*—grew in power (Sadat 1972). By the late eighteenth century, they had established their own mini-regimes, with a power base formed from the local urban Muslim population (Inalcik 1977, 27–52). In 1768 the Porte was forced to officially recognize their existence in exchange for obtaining army recruits and supplies from the provinces. In 1779 an early attempt was made to abolish the *ayans*, but the Russo-Turkish war of 1788–1792 forced the government to restore the *ayanlik* in 1790 and, by the early nineteenth century, the *ayans* threatened the foundations of the central administration. In 1808, the *sened-i ittifak*, a contract between the central authority and the powerful *ayans*, provided for the recognition of the local *ayans'* power to rule and place limits on the Sultan's authority.[7]

### The Serb Case

In the *pashalik* of Belgrade, after the Treaty of Belgrade (1739) and the return of the Ottomans, a total of 2,400 janissaries and 900 *sipahis* settled in (McGowan 1994, 685). They quickly turned toward financial extraction, illegal seizures of peasant land, and "protection" of the local villages. As a result, during the 1788–1791 war about 18,000 Serbs crossed the border and helped the Habsburg forces (Vucinich 1979, 308). During the 1790s, the Porte attempted a series of political reforms, including the confiscation of the estates; they granted the Serb population the right to elect elders in the villages and heads (*knezes*) in the communities, to act as representatives before the authorities. The amount of taxes paid to the state and the *sipahis* was fixed and the local prelates were given the right to serve as tax collectors. Serbs were also allowed to handle minor judicial questions, freely sell the surplus of what they produced, and build churches, monasteries, and schools. The right to bear small arms was confirmed and the authorities were prohibited from intervening in the Serb villages (Stojancevic 1982, 28–9). This local organization provided the first opportunity to voice the interests of the Christian local agricultural elites.

The socioeconomic struggle between rural and urban elements also cut along religious lines, the rural predominantly Christian, the urban, Muslim (Stoianovich 1989, 261–3). The *ayans* were therefore in direct conflict with the Christians because they attempted to assert their authority by collecting levies from the rural population. The janissary exercised a reign of terror over the countryside (Levy 1979, 326–8), with the usurpation of peasant holdings and tax obligations among the most serious of their offenses. Although the Porte had attempted to neutralize them, the 1801 Ottoman offensive against the powerful *ayan* Pasvanoglou of Vidin provided an opportunity for the janissary to reassert their power, and in 1804 they beheaded the leaders of the local *knezes*. This was the signal for the first Serb uprising: peasantry, pastoralists, and pig traders revolted in an attempt to "restore order" on behalf of the Sultan and against the usurpers of legitimate authority. Under these circumstances, the Serbs' initial assertion that they were fighting on behalf of the Sultan was not rhetorical. In fact, there is little evidence that national ideology played an important role as a motivational force before the 1840s (Stokes 1976; Meriage 1977; Paxton 1972).

The Serb military forces were a combination of bandits (*haiduks*) and ex-officers and soldiers of the Habsburg army (Skrivanic 1982). Although no reliable figures exist concerning the total number of the Serb military during the first Serb uprising (1804–1813), estimates vary from 28,000 to 60,000. By 1813 the Ottoman forces had crushed the rebellion and 110,000 Serbs fled to the Habsburg territories. A new revolt occurred in 1815, but this time, Prince Miloš Obrenović was successful—thanks to bribery and diplomacy—in winning autonomy from the Sublime Porte.

### The Greek Case

Traditionally, the organization of the Greek revolution is attributed to the nationalist secret society Philiki Eteria, instituted in 1814 in Odessa by three Greek merchants. However, a closer examination of the historical record reveals close connections between the Greek and Serb cases.

From 1785, the *ayan* Ali Pasha Tepelenli successfully consolidated his rule in Epirus, Southern Albania, and Thessaly; in 1804 he finally forced the warrior clans of the Souliotes to abandon their village confederation in Epirus and flee to the Ionian islands. Under his regime, the local bandits (*armatoli* and *klephts*) were forced to submit or cooperate with him. Many fled to the Ionian islands and offered their services as mercenaries to the French and the English, but after 1816, when the English disbanded their armed irregulars, they were eager to return home (Skiotis 1975, 318–9) and attempted to reach a compromise with Tepelenli. The time was right because the Porte was determined to crush the pasha, and he was in need of allies. Between 1818 and 1820, Tepelenli became aware of the Philiki Eteria's plan for an insurrection (in fact, he informed the Porte about it in an effort to appease the central bureaucracy), and he developed close ties with the conspirators (Arsh 1994, 317–54).

By 1820 Tepelenli was relieved from his duties, and when he refused to go, the Porte sent its armed forces after him. The Lion of Janina—as he was called—continued to resist in his citadel for 17 months. On 4 December 1820, Tepelenli concluded an agreement with the Souliotes, who then returned to Souli and fought alongside Muslim Albanian forces against the Ottoman army. A force of 3,000 Christians was joined by Muslim Albanian forces. Bribery and the pasha's strong resistance also contributed to the decline of Ottoman forces from 50,000 to only 10,000 (Skiotis 1975, 325; 1976, 104–7). In 1820 and 1821 the alliance between the Souliotes and Muslim Albanians faithful to Tepelenli was successful throughout Epirus, but it was terminated when the news of the Greek revolution in Peloponnesus (including massacres of the local Muslims) reached the Muslim Albanians (Krapsitis 1989, 229–307).

The descent of Ottoman forces upon Tepelenli brought plundering, extortion, and other forms of corvée on the villages. The local warlords, the *armatoli* of Rumeli, were eager to join the pasha's rebellion in order to drive the Ottoman forces out of their territory. In other words, the pattern that led to the Greek revolt was similar to the Serb rebellion. In early 1821, the *armatoli* of Rumeli (Androutsos, Tsongas, Varnakiotes, Stournares, Makres, Karaiskakes, Katsiko-giannes, and Panourgias) gathered together at Levkas and agreed to join the uprising (Skiotis 1975, 327). Elia Mavromichalis, the son of the prelate of Mani, represented Peloponnesus at the meeting. Soon afterward, bandits arrived in the Peloponnesus to prepare it for revolution.

The Peloponnesian bandits were desperate to return home. In Peloponnesus, between 1780 and 1800, an equilibrium was reached among the armed irregulars, the Muslim and Christian forces in service of the Muslim *ayan*s, and the local bandits. Under the threat of a French invasion during the late 1790s, the Ottomans invited Muslim Albanian forces in as a preemptive move against such a possibility (Alexander 1985, 77). The accelerated competition for extortion of money from the peasantry and the prelates led to protracted anarchy. In 1804–1805 the Porte issued orders for the swift persecution of the bandits, an announcement supported by the Patriarchate of Constantinople. The local Greek prelates and religious dignitaries joined forces and carried out an expedition against the *klephts*, killing 300 to 400 of them and forcing the rest to flee to the

Ionian islands. The dissatisfied bands of bandits presented a constant threat because they strongly desired to return home; their goal provided bandit leaders such as Theodoros Colokotronis a strong impetus to join the revolutionary conspiracy of the Philiki Eteria. The bandits were the forerunners of the revolution in Peloponnesus: In regions under the influence of the local prelates, there was not a strong desire to join the revolution and their participation was sometimes even coerced (Kontogiorgis 1977, 35).[8]

Other actors were prompted to join this coalition by economic considerations. The lifting of the continental blockade at the end of the Napoleonic wars had resulted in an economic crisis, with a serious decline in maritime commerce between 1816 and 1818. Specifically, on the island of Hydra the profit rate per ship fell from 116 percent in 1810 to 13 percent in 1817 (Kremmydas 1988, 130; 1980, 263–71). Greek shipowners were thus prompted to find other means of income, and to become partners in revolution. Agricultural exports were also adversely affected, reinforcing the antagonism between the Christian and Muslim prelates and providing the Christians with a desire for the obliteration of their Muslim adversaries.

The Greek revolution was thus the outcome of a number of local forces attempting to protect themselves from the misfortunes that the conflict between *ayan*s and central government had brought to their lands. A common pattern of landownership in the Serb and Greek cases aided the success of the revolts. In the *pashalik* of Belgrade and in "Old Greece" (i.e., Rumeli and Peloponnesus) the local Christian prelates were not large landholders, and were therefore not afraid of joining the revolutions. Once the Serb and Greek revolts were under way, the peasantry, hungry for land, joined in, and appropriated the Ottoman lands.[9]

## The Danubian Principalities

The Danubian principalities (Wallachia and Moldavia) were not an organic part of the empire, but were paying annual tribute to the Porte. The local Christian *boyars* (gentry) were allowed to retain and consolidate their holdings during the 1400–1800 period. The boyars were gradually successful in breaking up the communal association of the villages, turning the majority of peasants into quasi-serfs (Chirot 1976; Stahl 1980; for a very good summary, see Castellan 1989).

Initially, the amount of corvée remained lower than in the Habsburg lands. In the 1730s and 1740s, after the Russo-Ottoman wars and the occupation of the principalities by the Russian army, the peasantry began fleeing to Transylvania and the Banat (McGowan 1994, 682–3). The subsequent revenue crisis led to swift administrative action. In the Phanariot decrees of 1746 for Wallachia and 1749 for Moldavia, corvée was fixed at 12 days per year convertible to cash payment, whereas, later on, Prince Alexandros Ypsilantis set it at 12 days per year (in the Habsburg lands, annual *robot* labor ranged between 50 and 150 days). The Phanariot decrees formally put an end to serfdom and proclaimed the peasants' personal freedom. They did not necessarily alter the general socioeconomic situation, other than to put an end to peasant emigration to Transylvania and the Banat (Castellan 1989, 86–8; Lampe and Jackson 1982, 85). The boyars reinterpreted these decrees so that the actual length of obligations ranged from 25 to 40 days (Florescu 1968, 309). In return for their consent to serf "emancipation," the boyars increased the share of taxes paid directly to them. In 1818 the Caragea legislation increased the cash conversion tenfold and made settlement on estate land a privilege instead of a right for the peasant. Consequently, in the course of the nineteenth century dependence on the boyars increased (Quataert 1994, 866). Still, peasant dues remained lower than the Habsburg ones until the late nineteenth century.

The principalities were part of the Ottoman system delivering food supplies to Istanbul and were obliged to deliver considerable quantities of various goods often at fixed or unprofitable prices. The local aristocracy deeply resented this obligation and desired the principalities' disassociation from the Ottoman sphere of influence.[10] The principalities' association with the empire dated back to the 1500–1700 period, when significant cultural intertwining took place among the local Romanian elites, the post-Byzantine Orthodox Ottoman elites, and the high clergy. The growth of these ties was fostered by the migration of the remnants of the Byzantine aristocracy to the principalities, their intermarriage with the local landowning families, and the desire of the Romanian princes to be benefactors of the Ecumenical Patriarchate.[11] In time, a considerable portion of these elites merged through marriages and became hellenized. When, in 1711, the two *hospodars* (overlords) of the Danubian principalities, Constantin Brancoveanu and Dimitrie Cantemir, aligned themselves with the Russians against the empire, the Porte decided to replace the native princes with appointed ones. The Greek Orthodox families that became the beneficiaries of the Porte's decision came to be known as the Phanariots. Table 3 provides a listing of the families that, between 1711 and 1821, monopolized the princely title in the two principalities.

Phanariot rule has been a controversial topic in the literature.[12] In fact, the very term "Phanariot" in its contemporary connotation owes much to nineteenth-century historiography, which depicted the Phanariots as the source of everything evil in the principalities (Pippidi 1975, 231–9; for a traditional negative evaluation, see Seton-Watson, 1934). The key problem faced by the princes was short tenure: The average length of reign was 2.5 years. For example, from 1730 to 1769, Constantinos Mavrocordatos reigned six times in Wallachia and four times in Moldavia; the longest of these periods was only 6 months. The dwindling tenure of the princes was related to the increased payments required to obtain the seat: By 1750 the Moldavian throne cost 30,000 gold pounds and the Wallachian, roughly 45,000. This pattern suggests that the Ottoman government had a vested interest in frequent changes in the princely seats. Excessive taxation of the peasantry was the consequence of this system and led to peasant impov-

**Table 3**
**Distribution of Princes among Families, 1711–1821[a]**

| FAMILY | MOLDAVIA | WALLACHIA | TOTAL |
|---|---|---|---|
| Mavrocordatos | 8 | 9 | 17 |
| Ghika | 8 | 7 | 15 |
| Morouzi | 4 | 5 | 9 |
| Ypsilanti | 3 | 5 | 8 |
| Sutu | 3 | 7 | 10 |
| Racovista | 3 | 5 | 8 |
| Rosetti | 1 | 1 | 2 |
| Hangerli | 1 | 1 | 2 |
| Callimachi | 0 | 2 | 2 |
| Mavrogheni | 0 | 1 | 1 |
| Total | 31 | 43 | 74 |

[a]Not all princes were part of the Phanariot elite. For example, Nikolaos Mavrogheni was not part of this elite, and he was considered an outsider by the Phanariots (Vranousis, 1963, 19).

*Source*: Castellan (1989, 77).

erishment and deterioration of social conditions in both principalities. Part of the wealth went to the Porte, but some of it undoubtedly went into the pockets of the Phanariots themselves.[13]

As the preceding brief review suggests, the 1821 revolution was a complicated affair. The *hospodar* of Moldavia, Mihail Soutsos, was a member of the Eteria, and the Greeks in administrative and military posts were able to provide considerable support for the movement (Jelavich and Jelavich 1977, 41). In addition, the Eteria attempted to build a coalition between its own members and members of the free peasantry, who were involved in commercial activity and shared a common background with many Eterists (Constantiniu, 1984, 235). During the 1806–1812 Russo-Ottoman war, many independent peasants (*panduri*) had enlisted in the Russian army. Among these *panduri* was Tudor Vladimirescu, who, after the war, engaged in commercial activities and became a boyar. He had strong connections with military leaders in the principalities, who in turn were members of the Eteria. Vladimirescu entered into secret negotiations, and may have been initiated into the Eteria.[14]

On 27 January 1821, the dying Prince Alexandros Soutsos of Wallachia set up a provisional committee to serve as a caretaker government. Three of the committee's non-Eterist members—boyars Grigorie Brancoveanu, Barbu Vacarescu, and Grigore Ghika (who in 1822 became the first native prince)—immediately gave Vladimirescu a written promise of aid. This faction of the boyar class strongly opposed Phanariot rule, and it is probable that they wished to provoke a failed rebellion in order to embarrass the Phanariots.

On the night of 29 January 1821 Vladimirescu departed for Oltenia with the aid of the brothers Dimitrie and Pavel Makedonski, two military leaders highly influential among the *panduri*. His original mission was to reestablish order in a part of Oltenia where peasant unrest had been reported. Once there, however, he called for an uprising against the boyars; this call gained an overwhelming response from the peasants, who desired to overthrow the boyars and work the land for themselves. A total of 4,500 *panduri* enlisted in the army and, as Romanian peasantry joined the movement, this number eventually reached 20,000 (Constantinu, 1984).

By 12 March, Vladimirescu had crossed the Olt on his way to Bucharest. On 6 March 1821, Prince Dimitrios Ypsilantis, the leader of the Philiki Eteria, crossed the Prut into Moldavia with a small force consisting of mercenaries and Greek nationalists.[15] On 8 March 1821, in Jassy, he issued a proclamation that called all Greeks to "free their fatherland Greece and raise the Cross where the Crescent once stood." The revolutionary movement rested on a very fragile coalition between the nationalist movement of the Eteria and the native peasant movement. Vladimirescu's proclamation, issued on 29 January 1821, urged the population to rise against the oppressive rule of the government. He called for social reform and abolition of boyar privileges, changes justified in the name of justice and the Sultan (Brad-Chisacof 1988).

The forces of the Greek leader, Ypsilantis, moved into Wallachia and united with Vladimirescu, but the Greco-Wallachian cooperation soon broke down (Tappe 1973; Berindei 1973, 1979; Deletant 1981, 238–41). On 13 May, three Ottoman armies entered the principalities, and Vladimirescu sought to reach an agreement with the Porte. When Ypsilantis learned of this, he moved to capture and execute Vladimirescu, but his own forces were defeated at Dragasani on 19 June. Ypsilantis fled to Transylvania, where he was arrested by the Habsburg authorities. The beneficiaries of this attempt were the boyars, who were able to rid themselves of the Phanariots and have the princes elected among their own number.

In the Danubian principalities, therefore, the intersection of groups with different agendas (Moldavian and Wallachian boyars, peasants seeking their emancipation, and Greek nationalists) was not conducive to coherent revolutionary action. This was an outcome of the differences between the Ottoman Empire (where no hereditary landowning class existed) and Wallachia and Moldavia (where the boyars were hereditary large-estate owners). Whereas in Greece and Serbia the local Christian elites joined the rebellions, in the principalities the local elites refused to join a rebellion that sought to overthrow the basis of their wealth and power.

## TOWARD A MULTIDIMENSIONAL ANALYSIS: THE BALKAN REVOLUTIONS AS HISTORICAL CONJUNCTURES

The basic issues that have long preoccupied research concerning the Balkan national revolutions may now be discussed further. These include the role of expanding commercialization in the creation of political constituencies favoring independence from the Ottomans; the role of authority decentralization and the concomitant rise of the *ayan*s in providing the context for the outbreak of these movements; and the role of banditry in Balkan society. To this list, it is necessary to add the possibility of influences from Western Europe. To the extent that these factors contributed to these movements, then, the Balkan revolutions can be viewed conjecturally as outcomes of particular combinations of economic, political, military, and cultural factors.

The interpretation advanced here is an attempt to move the discussion beyond emphasizing one of these factors. As Held et al. (1999) have suggested, over the early modern period (1500–1840), globalization has been predominantly "thin"; for example, the relations among societies did not have the density and strong impact observed in later periods. This statement could lead to the argument that local–global relations were inconsequential. On the contrary, such relations were an important component of regional historical development. Using the Ottoman Empire as a test case, my argument aims to illustrate both the significance of such ties for the historical trajectory of the Balkans and the nonlinear, multifaceted nature of regional incorporation into the modern world-economy.

To study the determinants of the Balkan national revolutions in a manner that would be conducive to unveiling local–global relations, I use Michael Mann's (1986) image of "society" as consisting of overlapping economic, politico-military, and cultural-ideological power networks. In the following, I describe the manner in which these networks were influenced by relations with the Western European world-economy. In sharp contrast to the one-dimensional, economic approach advocated by some world-system theorists, the analysis is explicitly multidimensional. Politico-military, economic, and cultural-ideological networks are all considered to be potential determinants of the revolutions. My argument is built by a critique and revision of the two dominant interpretive models for social change in the Ottoman Empire: the incorporation thesis and the decentralization thesis.

The first model, the incorporation thesis, emphasizes the rise, over the eighteenth century, of a Greek Orthodox Balkan merchant class, which provided for a stratum relatively wealthy and open to communication with Western Europe. The traditional balance of power in the Ottoman system shifted as Balkan commerce slowly became concentrated in the hands of the Christians. The incorporation thesis suggests that the internal changes in the empire's social structure were driven by its gradual incorporation into the world-economy. Between 1750 and 1815, the expansion of commercial activity between the Ottoman Empire and Western Europe led to the economic incorporation of the empire into the modern world-system.[16] The thesis has important implications for the explanation of the national revolutions in the late-eighteenth- and early-nineteenth-century Balkans. According to world-system literature, the growth of the estate (*ciftlik*) system, increasing economic relations between the empire and Western Europe, and the rise of a Balkan commercial class of intermediaries are considered to have linked the empire with the capitalist world-economy and created a situation of dependency analogous to the Latin American case (Stokes 1980a). Balkan nationalist movements were the outcome of economic incorporation and the rise of new strata of merchants tied to global capital. This argument is a recasting of the Marxist perspective, suggesting the development of capitalism (and a class of Christian capitalist merchants) in the Balkans over the late eighteenth century.[17]

The problems associated with the incorporation thesis are both theoretical and substantive. Theoretically, there is insufficient consideration of the roles of the state, culture, and institutional factors (Skocpol 1977; Zolberg 1981; Robertson and Lechner 1985). Moreover, there are the problems of residual functionalism and teleology in Wallersteinian analysis (see, e.g., Sewell 1996). However, there are also substantive problems with regard to the Ottoman case. First, the size of the large estates has been overestimated. Free peasantry persisted in the Balkans, especially in more mountainous regions of the peninsula. Second, the existence of pastoral nomads in the Balkans created a social context similar to the stateless societies of the American Southwest (Hall 1989), thereby raising the possibility that such incorporation was far from linear. Finally, the incorporation thesis adopts a Eurocentric view of the Ottomans by suggesting a marginal role for the empire and its economic relations with Western Europe over the pre-1750 period. This interpretation is contested by research on the fifteenth- and sixteenth-century Ottoman Empire.

The second model stresses the patterns of decentralization of the Ottoman administration and the creation of Muslim and Orthodox Christian provincial administrative elites. The attempts by the central bureaucracy to reassert central authority over the local *ayans* provided the context for the Serb and Greek revolutions.[18] In this transformation from the traditional Ottoman estates to classes lie the origins of the social transformation in the region. In sharp contrast to the incorporation thesis, this model holds that the origins of social change were essentially internal. This model suggests that the evolution of the empire was driven by changes in its internal class structure, the weakening of the central government, and the usurpation of authority in the provinces by local Muslim officials (*ayans*), Christian prelates, and local bandits. Accordingly, socioeconomic shifts and changes within the political structure in the Ottoman Balkans provided the historical conjuncture responsible for the rise of national movements (Karpat 1972, 1973, 1982a; see also Chirot and Barkey 1984). Table 4 provides a simplified representation of the Ottoman social structure during the eighteenth and nineteenth centuries. A simple comparison of this table with Table 2 showing the Ottoman social structure during the Classical Age reveals the important social transformation under way. Basically, the old "estate" system, based on the divisions between *askeri* and *reaya*, faded away, and new class divisions became more important in the Ottoman social structure. Although this model captures important interactions between the empire's center and its regional elites, it fails to take fully into account the interactions between the Ottoman Empire and the Western European region.

**Table 4**
**Ottoman Social Structure in the Eighteenth and Nineteenth Centuries**

| Class | Muslims | Christians and Jews |
|---|---|---|
| Upper | Ottoman dynasty<br>Central and provincial<br>bureaucracy | The Patriarchs and Phanariots<br>The heads of the Jewish,<br>Catholic, and other millets |
| Middle | Local *ayans* and property holders<br>Merchants<br>Muslim community leaders<br>artisans, craftsmen, and<br>religious leaders (*ulema*)<br>Intellectuals | Merchants<br>Small-scale entrepreneurs<br>Landowners<br>Livestock breeders<br>Christian community leaders<br>Intellectuals |
| Lower | Apprentices in guilds and workers<br>Peasantry (mostly small owners) | Workers in small enterprises<br>Peasantry employed on the lands<br>of *ayans* or Christian<br>community leaders<br>Freeholding peasants |

Although neither perspective can fully account for the social processes that led to the Balkan revolutions, they are particularly useful as partial explanations. The socioeconomic processes associated with the incorporation thesis offer a useful insight into Ottoman–European economic relations; the decentralization thesis is indispensable for an understanding of the Ottoman state during the eighteenth century. In the next two sections, I review developments in both socioeconomic and politico-military networks. My discussion of the socioeconomic network focuses on the limits of the incorporation thesis by highlighting Ottoman–European economic relations in the fifteenth and sixteenth centuries, the limits of estate expansion, the particularities of the Balkan merchants, and the role of nomads in the Balkan economy. The discussion aims to narrow down the claims made by world-system theorists, in order to open up theoretical space for the role of additional factors in the analysis. My discussion of the politico-military network focuses on the issue of decentralization and the manner in which the Ottomans reorganized their bureaucratic system after the sixteenth century. This system allowed for the proliferation of banditry. In turn, bandits played a key role in the Balkan revolutions.

## THE ECONOMIC NETWORK: THE LIMITS OF INCORPORATION

During the eighteenth century, the rise of the *ciftlik* system in the Ottoman lands allowed local tax farmers, merchants, and members of provincial *ulema* to extend their economic grasp over part of the countryside.[19] These estates were not evenly distributed (Adanir 1989). They were present mainly in fertile regions or in the plains. In terms of sheer numbers, for example, during the late eighteenth and nineteenth centuries, the *ciftlik* system covered approximately 20 percent of the Bulgarian lands (Lampe and Jackson 1982, 36; see also, Palairet, 1997: 43–44). Often, an alternative strategy of financial extraction operated through the usurpation of landownership by various overlords who forced the peasants to give up their legal rights to the land, thus turning them into tenants (Crampton 1981, 175–80). But the independent uphill village continued to exist and, in the Serb and Greek lands, it remained the dominant type of land regime (Lampe 1989, 189).

Moreover, it is not solely the large estates' geography and size that casts doubt on the incorporation thesis. It is also the assumption that eighteenth-century commercial relations between the Ottoman Empire and Western Europe were qualitatively novel. In fact, research on the earlier Ottoman periods has suggested that socioeconomic contacts between Western Europe and the Ottomans were of particular importance. The fifteenth-century Ottoman state was one of the global powers of the time and was quite successful in expanding its authority in the Middle East (Syria, Egypt, and the Arab peninsula). In the sixteenth century, Portuguese and Ottomans combined to eliminate the Mamluk middlemen in East–West trade; at the same time, the French rivaled Venice for most favored nation in Ottoman ports (Brummett 1994, 25). The building of the Ottoman fleet in the early sixteenth century is directly linked to this pattern of competition and expansion. The fleet's purpose was to reinforce Ottoman control over commercial routes. Indeed, the Ottoman elites sought to exploit the traditional grain trade between the eastern and western Mediterranean through agents directly engaged in trade, developing connections with foreign merchants, or cooperation with or toleration of piracy (Brummett 1994, 139). In the early sixteenth century, the Ottomans were able to capture the main routes of the Eurasian trade in silk, spice, and copper.

The Atlantic expansion of the Western European states was an effort to develop an alternative to Ottoman dominance. The European Age of Discoveries and the concomitant influx of bullion from the New World led to the sixteenth-century "price revolution" in Western Europe. Although the influx of American bullion is said to have caused a steady price inflation in the Ottoman Empire (Barkan 1975), it is more likely that the inflation was a major mechanism of Ottoman finances (Gerber 1982; Inalcik 1978a).

As in other European states, the Ottoman Empire required hard currency to finance its standing army and navy. Moreover, during the wars against the Habsburgs in 1593–1606, the need for gun-bearing infantry resulted in a significant increase in the number of janissary troops from 7,886 in 1527 to 37,627 in 1610 (Inalcik 1994, 24). The changing nature of warfare increased military expenses from 57,707.666 *akca* in 1528 to 236,605,688 *akca* in 1670 (Karpat 1973, 50–1). It also contributed to the decline of the *timar* system. From 63,000 *timar* holders in southeastern Europe (and probably 200,000 altogether) in 1475, the number fell to a total of 40,000 (8,000 of them in the Balkans) by 1630 (Lampe and Jackson 1982, 26). It is indicative of the economic difficulties that, after the

1571 Lepanto defeat, the Ottoman state cut back its naval expenditures and never rebuilt its fleet (Inalcik 1994, 94–5).

From the sixteenth century onward, the Ottomans resorted repeatedly to currency debasement as a means of solving their fiscal crises. Between 1489 and 1616 the value of currency decreased by 140 percent (Karpat 1973, 50–1). Fiscal crises became a persistent feature of Ottoman life (Inalcik 1994, 97–9). In the second half of the fifteenth century, commercial concessions—referred to as capitulations—were granted to European merchants because the Levant trade brought badly needed cash into the empire (Inalcik 1978a, 92).

In the meantime, higher prices in the western part of the Mediterranean provided an irresistible pull for the export of agricultural goods, frequently in the form of contraband trade. In the late sixteenth and early seventeenth centuries, a series of mercenary revolts in Anatolia (known as the *celali* rebellions) contributed to a slowdown of economic activity and offered the opportunity for Western European merchants to expand their activities in Anatolia, rerouting agricultural goods from domestic to European markets. This transformation is reflected in the sudden rise of Smyrna (Izmir) from a post of 2,000 inhabitants in 1580 to a cosmopolitan port of 30,000 to 40,000 in 1650 (Goffman 1990). The introduction and expansion of cotton and tobacco cultivation (among other agricultural goods) catered to English, Dutch, French, and Venetian commercial interests. The export-based trade reconfigured the commercial landscape of western Anatolia, a process that intensified in the following centuries.

The example of Smyrna illustrates the fact that commercial relations between the Ottoman Empire and Western Europe were not an eighteenth-century novelty. Ottoman trade over this century remained almost stable in terms of value. In the meantime, the value of total world trade increased and, consequently, the global significance of Levant trade decreased (McGowan 1994, 725–8; 1981, 23). In the early seventeenth century, Venetian trade collapsed and French trade also went through a prolonged crisis between 1635 and 1650 (Goffman 1990, 97–137). The French eventually recovered and overtook the English, who were the empire's leading trading partner in the seventeenth century. Throughout the eighteenth century France was the empire's leading trade partner (Panzac 1992, 192). In 1717–1720 the Levant trade accounted for 13,500,000 livres out of a total French imports of 18,000,000; by 1786–1789 Levantine exports represented 30,200,000 livres out of 36,450,000 livres (Vakalopoulos 1973, IV:157–205; Gocek 1996, 88). Despite the rising volumes of external trade, the Ottoman market remained solid, with some sectors (such as the cotton industry) resisting foreign competition successfully (Panzac 1992). Domestic trade remained more voluminous than external trade until the early nineteenth century.

The rise of the Greek Orthodox merchant marine, one of the most important socioeconomic developments of the late eighteenth century, was the result of a favorable international economic conjuncture. In particular, the French, who were, from the 1720s to the 1760s, the main economic agents in the eastern Mediterranean, relied heavily on Greek Orthodox intermediaries. When, after

**Table 5**
**The Greek Orthodox Merchant Marine, ca. 1800**

| Port/Island | No. of Ships | Volume in tons. | Crew | Artillery |
|---|---|---|---|---|
| Hydra | 120 | 45,000 | 5,400 | 2,400 |
| Spetses | 60 | 19,500 | 2,700 | 900 |
| Poros | 4 | 600 | 120 | 24 |
| Psara | 60 | 25,500 | 1,800 | 720 |
| Mykonos | 22 | 3,300 | 440 | 130 |
| Patmos | 13 | 1,690 | 195 | 52 |
| Kimi | 25 | 4,500 | 450 | 60 |
| Skyros | 12 | 1,200 | 144 | 48 |
| Skopelos | 25 | 6,300 | 525 | 140 |
| Trikeri (Volos) | 12 | 2,100 | 216 | 48 |
| Limnos | 15 | 3,900 | 300 | 90 |
| Crete | 40 | 15,000 | 2,200 | 480 |
| Tinos | 11 | 880 | 132 | 44 |
| Thira | 32 | 2,560 | 480 | 128 |
| Andros | 40 | 2,800 | 400 | 80 |
| Galaxidi | 50 | 10,000 | 1,100 | 80 |

*Source*: Katsoulis, Nikolinakos, and Filias (1985, 135).

the 1755–1763 war and later on, during the 1788–1792 war, the French were forced to withdraw from the eastern Mediterranean, the Greek Orthodox islanders temporarily captured the majority of the trade for themselves.[20] The result was the growth of the Greek Orthodox merchant marine fleet from 150 in 1750 to 300 in 1780 and 500 in 1806 (Stoianovich 1994, 104). According to McGowan (1994, 737), 75 percent of the Levant trade during the Napoleonic period was carried by Greek Orthodox ships under various flags (see Table 5 for an evaluation of the merchant marine's size at the turn of eighteenth century).

The fleet was organized largely according to the guild system. Individuals contributed to shipbuilding and received a portion of the total profit. When the trip was successfully concluded, the shares were liquidated and distributed among the members (for descriptions, see Kontogiorgis 1982, 171–3 and Vakalopoulos 1973, IV:483–94). In some islands, wealth accumulation contributed to bitter disputes between wealthy prelates and the majority of the population. Maritime commerce remained a risky enterprise because of piracy in the Mediterranean and this was a prime reason for arming commercial ships with artillery. In effect, the line between piracy and entrepreneurship was not altogether clear; rather, the same people who would be merchants under favorable economic conditions turned to piracy when peaceful commerce was not profitable.

In addition to the Mediterranean trade, the Black Sea trade was also facilitated by the Kuchuk Kainarji treaty (1774). Following the treaty's stipulations, in 1783 the Black Sea was opened to Russian ships and Catherine the Great sought to attract Orthodox merchants to Russian ports such as Odessa. On 19 April 1795, Catherine issued a decree inviting Greek Orthodox merchants to trade and arranged for its translation into Greek and dissemination in the empire. Over the following two decades Odessa became a major center of Greek Orthodox commercial activity (Karidis 1981). By 1808 Russia had enrolled 120,000 Greeks as protected persons (Quataert 1994, 838). The Ottomans reacted to this policy fairly soon, and during the reign of Selim III (1789–1807), the great dragomans Jacob Argyropoulos and Dimitrios Mourouzis obtained permits (*berats*) granting special privileges to Orthodox Christian merchants in the empire.[21]

These commercial ties between the Ottoman world-empire and Western and Eastern Europe over the eighteenth century fostered the expansion of expatriate communities created from the search for social mobility and economic prosperity. Around the turn of the seventeenth century, approximately 200,000 Serbs, Greeks, Vlachs (pastoral nomads who lived all over the Balkans), and Slavs from Macedonia moved into the Habsburg lands.[22] Two main trade routes were developed: one toward the interior of the Balkan peninsula connecting the Balkan headlands with the Habsburg lands; and a sea route, connecting the ports of the empire with French, English, and Italian ports (McGowan 1981, 25; Vakalopoulos 1973, IV:182–203). The Greek Orthodox migrations of the eighteenth century closely correspond to these commercial routes (Spiridonakis 1977, 142).

These population movements were not determined solely by expanding commercialization. First, migratory peasant workers were a traditional, less permanent, type of population mobility, especially in Bulgaria and Macedonia. Workers left their homes in spring to work on farms or estates in the more fertile central and eastern areas of the peninsula, and returned home in late autumn (Stoianovich 1994, 63–4; Andoniadou-Bibikou 1979; Tomasevich 1955; Katsoulis, Nikolinakos, and Filias 1985, 70). Over the eighteenth century, the Ottoman-Habsburg wars (and subsequent fiscal oppression by armed irregulars), brigandage, and tax farming based on out-of-date records contributed to peasant flight (McGowan 1994, 681). In the Bulgarian lands, for example, during the Russo-Ottoman war of 1806–1808 an estimated 100,000 Bulgarians moved into Wallachia and southern Russia (Crampton 1981, 174).

Second, rapid population growth played a part in these migrations: The population of Wallachia, which had peaked at 300,000 in 1560, reached 700,000 by 1810, and 1 million by 1822 (Chirot 1976, 41, 83). The population of Greece almost doubled in the 100 years leading to the 1821 revolution (Spiridonakis 1977, 115–7). These demographic trends lend weight to Jack Goldstone's (1991, 400) argument that population increases in the early modern period have been the crucial factor in creating the social conditions for state breakdown, rebellions, and revolutions. Although there is no historical inevitability of state breakdown as a consequence of demographic pressures, Goldstone's explanation provides an alternative origin for the demographic-pressures observed in the later eighteenth-century Balkans: The inability of the Balkan lands to feed their expanding population forced their inhabitants to migrate. The expansion of pastoral nomadism in the peninsula, discussed in the next section, also contributed to population movements.

Given the massive nature of these migrations, it is necessary to draw a distinction between capitalist merchants and small-scale merchants and peddlers. Only the first can be said to be part of a global capitalist class. Indeed, most of them developed close ties with international capital and became assimilated into their host countries. The second group's migration was often forced due to economic conditions, and return to the homeland was a constant goal (Nikolopoulos 1988, 127).[23] As discussed in the next chapter, it was among members of this second group that nationalist feelings emerged during the early nineteenth century. For example, they formed the overwhelming majority of the Philiki Eteria. The Eteria's chronic financial difficulties are evidence that the movement was a reflection of the dissatisfaction of middle strata and small merchants, and not a conspiracy financed by the old established immigrant Greek Orthodox communities.[24]

This "middle" class of intermediaries was one of the most important political constituencies for the emergence of national movements. Still, the transition from the formation of this stratum to the formation of national movements is not linear. As discussed in length in Chapter 2, the ethnicity of these merchants is not clear. Although referred to by Westerners as Greeks, they were of diverse ethnic origin. The high status of the Orthodox Patriarchate and the predominance of the Greek element within the new merchant class meant that "Greek" became a prestigious identification for all merchants.

## THE POLITICO-MILITARY NETWORK AND PASTORAL NOMADISM

The traditional historiographic perspective suggests that the decline of the Ottoman Empire originated in the late sixteenth century and became most acutely felt over the next two centuries.[25] The traditional view has been that the empire's decline implied a decentralization of control over various provinces, with local administrators usurping authority for themselves. However, this model has been challenged by scholars suggesting that, instead of decentralization, the empire developed a bureaucratic organization involving state centralization. Because the Ottoman route to state centralization entailed considerable differences from the Western European model, earlier research failed to do justice to the Ottoman case.

Following Charles Tilly's lead, Karen Barkey (1994) has suggested that the Ottoman route to state centralization involved bargaining between the central bureaucracy and local leaders. The regional challengers were not "broken" as in Western Europe; rather, they were "housebroken," that is, they were continuously involved in negotiations and bargaining with the central authority in order to obtain symbolic and material benefits.

The Ottoman state responded to the sixteenth-century crisis in a variety of ways involving the reorganization of the administration and the intensification of taxation (Abou-El-Haj 1991; Barkey 1994; Inalcik 1980). Specifically, the urgent need for cash already mentioned led to tax farming, whereby individuals, most often members of the bureaucracy themselves, were granted the right of tax collection for a prolonged period of time. This eventually turned into lifetime appointments during the eighteenth century. The bureaucracy became the empire's dominant institution, and approximately 40 large households were able, by the late seventeenth century, to share the upper levels of Ottoman power among themselves (Abou-El-Haj 1991, 43–7; Gocek 1996, 22–31). During the eighteenth century, persistent warfare with Russia and the Habsburg Empire resulted in an acute need for cash, leading the Ottomans to request, however unsuccessfully, loans from Muslim and Christian states (Gocek 1996, 45–8).

The increase in taxation was not followed by peasant unrest because the system allowed young peasants to enroll in the army as mercenaries (Barkey 1994; Inalcik 1980, 286–7). These mercenaries often turned to banditry. Banditry was carefully manipulated by the Ottoman imperial system. The bandits eventually developed into a social category of their own, divorced of their peasant background, and did not hesitate to prey on the peasantry itself. Moreover, the expansion of nomadism in the empire offered support for banditry.[26]

In the eighteenth century, the powerful provincial *ayans* (Ali Pasha Tepelenli, Pasvanoglou, Mehmed Ali) who established their own mini-regimes relied heavily on such mercenary and bandit forces.[27] The rise of these provincial notables was an extension of the empire's bureaucratic organization. Over the sixteenth and seventeenth centuries, the office-households of the bureaucracy remained relatively centralized. But the necessity of the bureaucrats to safeguard their position against palace plots or dismissal and fear of confiscation led them to further their ties with the local notables, who were their traditional intermediaries with the population. The appointment of local notables as tax farmers strengthened their local power base (Gocek 1996, 60–2).

This group's behavior was the model for their counterparts in the Orthodox community, the local Christian prelates.[28] Under Ottoman rule, self-government (and tax collection) was transferred to the local level. The need for efficient tax collection led the Ottomans to assign the duty of tax collection to wealthy and prominent individuals in each community. This system offered the opportunity of tax usurpation (or multiplication) either by the prelates themselves or by agents of the central government.[29] Orthodox Christian and Muslim prelates were most often caught in the maelstrom of politico-military confrontations with each other, the central government, or local bandits. When Muslim and Christian notables were in conflict they would call on these outlaws for support of their own particular faction (for examples, see Kontogiorgis 1982, 351–70; for Peloponnesus, see Alexander 1985, 25, 38–40).

Known as *haiduks* or *klephts*, the Balkan bandits are viewed as symbols of popular resistance to Ottoman rule or as social bandits.[30] In reality, their ascent was a by-product of the organization of the local agricultural economy, whereby pastoral nomads moved with their large herds of sheep and goats from the lowlands to mountain pastures in April, and returned to the lowlands in October.[31] The economy of the pastoral nomads was based on the sheep and the goat, which were kept for milk, wool, and meat. Between the 1400s and the 1800s, in the mountainous areas of the peninsula (Kosovo, the mountainous areas of mainland Greece, and southern Albania) animal husbandry and pastoralism flourished (Arsh 1994, 31–91; Malcolm 1998).

In the *pashalik* of Belgrade, both agriculture and livestock raising were prevalent. Livestock was the main economic activity and agriculture prevailed in the areas of Stig, Krajina, the valley of Velika Morava, and in Krusevac Zupa. Corn-laden forests provided feed for swine, and the meadows grass for cattle and horses. During the late eighteenth century, the pig trade became the major commercial activity targeting the Habsburg markets. By 1800, an estimate of 200,000 heads per year were exported to the Habsburg lands (Pavlowich 1981, 41; Stojancevic 1982, 26). In southern Greece, the expansion of Ali Pasha Tepelenli's landed property favored the expansion of pastoralism. By 1821, he owned approximately 920 villages inhabited by 70,000 peasants; his flocks included 4,000,000 goats and sheep. His movable property was 150,000,000 gold francs and his annual income 30,000,000 francs (Moskof 1987, 58–9). Under the shadow of Pasvanoglou in Bulgaria, a similar trend developed: By the early nineteenth century, the shepherds of Kotel used to drive flocks of 10,000 to 30,000 sheep to graze on the pastures of Dobrudja (Crampton 1981, 178).

This lifestyle favored sheep stealing, robbery, and arms bearing, which in turn contributed to the development of a military class with its own ethos (Stoianovich 1994, 331–5).[32] In sharp contrast to the plains, mountainous regions—such as Kosovo, Mani (in Peloponnesus), Souli (in Epirus), and Montenegro—typically provided the terrain for challenging the local authorities (Kontogiorgis 1977, 18–22; Van Boeshoten, 1991a). In these regions, a clan-based society persisted, following its own customary laws, frequently involving the practice of vendettas among the different clans.

Montenegro, with its local archbishop serving as a de facto clan leader, is the best-known case of pastoral paramilitary societal formation. In 1834, Montenegro had 100,000 inhabitants and 20,000 rifles (Ferguson 1981; Stevenson 1971). Similarly, Mani in Peloponnesus was reportedly populated by close to

11,000 bandits at the turn of the nineteenth century (Alexander 1985, 64). The Greco-Albanian clans of the Souliotes in Epirus had the military strength of 2,500 men and received tribute from the neighboring villages. They fought the Ottoman forces in 1732, 1754, 1759, 1762, 1772, 1775, and 1789. Ali Pasha Tepelenli carried out legendary military expeditions against them until, finally, in 1803 he succeeded in destroying their basis (Skiotis 1976, 97; see also Krapsitis 1989, 54, 99–120). Similar clans were prevalent in northern Albania proper and the mountainous Kosovo plateau (Malcolm 1998; Arsh 1994).

Under these conditions, the Ottomans often employed the bandits as armed irregulars (*armatoli*) paid by the authorities in order to safeguard crucial commercial routes and passages (Skiotis 1975, 308–15). But there was no clear distinction between *klephts* (literally "thieves") and *armatoli* (or *haiduk*), because the same individuals might move between the two groups. Both "valued arms, and thrived on violence and open or veiled defiance of established autonomy" (Koliopoulos 1987, 26, 31–33; Baggally 1936, 1–27; Sanders 1979; Vucinich 1979).

Already mentioned in the brief review of the Serb uprising, Prince Miloš of Serbia was an extraordinary example of such a *haiduk* leader. His background was that of merchant, provincial leader, and bandit, activities that were fused rather than separated at the time. He consolidated his rule through negotiations with the Porte, often using bribery, and was interested in usurping authority and tax collection activities for himself. Since he did not know how to read or write he did not depend on the written word. He treated his administrators as his servants, and ruled by inspiring obedience through fear (see Petrovich 1976, I; Stokes 1976, 84–85; Castellan 1967 for a description of Serb dynasty, administration, and peasantry in the 1800–1840 period).

Within the *armatolikia*, a number of positions became hereditary; this led to the consolidation of a military class of captains, possessing flocks and land. By the early eighteenth century, bandits were present in 30 administrative areas in Bulgaria and Macedonia. By the end of the century there were eighteen *armatolikes* in Epirus alone (for a review, see Vasdravellis 1975, 16–7). As in Sicily (Blok 1974a), the rise of banditry was closely related to the bandits' ability to usurp authority for themselves from the local Christian or Muslim prelates. Their behavior in times of crisis was dictated not by the "national interest" but by their own customs and self-interest. For example, during the 1821–1828 Greek revolution, the *armatoli* of mainland Greece acted in an opportunistic manner, frequently withdrawing from the Greek camp or actively helping the Ottomans (when the military outcome in the region was in doubt). In addition, they would keep open lines of communication with the enemy while participating actively in the Greek cause, a type of insurance against possible Greek defeat (Petropulos 1976, 132). When organized fighting ceased (1827), virtually all the chieftains of western Rumeli submitted to Ottoman authority.

## A PRELIMINARY BALANCE SHEET

The three revolutionary movements exemplify the different impacts of the changes in the socioeconomic and politico-military networks and the way that these changes contributed to organized revolutionary activity. Although the incorporation thesis views these revolutions as closely associated with the expansion of the capitalist world-economy, the relationship between economic changes and social movements was mediated by the institutional and political context of the empire. Moreover, the economic changes of the eighteenth century were an extension of already established ties with Western Europe. From such a perspective, economic changes provided for the formation of such groups as the agricultural merchants and pig traders in Serbia and the Greek Orthodox shipowners and merchants. Although these groups tilted the Ottoman stratification system by assuming positions of relative prosperity, their actions were not determined by solely economic considerations. To arrive at a more complete understanding of their actions, it is necessary to account for their orientation, worldview, and identity formation. This is the task of the next chapter.

In the aftermath of the Ottoman bureaucratic reorganization of the sixteenth and seventeenth centuries, local Muslim leaders, bandits, and the central bureaucracy were involved in a web of constant conflict and cooperation. This web of association reflected the extent to which regional leaders sought privileges and rewards from the very central authority they challenged. Over the eighteenth century, the Muslim dignitaries (the *ayans*) that emerged and controlled for a period of time a considerable part of the Balkan peninsula, were the beneficiaries of this social pattern of center–periphery relations.

Armed bandits, mostly pastoralists or peasants associated with pastoral nomads, served as mercenaries for various competing sides. When the Porte moved to suppress two of the most powerful *ayans*, Pasvanoglou of Vidin and Ali Pasha Tepelenli, the local Christian elites and bandits found a good opportunity for revolt. Regional factors were the primary considerations in both the Greek and Serb cases. Because neither Serb nor Greek prelates were large landowners, they were not afraid of losing wealth and power by joining in the revolts—and they did so. In the Danubian principalities, however, Vladimirescu's peasant uprising met the strong reaction of the boyars, who saw in it a direct threat to their class interests. The Greco-Wallachian cooperation broke down relatively soon, leaving victory for the boyars, who gained the right to have the prince appointed from within their ranks.

If nationalism is defined as an ideology that is responsible for bringing together peoples of different backgrounds, there is little in the analysis thus far to suggest its existence. Rather, these revolutionary movements appear to be the product of socioeconomic changes, opportunities for military mobilization, and the general historical conjuncture.

Such an approach leaves the significant differences between the Serb and

Greek movements unaccounted for. The Serbs struggled for a long time, and were eventually successful only in gaining local autonomy and independence over their internal affairs. Serbia did not become fully independent until 1878. The Great Powers made occasional and opportunistic use of the Serb revolt, but were in general uninterested. This stands in sharp contrast with the Greek revolution, which led to Great Power involvement and the creation of an independent state in 1832, as well as to a wave of philhellenism throughout Europe (described in detail in Chapter 2). Although, there were many similarities between the Serb and Greek cases, there is little in the analysis thus far to help explain the differences in response to them by the great powers and the European public. This is because issues of ideology and cross-cultural communication have remained outside the scope of the analysis.

It is therefore necessary to listen to the agents themselves and inquire into their thinking. Until now, the voice of the agents has been replaced by the voices of the researchers, imputing motives and causes according to the agents' socioeconomic or politico-military position. The silent assumption is that human motives are essentially utilitarian and the possibility of action undertaken for altruistic motives is excluded. Religion, ideology, and mentality are played down in favor of class interest and individual profit.

While arguing in favor of an analysis focusing on the cultural-ideological dimension, however, it is important to state that the analysis thus far is not misguided or incorrect; it does provide a valid part of the necessary explanation. In other words, in the causal chain that this analysis follows, the economic, political, and military changes are properly considered to be necessary factors in the Balkan revolutions. However, they are not sufficient factors. To arrive at a complete explanation, it is necessary to incorporate the cultural-ideological network and its impact on these revolutions. The suggested line of explanation attempts to move beyond a juxtaposition of ideas and material factors, toward an explanation that incorporates economic, institutional, and cultural variables. It is exactly this task that is undertaken in the next chapter.

## NOTES

1. See Inalcik (1978b, 104–29), Itzkowitz (1977, 24), and Karpat (1973, 22). Karpat considers the *askeri* as open to non-Muslims but he adds that this was the case only by conversion (the ecclesiastical positions are the only exception). See Cvetkova (1975) for a discussion of reformist plans in the second half of the eighteenth century.

2. See Gocek (1996, 20–43) and Findley (1980, 3–40). For an overview of the Ottoman bureaucracy in the seventeenth century, see Faroghi (1994, 552–64).

3. McGowan (1981, 47) and Inalcik (1994, 114–8, 139–42). For an overview of the types of land ownership and their relationship to the earlier Byzantine system, see Tsopotos (1983, 60–107) and Cvetkova (1979a).

4. Cvetkova (1979a, 141) points out that the mediation of the state did not alter peasant dependency. Although this is true, state intervention introduced a new agent into social life, an agent largely absent in early Western European feudalism.

5. See Islamoglu and Keyder (1987, 59) and Asdrachas (1988b, 21–3). For a detailed description of the methods by which the *ciftlik* system was created from the *timar* system, see McGowan (1981, 56–79).

6. To cite an example, in 1801 Mouchli Giousuf Pashas of Serres owned 100 villages, half of them in the Struma valley in Macedonia; he was tax collector for the 11 larger villages and small towns of Chalkidiki (Moskof, 1987, 59).

7. It took the central government the next two decades to suppress the *ayans*. Sultan Selim III (1789–1807) undertook a major attempt at reform and this was continued by his successor Mahmud I (1808–1839). The janissary corps was relinquished in 1826 and under Selim III the foundations of a new army corps were laid. On the attempts to reform the Ottoman military and administration in this time period, see Shaw (1971; 1976, 260–77), Shaw and Shaw (1977, 1–55), and Lewis (1979, 40–103; 1965).

8. Karpat (1982a, 154) attributes peasant participation to incitement by the Greek prelates. Presumably this was because the prelates had little opportunity to move into the upper ranks of the Ottoman administration, and this served to strengthen their ties with their communities and their identification with the peasants. Unfortunately, this argument, however plausible, is not borne out by the evidence.

9. In pre-1821 "Old Greece" a little over 8 million "old *stremmas*" (close to 20% of 45,000 square kilometers) was equally divided between approximately 635,000 Christians and 65,000 Turks. In Peloponnesus the per capita landholding ratio between Greeks and Turks reached 20 to 1 (McGraw 1976, 114). In fact, Djordjevic (1965) considers the Greek and Serb revolutions to be peasant revolts motivated by the peasants' desire to overthrow the fiscally oppressive Ottoman regime.

10. Castellan (1989, 85) and Marinescu (1981, 289–319). The *divans* of Bucharest and Jassy opposed these obligatory deliveries. Petitions demanding a limitation and reduction of the principalities' obligations were drawn in 1774, 1782, 1783, 1785, 1786, 1787, 1791, 1793, 1803, 1818, 1822, 1824, and 1827 (Georgescu, 1971, 35).

11. Iorga (1985), Georgescu (1991, 58–72), Runciman (1968, 360–84), Zakynthinos (1976, 94–105), Subtelny (1986, 137–44), and Borsi-Kalman (1991, 7–13). In Wallachia, the reigns of Serban Cantacuzino (1678–1688) and Constantin Brancoveanu (1688–1714) accelerated the pace of Greek cultural influences (Deletant 1991, 190–2).

12. My discussion of the Phanariots draws heavily on Florescu (1968), Mango (1973), Papadopoullos (1990), Runciman (1968), Ionescu-Niscov (1974), Constantinu and Papacostea (1972), and Papacostea-Danielopolou (1986).

13. Runciman (1968) and Mango (1973) give conflicting views of the Phanariots when it comes to extraction of taxes from the principalities. Runciman writes that "every prince ended his rule a poorer man" and that the taxes extracted from the Wallachian and Moldavian peasantry ended up in the Porte. By contrast, Mango believes that the Phanariots themselves were appropriating this surplus. Constantinos Mavrocordatos' career supports Runciman's interpretation but Karatzas' career path supports Mango's. See Subtelny (1986, 36–41, 59–77) on the tribute in the pre-Phanariot period.

14. Camariano (1965) suggested that Vladimirescu was a member of the Eteria. Tappe (1973, 138) is certain that he was but Berindei (1973, 107) believes the evidence to be insufficient. In a lengthy overview of the Romanian bibliography, Oikonomidou (1982–1984) points out that Vladimirescu's plans were part of the Eterist plans. However, his call to the peasantry was so successful that the revolt was soon turned into a peasant uprising.

15. The conspirators initially offered the leadership position to Count Capodistrias,

who was the Russian foreign minister at the time. Capodistrias declined because he wisely predicted that the movement would be doomed. Ypsilantis was an officer in the Russian Army, and he hoped that Russia would intervene to save the Christian population. From the Ottoman point of view, the entire situation pointed to Russian involvement. For a review, see Jelavich (1991, 51–7).

16. See Wallerstein (1989, 121–89), Wallerstein & Kasaba (1983), Kasaba (1988), and Wallerstein, Decdeli, and Kasaba (1987). Similar accounts but with a more flexible viewpoint vis-à-vis the issue of relative autonomy of the state and other institutions have been put forward by Islamoglu and Keyder (1987) and Sunar (1987).

17. See, for example, Todorov (1986, 280–98); Moskof (1987, 77–84), and Kremmydas (1988). See Kordatos (1924/1991) for the original thesis and Stavrianos (1957, 335–48) for a closely related argument.

18. According to Karpat (1972, 244), "the relations of the *ayan*s with the bureaucratic order and their conflicting group ideologies formed . . . the central dynamics of the internal transformation which occurred in Ottoman society in the eighteenth and early nineteenth centuries."

19. See Mile (1979, 185–90) for Albania, Tsopotos (1983, 128–50) for Thessaly, and McGowan (1981, 121–70) on Macedonian *ciftlik*s in the 1620–1830 period. Stoianovich (1992, 26–7) reports the presence of *ciftlik*s in Macedonia and Thrace as early as the second half of the sixteenth century, and in Bulgaria by the 1750s, especially in Vidin, Lom, and Belogradchik. For general discussion on the *ciftlik* system and the introduction of maize into the Balkans, see Stoianovich (1992, 1–13).

20. Much of this was contraband trade, in theory illegal, but made possible because of the coalescence of interests among *ciftlik* owners, merchants, and "corrupt" administrators. The grain trade led to repeated food crises throughout the empire, leading to successive imperial edicts condemning the practice (Kasaba 1988, 18–22; Leontaridis 1987, 44–6; Gocek 1996, 90).

21. These privileges included customs relief, the right to wear special uniforms, the right to keep representatives in Smyrna and Salonika, and the right to conduct their affairs and appeal personally to the Sultan on behalf of their interests (Mantran 1977, 219; Vakalopoulos 1973, IV:426; Pantazopoulos 1988, 313). These benefits led to protests by Muslim merchants (Quataert 1994, 839).

22. See Vucinich (1979, 302), McGowan (1981, 90), and Papandrianos (1993, 19–29), and, for an overview, McGowan (1994, 647–50). By the middle of the eighteenth century, approximately 18,000 Balkan merchants are reported to be based on the Habsburg lands, mainly along the Ottoman border (Lampe and Jackson 1982, 60). Vakalopoulos (1973, IV:226) puts the figure at 80,000 families.

23. In his study of Greek Orthodox immigrants in the southern Slav countries, Papandrianos (1993) classifies them into three main categories: commercial intermediaries transferring goods between regions, large merchants, and small merchants and peddlers (other related occupations are also reported). On the ambivalent attitude toward expatriation, see Vakalopoulos (1973, IV).

24. For discussions, see Clogg (1981), Yanoulopoulos (1981), and Filias (1985). As Dertilis (1977, 43–54) argues, the incorporation of the Ottoman Empire into the modern world-economy does not necessitate the transformation of its socioeconomic structures.

25. The empire's decline brought with it important changes in the general socioeconomic structure of the Ottoman Balkans and has been a topic of discussion among re-

gional experts for a long time. For some of the most influential viewpoints, see Inalcik (1972; 1977; 1978b, 224), Cvetkova (1977), and Stavrianos (1958, 117–36).

26. Barkey's (1994) analysis focuses on Anatolia, but the general process she describes is quite helpful in understanding the situation in the Balkans, too. Oddly, in an earlier publication (Chirot and Barkey 1984), she adopts a negative view of the Balkan revolutions as unworthy of analysis.

27. Inalcik (1977, 27–52). In the Balkans, powerful *ayan*s were Pasvanoglou of Vidin, Mehmed the Old (succeeded by Kara Mahmud) in the *sanjack* of Skhodra (Shkoder), and Ali Pasha Tepelenli (for details, see Pollo and Puto 1979, 131–44; Malcolm 1998; Arsh 1994).

28. These prelates are known as *corbaci* or *chorzabazi* among the Bulgarians, and *cojabasi (kotzampastides)* among the Greeks. In the case of the Serbs, the same function was fulfilled by the tribal organizations known as *knezes* (McGowan 1994, 668–70; Sarres 1990, II:337–420; Kontogiorgis 1982; Asdrachas 1988a, 123–44; Vakalopoulos 1973; Karpat 1973, 150).

29. Thus, in 1809 the dragoman of the fleet Theodoros Rizos received 50,192 *gross* by the islanders on behalf of the central government. He did not turn the money over to the treasury, however, and the central government demanded the payment of the taxes by the islanders in full (Kontogiorgis 1982, 79). By the end of the eighteenth century, the prelate of the island of Naxos Markakis Politis forced the islanders to pay him 40,000 *gross* (three times the normal amount of taxes) as payment for his expenses (travels, briberies to the Porte, etc.) (Kontogiorgis 1982, 123–48).

30. See Hobsbawm (1959, 1969). For critical evaluations of the social banditry thesis, see Bolk (1974b), Koliopoulos (1980), Barkey (1994), and Van Boeshoten (1991b).

31. The pastoral lifestyle contributed to clan-based structures such as the well-known *zadruga* family (see Byrnes, 1976). The *zadruga* was not the outcome of the *ciftlik* mode of cultivation and is observed among Vlachs, Albanians, and Slavs (Todorova 1993). As Braudel (1972) has observed, for the Mediterranean as a whole the mountaineers were a group living on the fringes of civilization.

32. Around 1781, the Sofia authorities revived the custom of hiring mounted guards against the *haiduk*s from St. George's Day (6 May) to St. Demetrius' Day (26 October). This period corresponds with the seasonal movements of the shepherds, thus indicating that *haiduk* activity was related to the pastoral lifestyle (Cvetkova 1982, 324). The role of the seasonal movement between the two holidays is exemplified in the following Serb proverb: "On St. Demetrius' *haiduk*s disband, on St. George's *haiduk*s together band" (quoted in Stoianovich 1994, 64).

# 2

# A Multidimensional Analysis of the Balkan National Revolutions (Part II)

To address the issue of shifts within the cultural-ideological network of the Ottoman Balkans, it is necessary to discuss the relationship between the various "national awakenings" of the Balkan peoples and the key intellectual feature in eighteenth-century European intellectual life, that is, the Enlightenment. Conventionally, Eastern European literature (particularly the Balkan national histories) gives a broad interpretation to the Enlightenment, identifying it as a general trend toward literacy, social and cultural mobilization, and national assertion. This sweeping interpretation makes the Enlightenment almost synonymous with a "national renaissance" or an "awakening."[1] In such interpretations of the Enlightenment, different intellectual currents (millenarianism, liberalism, and romantic nationalism) are bound together. To avoid such a conflation, it is necessary to view the Balkan Enlightenment as an expression of the intellectual contacts with Western and Central Europe (Kitromilides 1983, 51–52). The Enlightenment was a social movement that emerged in European societies over the course of the eighteenth century—roughly between 1750 and 1799. It sought to replace the theocratic and authoritarian culture of the Old Regimes with a new culture that proclaimed itself to be secular, rational, and scientifically oriented. In the ideology of the ancient regime, societies were composed of corporate groups with distinctive rights and responsibilities; in the Enlightenment view, societies were composed of individuals who created social institutions by entering into voluntary contracts (Gay, 1966, 32–38; Bendix 1978). These principles were gradually applied to society at large, thus providing the context for the substitution of the rule of kings by that of the "people." The concept of "nation" emerged in close connection with this important shift in ideology and political legitimacy.

## ETHNICITY AND SOCIAL STRUCTURE IN OTTOMAN BALKAN SOCIETY

In most ethnically diverse societies, class and ethnicity are closely associated. Because only the more affluent, urban, and literate strata are in a structural position to be influenced by ideological currents (such as the Enlightenment), it is important to clearly establish the relationship between class and ethnicity in Ottoman Balkan society. In addition, given the fact that national identity is a relatively recent phenomenon, the issue of ethnicity should be approached in a nonnationalist manner. To do so, it is necessary to differentiate between modern forms of identity (such as national identity) and premodern forms of identity. As discussed in the Introduction, the concept of *ethnie* (or ethnic community) allows for such a differentiation.[2] Contrary to the situation in modern secular nations, characterized by a mass public culture, common economy, and legal rights and duties of their members, *ethnies* are predominantly premodern social formations. Membership in an *ethnie* does not necessarily lead to attributing political significance to ethnic differences.

I suggest that in the Ottoman Balkans, Greeks, Albanians, Bulgarians, Serbs, and Romanians were *ethnies* that were clearly aware of their differences. But, even if this proposition is accepted, it does not follow that modern nations are born out of an ethnic core (cf. Smith, 1986). In fact, at least in the case of the Greek Orthodox Christians, this model does not capture the complexity of the historical record. The key issue has to do not only with the existence of separate *ethnies* in the Balkans, but also with the manner in which social mobility and the division of labor affected the always fluid nature of ethnic identity.

Before the 1850s, social mobility frequently implied acculturation into the *ethnie* associated with a particular niche in the social division of labor. For example, in Macedonia, Serbia, and Bulgaria, class and ethnicity overlapped, resulting in the utilization of the terms "Serb" and "Bulgar" to denote the peasantry per se. Since most peasants were Slavs and most Slavs were peasants, class distinctions often became ethnic distinctions (Slijepcevic 1958, 82–96; Kofos 1964; Vermulen 1984; Shashko 1973). When Slavs moved into the urban world or became members of the middle classes, they generally shifted their identity to Greek. In Belgrade, for example, Serbian townsmen dressed in the Greek style, the Belgrade newspapers included the rubric *Greciia* (Greece), and the local Christian "higher strata" were Grecophone until 1840—at least according to Stoianovich (1994, 294; see also Karanovich, 1995, 31). In southern Albania and Greece during the late eighteenth and nineteenth centuries, thousands of Orthodox Albanians and Vlachs became completely Hellenized (Skendi 1980, 187–204). In the Bulgarian lands, during the second half of the eighteenth century, the domination of cultural life by the Ecumenical Patriarchate led to the promotion of Grecophone culture in liturgy, archives, and correspondence (Markova 1980).

For the Serb and Bulgarian *ethnies*, the Slavic clergy served as a depository of ethnic identity and the religious "cell schools" provided an elementary education in Old Slavonic. In 1762 the Bulgarian monk Father Paisi of Khilendar wrote his (later famous) *Slavo-Bulgarian History*, a call to cultural regeneration and revitalization of Bulgarian ethnic identity (Clark 1954; Pundeff 1969; Hristov 1974; Velchev 1981). Similarly, during the latter part of the eighteenth century, the Serb monk Dositej Obradović attempted to spread literacy and education among the Serbs (Pribic 1983; Jovanovic-Gorup 1991). In 1811, Obradović was appointed minister of education, and, although he kept this post for a few months until his death later in the same year, he is credited with giving a new direction to the newly created education system in Serbia (Karanovich 1995, 13).

The 1804 Serb uprising was a response to the administrative disintegration of the Ottoman Empire. National sentiments among the Serbs were largely absent before the 1840s (Stokes 1976; Meriage 1977). Major influences for the formation of a Serb national identity came from the communities of the Habsburg Serbs (Banac 1981; Stoianovich 1989). As the 1804 Serb uprising illustrates, the key difference between the Grecophone and Slavonic cases was one of reception. Obradović and Paisi were at the forefront of sociocultural transformation within the Bulgarian and Serb *ethnies*. The entire eighteenth century produced only five Serbian historians and three Bulgarian historians (with the exception of the chroniclers) (Petrovich 1970, 297–309). All Serb historians were natives of the Habsburg Empire. Jovan Rajić's *History of the Various Slavic People* (1794–1795) remained a seminal work for southern Slav historiography for the next fifty years, a testimony to the general low level of historical writing. Similarly, the rise of the Bulgarian national movement is closely associated with the ascent of a nationalist intelligentsia in the post-1825 period (Meininger 1974).

The establishment of secular schools indicates the beginnings of the transformation of the Serb and Bulgarian *ethnies* into modern secular nations. During the 1804 Serb uprising, the revolutionaries, most of them illiterate, realized the importance of education and proceeded to organize the first high school (Grand School or *Velika skola*) in the *pashalik* of Belgrade. The school was opened officially in 1808 (Pribic 1983, 47–48; Karanovich 1995, 12–13). By 1830, when it became an autonomous principality, Serbia had sixteen town schools and several village schools, with a combined enrollment of approximately 800 pupils and 22 teachers (Karanovich 1995, 25). In Montenegro, the first elementary school was opened by Vladika (prince-bishop) Njegoš in 1834 (Lederer 1969, 401). In the Bulgarian case the number of traditional religious cell schools rose from 35 in 1800 to 189 in 1834 but most of them continued to teach Old Slavonic (not modern Bulgarian). Later secular Bulgarian intellectuals received their education from a number of Greco-Bulgarian schools, which taught not only classical and modern Greek, but modern Bulgarian as well. The first secular school in Bulgaria proper was instituted in 1835 thanks to the contribution of Vasil Aprilov, a merchant from Odessa. Initially, Aprilov considered himself Greek and aided the 1821 Greek revolution. When in 1829 the Ukrainian I. Venelin published in Moscow his *History of the Ancient and Modern Bulgars*, the book had a profound effect on Aprilov, who became an advocate of Bulgarian revival. With the aid of the Greek bishop Ilarion, Aprilov founded in 1835 the first secular school in his hometown of Garnovo.

In the early nineteenth century, the migratory waves of Bulgarians across the Danube and into the Danubian principalities significantly affected Bulgarian cultural life (Nelson 1989; Velichi 1979; Crampton 1981). Bulgarian pupils received education in Bulgarian in local schools. In 1830 the merchant Vasil Nenovich founded the first Bulgarian school in Bucharest. In 1806 bishop Sofroni Vrachanski published in Rimnik in Wallachia the first printed book in modern Bulgarian vernacular (a version of the Greek liturgical book *Kiriakodromion*). In 1824, Peter Beron published in Brasov *Riben Bukvar*, a primer that was heavily influenced by the *Eklogarion Grekikon* of Dimitrios Darvaris. This primer helped standardize the language into a literary form (Lord 1963, 260–1; Georgeoff 1982; Loukidou-Mavridou and Papadrianos 1980). As these two key examples illustrate, Greek translations had a strong impact on the emerging Bulgarian literature (see also Alexieva 1993; Danova 1980).

Before the 1820s, then, most middle-class Balkan Orthodox Christians were either ethnic Greeks, were largely acculturated into the Greek *ethnie*, or were under heavy Grecophone influence. To inquire into the Enlightenment's impact in the Balkans requires the specification of those groups that were in a structural position to be influenced by it. Only literate middle or upper classes could have been exposed to the new ideas and have an adequate comprehension of them. Even if the peasantry did enjoy a tacit understanding of the new ideas, the barriers of illiteracy would not have allowed them to articulate it. Therefore, any examination of the Enlightenment in Ottoman Balkan society should take notice of the class-based nature of this intellectual movement. This means that the Enlightenment's impact on the Ottoman Balkans was mainly (but not exclusively) among Greek, Grecophone, or Hellenized strata.

This argument is bolstered by the peculiar situation that developed in the Danubian principalities. As discussed in Chapter 1, Wallachia and Moldavia were never under direct Ottoman rule and, as a result, their social institutions were different from those of Ottoman society (Todorov 1985). In sharp contrast to the Ottoman Empire, in the Danubian principalities there was the Christian landowning class of the boyars. Throughout the Phanariot period (1711–1821), high-ranking boyars were employed consistently in administrative positions in the two principalities. However, the more numerous lower ranking boyars (the *neamurile* and the *mazili*) were frustrated because they were only partially exempted from taxation and because of their exclusion from high offices (Cernovodeanu 1986, 253). For them, the desire to overthrow the Phanariot regime was related to the desire to advance their own socioeconomic position (Georgescu 1991, 73–5, 96; Jewsbury 1979; Oldson 1983; Fischer-Galati 1969).

The political conflict between the boyars and the princes was not along ethnic lines since Greek, Hellenized, and Romanian families were often themselves divided between the two sides. Indeed, the Greek influence was so strong that Greek had become the language of the court, the royal academies, the divine services held at court, politics, and polite company. Even those who were of Romanian origin spoke Greek as their primary language. The influence of the Phanariots and the Grecophone Enlightenment on the local boyars' reception of Enlightenment ideas was considerable (Dutu 1967; Borsi-Kalman 1991, 12–3). During the eighteenth century, there was a clear trend toward secularization, with secular books rising from 15.6 percent of all books published in the 1717–1750 period to 53.2 percent in the 1790–1800 period and 74.8 percent in 1820–1830 (Georgescu 1991, 113).

During the 1750–1830 period, three generations of authors, members of the high and middle nobility, middle classes, and clergy raised the issue of administrative reform in the principalities. Between 1769 and 1830, 93 percent of the petitions for reform programs were signed by members of these elite groups (Georgescu 1970, ix). Among those asking for reforms were intellectuals who articulated a new political ideology. This new ideology did not initially make any connections with the Daco-Roman "cult" of the Latinist School of Transylvania. Instead of the theory of the Latin origins of contemporary Romanians, scholars such as Mihail Cantacuzino or Naum Ramniceanu suggested that it was the Dacians (although Romanized), and not the Ancient Romans, that were the forefathers of the Romanian nation (Fischer-Galati 1964; Georgescu 1991, 115–8). The ideology of "enlightened despotism" reached the principalities in the form of numerous German works, especially those of Christian Wolff. The Phanariots modeled their authority after European "enlightened despotism"; whereas the boyars chose to accuse the Phanariots of "oriental despotism" or developed the notions of "fatherland," "awakening," "citizen," and promoted restricted constitutional government, autonomy, and limited sovereignty (Georgescu 1971, 67, 106–23).

In 1818, the Transylvanian educator Gheorghe Lazar left Transylvania for Bucharest to take over the school of St. Sava; he established it as a center for the propagation of new national teachings. In Moldavia an analogous task was undertaken by Gheorghe Asachi in 1814 (Borsi-Kalman 1991, 29). Before these dates, higher education in the principalities had been Grecophone. Following the end of the Phanariot administration in 1821, the strong Grecophone presence was not (nor could it be) eradicated. Even in 1840, 28 of the 117 private schools in Wallachia were Grecophone. During the 1820–1840 period, Greek influences were manifested in intellectuals' bilingualism, in the manuscripts of this period, and the plethora of Greek neologisms in the language (Papacostea-Danielopolou 1971, 89). However, Greek was slowly replaced by French and then by Romanian.

The presence of a local indigenous aristocracy in the two principalities reveals the close relationship between class position and the articulation of political ideologies. The very reason that, as Peter Sugar (1975) and Dimitrije Djordjevic (1975) have suggested, the Enlightenment's impact on Ottoman Balkan society was confined to the Greek and Romanian cases, is the fact that only members of these two *ethnies* were in a structural position to be directly influenced by Western European ideological currents.

## THE ORTHODOX CHURCH AND MILLENARIANISM

To identify the Enlightenment's impact on the Ottoman Balkans, it is necessary to outline the preexisting ideological currents. Traditionally, the key cultural institution of Ottoman Balkan society, the Orthodox Church, was seen as the depository of the Balkan nations' national identity during the Ottoman period. But the Orthodox Church was a guardian of faith alone (Stokes 1979). For the Byzantine world, there was only one emperor and his empire constituted an earthly manifestation of the Kingdom of Heaven.[3] In fact, the 1453 conquest of Constantinople was explained as God's punishment for the sins of the Orthodox Christians. The post-1453 millenarianism merged the notion of the reconstruction of the Christian empire with the idea of the Second Coming. With the Second Coming, the Ottoman Empire would collapse and God's earthly kingdom would be reconstituted (Daniilidis 1934, 113–20). The Second Coming was to take place in 1492; this belief was so strong that even patriarch Gennadius subscribed to it (Mango 1980, 212–4). A later prophecy predicted that only five sultans would reign over Constantinople and another oracle postponed it further until the reign of Mehmed III (1595–1603). In the seventeenth century, prophecies were that Constantinople would be liberated 200 years after its fall, whereas in the eighteenth century the years of 1766, 1767, and 1773 were cited as possible dates for the Second Coming (Mango 1965, 35–36; Stoianovich 1995, 93–113).

Among the Greeks, folk myths related the fall of Constantinople to supernatural events. Additional prophecies and oracles proclaimed the future liberation of the Orthodox Christians by a fair-haired people (*xantho genos*) (for an overview, see Clogg 1985). Legend has it that the patriarch Gennadius interpreted an inscription on the tomb of the emperor Constantine to be a sign of this future event. During the second half of the sixteenth century, this prophecy gained momentum and was widely disseminated during the reign of Mustafa I (1617–1618 and 1622–1623) and throughout the late seventeenth century (Stoianovich 1995, 103–4). In the eighteenth century, Russian rulers such as Peter the Great and Catherine the Great became the foci of Orthodox millenarianism. In about 1750, the monk Theoklitos Poliklidis published a pamphlet (*Aghathangelos*) foretelling the liberation of the Christians by the fair-haired people, who, at the time, were generally identified as the Russians (Nikolopoulos 1985).

Similarly, the Serb Church preserved the cult of Prince Lazar following the extinction of his dynasty and the conquest of the Serb lands by the Turks (1389). Poetry and oral tradition were gradually codified in the Kosovo legend. In the religious interpretations of the Kosovo legend, emphasis was placed on Christian martyrdom: "Lazar's death on Kosovo [field] was the atonement for all of Serbia's sins—sins that had called the wrath of God upon them in the first place and caused them to lose their state" (Emmert 1990, 121). In 1601 the Italian Mavro Orbini published his work *Il regno degli Slavi*, which included a long passage on the Kosovo legend. In 1722 Sava Vladislavić published a Slavonic translation of Orbini's history, and during the eighteenth century the legend gained popularity among the Serbs of the Habsburg and Ottoman lands (Emmert 1990, 105–23; Mihailovich 1991). In 1690 the Serbian Church canonized the royal Nemanjić lineage (except for Tsar Stefan Dušan) and throughout the eighteenth century the new piety grew in significance among the Serbs. In that century, Stanj, an elder of the Vašojević clan, also foretold the advent of a Serbian messiah, a dark man (*crni covjek*) who would liberate the Serbs. Other myths popular in Macedonia and Serbia envisioned the return of Kraljevic Marko—a fourteenth-century Serbian vassal to the Ottomans—who, according to legend, had temporarily withdrawn from earthly life in some secret cavern; when the right time came, he would rise and lead the Christians against the Turks (Banac 1981, 46–8; Stoianovich 1994, 169). As these examples illustrate, Orthodox millenarianism was a vision that tied together temporal and spiritual regeneration, and should not be confused with nationalism.[4] Millenarianism provided the official Church doctrine with a political orientation that led to a de facto recognition of Ottoman rule and at the same time denied—in principle—the Sultan's legitimacy.

By making all "Romans" (i.e., formerly Orthodox subjects of the Byzantine Empire) members of the Ottoman *Rum millet*, the Ottomans offered official sanction to the Church's Orthodox universalism, thus facilitating the legitimation of the Grecophone ecclesiastical elites over the Balkan *ethnies*.[5] In addition, after 1453, the Church assumed jurisdiction over the civil affairs of the Orthodox communities. Moreover, by virtue of his residing in the capital of the empire, the Ecumenical Patriarch was able to usurp—in an informal but effective manner—considerable power from the Orthodox Patriarchates of Alexandria, Antioch, and Jerusalem. In the hierarchical structure of the Eastern Church, the Ecumenical Patriarch ranked first, followed by the other Orthodox Patriarchates, the autocephalous archbishoprics of Cyprus, Pec, and Ohrid, and the local metropolitans (Papadopoullos 1990, 94; Sarres 1990, II:421–524). In the eyes of the higher clergy, the Orthodox Church was the only legitimate bearer of the Christian tradition. For centuries, the enemy was the Catholic Church, which consistently attempted to infiltrate the Orthodox world (Frazee 1983). Although the majority of the post-1453 publications were Grecophone, most of them were religious in nature: Their major function was to counteract Catholic propaganda (Koumarianou, Droulia, and Layton 1986).

The conflation of Greek ethnic identity with that of the *Rum millet* was an indispensable component of the Ottoman social system. This conflation is revealed in the ethnic Greeks' view of the ancient Greeks, the *Hellenes* (Ellines). They were considered to be mythical beings having extraordinary stature and power, capable of superhuman tasks. Popular folk tales dated the Hellenes' existence to the dawn of time. In sharp contrast to this ancient race, the contemporary Greeks called themselves Romans (Romaioi) or Christians (Kakridis 1989). Autobiographical writings of eighteenth-century secular and religious figures testify to the deployment of religious categories as a road map for a person's existence, suggesting a shared religious mentality among the Orthodox Christians (Kitromilides 1996). In the late 1790s, Balkan Orthodox Christians routinely referred to themselves as Christians and referred to Catholics as either Latins or, more commonly, as Franks (Arnakis 1963, 131). Within the Ottoman Empire, these Greek Orthodox (or "Greek") urban and mercantile strata were referred to by the Ottomans, the Church, and themselves as *reaya*, Christians, or Romans (Romaioi), that is, members of the *Rum millet*.[6]

In the European cartography of the fifteenth to eighteenth centuries, "Grecia" included Dalmatia, Serbia, Bulgaria, the coastal area of Asia Minor, Albania, and the Aegean islands (Karathanasis 1991, 9). For the Western audience in Germany, Austria, and Hungary, "Greek" (Greek Orthodox) was synonymous with Orthodoxy (Stoianovich 1960, 290). Regardless of their ethnic origins, most Greek Orthodox Balkan merchants of the eighteenth century spoke Greek and often assumed Greek names; they were referred to as "Greeks" in the sense that they were of the "Greek" religion. During the eighteenth century, the geographic dispersion and the urban nature of the Greek *ethnie* in the Balkan peninsula transformed the "Greeks" into a Balkan urban class (Svoronos 1981, 58). Hence, the "Greeks" were not only the ethnic Greeks but generally included all the Orthodox merchants and peddlers, many of whom were Grecophone or Hellenized Vlachs, Serbs, or Orthodox Albanians.

In 1766 and 1767, Patriarch Samuel, citing huge deficits and the involvement of the local pashas in the election of archbishops as his reasons, reluctantly included the autocephalous archbishops of Pec and Ohrid in the ecumenical seat. This expansion of the Patriarchate's authority has been interpreted as proof of Greek domination over the other Balkan peoples. However, according to the official documents of the Patriarchate, the prime reason for the incorporation of Ohrid and Pec was their decline resulting from the widespread conversions in the aftermath of the 1737–1739 Austro-Turkish war (Papadopoullos 1990, 89–90; Vakalopoulos 1973, 292; Angelopoulos 1983; Konortas 1998, 217–27).[7] The abolition of the two autocephalous seats further expanded patriarchal authority over the Balkan peninsula and enhanced the prestige and power of the Grecophone elites controlling the Patriarchate.

Their Greek Orthodox ecclesiastical culture did not signify national supremacy of one people over another but, rather, a political and religious system that recognized the classifications of the Ottoman system alone (i.e., Orthodox, Jewish, Muslim, Catholic). This mentality was shared by the only other power center in the *Rum millet*, namely, the Phanariots. Although Runciman (1968, 378–9) has suggested that the Phanariots attempted to "combine the nationalistic forces of Hellenism in a passionate if illogical alliance with the ecumenical traditions of Byzantium and the Orthodox Church," I believe that the Phanariots' ideological orientation should not be viewed as a precursor of modern Greek nationalism. At least two main points support this interpretation.

First, the Phanariots' worldview was dominated largely by Orthodox universalism. Early eighteenth-century Phanariot princes emphasized an ideology of service to the Ottoman Empire. For example, Nikolaos Mavrocordatos (1680–1730) in his novel *Philotheou Parerga* (written in 1718 and published in 1800) describes the Ottoman *millet* system in detail and, as a good administrator, he emphasizes the system's virtues and religious tolerance (Bouchard 1982; Kamperidis 1992; Kitromilides 1978, 26–32; Dimaras 1977, 263–81; Henderson 1970, 20–7). It is, in fact, difficult to reconcile this defense of the Ottoman *millet* system with a nationalist orientation.[8]

During the second half of the eighteenth century, this vision of "enlightened despotism" was most clearly articulated in the Danubian principalities by Dimitrios Katartzis, an intellectual and administrator in Bucharest. In a series of writings between 1783 and 1791, Katartzis performed the first political analysis of the situation of Balkan Christians under the Ottoman occupation. He rejected the argument that the *Romans* (members of the *Rum millet*) did not constitute a nation because they did not have an independent political community of their own. He argued that the identity of the Orthodox Christians was that of the *Rum millet* (Dimaras 1977, 177–243; see also Vranousis 1975; Dimaras 1975, 330–1, on Phanariot political ideology). Although they did not participate directly in the government, indirectly (that is, via the Phanariots and the Patriarchate) they enjoyed a number of privileges and rights. Therefore, the *Rum millet* was not an oppressed people that needed to be liberated; rather, its progress could be achieved under the "enlightened" rule of the Phanariot and religious elites. As late as 1824, the Phanariot Theodoros Negris defined Serbs and Bulgarians as "Greeks," all of them lumped together in one sentence with the inhabitants of Thrace, Macedonia, Epirus, and a number of Aegean islands and Anatolian cities (quoted in Skopetea 1988, 25).

Second, the Phanariot attitude toward political expressions of the Enlightenment was not unequivocally friendly. This attitude is exemplified by the Phanariots' stance after the French revolution. Following the Russo-Ottoman rapprochement of 1791 and the condemnation of liberalism by Russian authorities, the Patriarchate proceeded to condemn new "French" ideas. The Phanariots, although familiar with the new ideas and seemingly their advocates up to that point, appeared to change their minds. Dimitrios Katartzis did not hesitate to condemn Voltaire; Alexandros Mavrocordatos, founder of Masonic lodges in Vienna and Odessa, followed the trend of antiliberal ideas. When Evyenios Voulgaris, protégé of Catherine, ex-liberal turned conservative, wrote to Mavrocordatos and inquired of him "what he believed in," Mavrocordatos replied by sending him the Orthodox declaration of the Faith (Loukas 1991, 66). These developments point to the limits of the Phanariot ideology of "enlightened despotism."

Nationalism was absent among the members of the *Rum millet* prior to the 1750s. Neither the Phanariots, nor the high clergy, nor the Orthodox peasantry endorsed or advocated nationalist ideas. Millenarianism expressed the social organization of Ottoman society in terms of the religious-political division between rulers and ruled. The main focus of revolutionary ideology was the religious-political division between the Ottoman privileged class of the *askeri*—which by the late eighteenth century was almost entirely Muslim—and the subordinate class of the *reaya*—which was predominantly, although not exclusively, Greek Orthodox (Karpat 1973; Sarres 1990).

## SECULARIZATION, THE NEW INTELLIGENTSIA, AND THE HELLENIC IDEAL

Although in earlier centuries, literary activity was predominantly religious in nature, in the post-1750 period, Grecophone secular literary production rose from 25 percent of the total in the 1700–1725 period to 47 percent in the 1775–1800 period (Dimaras 1970, 54). This increase was closely related with the intensification of commercial interactions between the Ottoman Empire and Western Europe (Stoianovich 1960; Kasaba 1988; on the Greek immigrant communities, see Geanakopoulos 1976; Papadrianos 1993; Psiroukis 1983). Throughout the eighteenth century, the rise of a Balkan Orthodox merchant class of intermediaries and other petit-bourgeois professionals provided support for the emergence of a new Greek Orthodox Balkan intelligentsia. Book circulation in particular was greatly facilitated by maritime commerce. Successful editions sold up to 1,500 copies (Koumarianou, Droulia, and Layton 1986). Funding for publishing came primarily from wealthy merchants, but publishers also solicited subscribers for particular editions. Between 1749 and 1832 approximately 200 books were printed by subscription; of these, 150 contain lists of subscribers amounting to 30,000 people (Clogg 1980, 125–9). These 30,000 subscribed to more than 58,000 copies. But only 7 percent of these subscribers actually resided in the regions that would eventually become the kingdom of Greece (1832). The cultural ferment was largely confined to the Greek Orthodox diaspora in Italy, Central Europe, the Danubian principalities, Constantinople, and Smyrna.

Education was provided in a number of schools scattered over the Ottoman Balkans, but the most prominent institutions among them were the princely academies of Bucharest (founded between 1678 and 1688) and Jassy (founded in 1707) (Georgescu 1991, 112; Camariano-Coran 1974, 307–62). Their professors included some of the most influential members of a new Greek Orthodox Balkan intelligentsia, which emerged in the late 1750s. In a statistical analysis of 68 Enlightenment intellectuals, Nikolaidis, Dialetis, and Athanasiadis (1988) identified two clusters of intellectuals with distinct profiles. The first group consisted of Greek Orthodox authors born before 1757. They were usually clergy or educators (oftentimes both), and they studied philosophy, philology, theology, mathematics, chemistry, and physics. They had been educated mainly in Western Europe and the language of their discourse was archaic or Attic Greek. These scholars were primarily employed in mainland Greece, the Aegean islands, and Anatolia. The second group consisted of Greek Orthodox authors born between 1757 and 1772. They were mainly merchants or secular intellectuals associated with the merchants. They studied languages and geography; their place of study was Central Europe and the language of discourse was closer to the Greek vernacular. Their major places of employment were the Ionian islands, the Danubian principalities, and cities in Eastern or Western Europe. Among this younger group it is possible to locate those most influenced by Western "enlightened reason."[9]

This new Greek Orthodox Balkan intelligentsia was a stratum crossing ethnic frontiers. Intellectuals characterized as "Greek" were not necessarily of Greek ethnic descent. The Bulgarian Nikolaos Pikolos, the Wallachian Iosipos Moisiodax (born in Dobrudja), and the Vlach Dhaniil of Moshopolis are Enlightenment figures known for their non-Greek descent (Kitromilides 1985; Protopsaltis 1980; Argyropoulos 1984; see also Dutu 1973, 110–1, for further examples). Figures such as the Vlach Dimitrios Darvaris from Klisura in Macedonia exemplified the fluid boundaries of ethnic identity during the late eighteenth century. Darvaris published grammatical books and translations in Greek, Russian, German, and Serbian (Loukidou-Mavridou and Papadrianos 1980). Within Balkan society, class and ethnic lines overlapped to such an extent that Hellenism became a form of "cultural capital" (Bourdieu 1984) offering an individual access to circles of wealth and prestige. Hellenization implied the acquisition of cultural capital and the benefits associated with it. The diffusion of "enlightened reason" proceeded from the middle-class and Grecophone strata to the other sectors of Ottoman Balkan society (see Mackridge 1981; Camariano-Coran 1975; Boissin 1970, for further examples).

In sharp contrast to the representatives of the Enlightenment, the very word "philosophy" and its advocates became the targets of religious reaction. Again and again, the story repeated itself: An enlightened educator, often schooled in Europe, started teaching the new philosophy and soon came under attack by the conservative establishment. From Methodios Anthrakiotis' excommunication by the Holy Synod (1723), to Stefanos Doukas' "confession of faith" (1810), this conflict persisted. Conservative figures such as Athanasios Parios or Dositheos Vousilmas were the champions of the reaction (Gedeon 1976, 57–96; for discussions of specific cases, see Giannaras 1992, 179–86; Angelou 1988, 211–92; Kitromilides 1978, 477; Iliou 1986). The schools of Kidonies, Smyrna, and Chios—which were at the forefront of the new educational spirit—became targets of the religious opposition.[10]

Throughout the eighteenth century, the reemergence of classical antiquity in the discourse of the Western Enlightenment strongly influenced the secularization of the *Rum millet*. During the Enlightenment era, the *philosophes* saw history as the unraveling of human progress. Within this framework the ancient Greeks were looked on as the "fathers" of civilization. Reason, philosophy, and the individual's freedom to shape his or her personal destiny were the central features of ancient Greek culture. As a result, although throughout the eighteenth century the rest of Eastern Europe was depicted as an essentially "backward" region, travelers to the Greek lands emphasized and reinforced a romantic and nostalgic view of Greece (Gay 1966, 72–85; Wolf 1994; Augustinos 1994, 22–36).

The Hellenic Ideal was not thought of as necessarily connected with the territory of Greece itself; thus, the German intelligentsia, who also lacked patrons to finance trips to the Orient, developed an extremely academic attachment to ancient Greece. Between 1750 and 1820 German intellectuals fiercely adhered to the commonplace belief at the time, that what was worth saving from ancient Greece had been handed on to Rome and was now carefully preserved on the shelves of their libraries (Einser 1991, 76–8; Constantine 1984, 85–146). No German of literary note traveled in Greece until shortly before 1800. It was mostly French and British travelers who toured the ruins of the ancient Greek world, and for the most part, the Germans read their accounts, or studied classical sculpture in the museums of Dresden or Italy, or looked at pictures included in the travelers' books (Stoneman 1987, 120–7; Augustinos 1994, 91–2; Gay 1966, 84; Tsigakou 1981, 19). The Society of Dilettante founded in 1733–36 in London financed a series of expeditions that facilitated the Greek Revival. The publication of such books as the *Antiquities of Athens* in 1762 further increased the passion for ancient Greece (Stuart and Revett 1762–1816).

The travelers' perspective evolved significantly over the course of the eighteenth century. For French travelers in Greece during the 1550–1750 period, the modern Greeks were a separate entity set apart from their rulers by religion, language, and custom. Whether the modern Greeks drew sympathy or denigration, it was invariably on the basis of their affinity with or divergence from the ancient Greeks. This earlier predisposition was transformed in the last third of the eighteenth and the first three decades of the nineteenth centuries into Philhellenism. During this period, Philhellenism expanded to encompass the modern Greeks and evolved so as to resolve the tensions between the present and the past (Augustinos 1994, 148–72; Stoneman 1987, 136–42, 144). Of course, the modern Greeks needed the guiding light of the West, which was now the repository of the legacy of antiquity. The liberation of the Greeks was part of the European "civilizing mission" (Nicolaidis 1992, 45–71; Augustinos 1994, 131–2).

The sentimental attachment the French felt for the ancients was not the only seed of philhellenism. Of equal importance were the precepts of the Enlightenment, which posited a direct relationship between politics and culture. Only a people living under equitable laws administered by a wise ruler could form a progressive society and achieve cultural preeminence. Seen from this perspective, the modern Greeks were an oppressed people. First, they lost their independence to the Romans, then they were under the theocratic rule of the Byzantine emperors, and their sufferings culminated during their centuries-long subjection to the Ottomans. For example, Voltaire entertained Philhellenic sentiments born from his belief that Greek civilization had declined in the postclassical era as well as from his aversion to tyranny. Voltaire and the *philosophes* in general viewed the Ottoman Empire as a violator of the natural rights of man. Voltaire hailed Catherine's efforts to expand Russia to the south and drive the Ottomans out of the Balkans (Augustinos 1994, 139–47). Catherine's motives were not identical with those of Voltaire, since her plans for imperial expansion were part of a general policy of colonization. Catherine used the idea of the liberation of the Greeks as a means for gaining legitimacy for her wars against the Ottoman Empire (Seton-Watson 1934, 153; Venturi 1991, II:769–99; Batalden 1982, 94–5).

These Western intellectual currents did not escape the notice of the emerging Orthodox Balkan intelligentsia. For example, Charles Rollin's *Histoire Ancienne* (1730–1738), a 16-volume history of ancient peoples focusing particularly on the history of ancient Greeks, was an extremely influential text. Over the next 50 years, Rollin's history served as the major historical text for Grecophone schools (Kitromilides 1978, 84–9; Clogg, 1985: 13). Although there was some time lag in the translations, many works appeared relatively quickly (Clogg 1980, 111–2). With the proliferation of this historical knowledge, the genealogical, cultural, and intellectual ties between Orthodox Balkan peoples and antiquity became the foci of a critical reevaluation. The influence of the Hellenic ideal on the Greek Orthodox intelligentsia was most pronounced in the works of Moisiodax and Korais. Iosipos Moisiodax, who served as director of the princely academy of Jassy, diagnosed a twofold problem in Greek Orthodox culture. On the one hand, knowledge of the ancients' texts was fragmentary, as texts were largely unavailable; on the other hand, the ancients were revered without questioning. To cure these ills, Moisiodax pointed to the West as a place where new knowledge was created and which could provide a new model for southeastern Europe (see Kitromilides 1985 for an intellectual biography).

This modernist attitude is also revealed in Adamantios Korais' attempt to construct a new language suitable for a new nation. This new language was to be created via the purging of non-Greek words from the spoken vernacular and their replacement with ancient Greek words. Korais was the protagonist of the movement to transform the role of the classical heritage for the Greek Orthodox *millet* (Clogg 1985; on Korais see Jeffreys 1985; Chaconas, 1942; Henderson 1970; Dimaras 1977, 301–89; 1988, 193–213). For Korais, education in the classics served to prepare people for a democratic polity. Korais did not anticipate the 1821 revolt against the Ottoman state because he considered it necessary for an educated elite to emerge before a national democratic state could be successfully established. In 1805, Korais started the publication of translations of ancient Greek authors in the series of *Elliniki Bibliothiki* (Hellenic library), a project funded by rich Chiote merchants. In his introductions to the various volumes of the series, Korais had the opportunity to comment extensively on the project of reeducation and liberation. Under the influence of the Western Hellenic ideal, Korais suggested the term "Greeks" (Graikoi) as the proper designation of the Orthodox "Romans" (Romanides 1975, 47). There was an important discontinuity involved in this recommendation. By "Greece" the Western European intellectuals meant the ancient territory of *Hellas* alone, and not the entire world referred to as "Romania" or *Rumeli* by the Greek Orthodox Christians (Romanides 1975, 209). Hence, the identification of the "Romans" as "Greeks" was bound to create an important disjuncture between the intellectuals' version of "Greece" (the so-called Hellenic ideal) and the popular "Romeic" religious and political identity. Not surprisingly, the Phanariot-religious establishment was at odds with his project.[11]

For Korais, the need for modern Greeks to rediscover their historical origins was a reflection of a broader program of political modernization. By adopting the knowledge of the ancients that was preserved in the West, the modern Greeks could rise again and reconstitute themselves in their proper position in the world. Of fundamental importance to such a program was the assumption of continuity between the "ancients" and the "moderns." In Korais' writings, this continuity was strategically employed to establish the necessity for the modernization of the Hellenic world (Korais 1971; Clogg 1976). To become worthy of the sacred name they bore, modern Greeks needed to be "enlightened," an argument justifying Korais' modernist orientation without directly questioning the traditional ecclesiastical discourse. But even if cultural continuity with Orthodox philosophical tradition was to be preserved in principle, most of the Balkan Enlightenment emphasized Western scientific achievements in order to defeat Orthodox religious conservatism.

In the field of politics, this orientation manifested itself in the Enlightenment thinkers' employment of the term *Greek* or *Hellene* versus the traditional "Romeic" vision advocated by the Patriarchate. These conflicting visions are reflected in the employment of the terms "race" (*genos*) and "nation" (*ethnos*) in the writings of various authors during this period (Xydis 1969, 207–13; Dimaras 1977, 81–90; see also Zakynthinos 1976, 140–80; Pantazopoulos 1994, 48–51; Romanides 1975). The "race of the Romans" is more or less identical with the *Rum millet*; its employment reveals the use of the *Rum millet* as the relevant political and cultural unit of organization. The gradual employment of the words *Greek* or *Hellene* and the use of the term nation (*ethnos*) reflect the slow transformation of a religious to a secular identity.

## THE ERA OF REVOLUTIONARY LIBERALISM

Toward the end of the eighteenth century, the conflicts between liberals and conservatives intensified. The liberals had grown stronger and the Church could no longer intimidate its opponents into submission. For example, when in 1793 the liberal author Christodoulos Pambekis was excommunicated, he died without repenting and his friends commemorated him in the public gardens of Leipzig (Dimaras 1988, 154). The French Revolution in 1789 provided the impetus for a particularly stormy period of conflict (1790–1800) between conservatives and liberals in the Balkans (Dimaras 1977, 245–62; Gedeon 1976, 57–96).

To this period dates the "battle of the pamphlets." This intellectual battle revolved around the publication of a series of texts such as *Fraternal Teaching* (1798; see English translation in Clogg 1969), *Anonymous of 1789* (1789; reprinted in Dimaras 1977), or *Hellenic Nomarchy* (1980; originally published in 1806). These texts manifested the intense struggle over intellectual orientation. The proponents of the Enlightenment increasingly called for the overthrow of Ottoman rule (for "liberation") and this call deeply affected the Church's role and position. The vision of the new Orthodox intelligentsia postulated the sovereignty of a people in secular terms. In contrast, the Church advocated a deliberately nonnationalist, theocratic position. For its liberal opponents, this position amounted to nothing less than "voluntary slavery" (*ethelodouleia*).

The emerging liberalism was strongly connected with the proliferation of freemasonry, leading the Patriarchate to repeatedly condemn the freemasons.[12] At least since 1776 and 1777, Voltaire and freemasonry were associated in the religious anti-Enlightenment literature. By 1791 various pamphlets located Voltaire among the "shameless, talkative, Godless Franco-masons" and in 1793 the Patriarchate condemned the "infidel, Godless Voltaires. . . . [instruments of the] cunning and misanthrope Demon" (quoted in Loukas 1991, 57–8). Gradually, the Church's position became more austere; by 1816 the Enlightenment teacher and author Stefanos Doukas was forced to submit the manuscript of his *Physics* to censorship, and in 1817, Ignatios Skalioras, one of the Patriarchate's clergy in the West, issued a fierce attack on Korais. When Patriarch Grigorios V, an opponent of secular ideas, returned to the patriarchal seat (1818–1821), the pace of the reaction accelerated (Dimaras 1977, 60, 261; see also Iliou 1988). In 1819 the Church condemned the novelty of giving ancient Greek names to newborns and created a list of heretical books.

This conflict partially reflects the different positions of the proponents of each side: The Church was part of the Ottoman administrative system and fearful of ideas that could upset the empire's order, whereas the merchants, peddlers, intellectuals, and other petit-bourgeois groups were proponents of the new ideas (cf. Iliou 1986). Of course, the ideological conflict cannot be reduced to class positions, because support for education and promotion of the new "enlightened reason" did not invariably imply commitment to revolutionary activity (see Clogg 1981; Anonymous 1980). Rich merchants were willing to offer money for educational projects but were unwilling to risk their fortunes in an open revolt against the Porte.

The French occupations of the Ionian islands in 1797 to 1799 and 1807 to 1814, as well as the occupation of the Illyrian region (1806–1814) supported the influx of ideas from the West into the Balkan lands (Kitromilides 1990a,

29, 45). From Bonaparte's first Italian expedition, the image of Napoleon as the liberator became dominant. Adamantios Korais called on him to liberate Korais' fellow compatriots; in 1800, the liberal boyars of Wallachia and Moldavia addressed a similar call to him; and the Serbs repeatedly requested his help in their ongoing revolt against the Porte (Clogg 1969, 87–90; Kitromilides 1990a, 38–49). Under the influence of French revolutionary ideas, literary societies were formed to promote the new worldview and youth were encouraged to follow the new ideas. From Vienna, thanks to Greek and Serb diaspora merchant communities, French liberal ideas were brought into the Balkans by means of pamphlets, translations, and secret societies (Koumarianou 1995; Botzaris 1962, 71–81; Kitromilides 1990a, 56, 109–38). Following the example of the Jacobins, secret societies were formed in Constantinople (1794) and the Ionian islands (1797).

Rigas Velenstinlis' movement took place in the context of this generalized emulation of French ideas throughout the region. Velenstinlis conceived of the idea of an Orthodox revolution among the Balkan peoples that would result in the overthrow of the Sultan's authority and the creation of a "Greek" state in its place. His connection with freemasonic lodges has never been proven, but there is a clear influence of liberal ideas in his work. He served as professor in the princely academy of Bucharest, as governor of Craiova, and as secretary under the prince Nikolaos Mavroyeni (Camariano-Coran 1974, 447; Pantazopoulos 1994, 20–35; Vranousis 1957). He produced a series of literary and scientific works, including translations of European books.

Velenstinlis' *Grand Map of Greece* (Ellas) of 1797 identifies *Hellas* with the Ottoman Empire's "central lands" (i.e., the Balkans and Anatolia) and calls for the overthrow of the despots by the coordinated action of all Balkan peoples. In effect, the map transforms the *Grecia* of earlier (fifteenth- to eighteenth-century) European cartography into *Hellas*. But for Western European Enlightenment thinkers, there was an implicit continuity involved in the employment of the two terms (ancient Greeks = Hellenes); for Orthodox Balkan society, this transformation involved a rejection of the ecclesiastical unit of *Rum millet* in favor of a secular *Hellas*. In Velenstinlis' own work, *Hellas* appears as the secular, liberal facet of the *Rum millet*, the product of an intellectual mutation caused by the reception of the Enlightenment in the Ottoman Balkans.

For the creation of his *Grand Map*, Velenstinlis utilized one of the most famous and honored books of the Philhellenic discourse, Jean-Jacques Barthélemy's *Voyage du jeune Anacharsis en Grèce* (1788). Barthélemy was a prominent numismatologist, epigraphist, linguist, and Hellenist. His book was translated into several European languages and its successive editions testified to its popularity. The high point of the book's popularity was the author's inclusion in the Academie française in 1789 (Augustinos 1994, 38–9). The book describes the imaginary travels of young Prince Anacharsis in ancient Greece from 363 to 337 B.C.—in effect, providing a panoramic view of the ancient Greek world. Velenstinlis translated five of the eight chapters of the book himself and used the information provided in it to construct his *Grand Map* (Pantazopoulos 1994, 68–9; Vranousis 1957; Botzaris 1962).

These Western influences also extended into the realm of politics. Velenstinlis' plans reveal a strong liberal turn, as they freely utilize the slogans of the French revolution ("liberty, equality, fraternity"). He selected the French constitution of 1793 (the most liberal of the French constitutions) as his own model. In the new federation he envisioned, the idea of citizenship would provide for the peaceful coexistence of all Balkan *ethnies*. In his Constitution of the Republic of Hellas, "all people, Christians and Turks, are . . . equal" (Article 3); slavery is prohibited (Articles 2 and 18); freedom of religion for Christians, Turks, Jews, and others is guaranteed; and it is recognized that "the sovereign people are all the people of this state without distinction of religion or dialect, Greeks, Bulgarians, Albanians, Vlachs, Armenians, Turks, and every other race" (Article 7). Clearly aware of ethnic differences, Velenstinlis credited individual rights with making his Hellenic Republic possible. The constitution provides a system of representative democracy where voting is not restricted to the prelates (Articles 21, 28, and 29). He further connected this vision with the existing cultural trends of his time by selecting Greek as the major language of the republic, arguing that "it is the easiest to comprehend and learned by all the races of the state" (Article 53).

Velenstinlis' vision is an example of both the strong influence of liberalism among the Orthodox Balkan intelligentsia and the culturally defined nature of the Hellenic ideal.[13] The Hellenic ideal revitalized the identity of the Orthodox Balkan intelligentsia. In place of the religious Orthodox identity of the *Rum millet*, the new mentality postulated a secular one based on the knowledge of the West and the ideology of liberalism. The geographical space occupied by Velenstinlis' *Hellas* remains that of Orthodox Balkan society, a feature testifying to the Balkan character of his thinking. To implement his goals, he organized a Jacobin-style secret society. His efforts were unsuccessful; in 1798 he and his followers were arrested in Trieste. They were tortured by the Austrian authorities only to be turned over to the Ottomans, who promptly executed Velenstinlis and his followers. His capture and death elevated him to the status of a martyr for his contemporaries, but his plans were condemned by the Patriarchate in 1798 (Vranousis 1975, 450; Pantazopoulos 1994, 53, 98).

Following Napoleon's defeat (1815), the economic crisis of Ottoman trade hurt many petit-bourgeois commercial intermediaries and merchants. This frustrated stratum was attracted to French Jacobin-style revolutionary ideas. The medium of these people was the Society of Friends (Philiki Eteria), a nationalist conspiratorial organization founded in 1814 in Odessa by three Greek merchants. Allegedly the founders of the Eteria were Freemasons, but this has been corroborated for only one of them, Emanuil Xanthos. Nevertheless, its symbolism and mode of organization reveal heavy Masonic influences (Frangos 1973, 1975). The Eterists played into the millenarian beliefs that still dominated the Orthodox Balkans, and strongly implied that their goals were supported by Russia. Thanks to this multifaceted approach, the society was able to build a coalition among notables, bandits, clergy, and merchants. Since the "Greeks" constituted a group scattered widely over the Ottoman territory and since, for the peasantry, it was the religious identity that counted ("Greek" versus "Latins" or "Turks"), the goal of the Eterists appeared identical to that of Velenstinlis. That goal was to create a Balkan Orthodox Christian movement that aimed to replace the religious authority of the Patriarchate and the political authority of the Porte with a new secular and liberal authority inspired by the French revolution.

A number of conditions and events render this interpretation a plausible one. First, prior to the 1821 revolution the names *Hellene, Hellas,* and *Hellenic* existed in literary discourse but had not yet prevailed. They coexisted with the terms *Greek, Roman* (*Romios*), and *Grecia* (Politis 1993, 33). Second, the "nation" was frequently conceived of as identical to the *Rum millet.* Even as late as 1853, one of the participants of the 1821 revolution in Peloponnesus considered Serbia and the Romanian principalities to be as much a part of "Greece" as Peloponnesus (quoted in Skopetea 1988, 35). Third, if the scope of the 1821 rebellion is confined to the Ottoman Empire alone (that is, excluding the 1821 movement in the Danubian principalities), it was religious and not ethnic solidarity that shaped popular attitudes vis-à-vis the revolt.

In addition to the Greeks, of the other Ottoman Christian subjects, Bulgarian, Serb, and Montenegrin fighters participated in the 1821 revolts (Loukatos 1979, 1980; Todorov 1982; Traikov 1980, 49; Papadopoulos 1980). In accordance with the Eterist plan, Bulgarian villages and cities had been infiltrated by the Eterists (Todorov 1977, 37–8). The Eterists also initiated into their society those Bulgarians living in the principalities as well as those living in colonies throughout Russia, Constantinople, and Bessarabia. They aimed ultimately to provoke a general insurrection among the entire Bulgarian population. The Eterist Dimitrios Vatikiotis, a former officer in the Russo-Turkish war of 1806–1812, is credited with mobilizing a total of 14,000 Bulgarians. The Eterists attempted to gain the support of the Serb exiled leader Karadjordje, and after his 1817 assassination, they tried to gain the support of Prince Miloš of Serbia (Lukac 1979; Papadopoulos 1979; Botzaris 1962, 86–111; Stojancevic 1979). According to their "general plan" the Bulgarians would be joined by the Serbs (with Prince Miloš taking the lead). Although often uncoordinated and unfocused, Eterist agents undertook considerable efforts in northern Bulgaria to prepare for an armed uprising. In January 1821, these plans called for the mobilization of 10,000 Bulgarians with a simultaneous influx of 10,000 Serbs into the Ottoman lands.

Thus, the conspirators' organizational plans clearly suggest that the 1821 revolts were conceived of as a revolution of the Orthodox *millet* against the Ottoman authority structure. Significantly, both the Ottomans and the Greek Catholic islanders understood the revolts using the same frame of reference. On 4 April 1821, Patriarch Grigorios V denounced the revolt in the Danubian principalities and excommunicated the revolutionaries (Sutsos and Ypsilantis). However, he was held responsible by the Sultan for the actions of his flock and on 10 April 1821 he was hanged (Frazee 1987, 45–52).[14] Whereas Orthodox Christians throughout the Ottoman Balkans identified with the revolt, the approximately 16,000 Catholic Greek islanders living in Naxos, Tinos, Siros, and Thira did not participate in it. Although Ottoman rule was not welcome, they hesitated to identify with a movement that was predominantly Orthodox. The Catholic islanders continued to pay the annual tribute to the Porte, and the Pope's declaration of neutrality with respect to the conflict did not provide an incentive to participate in the revolt (Frazee 1979; 1987, 63).

## PHILHELLENISM AND THE FOUNDATION OF THE MODERN GREEK STATE

Perhaps the most important consequence of all the cross-cultural contacts just discussed is the impact of Philhellenism on the educated European public.[15] This impact predisposed Europeans favorably toward the 1821 Greek revolution. In turn, this predisposition eventually led to the European powers forcing the Ottomans out of the territory that later became the kingdom of Greece. In many respects, the 1821 revolutionaries won their victory not in the battlefield, but in the European salons of the time.

By the late eighteenth and early nineteenth centuries, Philhellenism was in full swing in Europe. In 1806 François-René Chateaubriand, former foreign minister to Louis XVIII, set out to travel to the Levant and his travel book, *Itinéraire de Paris à Jérusalem et de Jerusalem* (1811) became extremely popular.[16] Although he spent a mere 19 days in Greece, a substantial portion of the book was devoted to it (Eisner 1991, 96; Augustinos 1994, 172–86). Having read a good part of the travel literature beforehand, and immersed in the romantic gaze of time, Chatcaubriand provided an idealized image of Greece that served as background for his romantic contemplation of the past.

For Chateaubriand as well as for most French travelers, Greece's contemporary decline was not problematic. Their attitude contrasts sharply with the views of Moisiodax, Korais, or Velenstinlis. Its civilization had been transmitted to Europe, where it was preserved. This attitude was revealed in the travelers' mostly negative attitude toward all expressions of Byzantine Orthodox civilization. It is indicative of their perception that most of the early-nineteenth-century Greek paintings provided only a barely adequate representation of a temple or an architectural group. A painting was usually framed by a vaguely defined landscape setting, and the actual surroundings were replaced or modified according to the effect the artist wished to convey. After all, it was the legendary Greece rather than the contemporary reality that the European public preferred (Tsigakou 1981, 29, 46–7). During the 1821–1828 period, the "Greek cause" became a rallying point for liberals throughout the Continent. Romantic neoclassicism added a sense of adventure and pilgrimage. Published in 1821, Wilhelm Muller's *Lieder der Griechen* (Songs of the Greeks) sold over a thousand copies in six weeks; it was only the beginning of the Philhellenic fervor. Approximately 1,200 European (and a few American) volunteers descended on Greece during the revolution. Some of them were mercenaries, others were former officers in the French or British armies who felt homeless in post-1815 Europe, and still others were genuine romantics obsessed with classical antiquity.

Philhellenism was strongly colored by partisanship. The movement was strong among the German intelligentsia (professors and students), among the "left-wing" Whig liberals of Great Britain, among Italian *carbonari*, and among French Bonapartists (for details, see Dakin 1955; Woodhouse 1969). The members of the London Greek Committee were people who belonged to the reformist circles, and for many of them Philhellenism was a manifestation of their general political outlook. All the members of the British Parliament who were members of the committee were Whigs or Radicals, and Jeremy Bentham's name figured prominently among them. In short, it was the losers of the post-1815 European order who recognized the Greek cause as "the cause of Europe"—as a German pamphlet declared it (St. Clair 1973, 51–65). Not surprisingly, the Great Powers remained skeptical at the beginning. In 1820, liberal national revolutions erupted in Spain, Italy (Naples and Piedmont), and Portugal. The powerful and conservative Holy Alliance (Russia, Austria, and Prussia) viewed these movements as attempts to upset the post-1815 European order, and placed the Greek revolt in the same context (Pappas 1985, 15–17).

Between November 1821 and August 1822, 80 shiploads of volunteers departed from Marseilles for Greece. In France, at least six books of Philhellenic verse were published in 1821 and 18 in 1822 (St. Clair 1973, 53). The European governments acted in a hostile manner toward this movement; in fact, the German states' governments forced these activists to go underground. The fact that the most prominent Philhellene was Lord Byron, a romantic cultural rebel and prodigal son of the British aristocracy, is indicative of the "left-wing" orientation of the majority of the Philhellenes.[17] They were not the only ones, of course; neoclassicism brought over people of various political persuasions. In fact, the national rivalry among different nationals and the political rivalry between conservatives and liberals fragmented the Philhellenes into different groups bitterly arguing with each other. Thanks to the Philhellenes and Western European neoclassicism, the 1821 revolutionaries were successful in shaping public opinion favorably to their goals. European Philhellenism was not always identical with pro-Greek sentiment because the former was the outcome of complex political and cultural forces. In fact, many observers did not necessarily connect the ancient and modern Greeks with each other because the social condition of the moderns often aroused discontent, prejudice, and harsh judgment by the Europeans.

Many romantic writers championed the revolution with prose, poetry, music, and paintings. Most influential was Chateaubriand's *Note sur Grèce* (1824), a short pamphlet that called on European monarchs to go to the defense of Greece.

Byron's death in Messologi in 1824 further facilitated Philhellenism mainly in France, where he had acquired a considerable reputation as a great literary figure. The rising romantic movement found in Byron's "martyrdom" and other massacres of the war a suitable terrain for artistic expression.[18] This cultural movement brought the Paris Greek Committee to the center of the Philhellenic movement throughout the Continent. Created in February 1825, the Paris Greek Committee raised in three years about $325,000 (St. Clair 1973, 267, 270–2; Pappas 1985, 22). The Paris Committee was largely composed of Liberals and Orléanists, but it attracted support from many among the French aristocracy and it helped to tilt the European public in favor of the Greeks.

France and the United States were two natural allies for the revolutionaries. During the 1821 revolution, the Messina Assembly sent a message to the United States, considering the republic its ally (Pantev, 1977, 26–7). Adamantios Korais was an acquaintance of Thomas Jefferson and asked for American support during the 1821 revolution on the basis that the Greeks were fighting for goals identical to those of the American revolution (Lazou 1983, I:85–102). Although American aid, Philhellenes, and missionaries did arrive, the geopolitical position of the United States weakened its influence. Instead, it was France that played the leading role in the Philhellenic movement.

After the 1820 revolts in Italy and Spain had been suppressed, and after the initial Greek victories of the 1821–1823 period, the French and British governments reacted to Philhellenic pressure and contemplated the possibility of an independent Greece. Fear of the new state serving as a Russian puppet led them to an ambivalent policy toward philhellenes and the Greek movement. By 1825, Russian policy was reversed in favor of the revolutionaries and on 4 April 1826 an Anglo-Russian protocol on Greek affairs was signed at St. Petersburg.

While in 1823–1824, the notables and bandit leaders in Peloponnesus and Rumeli proceeded to fight among themselves over power and authority, Egyptian troops were called in by the Sultan. They landed in Peloponnesus (1825) and were successful in recapturing most of the lost territories. But whereas on the military front the combined Ottoman and Egyptian forces were finally successful, the propaganda war had been won by the Greeks. Eventually, this led to the reversal of European policy. British Foreign Minister George Canning used the rumors that Ibrahim Pasha, the leader of the Egyptian forces and son of Mehmed Ali, ruler of Egypt, was going to ship the Greek population to Egypt and repopulate the country with Egyptians to argue that the threat of barbarism could no longer go unopposed. Invoking the argument that the Ottomans had de facto lost control over the rebellious territories, he argued in favor of Greek national self-determination (Cunningham 1978; Kakambouras 1993; Schwartzberg 1988a, 1988b).

Diplomacy took over this process and resulted in the 1825 London protocol. The protocol's secret article contained the obligation of the Great Powers to force a truce between the Ottoman-Egyptian army and the Greeks. Soon, the subversion of the truce by Greek forces frustrated the Ottoman-Egyptian fleet and aggravated the situation. Although the European leaders did not anticipate it, the attempt to force the armistice led to the battle of Navarino (1827) and the destruction of the joint Ottoman-Egyptian fleet (for a description, see Woodhouse 1981). Following Navarino, the Greek cause was in effect successful because Muslim forces lacked the means to implement their mission. The Russo-Ottoman war (1828–1829) and the political rivalry of the Great Powers shaped the nature of the newborn state. Following the assassination of the first governor, Ioannis Kapodistrias (1828–1831), Greece became a kingdom to be ruled by a German prince who, since he was not Orthodox, could reassure England and France that the new state would not end in the Russian sphere of influence.

## CONCLUSIONS

Nationalism was absent in the Orthodox Balkan society of the Ottoman era. The sociopolitical organization of the Orthodox Christians (the *Rum millet*) was instrumental in highlighting the religious differences among the Balkan peoples. Romanians, Bulgarians, Serbs, Albanians, and Greeks were *ethnies* whose identity could shift from one to another without a change in the peoples' status vis-à-vis the Sublime Porte. Ethnicity was also associated with the division of labor and was frequently situational. Middle-class and urban Greek Orthodox Christians were generally self-identified as "Christians" or "Romans," while Western sources tended to refer to all Greek Orthodox Christians as "Greeks." The religious and secular elites of the *Rum millet* operated within this frame of reference. Although Grecophone, these elites emphasized their role as leaders of the *Rum millet*; they used religious instead of ethnic identity as their main inscriptive criterion. Concomitant with this Orthodox universalism, millenarianism was also prevalent among the Greek Orthodox Christians. The subjugation of the Christians under the Ottomans was seen as divine punishment for their sins; "liberation" was expected to occur simultaneously with the Second Coming. The considerable discontinuity between millenarian ideology and modern nationalism suggests that the power struggle of the Orthodox Christians against the Muslim Ottomans should not be conceived of as an expression of nationalism. That is, during the Ottoman period, Christians may have desired their liberation from the Ottoman rule, but this was a religious and not a national dream of liberation.

During the second half of the eighteenth century, intense cross-cultural contacts between the Ottoman Empire and Western Europe had a significant impact on the *Rum millet*. These contacts can be grouped into two categories: the ideological currents of the Enlightenment and the more diffuse revolutionary expectations that proliferated with the outbreak of the French revolution. The Enlightenment was transplanted into the *Rum millet* by a group of Orthodox and mainly Grecophone intellectuals during the second half of the eighteenth century. This new intelligentsia was not composed of individuals of ethnic Greek descent alone; many of them, however, were participants in the Grecophone culture of the time. The reception of the Enlightenment by the Orthodox Balkan society led to a growing trend toward secularization and critical thinking. Knowledge was valued as an end in itself and tradition was no longer uncritically accepted. The central place of ancient Greece in the Western Enlightenment led to a reconstitution of the relationship between the modern "Greeks" (Greek Orthodox) and the ancient Greeks (Hellenes). Adamantios Korais urged the Greeks to become educated through Western "enlightened reason" in order to become worthy of bearing this glorious name. The ecclesiastical establishment and many Phanariots opposed these new ideas since they correctly perceived that secularization would shift the religious foundation of solidarity among the members of the *Rum millet* and lead to the delegitimization of the Church and the Phanariots.

The French revolution intensified this battle between conservative and liberal Greek Orthodox elites and represented the second main source of inspiration for the new secular Greek Orthodox intelligentsia. A heated conflict broke out between conservatives and liberals in the 1790–1800 decade, during which the Church did not hesitate to condemn the Godless "franco-masonic" ideas, while proponents of the "enlightened reason" accused the Church of "voluntary slavery." During this decade there was the first explicit attempt to theorize an alternative to the Ottoman state and to organize a movement toward its overthrow. Rigas Velenstinlis conceived a Grecophone liberal democracy encompassing the Ottoman Empire's "central lands" (the Balkans and Anatolia) and promised religious tolerance and civil liberties to peoples of all religious and ethnic affiliations. His plans were not successful, but his attempt set the stage for the formation of the Philiki Eteria in 1814. The Eteria built a coalition among different Balkan *ethnies* and organized an Orthodox Balkan uprising in 1821.

Both in Velenstinlis' movement and in the 1821 revolutions, the identity of the Orthodox Balkan peoples is thought of as "Greek" (Greek Orthodox). However, instead of the religious connotation of this term, a secular interpretation was put forward. This reinterpretation suggested that Hellenism constituted a new cultural configuration defined in terms of Grecophone letters, Western European "enlightened reason," and liberalism. The secularization of the *Rum millet* had already proceeded far enough for these new concepts to appear, but was not deep enough for all the Balkan *ethnies* to be conceived of as being equal partners. This is why the considerable ambiguity surrounding the definition of the "Greeks" persisted until the foundation of the Greek kingdom (1832). In the broadest sense, the "Greeks" can be all the members of the *Rum millet*.

However, if a secular (as opposed to a religious) interpretation is given to the term "Greek," it is inappropriate to use it to characterize the Orthodox Balkan Christians who were not ethnic Greeks. But this contradiction was not transparent prior to the 1830s. As shown in this chapter, the (Ottoman) Serb, Bulgarian, and Romanian educational mobilizations gained momentum only after the 1821 revolutions. Instrumental for its acceleration was the removal of the Phanariots from the administration of the Danubian principalities. Although for the next two decades the presence of Greek culture and language remained strong, the rise of the Latinist movement implied a steady decline of the importance of Greek as a literary medium. Furthermore, the model of the administration of the post-1821 Danubian principalities was employed as a reference point for an independent Bulgaria. As early as 1829 the Russian commander Alexander Pavlovich, after contacts with Bulgarians active in the principalities, recommended to the Tsar the organization of Bulgaria as an autonomous principality similar to the Danubian principalities. In the course of the nineteenth century, Bulgarian and Albanian national societies flourished in the principalities (Velichi 1982; Iancovici 1971a, 1971b).

These mobilizations were significantly aided by the secularization of the Greek Orthodox intelligentsia. In transforming the religious identity of the Greeks into a secular one, the Greek Orthodox intellectuals of the time also circumscribed the boundaries of Grecophone cultural influence. Also, with the urban, mercantile, and educated elites endorsing a secular identity, the *Rum millet* lost legitimacy in the eyes of its most prominent members. Therefore, although Grecophone cultural influences were dominant in the Balkans, the cultural mobilization of the Orthodox Christians was not limited to Grecophone or Hellenized strata. In fact, the Romanian, Serb, and Bulgarian cases illustrate both the dominant nature of Grecophone culture in this period and the fact that the process of secularization entailed a revitalization of ethnic identity similar to the revitalization of Greek identity.

There are two main implications of the interpretation proposed here. First, at least until the early nineteenth century, it is perhaps more salient to refer to one Balkan Enlightenment instead of various national Enlightenments. Elements of a significant cultural differentiation among the Greek Orthodox Balkan intelligentsia were not present until that time. Suggesting this reconceptualization also makes it possible to analyze the complex relations between class and ethnicity within the Ottoman *Rum millet*. Second, the absence of serious ideological antagonisms among the Balkan intelligentsia during the Enlightenment period suggests that the intense ethnic and national rivalries among the Balkan peoples are a phenomenon that emerged during the second half of the nineteenth century; this is discussed in detail in Chapters 4 and 5.

The Enlightenment's historical significance consisted precisely in the fact that it aspired to transform Ottoman Balkan society according to the model of Western culture, thus integrating the European periphery into a common "Europe." The transmission of the Enlightenment in the Ottoman Balkans was the first attempt at Westernization by a peripheral non-"Western" society, a prelude to cultural processes that have transformed the globe over the last two centuries. To rule over various *ethnies* entailed the subordination of ethnicity to religion. Once this hierarchical system collapsed, the *millet* system was bound to experience a crisis of legitimacy. It does not mean, however, that the model of the nation-state was the only one available or that it should be presented as the most advantageous one. Given the ethnic intermixing of the Balkan lands and Anatolia, the postulate of ethnic homogeneity would have seemed strange to the peoples of the times. Therefore, two different roads were open to the Balkan peoples in the aftermath of the 1821 revolution: that of creating ethnically homogeneous states and that of establishing some type of federation.

## NOTES

1. For examples, see Turczynski (1972; 1975), Lancek (1983), Otetea (1970), Kossev, Hristov, and Angelov (1963), and Dutu (1976).

2. An *ethnie* may have, to differing degrees, the following characteristics: a collective proper name, a myth of common ancestry, shared historical memories, some elements of common culture (such as language or religion), an association with a specific homeland, and a sense of solidarity (Smith 1991, 21, 40; Smith 1986).

3. For a discussion of the Byzantine legacy, see Jekins (1967). With their 1204 conquest of Constantinople, the Crusaders of the Fourth Crusade shook this universalistic vision. Following 1204, the emperors of Nikea targeted the Greek *ethnie* as their major constituency and employed once again the word *Hellene* (previously used to signify "pagan") as an instrument for their own legitimacy. The reconstruction of the Byzantine Empire in 1261 put an end to this trend toward Greek proto-nationalism. For the next two centuries, the conflict between Orthodox Byzantine universalism and the newborn Greek proto-nationalism persisted. Two factors helped the resolution of this ideological struggle. First, in 1453, the conquest of Constantinople by the Ottomans led to the extinction of the secular Byzantine elites that promoted the ecclesiastical union of the Catholic and Orthodox churches. Second, among the Grecophone intellectuals of the time, the proponents of ecclesiastical union with the West (such as the philosopher Plithon) failed to gain sufficient popular and institutional support. Both factors helped Orthodox religious mysticism gain the upper hand and establish itself as the main current of thought among Orthodox Christians (Vakalopoulos 1961; Giannaras 1992; Daniilidis 1934).

4. Orthodox millenarianism has been misinterpreted as a manifestation of nationalism (Voyatzidis 1953; 1965). This assessment has been revised (see Mango 1965; Ahrweiler 1988; Iorga 1985).

5. The *Rum millet* included large segments of people who belonged to different *ethnies* (Clogg 1982, 185–6). In fact, the considerable variation in local dialects and languages strengthened the religious component of the system. Moreover, what I am referring to—somewhat anachronistically—as the *millet* system in this chapter constituted a model of social organization that was developed over a long time. It is likely that the word "millet" was not in use in the early stages of this system; its widespread employment is a nineteenth-century phenomenon (Braude 1982). See Konortas (1998, 121–64) for a discussion of the evolution of the relationships between the Ottoman state and the Patriarchate.

6. The name *Roman* was a legacy of history, however, not a factual identification of race or ethnicity. Even to this day, the patriarchs of Constantinople, Antioch, and Jerusalem are referred to as "Roman" patriarchs. The terminological confusion of the terms "Romans" and "Greeks" owes much to the political rivalry between Western Europe and the Byzantine Empire, a rivalry that emerged during the course of the Middle Ages. The term *Roman* originally indicated a political designation, that is, a citizen of the eastern Roman Empire (since the western part collapsed in the fifth century). Since Charle-

magne's reconstitution of the western Roman Empire in 800, Western Europeans began employing the term "Greek" to denote the Romans of the eastern Roman Empire—causing in the process the outrage of the eastern Romans (i.e., Byzantines) (Romanides 1975, 281; Gill 1980, 68). The Ottomans used the term *reaya* to mean all land cultivators regardless of religion; in practice, in the Ottoman Balkans, it meant the Orthodox Christians.

7. Runciman (1968, 376–80) considers this expansion the outcome of Phanariot influence aiming at the restoration of Byzantium. See Hupchick (1993) for a similar interpretation. In the Serb case, successive migrations to the Habsburg territories in 1690 and 1737 reduced the population. In both cases, the Serb clergy aided the Habsburgs against the Ottomans; this led to the 1737 decision of the Ottomans to replace the Serb high clergy with Greeks (Jelavich 1983, I:93–95; Arnakis 1963; Pijakov 1968).

8. The same attitude was expressed by Nikolaos' son, Alexandros Mavrocordatos, who wrote in a letter: "We conform to the prescription of the Gospel 'Render unto Caesar the things which are Caesar's'; it is not the custom of us Christians to confuse what is temporary and corruptible with what is divine and eternal" (quoted in Mango 1973, 51). See also Lazarescu (1975, 79–94) and Daniilidis (1934, 165–8, 240–4).

9. The eighteenth-century Greek clergyman Evyenios Voulgaris, arguably the most important Enlightenment figure in the Balkans, stands out as a "bridgehead" between the two groups. For further discussion on Voulgaris' life and scholarly activities, see Roudometof (2000a).

10. The Church's objections to Enlightenment included first, the charge of atheism and the fear that new attitudes would weaken the strong anti-Catholic stand of the Orthodox Church. Moreover, the Church feared that new theories, such as heliocentrism, would shake the Church's central position in the worldviews of the believers. Second, there was a general perception that antiquity's knowledge was superior to modernist knowledge. Third, the Church's objections emphasized the socioeconomic conflict between the groups associated with science (merchants and other new strata emerging in the course of the eighteenth century) and the established religious elites of the *Rum millet* (Makridis 1988, 265–82).

11. On the bitter conflict between Athanasios Parios and Korais, see Giannaras (1992, 181). See also Giannaras (1992, 215–29) for a negative evaluation of Korais. As already discussed, one of the most prominent Phanariot intellectuals of the time, Dimitrios Katartzis, categorically rejected the Hellenic thesis in favor of the "Romeic" identity. Whereas Korais struggled to transform the religious Romeic identity into a secular one, the Phanariot Panagiotis Kordikas insisted in 1818 that it was "through the Holy Faith [that] the Hellenic Race was saved from ultimate disappearance," and that national identification via the Christian religion has become "such an essential feature of the Nation, that a Hellene ceases to be recognized as a Hellene if he ceases to be recognized as a Christian" (quoted in Politis 1984, 30). Kordikas was an educated Phanariot who came into direct personal and ideological conflict with Korais (Dimaras 1977, 349–61).

12. The first Masonic lodge opened in Galata in Constantinople in 1744. In the Ionian islands Freemasonry was instituted in 1740; in the principalities, foreign Freemasons existed as early as 1743, and the first Romanian lodge was founded in Jassy in 1772 (Gedeon 1976, 104; Georgescu 1971, 32 n.3). Both Greek Orthodox and Western merchants enrolled, accelerating the process of acquainting the new Greek Orthodox aristocracy with Western liberalism.

13. See Daskalakis (1979) and Vranousis (1957) on Velenstinlis' life and the infor-

mation obtained by the Austrian authorities (see Botzaris 1962 for a brief overview). See Kitromilides (1978, 265–312) and Pantazopoulos (1994, 61–92) for analyses of the liberal nature of Velenstinlis' works. Kordatos (1983) is perhaps the first researcher to put forward the notion of Velenstinlis as a visionary of a Balkan federation. For a critical overview regarding this claim, see Pantazopoulos (1994, 51).

14. Karpat (1986, 150) maintains that this was the result of Sultan Mahmud II's "mis-understanding" a national revolt for a religious one. However, the Ottomans were not informed regarding the secular trend signified by the rise of Hellenism. In 1826, Iakovos Rizos Nerulos recounted that in the early stages of the 1821 revolution, when the word "Hellenes" (and not "Grecs") was used, the Ottomans did not recognize the name and were wondering who these people were (quoted in Politis 1993, 34).

15. This subsection draws heavily on Roudometof (2000a).

16. Contrary to the praise with which the book was received among the European public, Dionysios Avramiotti, a Greek doctor, did not hesitate to expose its inaccuracies in a critical treatise published in Padua in 1816. Although a good deal of the disagreement between the French visitor and the Greek doctor was personal, their individual divergences exemplified the divergent meaning of the Hellenic past for Europeans as opposed to modern Greeks. For the former it was a field of archeological and scholarly study and a source of artistic and poetic themes; for educated Greeks, their Hellenic heritage was a relatively new discovery from which they derived pride and dignity (Augustinos 1994, 189).

17. On Byron's contribution to the philhellenic movement, see Woodhouse (1969, 401–20), St. Clair (1973, 138–85), Cunningham (1978), Dakin (1955, 42–79), and Kakambouras (1993).

18. In Paris a lyrical tragedy, *The Siege of Corinth* (October 1825) opened with music by Rossini and Pichald's tragedy *Leonidas* was performed at Theater Français (November 1825). Delacroix painted a series of pictures inspired by the war, including his famous *Scenes from the Massacres of Scio* (inspired by the Ottoman massacres of Chios in 1822), a picture exhibited at the Salon (1824) and brought by the king to the Louvre (St. Clair 1973, 267–70). See Tsigakou (1981) for a discussion of the aesthetic dimension.

# 3

# The Pursuit of Citizenship

Do not think that we consider this corner of Greece as our country, or Athens as our capital, or the Parthenon as our national temple. The Parthenon belongs to an age and a religion with which we have no sympathy. Our country is the vast territory of which Greek is the language, and the faith of the Orthodox Greek Church is the religion.

An Athenian Greek to Nassau Senior, 1857–1858,
quoted in Clogg 1988, 253

We, who have always inhabited this geographical unit which is composed of the Balkans and Asia Minor, are divided in small nations and states . . . we fight constant wars among us . . . and do not see that with these wars we incite the appetite of the foreigners for our land . . . that is why none of us can stand on his feet. . . . I was thinking more frequently this at Constantinople . . . and I could see no other way to save ourselves but to form an association against foreign pressure.

Athanasios Souliotis, Greek officer and activist, 1916,
quoted in Xanalatos 1962, 281

[East and West are] not geographic terms but qualitative terms which denote a difference in cultural principles which have become active forces in the history of mankind.

Ivan Aksakov, Russian Panslavist (1853), cited in Petrovich 1956, 71

We have made unsuccessful attempts to convert the non-Muslim into a loyal Ottoman, and all such efforts must inevitably fail, as long as the small independent states in the Balkan peninsula remain in a position to propagate

> ideas of separatism among the inhabitants of Macedonia. There can therefore
> be no question of equality, until we have succeeded in our task of Otto-
> manizing the Empire—a long and laborious task, in which I venture to
> predict that we shall succeed after we have at last put an end to the agitation
> and propaganda of the Balkan States.
>
> Talat Bey (later pasha and Grand Vizier) at the 1910 convention
> of the Committee of Union and Progress in Thessaloniki,
> quoted in Lewis 1979, 218

In the last chapter, I suggested that liberalism, secularization, and the Enlightenment had a profound effect among the Orthodox *millet* of the empire. Consequently, the Orthodox *millet* began to disintegrate and nation-states were
formed from the Balkan provinces of the empire. By 1832, the process of fragmentation had already begun with Serbia, Greece, and the Danubian principalities outside the Porte's administrative control. Greece was an independent state;
Serbia and the principalities remained formally affiliated with the empire. It was
evident that, unless drastic measures were taken, the process of disintegration
would continue. The problems associated with adopting the form of the nation-
state in an ethnically heterogeneous region were realized early on by the local
statesmen.

In this chapter, I discuss attempts to employ the discourse of *citizenship* in
order to build state units that would incorporate the heterogeneous population
of the Balkans. Of course, citizenship could be founded on membership in one
of the rivaling Balkan nation-states. As is discussed in Chapter 6, the development of citizenship in the Balkan nation-states gained momentum in the post-
1878 period, precisely at the time when visions of interethnic citizenship were
frustrated.

However, for the population still under Ottoman control, there were other
alternatives. For them, citizenship could be pursued on a multiethnic and multicultural basis, along the lines suggested by Rigas Velenstinlis in the 1790s
(Todorov 1995, 1–9; 1991, 94). The plans pursued entailed two different conceptions of citizenship. On the other hand, there were attempts and plans to
establish a type of *transnational* citizenship, in the form of federalism (including
Yugoslavism) or Pan-Slavism. On the other hand, there was a long and serious
attempt by the *Tanzimat* reformers, Ottoman Greeks, and the Young Turks to
develop a model of *interethnic* citizenship.

In the pre-1878 period, the structural and cultural transformation of the
Greeks, Bulgarians, and Serbs into full-fledged nations was largely incomplete.
This process continued until the early twentieth century and thereafter. Consequently, the pursuit of transnational or interethnic citizenship was a viable option.

## FEDERALISM IN THE NINETEENTH-CENTURY BALKANS

During the first half of the nineteenth century, the Greek and Bulgarian national movements preserved a strong cooperative spirit in their plans. In the Greek kingdom, a number of secret societies and organizations were formed (e.g., the Thrace-Bulgarian-Serb Committee, Macedonian Society, Big Brotherhood, Philorthodox organization) (Todorov 1991, 94–7; 1995, 32–43; Papadopoulos and Traikov 1984, 573–82; Jelavich 1966, 89–102). Their goal was the liberation of Thessaly, Macedonia, and Thrace and their means for accomplishing it was a general Balkan uprising. Young Bulgarian nationalists readily pursued interethnic cooperation as a means of achieving Bulgarian independence (Tzvetkov 1993, 1:409–14; McDermott 1962, 119; Dimof 1974, 180–1; Genchev 1977, 72–85).

This spirit of interethnic cooperation, usually entailing the seeds of a federal organization, remained alive until at least 1878. International events throughout this period shaped the direction of these visions and provided the context for rounds of usually failed discussions.[1] In the 1860s and 1870s, the Italian unification influenced Greek political thought. Following the slogan *Italia fara da se* Greek writers developed the concept "the Orient to the Orient" as a political principle that entailed the rejection of foreign intervention and the solution of the national question through the efforts of the local peoples. In 1861–1962, a series of projects and pamphlets appeared, many advocating Balkan federalism, but also confused as to their ultimate goal (Liakos 1985, 125–9; Todorov 1991, 98–9). Adopting the model of the Italian committees, Greek, Greco-Slavic and Graeco-Albanian committees were set up in southern Italy, Albania, Epirus, and Smyrna. They aimed at the organization of a joint Balkan revolution and the coordination of activities among Slavs, Greeks, and Albanians (Liakos 1985, 159–64).

In the early to mid-1860s, the Serb prince Mihailo attempted to organize a confederation or federation of the Balkan peoples.[2] Mihailo's plan involved the attempt to create a broader South Slav federation incorporating not only the Habsburg Slavs but also the Bulgarians. Early Bulgarian nationalists such as Vasil Aprilov, Ivan Seliminski, and Ivan Dobrovski viewed Slavic identity as a major part of modern Bulgarian identity (Shashko 1974b, 138–40; McKenzie 1985, 297–330). With the support of Russian Pan-Slavists and that of the Serbs and Prince Mihailo, the conservative Bulgarian community of Bucharest put forward the plan of a Serbo-Bulgarian or Yugoslav kingdom to be created under the leadership of Prince Mihailo. On 17 April 1867, 35 Bulgarian representatives assembled in Bucharest and adopted this proposal (Shashko 1974b, 144; Stavrianos 1944, 93–103). Georgi S. Rakovski, the leader of the Bulgarian nationalist movement, rendered his support to Prince Mihailo and even formed a Bulgarian Legion to fight the Ottomans. However, while in Athens in 1863 to conduct negotiations with the Greek government, Rakovksi learned of secret Serb–Greek agreements providing for acquisition of what Rakovski considered to be Bulgarian lands by the Greeks and the Serbs. The Bulgarians accused the Serbs of following a policy of Pan-Serbianism and this led to an estrangement between Serb leaders and Bulgarian nationalists (Trajkov 1984, 105; Shashko 1974b, 141; McKenzie 1985, 319; Stavrianos 1944, 88). After Rakovski's death in 1867, the greatest adherent of South Slav unity was Liuben Karavelov. Karavelov supported the Serb–Bulgarian cooperation and while living in Belgrade from 1867 to 1869 he found himself in agreement with Serb nationalists concerning the problem of South Slav unity. Other Bulgarian leaders gradually abandoned this project.[3]

In the 1850–1878 period, Pan-Slavism influenced the direction of the Serb and Bulgarian movements, which sought to foster their ties with Russia. Although Pan-Slavist feelings had existed since the seventeenth century (Petrovich 1956, 9–14; Fadner 1962, 73–88, 91–105; Zlatar 1990), Pan-Slavism as an organized intellectual movement emerged in the early nineteenth century.[4] In the second half of the nineteenth century, Pan-Slavism was strengthened by the absorption of romantic nationalism into the Russian literary and political scene (Greenfeld 1991). Pan-Slavists such as Ivan Aksakov, whose statement is quoted in the beginning of this chapter, postulated a prehistoric Slav unity and urged the various Slavic groups to reconstruct this cultural and political unity. Although they were not—strictly speaking—Russian nationalists, Pan-Slavists often suggested that this unity could be achieved under the auspices of Russia (Fadner 1962, 53, 109).[5]

Pan-Slavism emerged as an articulated movement after the Crimean War (1853–1856) and gained momentum as an intellectual movement in the 1860s and 1870s, albeit without a clear political focus. In 1867 the Moscow Slav Congress offered the opportunity to Slavs from all over Europe to come together for a period of almost a month in a series of informal gatherings and celebrations. Despite the rejoicing of all the participants, it was clear that no single group was willing to give up elements of its individuality in order to become absorbed into the Slavic unity of the Pan-Slavists (Petrovich 1956; Fadner 1962, 241–92; Milojkovic-Djuric 1994, 54–95).

Pan-Slavist ideology met Russian foreign policy objectives in the work of the Russian ambassador in Constantinople (1864–1877), Count Nicholas Pavlovich Ignatiev. Ignatiev was the architect of Russian intervention in favor of the Bulgarian national movement; his contribution is discussed in Chapter 5. When, in the aftermath of the 1875 revolts in Bosnia-Herzegovina, Serbia went to war against the Ottoman Empire, Pan-Slavist feelings were aroused in Russia (Miliojkovic-Djuric 1994, 96–123; on the 1875 crisis, see Sumner 1962). The Slavic committees organized a wave of informal aid to Serbia; this included money, arms, volunteers, and army officers. The Slavic committees sent 4,303 volunteers to Serbia, although only about half of them reached the front (McKenzie 1967, 122; Jelavich 1991, 170–8).

Pan-Slavist feelings were soon frustrated. The Russian volunteers' paternalistic attitude vis-à-vis the Serbs caused the Serbs to regard them as worse than the Turks. Relationships between Russian volunteers and Serbs turned sour; the former accused the Serbs of lack of courageous spirit and the Serbs were dismayed by the Russians who ended up in Belgrade's cafés instead of the front. In addition, the socioeconomic and cultural differences between Serb and Russian societies became apparent (Milojkovic-Djuric 1994, 118). The Serb-Ottoman war ended with a Serb military disaster and only the Tsar's immediate threat of force prevented the Ottomans from marching to Belgrade. By 1876, Russian public opinion and policy changed from support to Serbia to support for a future Bulgarian state (Durman 1987, 44–52; McKenzie 1967, 146–7).

Although dipomats worked to resolve the 1875–1876 eastern crisis throughout 1877, the failed Bulgarian uprising of April 1876 contributed to Russia's tilting toward war. The Russo-Ottoman war led to the signing of the San Stefano Treaty (1878) and the emergence of a "Greater Bulgaria" that subsumed most of the European part of the Ottoman empire. Following European reaction and strong protests by the other Balkan states, this treaty was revised and the new Treaty of Berlin returned Macedonia to the Ottoman empire. Instead of an independent Bulgarian state, two principalities were created: Bulgaria and Eastern Romilia. (The two were eventually united in a bloodless coup in 1885.)

In exchange for the assignment of Bulgaria to the Russian sphere of influence, the Habsburg Empire was granted the administration of Bosnia-Herzegovina and Serbia was assigned to the Habsburg sphere of political influence. During the reign of the prince and later king Milan, Serb nationalists continued to view Russia as the protector of all South Slavs. Prince Milan's endorsement of the prescribed policy of submission to the Habsburg monarchy and his growing Russophobia made Milan the target of Serb nationalist reaction. Since the possibility of expanding Serbia territorially into Bosnia was precluded because of its occupation by the Habsburgs, Prince Milan attempted to satisfy Serb territorial aspirations to the south, toward northern Macedonia or southern Serbia (Jelavich 1962b, 162–204).

Following the creation of the principality of Bulgaria (1878), Russian policy began a slow collision course with Bulgarian nationalism. Although Bulgarian nationalists always considered the Berlin treaty unfortunate and were determined to undermine it, they were not Pan-Slavists.[6] Russian attempts to dominate Bulgarian political life in the post-1878 period led to a Russo-Bulgarian estrangement (Durman 1987; Jelavich 1991, 178–96). Under the reign of Prime Minister Stefan Stambolov (1887–1894), this gap grew into full-scale political confrontation (Perry 1993). Cooperation was restored only after Stambolov's removal from office in 1894. Over the 1850–1878 period, the growth of political and cultural connections between Russia and the Balkan Slavs fragmented solidarity among the Eastern Orthodox Christians of the peninsula. The Greeks considered the new turn in Russian policy to be abandoment by their former protectors, a turn of events that fostered visions of Greco-Ottoman cooperation in the 1870s.

Following the 1878 San Stefano Treaty, Bulgaria, Serbia, and Greece became involved in a bitter conflict over Ottoman Macedonia. Each state claimed this region for itself and this disagreement left little room for visions of solidarity to develop. Dissenting voices within these countries advocating the idea of a federation belonged to the Left. In Serbia, the socialist leader Svetozar Marković and his followers advocated social reform in internal politics and in foreign policy they advocated the formation of a Balkan republican federation (Mc-Clellan 1964). Dimitur Blagoev, the leader of the Bulgarian socialists, also be-came one of the greatest adherents of Balkan federation. Blagoev opposed a union between Serbia and Bulgaria that would be the result of governmental action and advocated a union similar to that of the United States (Shashko 1974b, 154). Within the Greek kingdom, pro-federalist ideas were put forward by a number of intellectuals involved with the left-wing Radical party of the Ionian islands. Following the unification of the islands with the Greek kingdom (1864), these intellectuals joined the Greek political scene. They advocated so-cial reform in domestic affairs and federalism in foreign policy. By the 1880s and 1890s, forerunners of socialist ideas came to the forefront of the federalist solution (Todorov 1991, 101–6; 1984, 529–37; 1995, 110–38). These groups of intellectuals and reformers were closely involved in the formation of the society "Eastern Federation" (1884), whose goal was to promote the union of the Balkan peoples. The society developed contacts with Romanians, Bulgarians, and Serbs; it also published a newspaper whose circulation was soon banned in the Ottoman lands. Its goal was a peaceful solution of the Macedonian Question (see Chapter 5) that divided the Balkan peoples at the time. The society called for the for-mation of an Albano-Macedonian state in the context of a broader Balkan fed-eration as a means of avoiding the bitter conflict of the Balkan states among themselves.

Of all these visions, Yugoslavism was the only one to eventually succeed. It was mostly propagated by intellectuals and other national leaders who fostered it as a means to accomplish their own particular goals. Initial fragments of Yugoslavism can be detected in the Croat Illyrian movement of the 1830s. How-ever, the Illyrian movement was restricted to Croatia with little following outside the region. Its ethnocentrism and narrow social and ethnic bases were among the main causes of its failure.[7] If *cultural* Yugoslavism was a moot concept during the nineteenth century, *political* Yugoslavism found fertile ground within the Habsburg monarchy where it was possible to advocate "trialism" (e.g., the reorganization of the Habsburg Empire into three state units, that is, Austrian, Hungarian, and Yugoslav) as an alternative to dualism (Austria and Hungary). The weakness of Croatian nationalism throughout the nineteenth century was a major factor contributing to the appeal of trialism. Croatia lacked an army of its own, strong international protectors, and a popular national movement. Its national movement was initially dominated by middle and lower gentry, sup-plemented by an upwardly mobile bourgeoisie (Jelavich 1967, 83–7).

The first rapprochement between Croats and Habsburg Serbs occurred in the context of the 1848 revolutions, when the two sides cooperated with each other—both of them hoping for autonomy from Vienna (Adler 1979, 276–7;

Jelavich 1967, 93; Vucinich 1967, 5–6). In fact, the Vojvodina Serbs were granted regional autonomy on 6 November 1849 by the Habsburg monarchy; however, as soon as the 1848 Hungarian revolution was crushed, the Habsburgs reneged on their promises and the Serb Vojvodina existed only as an administrative area with no real autonomy given to the Serb community. Following the 1859 Habsburg defeat in Italy, the Habsburgs sought a reconciliation with the Hungarians, and on 29 December 1860, the emperor abolished the Serb Vojvodina and granted its territory to Hungary. In the 1860s, the Vojvodina Serbs repeatedly expressed their desire for regional autonomy from Hungary to no avail.[8] During the early 1860s Catholic bishop Josip Juraj Strossmayer espoused the idea of South Slav unity within the boundaries of the Habsburg Empire; and he was the first to employ the term "Yugoslav." Bishop Strossmayer and the Croat historian Franjo Rački were the most prominent members of the Croatian National Party during the 1860s. Strossmayer hoped to achieve the Serbo-Croatian union through a church union: The Serbs were to recognize papal supremacy and the Croats to introduce Slavonic language in church services (Vucinich 1967, 19). In 1874, these efforts culminated in the establishment of the Yugoslav Academy of Arts and Sciences in Zagreb. However, this activity did not imply a desire to unite Croatia with Serbia proper. The Serb question was undoubtedly most vexing for the Croats. With Serbs dispersed in Dalmatia, Croatia-Slavonia, Vojvodina, and Bosnia-Herzegovina, the Croats had to come to terms with the fact that many of the provinces claimed by them were not inhabited solely by Croats. Yugoslavism was a concept that allowed for the assertion of Croatian state rights without being dismissive of the Serbs.[9]

World War I (1914–1918) forced the situation in the Habsburg territories and led to proclamation of the kingdom of Serbs, Slovenes, and Croats (1917), which was eventually renamed Yugoslavia in 1929. The problems posed by the construction of a common state plagued Yugoslavia during the interwar period. These problems are reviewed in Chapter 7. Suffice it to say, as the discussion has illustrated thus far, Yugoslavism was a popular vision in the Habsburg territories. In terms of the general outcome of federalism, it is plain that geopolitical rivalry among Belgrade, Athens, and later on, Sofia prevented the articulation of long-term meaningful solutions. Moreover, international interventions most often contributed to further complication of these rivalries. Finally, federalism was increasingly at odds with the prevailing international trends of the time. As the European system of nation-states was consolidated, the international environment was becoming less favorable to interethnic citizenship (cf. McNeill 1985; Hobsbawm 1990).

## OTTOMANISM, ECONOMIC DEPENDENCE, AND CONSTITUTIONALISM

While federal plans were mostly unsuccessfully pursued, the Ottoman Empire was undergoing a significant economic transformation in the course of the nineteenth century. Until 1820, volumes of intraregional trade within the empire as well as trade with Russia and Egypt were higher than those with central and western Europe (Pamuk 1987, 8, 130). In the early 1820s the ratio of total Ottoman exports and imports to overall volume of production was well below 5 percent. From 1820 to 1853 the Ottoman trade came under British hegemony. The 1829 Treaty of Adrianople led to the collapse of the Ottoman supply system in the Danubian principalities and in 1838 the British–Ottoman treaty included a 5 percent import tariff versus 12 percent tax imposed on local products (Tsoukalas 1987, 279–80; Stavrianos 1958, 320; Pamuk 1987, 11–12). The most important article of this treaty was the abolition of the foreign trade monopoly system and of the governmental ability to impose restrictions and additional customs or duties. Subsequently, British exports grew from 1 million pounds in 1825 (versus 1.2 million in Ottoman exports) to 8.4 million pounds in 1852 (versus 2.2 million in Ottoman exports). Although many researchers suggest that the end result of the rising volumes of trade with the West was the empire's gradual economic decline, Palairet (1997, 42, 53–57) argues that the Ottomans' nineteenth-century economic record is mixed. That is, while some older traditional industries did decline, their decline was balanced by the rise of new industries, many of whom operated in small cities in the Ottoman Balkans.

Even if this interpretation is adopted, there is little doubt that commercialization had a serious impact on the socioeconomic position of the empire's various groups and religious communities. From 1826 to 1860 the bureaucracy granted open access to Ottoman markets in exchange for relative freedom from interference with domestic affairs (Quataert 1994, 763, 828–32).[10] Ottoman trade with Western Europe doubled between the 1850s and 1870s and by the second half of the nineteenth century, the large port cities of Saloniki, Constantinople, Trebzond, and Smyrna were transformed as a result of the increased trade (*Review* 1993; Moskof 1978; Asdrachas 1988b; Kremmydas 1972). In the early 1910s, almost 14 percent of GNP and more than 25 percent of agricultural production was being exported. The ratio of imports to GNP was approximately 18 percent (even higher in coastal areas).

From the 1850s onward, inflows of foreign capital were made available for state borrowing and contributed significantly to growing state dependence on foreign capital. Institutional arrangements strengthened this trend. For example, the monopoly on print paper currency was transferred to the Ottoman Bank in 1863 (this linked the empire to the gold standard) and in 1866 foreigners were granted the right to purchase agricultural land. In 1862 the Ottoman debt reached a total of 10 million English pounds; it was paid back by an international loan in 1865. However, by 1872 the debt once again reached 10 million pounds, eventually climbing to 16 million pounds by 1874. As a result, in the early 1870s, the Ottoman state became heavily dependent on the banking elite's providing the funds for financing the soaring Ottoman deficit (Pamuk 1987, 12–3, 17; Exertzoglou 1989, 15–58).

The non-Muslim *millet*s (mostly Greeks and Armenians) provided the commercial intermediaries between the Western powers and the local economy. During the earlier centuries, Western merchants used Christians and Jews as intermediaries because members of these communities were willing to become protégés of foreign powers in order to escape the threat of property confiscation by the Sultan. Some prominent examples of this trend have already been mentioned in Chapter 1. Moreover, Russians and Habsburgs competed with each other to attract merchants to their territories and offered the protégé status as a recruitment mechanism (for details, see Gocek 1996, 96–7). Because the import-export trade brought considerable profits, the earlier trend of merchants' becoming protégés of foreign powers was reinforced. The advantages offered by the protégé status (freedom from administrative extortion and interference, exemption from tariffs, and exemption from other obligations to the empire) led to the non-Muslim merchants' gaining a considerable advantage over the Muslims (Karpat 1972, 258–61; Berkes 1964, 139–44; Issawi 1982, 261–86).

Commercialization implied a steady improvement and greater prosperity among the Christian middle strata and deterioration of living conditions for the peasant or urban Muslim strata who could no longer compete with them (Karpat 1982b, 394; Panayotopoulos 1983, 87–128; Gocek 1996, 110–6). Ottoman Greeks were rapidly becoming identified with the urban strata: According to the post-1922 declarations of the Ottoman Greek refugees, more than 50 percent of the Greek population was urban (Tsoukalas 1987, 289). By 1914 Greeks were responsible for 50 percent of capital investment (the Armenians were second with 20%) (Alexandris 1983, 32). By 1910–1912 the Greek Orthodox population of Anatolia was close to 1.5 million.[11] To this number should be added the Ottoman Greeks of Constantinople, Thrace, and Macedonia.[12] By 1914–1915 the official Ottoman statistics reported a total of 1,729,738 Ottoman Greeks throughout the empire. Although wealthy capitalists were prominent among them, the Greek Orthodox, Armenian, and Jewish *millets* consisted mostly of petit-bourgeois elements. For example, in the second half of the nineteenth century, the Greeks in Constantinople numbered between 200,000 and 400,000.[13] In 1868, 30 percent of the freelance professionals and 33 percent of the handicraft producers of Constantinople were Ottoman Greeks (Svolopoulos 1994, 67–8; Exertzoglou 1989, 15–24).

While the market forces were becoming identified with Ottoman Greek capital, the state was becoming Muslim. For the urban Muslim population, employment in the bureaucracy was one of the few areas (or sectors) in which they had an advantage over Ottoman Christians. Between 1777 and 1797 there were only 869 clerks in the central scribal offices in Constantinople. The total number of personnel is estimated to have been around 1,500. With the reforms of Selim III (1789–1807) and Mahmud II (1808–1839) and the dismissal of the Phanariot interpreters in the aftermath of the 1821 revolution, the translation office in the Ministry of Foreign Affairs was filled with Muslims (Findley 1980, 58–63, 133–4). In the 1830s, this office offered the opportunity for a number of Ottoman Muslims to learn foreign languages (mainly French). Some of the new bureaucrats served as ambassadors of the government in European capitals and were strongly influenced by their European experience. By the end of the nineteenth century the total number of officials is estimated to have been between 70,000 and 90,000 (Findley 1989, 22–3; 1980, 65). This tremendous increase in size reflected the changing nature of the bureaucracy, but its increase also provided for civil service positions. The political evolution of Ottoman institutions has to be understood against this polarization between a predominantly non-Muslim middle strata and a predominantly Muslim civil service sector.[14]

During the nineteenth century, the Ottoman bureaucracy was responsible for initiating a program of state-sponsored modernization in order to build civic ties among the empire's population. In 1839, the first major reform effort took place with the proclamation of the *Hatt-i Serif* of Gulhane. The edict declared that all subjects regardless of religion must have guarantees for their security of life, honor, and property, that trials must be public and according to regulations, that confiscation was abolished, that an orderly system of taxation would take the place of tax farming, and that a regular system of military conscription must be established.[15] It was accepted with high hopes by the Christians but the postulate on equality was received with hostility by the Muslim population. Moreover, the representatives of the old order—religious officials and province adminis-trators—did not welcome the edict.

The second major effort took place following the Crimean War (1853–1856), when the European allies of the empire (Austria, France, and England) pushed the Porte to take reform measures. This second reform effort was undertaken by Ali and Fuad pashas who were in control of the government for most of the time during the 1850s and 1860s. In the *Hatt-i Humayun* (1856) the aboli-tion of tax farming and bribery was again promised and the equal liability of Muslims and non-Muslims to military service was reiterated. A note annexed to the *Hatt-i* repeated the 1844 declaration that apostasy from Islam would not be punished by death (Davison 1963, 55). Other stipulations included the strict observance of annual budgets, the establishment of banks, the employment of European capital and skills for economic improvement, the codification of penal and commercial law and reform in the prison system, and the establishment of mixed courts to take care of a greater proportion of cases involving Muslims and non-Muslims.

The *Hatt-i* illustrated the concept of *Osmanlik* (Ottomanism) at work and, although religious phraseology found its way into the edict, the concept of pa-triotism or "compatriotism" among the Ottoman peoples was also introduced. Following 1856, *Osmanli* was a term applied to all the peoples of the empire, irrespective of their status. Muslim Turks were now referred to both as *Osmanli* and also as *kavim* (people) (Kushner 1977, 22–3). The term *millet*, which pre-viously denoted religious communities, came to be used as a rough equivalent to "nation" or "people." The term gradually became applicable to the Muslim Turks as well as the Ottoman Christians and Jews. The *Hatt-i* extended popular representation. At both the provincial and communal councils there was to be a fair choice of Muslim and non-Muslim representatives, the Supreme Council of Judicial Ordinances was to include representatives of the non-Muslim *millets*, and the *millets* themselves were to be internally restructured.

The edict met the strong opposition of the Muslims and was depicted as the outcome of outside pressure on the government. Innovation was not welcomed by traditional Islam and these reforms faced reaction not only from Muslim theologians but also from local officials and the common folk (Davison 1963, 65–6). The educated bureaucrats who promoted these reforms were at the forefront of Ottoman Muslim modernization. Of the 95 persons who occupied top positions in the Sublime Porte during the 1826–1878 period, 46 percent belonged to the high strata and 42 percent received some type of special training for civil servants (Todorova 1976, 103–44). In sharp contrast, the majority of the Ottoman Muslims lagged behind in comprehending the reform agenda. According to a contemporary observer, 90 percent to 95 percent of the Muslim population was illiterate (Davison 1963, 69, 177). For them, the assumption that infidels (non-Muslims referred to in a derogative manner as *giaur*) would be equals to the Muslims was in contradiction to the *millet* system and the privileged position awarded to Muslims in it.

In the following years, the central bureaucracy followed up most of these declarations by adopting specific measures to achieve the "merger" of Christians into Ottomanism (Safrastjan 1989, 34–44; Davison 1963; Lewis 1979; Shaw and Shaw 1977). Of these measures the most unfortunate one was the attempt to create equality in the military service. This proposal was resented both by Christians (who preferred to pay a poll tax instead) and Muslims (who refused to be under the command of infidels), and it was never implemented. In addition, in the 1860s the government attempted to bring the educational system under its control. The goal was to create joint schools in which both Muslims and non-Muslims would participate. This effort met the strong opposition of the minority groups and was never fully implemented. Since the Christian communities were in close contact with the West, secular education provided them with an advantage over the Muslims. By 1896 there were 31,000 pupils in Muslim middle schools compared to 76,000 non-Muslims (Issawi 1982, 277; Shaw and Shaw 1977, 112–3). Given this discrepancy, it is not surprising that a unified educational system was not welcomed by the Ottoman minorities.

The cases of Crete and the *villayet* of Danube illustrate the problems posed by the *Tanzimat* reform in the provinces (Kalliataki Mertikopoulou 1988; Safrastjan 1989, 35–7). In both places "equality" meant equal participation of Muslims and non-Muslims in the councils—irrespective of the population ratios. Furthermore, local Muslim elites were able to sabotage reform efforts through their participation in the council, whereas frequently the Christian representatives were handpicked by the administration or elected in "rigged" elections (Davison 1968, 98–9). Furthermore, the policy of the Ottoman reformers brought them into conflict with the traditionally oriented bureaucrats who—since they did not know French—tended to gather in the lower positions. This created a structural contradiction within the bureaucracy: The low officials loathed their superiors and did not feel disposed to carry out the *Tanzimat* program. Even in the Foreign Ministry (where knowledge of French weighed heavily) 30 percent of the positions were filled from this conservative group of officials (Findley 1980, 202–9). Over the post-1856 period, although new positions were filled by non-Muslims, their employment remained limited. Compared to traditionally oriented Muslims, they were better treated, but they were not treated as well as Western-oriented Muslims (Findley 1982, 339–68; 1989, 87–130).

Nevertheless, the reconstruction of the empire was to the benefit not only of the bureaucracy but also of Ottoman Christian capital. Foreign financial control over the empire increased during the nineteenth century. In the 1850s the already accumulated debt was further increased because of the need to finance the Crimean War (1853–1856). The loans were contracted under unfavorable terms (10–12% interest rate).[16] Between 1869 and 1875 the state borrowed more money than its estimated revenues and, as the 1873 recession further restricted capital availability, this led to an acute financial crisis. The chronic debt created by the budget deficit was also accelerated by bad financial management in the 1870–1875 period, leading to the 1875 bankruptcy (for an overview, see Exertzoglou 1989, 59–71). The development of trade and finance led to the consolidation of a money-owning Greek Orthodox elite (the so-called Galata bankers) with strong international connections: In an 1868 census a total of 68 private money-lending companies was recorded. In the 1870s this elite exercised significant control over the four main Ottoman banks (e.g. Société Générale de l'Empire Ottoman, Credit General Ottoman, Bank of Constantinople, and Société Ottomane de charge et de valeurs) (Exertzogou 1989, 15; Svolopoulos 1994, 70).

Two groups of reformers emerged in the 1860s and 1870s. The first group consisted of Muslim liberal intellectuals (the "Young Ottomans") who criticized the *Tanzimat* reformers for their lack of bold leadership (Kushner 1977, 5; Davison 1963, 173–5; Berkes 1964, 202–18).[17] The second group were Ottoman Greeks, members of the banking elite of Constantinople, who desired the reorganization of the Ottoman empire and its gradual mutation into a new Byzantium. The Greco-Ottoman cooperation took place under the veil of Masonic lodges in Constantinople. Cleanthis Skalieris, a Greek banker with close ties to France, cooperated with Ahmed Midhat pasha, the former governor of the Danube *vilayet*, and heir apparent Murad in this project. Murad became a Mason (20 October 1872) and this offered the opportunity for the creation of joint Graeco-Turkish lodges (Svolopoulos 1980, 441–57). From 1872 the lodge "Progress" operated in Turkish every third meeting and a new lodge instituted by Skalieris worked exclusively in Turkish.

On 10 May 1876, following the revolts in Bosnia-Herzegovina, the *softa*s (theological students) rioted outside the Sublime Porte demanding the dismissal of the Grand Vizier Mahmud Nedim pasha and the Chief Mufti Hasan Fehmi Efendi (Lewis 1979, 160). This bloodless coup was successful and on 30 May

1876 Prince Murad ascended to the throne as Murad V. The "Young Ottomans" who provided the inspiration for constitutionalism, however, had to share power with the former provincial governor Midhat pasha and other members of the Ottoman and Greco-Ottoman elites (Hanioglu 1995, 34–5; Loukas 1991, 150–64). The preliminary measures for the implementation of the constitution and related reforms were undertaken by Skalieris with the assistance of lawyer Francis L. Aimable, former diplomat A. Holinsk, Midhat pasha, English ambassador S. G. Eliot, and Iranian ambassador Malkum (Hanioglu 1989, 187). The Ottoman Greek population enthusiastically endorsed the constitution especially because they believed that it would provide a shelter against rising Bulgarian nationalism (Alexandris 1980, 376–9; Svolopoulos 1994, 27). When Midhat pasha visited the non-Muslim religious leaders, the Ecumenical Patriarch greeted him as the rejuvenator of the Ottoman Empire.

In the meantime, popular support began dwindling when it became known that equality would be granted to non-Muslims. The principal opposition came from the *softa*s. Although among Midhat's most vocal supporters only a few months before, they realized for the first time that constitutionalism would bring the equality of Christians and Muslims (Devereux 1963, 39). On 31 August 1876 Murad was declared mentally unstable and deposed. Following his deposition and the ascent of AbdulHamid II, the plan of constitutional reform was still not dead. Midhat pasha was able to pressure AbdulHamid into approving the constitution but the Sultan was able to introduce the notorious article 113, which gave the Sultan the power to banish from the empire without trial or other legal procedure anyone of whom he had doubts. Midhat pasha was able to secure the constitution just in time to present it to the international conference that was discussing a variety of issues dealing with the fate of the empire. In 1875–1876 the revolts in Bosnia-Herzegovina and the war between Serbia, Montenegro, and the empire were the first international incidents. They were followed by the Bulgarian uprising of April 1876, which was brutally crushed; the massacres that ensued turned European public opinion against the Ottomans. Midhat's diplomatic maneuver failed when the European powers refused to accept the Ottoman argument that because a constitution had been established there was no further need for intervention.

In the midst of the Eastern Crisis of 1875–1878, the Parliament came into session on 19 March 1877. The representatives endorsed the concept of Ottomanism and rejected foreign interference on behalf of non-Muslim minorities. In fact, the Ottoman Greek deputies sided with the empire against Russia in the 1877–1878 war and even called for the enlistment of non-Muslims in the Ottoman army (Alexandris 1980, 380–1). In the first session, the desire to criticize the government was subdued but in the second session, critics of the government gained the majority and proceeded to castigate the ministry for its poor performance. This action grew out of the Russo-Ottoman war of 1877 and the disaster that it brought to the Ottoman forces. In the aftermath of the war some 200,000 to 300,000 Muslims from Serbia, Bulgaria, and the rest of the Balkans were killed and more than 1 million Muslims were made refugees (Karpat 1982b, 398). Following the Parliament's decision to publicly criticize the government (and thus indirectly the Sultan, who appointed the ministers), AbdulHamid suspended the Parliament by a decree of 14 February 1878 on the grounds that an extraordinary condition of crisis impelled him to do so.[18] The Sultan had acted in accordance with the constitution; however, this action served as a pretext for establishing AbdulHamid's personal regime during the 1878–1908 period. During this period, proponents of parliamentarism were persecuted and police spying, censorship, intimidation, and bribery were used to silence the proponents of reform. Whereas the *Tanzimat* leaders had attempted to establish loyalty to the empire as the common fatherland (*vatan*), AbdulHamid II strongly emphasized that loyalty was owed to the Sultan and not to the fatherland (Kushner 1977, 51; Palmer, 1993, 173–175). His regime consciously used Pan-Islamism and religious conservativism to gain legitimacy.[19]

## THE YOUNG TURKS AND OTTOMANISM

Over the second half of the nineteenth century, European influences begun to push Muslim Ottoman intellectuals in a direction far removed from Abdul-Hamid's policies. They were influenced by nineteenth-century romantic nationalism as well as Orientalist writings that pointed out the close affinities among the Turkish peoples. Contacts with Central Asian Turks threatened by Russian and Chinese expansion facilitated Pan-Islamic sentiments but also raised awareness among the Ottoman Turks regarding Turkish common ethnic identity (Kushner 1977, 7–11, 41–80; Hanioglu 1995, 10–26). Whereas religion had been the dominant concern in Ottoman thought, during the 1850s and later, "science" became the new dominant concept.

The Young Turk movement attracted both Muslims and non-Muslims, united in their opposition to AbdulHamid but with great differences in outlook and ideology. The movement originated in 1889 when a group of students at the Imperial Military Medical School formed a conspiratory society. The Young Turks' sudden rise was the outcome of the state-sponsored policy of Westernization. Between 1830 and 1860 the expansion of a Western-style educational system offered the opportunity to young Muslim students to become socialized into Western science and knowledge (Gocek 1996, 68–80). The rationale was to provide the empire with competent people schooled in Western models of warfare, science, and medicine. However, instead of blind loyalty to the Sultan, this group developed an adherence to the abstract concept of the "fatherland."

By 1892 they forged ties with opposition leaders in exile and by 1895 they published an official declaration of their goals, under the banner of the Committee of Union and Progress, in the dissident journal *Mecheveret* in Paris (Ramsaur 1957, 14–16, 24). In 1894, Geogrios Skalieris (son of Cleanthis Skalieris), N. Igglesis, Sp. Spanopoulos, and others were encouraged—by the Greek ambassador Mavrocordatos, the French ambassador Paul Cambon, and the English ambassador Philip Currie—to revitalize Cleanthis Skalieris' earlier lodge, the Light of the Orient. Their plans involved the reconstruction of the empire into an Eastern Greco-Ottoman state. This lodge was in cooperation with the early Young Turk opposition. By 1896 this lodge's activities were coordinated with its sister lodge in Athens. In publications indirectly sponsored by this group, a series of articles appeared in support of the deposed Sultan Murad V and the constitution (Loukas 1991, 203–4; Hanionglu 1989, 188–9; 1995, 35–41). By 1896 the Young Turks had orchestrated a coup against the Sultan. However, their plans were revealed to AbdulHamid's agents and the police arrested most of the conspirators (Ramsaur 1957, 31–5; Hanioglu 1995, 200–12).

In the early 1900s, the exiled Young Turks were divided into two groups: the nationalistic fraction led by Ahmed Riza, who advocated centralization and educational reform; and the liberal fraction led by Prince Sabaheddin (1877–1948) (Berkes 1964, 305–12; Hanioglu 1995, 173–99; Ramsaur 1957, 66–93). Riza, Cevdet, and their followers were influenced by Gustave Le Bon's elitist theories and by racist theories prevalent in German circles. Their elitism stood in sharp opposition to their endorsement of parliamentarism. Sabaheddin was one of the two sons of AbdulHamid's sister. Like Riza, he was influenced by French sociologists. But Sabaheddin followed the writings of Edmond Demolins (1852–1907) and thought that the source of the Ottoman troubles was the absence of an individualistic culture. For him, education should follow the Anglo-Saxon system and provide for the development of the entrepreneurial spirit and an individualistic ethos. Thus, Sabaheddin came to develop a liberal ideology that put him at the other end of the political spectrum. In the 1902 congress Sabaheddin was able to gain the support of a majority of Turks, Greeks, Albanians, and Armenians and leave Riza's more nationalistic faction to the opposition (Hanioglu 1995, 38–41, 198–9; Zurcher 1984, 16–8; Alexander 1980, 387). Riza's faction gained the upper hand in the organization after the 1902 congress. By 1906 the liberal faction created its own organization, thus allowing Riza's faction to inherit the movement's official title (Hanioglu 1995, 214).

Although these factions became influential after the 1908 Young Turk revolution, it was the military officers stationed in Thessaloniki (Saloniki) who initiated the overthrow of the Sultan. Among them, discontent grew as the Macedonian Question became the focus of international and Balkan politics after 1878. In 1903 the IMRO (a terrorist organization founded in Thessaloniki in 1893) orchestrated the 1903 Illinden uprising (for details, see Chapter 5). The European powers did not intervene and the uprising ended in bloodshed. Following the uprising's suppression by the Ottoman forces in October 1903, Franz Joseph of Austria-Hungary and Tsar Nicholas II of Russia met at Murzsteg and sponsored a new set of reforms for the province. The Murzsteg Program reorganized the gendarmerie under the control of a foreign general supported by a staff of foreign officers. Ottoman authorities were obliged to rebuild those houses and churches that had been destroyed during the rebellion. The presence of foreign officers undermined the authority of the central government without bringing a more efficient administration. The imposition of European military advisers and financial experts, who often exhibited a condescending and patronizing attitude toward Muslims, was a humiliation for Ottoman officials and fueled complaints against the Sultan (Gawrych 1986, 309–10).

Other complaints within the army included favoritism in promotions and lack of regular payments. Soldiers were frequently forced to fend for themselves to avoid starvation. The resulting low morale led to frequent troop desertions, a major problem for commanders in the field pursuing Greek and Bulgarian bandit gangs. In the midst of this malaise, many young officers wanted a free hand to reassert Ottoman authority. Using the Freemasonic lodges for their purposes, they were able to build a secret organization that aimed to restore the 1876 constitution.[20] In 1906, the young Mustafa Kemal (later Kemal Ataturk) founded the secret society *Vatan* (Fatherland) in Damascus (Ramsaur 1957, 94–100). In 1906 ten men (mainly officers) established in Thessaloniki the Ottoman Freedom Society.[21] In 1907 this group merged with the exiled Young Turk groups led by Ahmed Riza and the *Vatan* group to become the Ottoman Society of Union and Progress, more commonly known as the Committee of Union and Progress (CUP) (Ramsaur 1957, 121; Gawrych 1986, 311–2; Kitsikis 1990, 91). By 1908 the Young Turks appealed openly to the Christian population of Macedonia to join their conspiracy (Vakalopoulos 1988, 190–1). Over the summer of 1908 the conspirators' plans succeeded. Senior Captain Niyazi Bey provided the spark for the rebellion when he raided an army depot in Resne on July 3 and then fled to the mountains of Macedonia with approximately 400 men. The Third Army Corps revolted and a series of ultimatums were sent to the Sultan demanding the restoration of the 1876 constitution. On 23 July 1908, in a surprisingly short period of time, AbdulHamid acceded to their demands.

During the 1908–1913 period, although the Young Turks dominated the political arena, the cabinet was largely filled with members of the traditional Ottoman bureaucracy. The Young Turks (under the banner of the CUP) came to rule directly only in 1913. The vast majority of the CUP leaders, approximately 90 individuals, lacked any roots in the Ottoman establishment (Gawrych 1986, 313). For example, Enver, later one of the famous CUP leaders, was only 27 years old in 1908 and was the son of a bridge guard in Constantinople (Kitsikis 1990, 93; Palmer 1993, 203–204). The Young Turks were outsiders who swept into power in 1908. Because of their inexperience and youth (their average age was around 30) they lacked the confidence to assume direct leadership. In a status-dominated society, it would have been a sacrilege for people of such humble origins to assume positions of leadership.

Initially, the restoration of the constitution was greeted with joy throughout Europe and the empire. The Young Turks were pictured as reincarnations of the legendary French revolutionaries united behind the slogan of "Freedom, Equality, Justice, and Fatherland" (Farhi 1971, 277; Miller 1936, 476). The revolution was enthusiastically accepted by politicians in the kingdom of Greece as well as by Ottoman Greeks.[22] The impetus for Greco-Ottomanism came from the visible threat of Bulgaria's conquering most of Macedonia and Thrace and from the Young Turks' initially friendly attitude toward minorities. Its most articulate proponents were Ion Dragoumis and Athanasios Souliotis. Ion Dragoumis served as Greek consul in Macedonia, where he became a close friend of Athanasios Souliotis, a Greek officer and head of the Greek Organization of Thessaloniki (1906–1908). Both were involved in fighting Bulgarian bands in Macedonia. In 1908, they moved to Constantinople, where Dragoumis served at the Greek Embassy and Souliotis headed the Organization of Constantinople (O.C.), a club formed to combat the Bulgarian nationalists in Thrace.[23]

Dragoumis was an influential figure in terms of both his writings and his political activity. Jointly with Souliotis he developed the notion that Greeks and Turks were brothers who shared the same cultural heritage. As in Skalieris' case a few decades earlier, they were attracted more to the old universal or "Byzantine" vision of the *Rum millet* and less to the state-sponsored Greek nationalism advocated by Athens. They believed that the cultural syncretism they called for was a tangible and realistic goal. Souliotis' statement at the beginning of this chapter provides a concrete example of their approach to the "nationality question." To be sure, they believed that the Greeks would dominate any pact or association like this, but they thought that this would be a matter of cultural, educational, or economic superiority. Dragoumis condemned state-sponsored Greek irredentism and advocated that the "nationalities" of the empire continue to live under Ottoman rule once their rights were officially recognized. After the 1908 revolution, Souliotis and Dragoumis attempted to build a coalition among the Greek government, the Patriarchate, and the Ottoman Greeks in order to promote this goal. Between 1878 and 1908, the Patriarchate supported the Greco-Ottoman orientation (Alexander 1980, 385–95; Boura 1983, 69–83).

But the attempt to coordinate action between Ottoman Greeks and the Greek state was not successful. Already initial clashes between the CUP and the Ottoman Greeks had taken place over the issue of representation in the 1908 elections. The electoral law stipulated one deputy to every 50,000 males and eliminated any formal quota arrangement. Although the goal was to eliminate any formal division among Ottoman citizens, the Orthodox minorities feared that their political participation would be hindered (Kayali 1995, 268).[24] This early dispute was further exaggerated by the interference of the Greek diplomatic corps, who crafted a 16-deputy bloc determined to preempt any attempt at reconciliation. This bloc successfully canceled negotiations between the CUP and the Greek community.[25] As their number dropped with each new election, this bloc gradually came to control all Ottoman Greek deputies. From 26 Ottoman Greek deputies in the 1908 Parliament their number dropped to 18 in 1912–1914—of whom 12 were in favor of the Greek irredentists. After 1912, the Unionists began to call the Greco-Ottomanists "Byzantinists" (*Bizanscilar*), an unkindly term that led to further alienation (Alexandris 1980, 395–6). By 1918–1922 the shift toward the Greek irredentist camp was complete. The success of the Greek state in controlling Greco-Ottoman tendencies may be attributed to a new generation of middle-class Greek Orthodox professionals and merchants, many of whom had dual citizenship or were Greek citizens. This group rose gradually in the late nineteenth century and was definitely oriented toward the Greek state, in sharp contrast to the older pro-Ottoman Greek Orthodox strata (Anagnostopoulou 1997, 301–18).

Most of the minority representatives (Greeks, Bulgarians, Armenians) were aligned with Prince Sabaheddin's Liberal party that advocated "administrative decentralization and personal initiative." In the 1908 elections, the Liberals lacked the CUP's organization and won only one deputy. Soon after the elections, reaction to the CUP secularization agenda led to a coup orchestrated by lower-ranking *ulema*, mosque functionaries, students of religious law (*softas*), the Sufi dervishes, and the petit-bourgeois elements under their influence (Farhi 1971, 279–81; Palmer 1993, 205). Ironically, the Ottoman Christians tacitly supported religious conservatives because both groups were united against the CUP. The coup broke up on 13 April 1909 when the First Corps, stationed in Constantinople and not infiltrated by the CUP, mutinied and was successful in removing key officials from their posts. The restoration of the *Seriah* (Islamic law) served as a political slogan and for a moment it seemed that the CUP was going to lose control of the situation. Soon, however, reinforcements arrived from Thessaloniki, commanded by Mahmud Sevket pasha (a 53-year-old general who was not a CUP member), with whom were Niyazi and Enver, the two key CUP leaders, who had returned posthaste from the Ottoman Embassy in Berlin on hearing the news. The deliverers reached the capital on 23 April, and occupied it, after some clashes with the mutineers, on the following day (Lewis 1979, 216).

Subsequently, the army generals and Mahmud Sevket pasha himself became important political actors until 1913, when the lower-rank officers of the CUP were able to return to power.[26] Following this political realignment, governmental policy moved decisively toward centralization. The *Osmanli* (i.e., Ottoman) language and culture was to become sanctioned by the state. Initially, the Young Turks did not have a clear ideology and a number of ideological currents were pursued, ranging from Pan-Islamism to Pan-Turkism (Ergil 1975, 44–9; Alp 1917; Berkes 1964, 305–46; on Pan-Turkism see Arnakis 1960, 19–32; Landau 1981, 7–71). In terms of political program, there were three alternative ideological options: Westernization (and political Ottomanism), cultural Ottomanism, and Islamicism. The first of these alternatives was advocated by the "Liberal Entente," a coalition of the Liberal Party, deputies who defected from the CUP, and the non-Muslim minorities (Kayali 1995, 272–3). The second alternative was advocated by the CUP; it translated into centralization and cultural homogenization of the empire's minority population. The third alternative was advocated by conservative religious elements who resented CUP's secularization policies. Over the 1908–1912 period the CUP policy was one of cultural Ottomanism and centralization and was opposed by the other two parties.

Instrumental for CUP's political expression and gradual evolution was the social and political environment out of which the movement emerged. Ottoman Macedonia was the province that had suffered most in terms of guerrilla warfare, terrorist attacks, plundering, and assassinations.[27] The army officers leading the CUP should have been able to pacify the province. Among them, hard-core attitudes advocating forceful suppression of the bandits were the rule. For many officers, the CUP represented the forces of good engaged in a cosmic struggle against the enemies of the Ottoman homeland and nation (Gawrych 1986, 320–1; Vakalopoulos 1988, 218–61). In Ottoman Macedonia, after a brief interlude of peace, political and military conflict erupted once again and the Young Turks decided to respond forcefully. Within the span of a few months in 1909 Parliament passed a series of repressive legislative measures aimed at government centralization and the "Ottomanization" of the non-Muslims.[28] By 1910 the CUP decided to forcefully disarm the Christian population in Macedonia, whereas the Muslim population would remain armed. The result was that by the end of 1910 and early 1911 Bulgarian, Greek, and Armenian activists joined forces to resist what they considered to be repressive CUP measures (Mazarakis-Ainian 1986, 159; Vakalopoulos 1988, 372). In particular, the Bulgarian–Greek coalition was a premonition of the broader Balkan cooperation in the 1912–1913 Balkan wars.

When, in 1910, Mahmud Sevket pasha became the minister of war, the tendency to solve the nationality problem by the use of force gained momentum and additional legislation curbing the freedom of expression was passed.[29] Increasingly, CUP's cultural Ottomanism implied the assimilation of the minorities (Lewis 1979, 218; Ahmad 1982, 411). The parliamentary debates on the unification of the educational system, the abolition of ecclesiastical privileges, and the law of associations illustrated the differences between the two sides. For the CUP, these "privileges" were a relic of the past that created a structural inequality in favor of the Christians and should be abolished. For the minorities, the community organizations were the units reassuring their survival as distinct groups. For example, minorities desired the recognition of their schools by the state. Christian deputies called for adherence to the 1908 declarations; the O.C. (the Souliotis–Dragoumis group) was in the forefront of these requests for equal rights (Mazarakis-Ainian 1986, 160; for a detailed discussion, see Anagnostopoulou 1997, 467–93).

Increasingly the CUP became frustrated with official Ottoman policy and attempted to form its own government. The CUP manipulated the April 1912 elections and the opposition groups were able to elect only 6 out of the 275 deputies (Lewis 1979, 222; Ahmad 1969, 103; Kayali 1995, 273–7). But in October, the Balkan wars erupted. The allied forces of Serbia, Montenegro, Bulgaria, and Greece defeated the Ottoman forces and the empire lost the overwhelming majority of its European provinces. With this turn of events, Ottomanism lost its practical appeal. By 1918 the empire had shrunk to the territory of Anatolia, where the influx of Muslim refugees further increased Muslim demographic predominance. Moreover, Anatolia's non-Muslim population consisted mainly of Ottoman Greeks and Armenians. In the aftermath of the Balkan wars, Turkish nationalism began to emerge as a potent intellectual force. The eventual transformation of the empire into modern Turkey is discussed in Chapter 7.

## INTERETHNIC AND TRANSNATIONAL CITIZENSHIP: AN ASSESSMENT

The secular idea of the "nation" entails the exaltation of the "people" as determinants of the national will. However, in principle the designation of the specific cultural attributes of the "people" remain a matter open to debate. As discussed in Chapter 2, for the peoples of southeastern Europe, the issue of the "popular will" had been raised at least since Rigas Velenstinlis' writings in the early 1790s. Given the ethnic intermixing of the various cultural groups, the proposition that ethnic coexistence should accompany popular participation in government was not a far-fetched idea, but a notion that grew out of the reality of Ottoman cultural life. The failure of the discourse of *citizenship* to take roots in southeastern Europe was not due to the absence of civil society, democratic values, or cultural attributes. Political and economic reasons lie at the heart of this failure. During the nineteenth century, there was no shared basis for a federation. Usually, federalism served as a political slogan or weapon to further the political goals of a particular nation and there was no deep commitment to the concept. The proliferation of local power centers (Athens, Sofia, Belgrade, Bucharest) in the Balkan peninsula implied the intensification of geopolitical rivalry. No local center would surrender its claims to the Balkan territories and this acted as a counterforce to visions of Balkan unification.

With this in mind it is possible to gain a better perspective on the Yugoslav solution—the only program that was implemented in 1918 with the creation of the kingdom of Serbs, Croats, and Slovenes. As discussed in Chapter 7, the kingdom of Serbs, Slovenes, and Croats was achieved by suspending the true conflict between Serb and Croat elites through the ideological construct of Yugoslavism. The meaning of Yugoslavism, whether it entailed subordination to Serbia or a federation among different political units, remained conveniently vague so as to facilitate the acceptance of the program by all sides. The problematic nature of Yugoslavism should be understood as a manifestation of the broader regional failure to develop a genuine commitment to interstate cooperation, other than the opportunistic alliances that served short-term geopolitical interests.

The reasons for the failure of *Tanzimat* (and Greco-Ottomanism) were less political and more economic. The ideology of Ottomanism developed by the *Tanzimat* reformers and espoused by Greco-Ottoman activists offered a viable political solution. In fact, in this chapter, I have emphasized the specifics of Greco-Ottomanism to discredit the assumption that Ottoman minorities were monolithically attracted to the nationalisms of the Balkan nation-states. This assumption forms the basis of numerous interpretations and the evidence reviewed in this chapter shows it to be incorrect.

Bourgeois democracy and equality inevitably led to the strengthening of Christian influence; not surprisingly, wealthy Ottoman Greeks were among its proponents, as well as Ottoman bureaucrats, who hoped that political reorganization would prevent the spread of nationalism among the Ottoman Christians.[30] But, for the traditionally oriented Muslim population, such a solution entailed a loss of status without any meaningful gain. Insofar as the Muslims monopolized the ruling institutions, their financially inferior position could be rationalized: Even if the Christians were wealthier, the state remained Muslim. But if equality was implemented, the increasingly impoverished Muslim population would have no domain to claim as its own and its status would suffer a blow of unimaginable proportions. In this regard, the 1876 failed effort is testimony to the liberals' lack of a genuine political basis among the Ottoman Muslim population.

When the Young Turk movement finally gained power in the 1908 July revolution, Ottomanism resurfaced, but this time, the Young Turks supported a concept of *cultural* Ottomanism that implied the absorption of the non-Muslim groups into Ottoman Muslim society. By that time, the central bureaucracy's failure to gain legitimacy in the eyes of the Christian population had greatly strengthened the appeal of Balkan nationalists among the Ottoman Christian population. The major representatives of the Young Turk movement, military officers and petit bourgeois strata, were in direct competition with the Greek Orthodox middle strata. While proponents of Greco-Ottomanism and liberal Young Turks espoused a policy of *political* Ottomanism (i.e., multiculturalism), the *cultural* Ottomanism of the Young Turks implied assimilation. The reasons for the empire's collapse lie in the political and economic conflict between the predominantly Muslim bureaucracy and military officers and the urban Orthodox middle strata. This conflict did not allow for an "identity of interests" to develop. On the contrary, the absence of cross-cutting cleavages reinforced the overlap between socioeconomic position and ethnicity. Most of the Ottoman Muslims and Young Turks occupied positions associated with the state and most of the Ottoman minorities were associated with the market and the free professionals.

Finally, a major contributing factor in this failure is the infiltration of nationalist ideologies into the empire's territory from the new Balkan states. Ottomanism failed because, as I describe in the next two chapters, the propaganda of the Balkan states and their irredentism were ultimately successful in claiming the loyalty of the Ottoman Christian population.

## NOTES

1. In the aftermath of the failed Hungarian revolt of 1848, Hungarian nationalist leader Lajos Kossuth put forward a proposal for a Danubian federation among Hungary, Romania, Serbia, and Croatia (Djordjevic 1970b, 119–45; Liakos 1985, 68–71; Stavrianos 1944). The plan failed to materialize because the Hungarians of the Habsburg

Empire felt that it could jeopardize their privileges in the Habsburg regime. In 1849 the Hungarians had refused to make concessions necessary to win the cooperation of their Romanian and Serb allies. Similarly, the Serbs and Romanians were willing to entertain these plans in 1853 and 1859 because of the favorable international situation (Stavrianos 1944, 82–83). Among the South Slavs, different projects were put forward by Mihailo Polith-Dešanći, a Vojvodina Serb; Svetovar Milesić, leader of the National Party; and the Croatian Imro Ignatijević-Tkalać (Djordjevic 1970b, 30–4 for an overview; also Liakos 1985, 71–2).

2. Mihailo concluded alliances with Montenegro and Greece and a friendship pact with Romania. At the brink of war for some time, Mihailo—whom McKenzie (1985, 243) describes as an indecisive leader—was finally persuaded by the Habsburgs to abandon his military designs. Still, part of the rationale for aborting this plan was the Balkan states' lack of military capability (Stavrianos 1944, 103–4; McKenzie 1985, 313–4). Using the threat of war, however, the Serb diplomatic entourage was able to secure the evacuation of the remaining Ottoman garrisons from Serbia in 1867 (McKenzie 1967, 11–5; 1985, 306). Prince Mihailo was murdered the next year and under Prince Milan's regency (1868–1873) nationalist plans dwindled. For overviews, see McKenzie (1985, 240–347), Stavrianos (1944, 84–122), and Liakos (1985, 173–7).

3. Vasil Levski promoted Bulgarian self-reliance and Stefan Stambolov, who later became prime minister of Bulgaria, wrote a number of articles in the pre-1878 period, in which he supported South Slav solidarity but opposed Serb "hegemony." Stambolov thought that Serbia ought to give up its pretensions of being the Piedmont of the Balkans in order to secure the cooperation of the Bulgarians (Shashko 1974b, 150–2; Stavrianos 1944, 118–9).

4. Its first stirrings occurred in Czechoslovakia, Slovenia, and Poland where in the first half of the nineteenth century intellectuals appropriated the "folk" ideology of Johann Herder to revitalize their own respective cultures (Kohn 1953, 9–100; Milojkovic-Djuric 1994, 8–53). In early nineteenth-century Russia, Pan-Slavist themes were connected with liberal and democratic ideas and were condemned by the Tsar (Fadner 1962, 145).

5. In 1869 Nicholas Danilevskii, in his *Rosiia i Europa*, envisaged such a political union of 125 million people that would include most of all nations of Eastern Europe (Fadner 1962, 314–38; Petrovich 1956). The goal was to create a union similar to the German Confederation and counter Bismarck's impressive achievement. This union incorporated many non-Slavic peoples (Greeks, Romanians, Magyars) whose inclusion was justified by a variety of historical and political arguments.

6. Palgrave, the British representative in Bulgaria, wrote that "Pan-Slav agitators, did any such exist here, would be as ineffective as in Belgium or Holland" because "the inhabitants of the Principality have no sympathy or care for any race whatever" (quoted in Black 1943, 153).

7. Jelavich (1967, 90), Despalatovic (1975, 87–8), and Adler (1974b, 98). There was sufficient ambiguity in Illyrianism to lead Djordjevic (1980, 6) to the viewpoint that the Illyrians "were Yugoslavs when preaching . . . cultural Yugoslavism, Croats when fostering the political unification of Croatia in the framework of the Habsburg Monarchy." Although there was some interest in the Illyrian movement by Habsburg Serbs, there were significant obstacles to its acceptance. First, when the Illyrian movement surfaced, the Serb communities were involved in the literary controversy surrounding Karadžić's linguistic reforms; that is, whether his reformed language was to triumph over Church

Slavonic (see Chapter 4). Second, some Serb writers viewed the Illyrian movement as a tool of the Roman Catholic Church (Despatalovic 1975, 133–5; Banac 1984, 79).

8. During the 1860s, the liberal Svetovar Miletić and his newspaper, *Zastava*, were the soul of resistance to Hungarian rule. Miletić was the organizer of the Liberal Party. His program demanded equal rights for all Hungarian minorities. With the emergence of political liberalism, the Vojvodina Serbs were gradually drawn into the orbit of greater Serb nationalism (Adler 1979, 281; Dedijer et al. 1974, 342–3; see also the discussion in Chapter 4). These demands were initially framed as a continuation of the religious privileges granted to the Orthodox community following the Great Migration of 1690.

9. Jelavich (1967, 96–7), Rusinow (1995, 359–60), and Banac (1984, 85–9). The alternative to Yugoslavism was the Party of Right (or *Pravastvo*), led by Ante Starhević and Eugen Kvaternik, who stressed ethnic rights and advocated Croatia's total separation from the Habsburg empire. Starhević and his party showed a strong revulsion for everything Serbian or Slavic. Starhević repeatedly used the term "Slavo-Serb" as a derogatory expression to designate anyone he regarded as an enemy or a traitor to the Croatian cause. He even wrote an article entitled *"Ime Serb"* (The Name Serb) in which he denied the historical validity of the name, and objected to its use. In his view, the Serbs were Croats who had gone astray by becoming Orthodox; his purpose was to bring them into the Catholic Croat fold.

10. The bureaucracy responded to trade liberalization by adopting a state-sponsored program of industrialization in the 1840s. Initially, the program appeared to be working, but mismanagement and the low cost of foreign imports prevented the creation of an indigenous industry (Clark 1974, 65–76).

11. According to McCarthy (1983, 111–2), by 1911–1912 the Ottoman Greeks of Anatolia were 1,254,333 (excluding those who were not Ottoman citizens). The estimate is based on Ottoman census figures. Using the 1910–1912 patriarchal census, Kitromilides and Alexandris (1984/1985, 28) estimate 1,547,952 people. For further comments on the controversy over the numbers, see McCarthy (1983, 89–99; cf. Kitromilides and Alexandris, 1984/1985, 9–44).

12. Veremis (1980b, 12) reported that according to the 1912 census there were 2,452,151 Ottoman Greeks in Anatolia and Constantinople. The reliability of the initial Greek estimates is questionable (McCarthy 1983, 89–99; cf. Pentazopoulos 1962, 19–32). During the nineteenth century, a wave of immigration from the kingdom of Greece and the Aegean islands contributed significantly to the increase in Greek population, mainly in western Anatolia (for details, see Anagnostopoulou 1997, 109–22, 137–238).

13. By 1914–1915 the Ottoman statistics report a total of 205,762 Ottoman Greeks out of a total of 909,978 (Muslims were 560,434) (McCarthy 1982, 69). Because these figures do not count Greeks residing in Constantinople who were not citizens of the Ottoman state, it is almost certain that the Greeks' number was higher (cf. Svolopoulos 1994, 38).

14. Gocek (1996, 80–6) considers this group a "bureaucratic bourgeoisie" and contrasts it with the predominantly minority-based "commercial bourgeoisie." Her terminology is not adopted here, because of the problems associated with inserting a Western-style term into a quite distinct social formation (cf. Gocek 1996, 4–11). The analysis in this chapter builds on the contrast between the two groups, and in this regard it is quite close to Gocek's analysis.

15. The text of the *Hatt-i* is reprinted in Kitsikis (1982, 217–9); see also Davison

(1963, 40). On negative reaction to the issue of Muslim–Christian equality, see Davison (1954, 844–64).

16. Quataert (1994, 763, 773), Exertzoglou (1989, 15–58), and Shaw and Shaw (1977, 122, 155). From 1863, with the establishment of the Ottoman Imperial Bank, this control was accelerated. During 1867 and 1874 the industrial Reform Commission attempted unsuccessfully to restore some of the monopolistic practice of the guilds.

17. The first attempt to constitute the Young Ottomans as an organized group took place in 1865 in Constantinople, when a group of 6 individuals held a meeting and established a secret society that in later years reached a total of 245 members (Lewis 1979, 152–3; Davison 1963, 194; for overviews, see Mardin 1962 and Berkes 1964). With Namik Kemal as their best exponent, this group advocated some form of constitutional government as a means of removing control of the government from the hands of Ali and Fuad pashas.

18. The 1876 constitution was granted by the Sultan and did not provide for genuine democracy. The Sultan was above its provisions and the assembly could not vote down the government (Berkes 1964, 249, 346–8; Devereux 1963; Karal 1982, 387–400). The decision to prorogue Parliament may have been based on the fact that—once the Ottoman concessions to the Russians would be known—it would be very difficult to silence the critics in the opposition.

19. Islamic agitation began in 1877–1878 in Constantinople and rapidly gained support among the victims of the war (Karpat 1982b, 404–6). AbdulHamid used his title as *caliph* (supreme religious leader) to affirm his absolutism. For a review, see Deringil (1991).

20. Although Macedonia was the seedbed of the rebellion, it was not the only place where this attitude was expressed. In eastern Anatolia, frequent clashes among Kurds, Armenians, and security forces unsettled the local society and provided fertile ground for the growth of revolutionary activity against the Sultan. In 1907, a group of army officers and civilian officials founded a clandestine society in Enzurum with the goal of restoring the 1876 constitution (Gawrych 1986, 311). In 1901 the revitalization of the Italian lodge *Macedonia Resota* in Thessaloniki resulted in the recruitment of a number of Young Turk personalities such as Talat Bey (who later became prime minister), Rahmi Bey (who became governor of the Smyrna *vilayet*), Ahmed Naki Bey (later Turkish ambassador in Paris), and others (Loukas 1991, 205; Zurcher 1984, 19–21).

21. The Young Turks' activities were made known to the Greek consuls in Macedonia, who, in turn, informed the Greek government. Although the Young Turks called for the Greeks to join the movement, the consuls advised caution because in case of failure the Christians risked severe punishment (Panayotopoulos 1980, 87–95). On the other hand, the Young Turks never clarified the meaning of the "cooperation" they sought and whether it involved power sharing.

22. In the Greek kingdom, Freemasons and influential political figures (D. Rallis, the leader of the parliamentary opposition; K. Mavromichalis; and G. Blatazis), instituted the Greco-Turkish Constitutional Union (November 1908) aiming for the restoration of the earlier Greco-Ottoman vision of 1876 (Kitsikis 1990, 101–3; Loukas 1991, 207). In fact, when Rallis visited Thessaloniki, to the dismay of the Greek officers present, he endorsed the Young Turks' agenda of Ottomanism (Kitsikis 1990, 131–3).

23. Xanalatos (1962, 280). See also Kitsikis (1990, 105–15). Greek and Turk historians have interpreted these visions as just another version of Greek nationalism (Vakalopoulos 1988, 18–20; Ahmad 1982, 406; cf. Souliotis-Nikolaidis 1984).

24. According to the Ottoman census of 1914, there were 520,424 Muslims and 389,553 non-Muslims in Constantinople. Part of the dispute concerned the status of Greek citizens, estimated at 65,000 in 1912, who were not recorded by the Ottoman census (Alexandris 1983, 50).

25. The events that occurred shortly after the July revolution further damaged prospects for a "Greco-Ottoman" scheme. On 5 October 1908 Bulgaria declared its independence and 24 hours later Austria-Hungary announced its formal annexation of Bosnia-Herzegovina; Crete declared its union with the kingdom of Greece. Although Prince Sabaheddin was in favor of the union, Talat Bey reacted strongly, asking for the Greek kingdom not to "backstab" the empire (Gawrych 1986, 313; Loukas 1991, 216–7).

26. Kitsikis (1990, 87–96) and Palmer (1993, 210–14). Kitsikis considers the 1908 movement an expression of the Turkish bourgeoisie. The movement aimed for a genuine cohabitation of Christians and Muslims, but Kitsikis argues that after the 1909 coup, conservative elements were in full control of the government. On the contrary, Lewis (1979, 217) suggests that it was the CUP that came fully into power. The difference is one of perspective: Kitsikis considers the young middle-class officials as the real power behind CUP and the older generals as a conservative group.

27. For example, between 1 March 1906 and 1 March 1907 there were 733 assassination attempts made by Bulgarians and 601 by Greeks. The following year (1 March 1907–1 March 1908) there were 829 assassination attempts by Bulgarians and 586 by Greeks (Vakalopoulos 1988, 228).

28. For example, the legislation on associations forbade the formation of political clubs or associations that had an ethnic basis or a national name; the Law for the Prevention of Brigandage and Sedition authorized the formation of special military units to be used for disarming and suppressing Greek and Bulgarian bands in Rumelia and Armenian bands in eastern Turkey. Passed on 8 May 1909, the Law of Vagabonds and Suspected Criminals allowed the police to detain suspects for up to 48 hours; it also empowered the government to imprison participants in bandit gangs for 10 years and execute leaders of such organizations. Families of those participating in guerrilla activity could suffer punishments for the actions of their members. The army established "pursuit battalions" to find and disarm bandit gangs (Ahmad 1969, 61–2; Gawrych 1986, 323).

29. Gawrych (1986, 322). The Law on Public Meetings expressed this momentum: It required the organizer to present a written declaration stating his name and profession, and indicating the place, date, and time of the meeting, thus in effect making any public protest impossible. Similarly, the Law on the Press and Printing Establishments, although not actually censoring the newspapers, significantly restrained the freedom of the press. Last, an antistrike law checkmated any action that might have been taken by the growing labor movement (on CUP's attitude toward the Thessaloniki labor movement, see Moskof 1978, 191–8).

30. This point has been made by N. Batzaria, a Macedonian Vlach and leading CUP member, who stressed that Ottomanism and liberalism appealed to the Christians because they believed that it could aid them in achieving control over the political institutions (Karpat 1975, 294).

# 4

## Invented Traditions, Symbolic Boundaries, and National Identity in Greece and Serbia, 1830–1880

In this chapter, I examine the articulation of nationhood in the emerging national societies of Greece and Serbia. These two small nation-states are similar because they were both carved out of former territories of the Ottoman Empire. Their populations were composed overwhelmingly of illiterate Orthodox peasantry with a thin layer of intelligentsia. Moreover, the formative stage of each occurred over the course of the period between 1830 and 1880. Because they were the only autonomous or independent Orthodox Christian states in the region, their historical development has had a significant impact on the rest of the Ottoman Balkans. The fundamental issues examined in this chapter are twofold. First, I examine the redeployment of religious categories to build a new secular national identity on behalf of the state. Second, I examine the intelligentsia's efforts to provide an intellectual edifice that would promote the transformation of Orthodox religious identity into secular national identity. With respect to this latter issue, I discuss the intelligentsia's efforts to manipulate symbolic boundaries in order to produce a collective redefinition of parts of the Ottoman Empire as "unredeemed" territories of the Greek and Serb nations.

### THE RELIGIOUS REVIVAL IN GREECE

During the post-1832 period, the kingdom of Greece witnessed an intense conflict between modernizing efforts and local conservatism. This conflict involved cultural, religious, and political dimensions:

In matters of dress and style of life the contrasts were most noticeable. Some, in the manner of Europe, wore the black redingote, slept on beds and sat on chairs, and took their meals with their wives. They spoke at least one European language. Others, the vast majority, slept on mats or out-of-doors, and squatted on pillows. They kept their wives well covered and lived socially apart from them. . . . Differences in the realm of ideas were harder to define but no less real. For instance, those who enjoyed any contact with Europe thought of statehood in terms of nationalism, centralization, bureaucracy, perhaps constitutionalism. For the indigenous elements, the machinery of the Ottoman state—pashaliks, captanliks, maybe theocracy—was quite satisfactory if possessed exclusively by Greeks in general or by a particular class of Greeks. (Petropulos 1968, 37)

This basic schism between the two cultural orientations can be expressed as a discrepancy between the "Romeic" and "Hellenic" identities (Hetzfeld 1982, 19–21; Giannaras 1992; Politis 1993; Dimaras 1985, 345). This discrepancy can be seen in constitutions and national assemblies over the 1821–1827 period where the term "nation" was given a twofold meaning: a broad one, including all members of the *Rum millet*; and a narrow one, including the revolutionaries and their prospective state (Skopetea 1988, 35–38). The Romeic identity expressed the local Orthodox and conservative part of the new nation; the Hellenic identity expressed the cosmopolitan, modernist, and "Western" part of the nation.[1]

The initial goal of King Otto's German regency administration (1833–1837) was to suppress the local bandit-rulers and construct a modern centralized state. According to nineteenth-century European mentality, the regency "believed that being civilized was being European [and] interpreted the Greek Revolution as an attempt to adopt European forms and customs" (Petropulos 1968, 162–4).[2] The Bavarian administration organized a Bavarian-dominated army and offered considerable technical assistance in road building, gardening, husbandry, and the construction of private and public buildings. Under the regency, new buildings were erected in Athens, most of them imitations of nineteenth-century German neoclassicism (Giannaras 1992, 256–8).

These new buildings embodied the mentality of the Bavarian administration and the Western-trained intellectuals. This mentality rejected the Byzantine Ottoman tradition in favor of a revival of classical Greece. Accordingly, the new Greece that emerged after 1821 was a continuation of ancient Greece; and had no spiritual ties with the Byzantine Orthodox tradition. Characteristic of this assumption was the intellectuals' viewpoint vis-à-vis the place of ancient Macedonians in ancient Greek history. During the 1794–1841 period, at least 14 intellectuals (among whom were prominent figures such as Panagiotis Kordikas, Adamantios Korais, Alexandros Soutsos, Georgios Kozakis-Tipaldos, and Iakovos Rizos-Nerulos) expressed the opinion that the ancient Macedonians were not part of the ancient Greek world (Politis 1993, 40–2; Dimitrakopoulos 1996). The Macedonians were considered conquerors of ancient Greece, the first of a series of invaders that kept the region under their rule for more than two millennia.[3]

However, those who championed the Byzantine Orthodox tradition contested this "Hellenic" viewpoint. Among them were three groups of nonindigenous Greeks (i.e., those born outside the kingdom's boundaries) crowded within the state: old bandit warriors, refugees from the 1821 revolution, and pro-Orthodox intellectuals (Skopetea 1988, 43). In particular, bandits and refugees were in direct competition with the indigenous Greeks (i.e., those born in the kingdom) for the limited resources of the state and the land; unlike the indigenous Greeks, they could not view the "nation" as identical with the state. For them, national resurrection was still incomplete. When in 1838 the royal administration agreed to the establishment of March 25 (Annunciation Day) as the national holiday, these groups used the occasion to illustrate the close connection between Greek identity and Orthodoxy (Dimaras 1985, 161). Contrary to the deliberate undermining of this holiday by the state authorities, private-sponsored celebrations took place in the 1839–1842 period. In this period, the tragedy *Rigas*, written by Ioannis Zambelios, became a focal point for March 25 celebrations because it implied the continuity of the liberation struggle. By 1843, Rigas Velenstinlis became "the first martyr" of the Greek cause—as a poem read in that year's celebration declared him to be.

Because religion was the peasantry's prime cultural and political marker, the regency attempted to create an Orthodox national church under the control of the state so that the people would not be under the influence of an ecclesiastical leader (i.e., the Patriarch), who was a civil servant of the Ottoman state. In doing so, the regency imitated the German model of state-sponsored church, although the Enlightenment thinker Adamantios Korais had put the original idea forward many years ago. One of his followers, Theoklitos Pharmakidis, helped Regent Ludwig von Maurer organize the establishment of the new church. By 23 July 1833, 22 bishops (most of them picked to ensure a favorable outcome) approved the creation of an autocephalous church closely tied to the state (Frazee 1987, 134–41; Petropulos 1968, 184–9). According to the new constitution of the church, state agencies assumed close control over church activities. The next step undertaken by the regency was the consolidation of monasteries. The government shut down all 412 small-size monasteries and consolidated the monks into 148 monasteries (Frazee 1987, 156; Giannaras 1992, 272–5). This consolidation was violent: The Bavarian army took the initiative to forcibly expel the monks from their monasteries and incited discontent among the population.

In addition, the activities of Protestant and Catholic missionaries raised the issue of the role of the state in safeguarding Orthodoxy against "heretical" propaganda. Plans were undertaken for the foundation of a Protestant university in Athens by J. King. Under the regency, approximately 112 Protestant publications were approved as adjunct schoolbooks. Members of the British and Foreign Bible Society had been arriving in Greece since 1827. In 1834 the Bible Society published a translation of the Old Testament into modern Greek; Neophytos Vambas, a prominent Enlightenment figure, was the translator. By 1836, 45,000 copies of the translation had been published (Giannaras 1992, 278–80; Frazee 1987, 189–92). The controversy created about the translation centered on the significance of providing "unmediated" access to the Bible. The Orthodox defenders considered the translation inaccurate and insisted on the Greek version of the Bible as the only legitimate one. The practice of translating the Bible into the local vernacular was conceived of as an attempt to convert Greeks to Protestantism (Petropulos 1968, 424–6). In 1841, Ms. Hill, the wife of the American missionary John Hill, wrote to her husband that a number of Greek girls enrolled in their Athens girls' school were converted to Protestantism. The letter was leaked to the Greek press and caused another round of accusations concerning the missionaries' activities.

The protection offered to the Greek Catholics, whose monasteries were exempted from the consolidation; the fact that the regency and the king were not Orthodox; and the suppression of the local bandits (many of whom had fought in the 1821 revolution) created the widespread impression of an attack on Orthodox traditions. In such a climate the separation of the Greek Church from the Patriarchate was understood as the first step in a conspiracy aiming to convert the people into Protestantism and Catholicism. The combination of the reaction to centralization by the regional power centers and the popular discontent produced 14 peasant revolts between 1833 and 1852 (Aroni-Tsichli 1989). Most of them were a reaction against taxation or were incited by local overlords who demanded financial rewards from the state. The revolts employed the rhetoric of the struggle against an "infidel" (non-Orthodox) administration in favor of the protection of local religion and custom. As in post-1789 revolutionary France, peasantry followed their traditional local leaders in a struggle against customs and laws that were alien to them.

In October 1834, the Greek priest Constantinos Oikonomos arrived in Greece. Trained in Russia, he was the most prominent ecclesiastical author of the nineteenth century.[4] He quickly became the soul of Orthodox resistance to the new ecclesiastical arrangement. In this struggle and throughout the 1834–1850 period, Oikonomos and Pharmakidis were the main opponents; in their writings, they clashed head to head in almost all domains and their struggle expressed the intense conflict between Western trends and Eastern Orthodox conservatism.[5] By supporting the Greek national church, Pharmakidis was accused of introducing the doctrine of ethnonationalism (*ethnofuletismos*) into Greek Orthodoxy.[6]

Inspired by the regional resistance to state centralization, the church question, and King Otto's attempt to follow a pro-Russian policy during the years 1837 to 1839, a secret society (Philorthodox Society) was formed in 1839. The society aimed at the liberation of Epirus, Thessaly, and Macedonia. It had close ties with the Russian representatives and was organized according to the models of the Philiki Eteria. Its members were inspired by the millenarian prophecies of *Agathangelos*, that is, of a restoration of the Orthodox Empire in the East (Jelavich 1966; Frazee 1987, 193–5; Nikolopoulos 1985, 49–50; and Giannaras 1992, 295–6). They aimed at the convocation of a national assembly and, if faced with royal opposition, they planned a palace coup backed by popular insurrection. Nothing came of these early plans.

During this period, nevertheless, Kolletis' "French" party became closely associated with irredentism. Ioannis Kolletis was a Greek Vlach politician from Epirus, and his main following was among the old bandits and warriors, a class permanently committed to a war policy. Raiding was a way of life for most of them and with the Turks absent, their raids could hardly be justified as "revolutionary" activity (Petropulos 1968, 357). By 1842, this "French" party came to an understanding with the "English" pro-Western party of Mavrocordatos, in order to force the issue of a constitution. In 1843 this alliance of regional elites, conservative Orthodox pro-Russian, and Western pro-English politicians forced King Otto to grant a constitution.

In the constitutional assembly that followed the revolution of 3 September 1843, the issue of national identity occupied central stage owing to the proposal to consider all nonindigenous Greeks as noncitizens of the state and therefore ineligible for civil servant positions (Dimakis 1991, 51–3, 60–2). The issue revealed the strong partisan antagonism among different factions and the fact that civil sector positions served as "booty" for those in control of the government. Old warriors who had been excluded from government posts were eager to share in the administration and provide posts for their own clients. The characteristic statement "they had enough of a meal, now it is our turn" (*arketa efagan autoi, tora einai i seira mas*) summarized the viewpoint of the indigenous movement.[7] This resentment overlapped with the strong dislike of these strata for the Westernized Greeks who occupied such posts (the so-called intellectuals). In the context of debating this proposal, Kolletis, himself a nonindigenous, gave his famous speech that proclaimed that

the Greek kingdom is not the whole of Greece, but a part of it, the smallest and the poorest part of Greece. Autochthon [indigenous] then is not only an inhabitant of the kingdom, but also one from Jannina, Thessaly, Serres, Adrianople, Constantinople, Trebzond, Crete, . . . in general every inhabitant of land which is Greek historically and ethnically . . . The . . . struggle did not begin in 1821; it began the day after the fall of Constantinople; fighters were not simply those of 1821; fighters were and are always those continuing the struggle against the crescent for 400 years. (quoted in Augustinos 1977, 14)

Kolletis' speech is generally considered to be the first open proclamation of the Greek "Great Idea."[8] It blended millenarian hopes of a restored Christian Empire with secular Greek state-sponsored nationalism; it gave the masses a clearly understandable vision while it transformed millenarianism into modern nationalism.[9] The impact of the mixed religious-political revival continued to be felt throughout the nineteenth century.[10] In 1850, the Patriarchate recognized the autocephaly of the Greek Church; in 1852, the new constitution of the Greek national church was approved. This ended the conflict between Orthodox conservatives and Western liberals: The conservatives succeeded in uniting the national church with the Patriarchate even if only in form and not in substance; the liberals preserved the substance of the 1833 church constitution. Even if at first glance the conservatives appear to have won only a hollow victory, the true losers were the liberals (Skopetea 1988, 131). Although in form the Church became independent from the Patriarchate, its autonomy was surrendered into the hands of the state. By controlling the Church, the state was effectively in control of the most important social institution.

In a close alliance with each other, policy makers and the Church hierarchy proceeded in safeguarding Orthodoxy from liberal critics and Protestant infiltrations. In 1837 daily prayer was instituted by decree for all public schools (Perselis 1997, 79). In 1852, J. King, the Protestant missionary, was prosecuted for proselytism. In 1854, a ministerial decree ordered the reading of religious books in schools at least on a weekly basis; in 1856 another decree declared the religious education of the students to be a state responsibility (Perselis 1997, 94–5). The same year the author Andreas Laskaratos (1811–1901), born in the Ionian Islands, published his book *The Mysteries of Kephalonia*. The book, as did other works by the same author, castigated superstition and religious fanaticism. The author was excommunicated by the Church (Dimaras 1988, 325). By 1857, the high school regulations obliged the students to church attendance every Sunday and holidays; in 1855, 1865, and 1871 suggestions were publicly made to give the priests the right to serve as teachers (for further discussion, see Perselis 1997, 107–31). In 1874 and 1877 two laws were submitted to parliament proposing that public education be turned over to the clergy. In 1866, the author and critic Emmanouil Roidis published his book *Papisa Ioanna*. The book was the product of liberal thought and was highly critical of religion; its erotic scenes were considered scandalous at the time. The timing of the publication was also critical; just a few months earlier the publication of Renan's *Life of Jesus* had drawn the Church's negative reaction. Roidis' book also earned its author excommunication from the Church (Dimaras 1988, 331–2; 1985, 389–90). By 1879, Roidis wrote that church and state had in effect merged with each other (Skopetea 1988, 133).

Out of this redeployment of Orthodoxy rose the need to reconcile the Byzantine Orthodox tradition with the Western idea of a secular Greek identity. A second important reason for such a reconciliation was the necessity of clearly articulating a "national mission"; that is, to provide an ideological justification for the unification of Greek Orthodox Christians under the auspices of the Greek state. A third—and perhaps more important—reason was the challenge to modern Greek identity by Jacob Philip Fallmerayer.

The challenge that Fallmerayer posed to the newly born Greek identity represented the broader cultural transformation of the period and the gradual rise of romanticism with its concomitant reevaluation of the people (*Volk*) as the fundamental representatives of "authentic" culture.[11] In 1830, Fallmerayer published his *Geschite der Halbinsel Morea wahrend des Mittelalters*, in which he put forward his "Slavic" theory; that is, the argument that during the Middle Ages the Slavs overran the Balkan peninsula and, therefore, the contemporary Greeks are descendants of these Slavs and Albanians. He attempted to provide proof for his theses through a combination of original sources and linguistics, deriving evidence out of Slavic toponyms in southern Greece. Furthermore, his argument blended a "racial" thesis (i.e., that the modern Greeks are not racially connected with the ancients) with a cultural thesis (i.e., that the modern Greeks do not share the cultural traditions of the ancients) (Veloudis 1982, 28–36; Herzfeld 1982, 75–7). He strongly criticized philhellenists for their obsession with classical antiquity and for their lack of attention to contemporary reality. In addition, there was a political agenda present in his work. Fallmerayer was an ardent German liberal and proponent of democracy. He was even elected deputy in the 1848 Frankfurt parliament and then fled to Switzerland. His politics cost him his university chair. Because a liberal united Germany would not be able to resist Russia's territorial ambitions, any obstacle to these ambitions was welcome. The Greek state could only be a "Slavo-Greek" state which could be enlightened only by "Kiev." Modern Greece was a facet of Russian expansionism (Pan-Slavism) and therefore, by implication, Greek nationalism was unwelcome. Ottoman Turkey should serve as a fortress against Pan-Slavism, and by implication against Greek territorial ambitions.

The need to provide a plausible reply to Fallmerayer is generally recognized as a central motivational factor in Greek scholarship. However, in doing so, Greek authors had to resolve the internal contradictions of their own culture. Historiography and folklore studies were the two main areas where unity and continuity were to be found.[12] Prior to 1840 there was practically no indigenous tradition of historiography.[13] The most impressive outcome of the Greek reaction to Fallmerayer was the flowering of folklore studies; "most, if not all, of the volumes of 'national folklore' which appeared in the years between Fallmerayer's *Geschichte* and the beginning of the twentieth century were directly inspired by the goal of proving 'the German' wrong" (Herzfeld 1982, 80; for details, see Veloudis 1982, 47–63; Herzfeld 1982, 75–96). The attempt to refute him, however, led to Fallmerayer's exercising a considerable influence on his critics' thinking. The Greek romantic historiography and folklore research that emerged in the post-1850 period blended two ideas which, at first sight, might appear irreconcilable: that there is a fundamental continuity between ancient and modern Greeks; and that the historical territory of the Greek nation is identical with the space occupied by the former Byzantine Empire. The reconciliation of the two premises was accomplished because of the influence of romanticism on the new discourse. Whereas Enlightenment authors, such as Korais, viewed the nation as a process, the new romantic approach viewed the nation as an eternal static entity.

## GREEK ROMANTICISM AND THE GREAT IDEA

In 1852, Spiridon Zambelios published his collection of folk songs, a book noted for its lengthy (595-page) introduction. Zambelios proposed a threefold classification of Greek history: ancient, medieval, and modern. Past and present were conceived as united: on the book's cover, there is a picture of bandits and priests armed with swords and holy icons conducting a siege of Constantinople, while, at center stage, Constantinos Palaiologos, last emperor of the Byzantine Empire, guides them forward.[14] After the fall of Constantinople, Zambelios argues, "the race is in captivity, the nation remains standing." Henceforth, "the sword and the song" become its two inseparable companions. Folk songs, therefore, are the expression of national resistance and illustrate national continuity.

These premises provided folklore research with its national significance and its internal logic. The goal of the discipline was to provide evidence of national continuity by recovering the past and integrating it into the present "folk" culture. The first important transformation undertaken by folklorists was the clearcut separation of *klephts* and their tradition from ordinary banditry.[15] The ancient Greek word *listis* was reintroduced into Greek in order to denote the existing reality of banditry and the word *klepht* was redeployed so as to signify the warriors who resisted Ottoman rule. The *klephts* were separated from their social context and depicted as national heroes. Their heroism provided an example of the survival of the ancient Greek military valor. Their songs became part of the national treasury.

While folklorists attempted to use the present to establish a tie with the past, the Greek romantic historiography of the nineteenth century attempted to create a history that could prove the unbroken continuity of the Greek nation (thereby refuting Fallmerayer) and would aid the articulation of the Greek "Great Idea." In 1853, Constantinos Paparrigopoulos published a school textbook where he reversed the thesis that antiquity ended with the conquest of ancient Greece by the Macedonians: "The Macedonians," he wrote, "although they are not mentioned in the earlier eras of Greek history, were nevertheless Greeks" (quoted in Politis 1993, 44). The reevaluation of the Macedonians was directly related to the need to provide the idea of Greek unity with a reference point in the Hellenic past. The Macedonians united the fragmented ancient Greek states and transplanted ancient Greek civilization in the East. Modern Greek nationalism needed this unity—symbolized by Alexander the Great—in order to provide for an ideological justification of the idea of Hellenic unity in the present. Together with Zambelios, Paparrigopoulos was the most influential historian in modern Greek history.

Paparrigopoulos was born in Constantinople and therefore, was not an "indigenous" Greek. He was a protégé of Ioannis Kolletis, the defender of the "nonindigenous" Greeks (Dimaras 1986, 119–24). Initially Paparrigopoulos worked as a civil servant, but after the 1844 Parliament decision to restrict the eligibility of these positions to "indigenous" Greeks he was fired. He turned to the teaching of history as an alternative, and occupied the position of high school principal in Athens. In 1850, in order to gain a university seat, he submitted a monograph to the University of Munich asking to be given the title of professor. This was granted and following the acceptance of the title, he was hired onto the philosophical faculty of the University of Athens (Dimaras 1986, 117–28, 138–9). From early in his career, the basic concepts that preoccupied his thought were those of Greek historical mission, unity, the Great Idea, and the Eastern Question. Paparrigopoulos' version of Greek history, published during the 1860–1874 period, was grounded on the assumption of an unbroken historical continuity between the ancient and the modern Greeks. His historical narrative bridged the gap between the ancient world and the modern era by reinterpreting medieval Byzantium as a manifestation of Hellenism during the Middle Ages. Indeed, he believed that the term "Byzantine" was suspect since it concealed the Hellenic character of the Eastern Roman Empire (Dimaras 1986, 186). Thus, the narrative of Greek ethnogenesis stretched over a period of 3,000 years, assuming a fundamental continuity that transcended the different historical periods.

An indispensable component of the unbroken historical continuity thesis was the Hellenic character of the ancient Macedonian kingdom. Alexander the Great was the hero who brought "enlightenment" to the barbaric Orient and this led to the flowering of Hellenic letters in the eastern Mediterranean. The Byzantine Empire was conceived of as the product of the combination of Hellenic culture with the ideas of Eastern Orthodoxy. This was the second glorious era of Hellenism, one that came to an end with the conquest of Constantinople by the Turks.

The fundamental goal of this reinterpretation of Greek history was the reevaluation of Orthodoxy and its recovery from the harsh criticism of the Enlightenment. Politically, Greece was viewed as the inheritor of Byzantium and by extension, as the legitimate inheritor of the Ottoman Empire; with respect to Russia and the Balkan Slavs, Greece gained a considerable element of prestige as the legitimate inheritor of the earlier Byzantine tradition. The vision put forward is accurately captured in a new word created by Zambelios: "Greco-Christianic" (ellinochristianikos), a term denoting the identification of Greece with Orthodoxy (Dimaras 1985, 461). In this recasting of the role of religion in social life, Orthodoxy was viewed as a central feature of Hellenism. Constantinos Paparrigopoulos was an ardent nationalist. He was frequently involved in the political debates of his day and was co-founder of the Society for the Propagation of the Greek Letters (1869), one of the major nationalist organizations of the late nineteenth century (Dimaras 1986, 241; Vergopoulos 1994, 180–3). The society's actions were for many years dominated by Paparrigopoulos. Its goal was to "strengthen Hellenism in the areas that [other] . . . nations attempt to usurp" (quoted in Dimaras 1986, 241)—that is, mainly in Bulgaria and Macedonia. Paparrigopoulos considered that his duty was "national as well as scientific" (quoted in Politis 1993, 147). Indeed, that was the case.

The publication of the *History of the Greek Nation* over the years 1865 to 1874 was partially financed by state agencies and national societies and provisions were made for copies to be distributed to the municipalities and to Athens University. In 1877 Parliament allocated 6,000 drachmas to finance a French translation of the book (*Histoire de la civilisation hellenique*, 1878). By 1879 a conference was held in Athens with the participation of all Greek associations active outside the kingdom of Greece; Paparrigopoulos masterminded the project of coordinating their efforts to turn his *History* into a foundational text. In 1882, the Historical and Ethnological Society of Greece was founded with the goal of "proving" the unbroken unity and continuity of Hellenism from antiquity to the present (Vergopoulos 1994, 180–1; Dimaras 1986, 227–34). Over the course of the next years Paparrigopoulos' narrative became the "official" history of modern Greece—and has remained largely unchallenged to this day.

The Greek national mission was clearly stated in Kolletis' 1844 speech: "By its geographical position Greece is the center of Europe, having on its right the East and on the left the West, it is destined to enlighten the East through its rebirth as it illuminated the West through its fall" (quoted in Augustinos 1977, 14). In the following years, the "enlightenment of the East" became the notion most closely affiliated with the "Great Idea." The geographical territory the Greek state should occupy was by no means clear-cut.[16] Paparrigopoulos' work, by identifying Greece with the earlier Byzantine Empire, also supported the maximum of the Greek claims in every direction. The discrepancy between the means of the small weak Greek state and the grandiose dreams that the Greeks themselves were imagining was a constant source of complaint for the critics of the new state.[17]

Throughout the nineteenth century, the expansion of the educational system in the kingdom of Greece and in the Ottoman Empire aided the "awakening" of Greek identity. In the Greek kingdom, although in 1830 only 8 percent of children attended elementary school, the number rose to 29 percent by 1855, 40 percent by 1878, 53 percent by 1895, and 72 percent by 1908 (Tsoukalas 1987, 392). Similar high numbers are observed in secondary education and university attendance.[18] Since its establishment in 1834, education in primary and secondary schools was free, a development that facilitated social mobility. But education used the *katharevusa* version of Greek (i.e., a "purified" version of Greek with heavy borrowings from ancient Greek) and not the spoken vernacular known as *demotiki*. The strengthening of *katharevusa* was the indirect consequence of the neoclassicism dominating early nineteenth-century cultural life. It symbolized the regeneration of ancient Greece in its most formal aspect (language) (for discussions, see Iliou 1989; Mouzelis 1978; Tsoukalas 1987, 527–68). Although Korais, the original creator of *katharevusa*, wished to create a fusion between modern and ancient Greek, his creation was turned into an im-

**Table 6**
**Time Allocation per Course in Secondary Education***

| COURSE | 1836 | 1867 | 1884 | 1914 |
|---|---|---|---|---|
| Ancient Greek | 70 | 94 | 78 | 57 |
| Modern Greek** | -- | -- | 14 | 20 |
| Latin | 22 | 18,5 | 14 | 14 |
| History | 14 | 17 | 14 | 17 |
| Mathematics | 21 | 26,5 | 22 | 27 |
| Philosophy & Religion | 15 | 17 | 16 | 21 |
| Other | 46 | 35 | 44 | 55 |
| TOTAL | 188 | 207 | 202 | 211 |

*hours spent per course weekly over a seven-year period.
**Modern Greek refers to *katharevusa*, which was the official language of the Greek kingdom. It is revealing that while Ancient Greek was taught since the system's creation, *katharevusa* was only taught since 1884.

*Source*: Tsoukalas (1987, 555).

itation of ancient Greek that was incomprehensible to the vast majority of the people. *Katharevusa* provided for symbolic distinction between elites and masses in the new state. Table 6 illustrates this cultural trend.

Only after 1888, with the publication of the novel *To Taxidi* by the Greek author Psicharis, did a reform movement begin.[19] The *demoticist* movement attempted to establish the spoken vernacular in place of *katharevusa*; it was a long and bitter battle that was resolved only in 1975 with constitutional guarantees that *demotiki* was the official language of the Republic of Greece. Throughout the Ottoman Empire, the Grecophone communities enjoyed their own educational institutions even prior to the establishment of the Greek kingdom. By 1861 there were 726 Greek schools in the Ottoman Empire, with 903 teachers and 34,939 students (Augustinos 1992, 153). In 1861 the foundation of the Hellenic Philological Society of Constantinople aimed specifically at exploring the new circumstances created after the 1856 reform edict (Mamoni 1975, 104). The society aimed at the cultural cultivation of the Christians in the Ottoman Empire and proved so successful that similar organizations from within the Greek kingdom imitated it. By 1871, the society, under new regulations, assumed the task of coordinating educational activities throughout the empire (Augustinos 1992, 179). During the 1860–1870 period, more societies were founded throughout the empire and in 1869 the sultan officially recognized the right of Orthodox communities to set up educational institutions.[20] With the exception of Smyrna, where educational societies had operated since 1838, most other organizations were founded after 1861.

In Athens, the Society for the Propagation of the Greek Letters was the semi-official organization responsible for education in Macedonia and Thrace. The society was officially entrusted by the Greek Foreign Ministry with this task; in 1886 its official responsibilities were transferred to the Committee for the Strengthening of the Hellenic Church and Education and the society continued its activities as a private organization. Since 1870, the Greek state financed schools in Epirus, Macedonia, and Thrace.[21] During the same period, Bulgarian organizations opened their own schools in Macedonia and Thrace; this led to a sharp conflict between Greeks and Bulgarians. Especially in regions where the population was ethnically mixed, one finds a disproportionate number of schools because schools could be most useful in these contested regions. In Macedonia alone, the number of students in Greek schools increased by sixfold in the 1877–1904 period. It should be noted that the use of *katharevusa* by the Greek state and the emphasis in school curricula on ancient Greek were important obstacles in the success of Greek schools in the Ottoman Empire. For example, in Macedonia, Greek students did not learn to speak modern Greek (*demotiki*) because they were taught Attic Greek or *katharevusa*, both of them in effect dead languages (Tsoukalas 1987, 549). Although the activities of the societies and the financing of schools by the Greek state significantly encouraged the creation of educational institutions in the Ottoman Empire, the proliferation of schools was significantly slower than in the Greek kingdom and only in Smyrna and Constantinople was the rate of their increase comparable to that in the Greek kingdom (Tsoukalas 1987, 464; for Smyrna, Augustinos 1992, 158–62). The establishment of educational institutions received a boost from the contributions of the rich Greek diaspora both within the kingdom and within the empire (Tsoukalas 1987, 488).

With the building of this educational apparatus, national mobilization, education, and literacy became blended. This fusion is exemplified in the work of Leon Melas, an Epirote Greek, who became an important figure in the Greek judicial system. His book *O Georstathis* (1858) was a combination of nationalism and moral teachings and was widely circulated in Ottoman Greek communities. Gerostathis was a fictional character born in Epirus and educated in Janina. He traveled abroad, engaged in commerce, and became acquainted with all the wonders of the world and progress. But he never forgot his homeland or neglected his cultural heritage; he specifically took pleasure in learning about ancient Greece while holding to the Orthodox faith. *O Gerostathis* "crystallized and established the underlying intellectual justification and social purpose of education in the Greek world" (Augustinos 1992, 172). It exemplified Zambelios' Greco-Christian fusion.

Taken in combination, the societies, the educational system, folklore research, and history (which was taught in the Greek schools), gradually transformed the diffuse solidarity of the *Rum millet* into a new form of national identity. This identity was predicated on the reunification of the classical Enlightenment "Hellenic" vision with the Byzantine Orthodox tradition. Paparrigopoulos' and Zambelios' writings provided for this reconciliation. They successfully transformed the *substantive* problem of the transition to modernity into a *formal* problem of historical continuity; the issue was to "prove" that the modern *Rum millet* was the inheritor of both classical Greece and the Byzantine past, a thesis aptly captured by Zambelios' term "Greco-Christianic."

## SERBIA: A PIEDMONT FOR THE SOUTH SLAVS

The emergence of the principality of Serbia as a possible Piedmont for the South Slavs was slow and gradual. As with modern Greece, a distinction was indeed made between the Serbs of the principality, the so-called Serbians (*Srbijanci*), and Habsburg and Ottoman Serbs (*Srbi*) (Rusinow 1995, 356; Skopetea 1988, 387–96). To bridge the gap between the two groups was the goal of the Serb national ideology.

By 1830, Prince Miloš Obrenović had succeeded in winning autonomy for the principality of Serbia. In his attempt to control local rebellions and ensure his own position, Miloš harshly persecuted all those opposing him, employing murder, torture, and deceit to affirm his own authority (Petrovich 1976, 1:103–20; Djordjevic, 1970a, 74–8; Dedijer et al., 1974, 280–1). Controlling a variety of administrative positions and commercial monopolies, he turned himself into the richest person in Serbia. In his effort to centralize the state apparatus, Miloš allowed for the creation of a new social force that was to play an instrumental role in Serbia's political evolution. This force was the state bureaucracy. State employees increased from 24 in 1815 to 492 in 1837 and 1,151 in 1842 (Stokes 1975, 4; Stoianovich 1959, 246). Most of them came from the Serb community of Vojvodina and they were called *prečani* ("men from across") or more unkindly *nemačkari* (from the word *nemči*, i.e., Germans). Education and privilege separated the newcomers from the peasant population (Petrovich 1976, 1:142; Skopetea 1988, 374–81; Stoianovich 1959, 242–8). In this group Miloš' terrorist tactics were deeply resented. In 1832, Vuk Karadžić, the legendary collector of Serb folk poetry, counseled Miloš to establish a government separated from his own household, to end the corvée in Miloš' estates, to establish schools, to end his own private enterprises that competed with those of other merchants, and to give the people a constitution (Petrovich 1976, 1:143–4; see Wilson 1970, 253–68 for the complete text of Karadžić's letter).

But Miloš could not be influenced by words alone. Bureaucrats and local notables combined their efforts to force Miloš to grant a constitution. In 1835, their efforts were successful. Written by Miloš' secretary, Dimitrije Davidović, the so-called Davidović Constitution was the first step toward power sharing in Serb political history. Because this constitution was too liberal for the international standards of the period, it caused the involvement of the Great Powers and the Ottoman government in Serb politics. After 3 years of diplomatic maneuvers, it was replaced by the 1838 constitution (also known as the Turkish constitution). This constitution took the form of an "organic statute" and established a 17-member council. The cabinet was made responsible to the council and not to the prince, thus effectively curbing Miloš' authority.

This was a victory for Miloš' opponents, by now known as Constitutionalists (Djordjevic 1970c, 84–93; Petrovich 1976, 1:156–8). Unwilling to compromise, Miloš resigned and after a 3-year period of rule by his sons, the Constitutionalists were able to remove the Obrenović dynasty from the throne and return Alexander Karadjordjević, son of the legendary hero of the first Serb uprising, to the throne. The principal personalities among the Constitutionalists were Vučić, Avram Petronijević, the brothers Aleska and Stojan Simić, Hadzi-Milutin Garašanin, and his son, Ilija (Dragnich 1978, 23; McKenzie 1985, 24–42). During the 1842–1858 period, the Constitutionalists—in reality a small, elite group—held the real power because Alexander Karadjordjević was not an effective leader and lacked a large following. Over the 1842–1847 period, Ilija Garašanin in particular became an almost indispensable administrator.

The principality of Serbia underwent major social changes in the first half of the nineteenth century. The traditional extended family, the *zadruga*, began to collapse.[22] Urban settlements were Serbianized and Belgrade ceased to be a city dominated by Greeks, Hellenized Vlachs, and Turks. In addition, Serb migration from the Habsburg territories and Bosnia-Herzegovina into the principality aided the creation of a national nucleus.[23] During the 1842–1858 period the Constitutionalists initiated a program of modernization "from above" to educate the people and improve the social conditions in the country (for a review, see Kuranovich, 1995). A major change pertained to the civil service: Whereas Prince Miloš treated civil servants harshly, the Constitutionalists guaranteed tenure to them. They were also granted special rights and privileges; for example, bureaucrats could not be dismissed without cause. The result was a hunger for civil service positions (Djordjevic 1970a, 94–7; Dragnich 1978, 25–6).

The physical consolidation of ethnic Serbs into one state was accompanied by a national revival that sought to revitalize Serb ethnic identity and transform it into a modern secular national identity. The first step was the establishment of a Serb Orthodox Church organization in the principality. Between 1815 and 1830, Prince Miloš assumed de facto leadership in Serb ecclesiastical affairs (Petrovich 1976, 1:210–13; Vavouskos 1979). Miloš was highly observant in his religious duties and issued decrees forcing the population to follow his example. He took measures to fight ecclesiastical corruption and to force Old Church Slavonic (instead of Greek) as the official language in church services. He procured five bells for the Belgrade Orthodox cathedral and obtained permission to have the bells ring (1830); the ringing of church bells was prohibited in the empire and the action was pregnant with religious and national symbolism. Moreover, Miloš obtained from the Sultan (1830) a decree recognizing the internal autonomy of the Serb Church. In 1833, Peter Jovanović was consecrated bishop of Belgrade by Patriarch Constantine I. On this occasion, the Serb Patriarch was elevated to second rank in the hierarchy of the Eastern Church (from the twelfth rank it previously held). The establishment of a state-sponsored independent Serb Church reaffirmed the replacement of Greek by Old Slavonic as the official language of services. With all these actions, Miloš facilitated the redeployment of Orthodoxy as an integral part of Serb identity.

The most explicit revitalization of Serb identity, however, took place among the Vojvodina Serbs. Their ethnoconfessional community, instituted after the Great Migration of 1690, was organized under the leadership of the archbishop of Karlowitz. Among them, there was an extensive middle class that was greatly involved in the 1804 Serb uprising (Banac 1981; Adler 1979). Vojvodina was also the place where the first Serb printing press was set up. In 1769 the Habsburgs permitted the establishment of a Serb press in Vienna. During the 1770–1800 period, this press published 325 books in Serbian, of which more than 100 were original works (Adler 1974a).

The cultural revival of the Habsburg Serbs was mainly the accomplishment of the literary society Matica Srbska. Founded in 1825–1826, the society and its major publication, the journal *Ljetopis* served as the key Serb intellectual and cultural vehicle for the following 50 years. Initially, intellectual mobilization was extremely difficult because the Serb activists found themselves in the difficult position of having no readily available audience interested in their cultural and literary activities. In many respects, they had to create this audience in order to sustain the society (Kimball 1969). Another difficulty was the conservative pro-Orthodox and Russophile attitudes of the community. Karadžić's modern version of Serbo-Croatian was not readily accepted; and many in the community persisted in advocating the use of Old Church Slavonic. From 1835 forward, however, the society was able to assert its role and provide an outlet for a variety of publications. Most of its publications were universal or national histories, reprints of the works of Dositeij Obradović, and Serb plays and poems.

The major cultural theme explored by Serb literature throughout the nineteenth century was the Kosovo legend. The folk songs of the Kosovo battle (1389) were prominent in the four-volume folk song collection published by Vuk Karadžić. In fact, Karadžić wrote that he did not find many songs predating Kosovo and he attributed it to the shock caused by the battle.[24] These folk songs provided the most elegant example of Serb medieval poetry. Through his collections of folk poetry, Karadžić exercised considerable influence on Serb intellectual evolution: The collections were not the product of impersonal classification; rather, they reflected and shaped growing Serb nationalism (Barac 1973, 89). In the Kosovo circle, the original emphasis had been on Prince Lazar's martyrdom, in his desire to sacrifice himself in order to purify Serbia. But by the late eighteenth century and the nineteenth century, the Kosovo legend was reinterpreted (Emmert 1990, 105–23; Mihailovich 1991, 142–50). The version that was popularized among Vojvodina Serbs in the eighteenth century was a moral tale: a quarrel breaks out between Prince Lazar's daughters that creates a conflict between Lazar's two prominent knights, Vuk Branković and Miloš

Obilić. Vuk accuses Miloš of treason; during Lazar's banquet, Miloš pledges to prove his loyalty to Lazar; then Miloš flees to the Turkish camp and assassinates Sultan Murad. Lazar exhorts his men to bravery; the battle then follows. Lazar is killed in the battle while Vuk Branković, the real traitor, abandons the Serb side and joins the Turks. In this version, the Kosovo tale is a story of love, bravery, treason, and sacrifice for the nation.

In his poems, *The Ray of Microcosm, Mountain Wreath*, and *Stephen the Small*, Prince Njegoš of Montenegro blended the millenarianism of the original Kosovo legend with modern nationalist ideology, providing an epic synthesis that was to have a lasting effect on Serb identity.[25] In his reinterpretation, Njegoš conceived the battle for national independence as a manifestation of the cosmic battle between Good and Evil, Light and Darkness. The Serbs were a nation carrying the cross of martyrdom through the centuries. In *Mountain Wreath* (1847), the most famous of his poems, Njegoš reinterpreted the legacy of the Kosovo battle. The poem was based on a historical event: a battle between Montenegrin fighters and Montenegrin renegades (converts to Islam). Heroism, bravery, and devotion were the sentiments dominant in the epic. Whereas in the earlier tradition, God forced Prince Lazar to choose between the heavenly and the earthly kingdom, Njegoš conceived Kosovo as the constant destiny of the Serbs.[26] This theme is similar to the one that the Greek Ioannis Kolletis invoked in his 1844 speech in the Greek parliament. In both cases, the obligation of the good patriot was to carry on this eternal conflict between Serb (or Greek) and Turk. This moral imperative was codified in an epic poem declaring that "whoever is a Serb of Serb blood . . . and he comes not to fight at Kosovo . . . May he never have the progeny/ His heart desires, neither son nor daughter; / Beneath his hand let nothing decent grow . . . Until his name shall be extinguished!"[27]

In Njegoš *Mountain Wreath*, this call to arms took the form of the resolution of Serbia's cosmic misfortune. Good and light battle in history against evil and darkness: "The Crescent and the Cross, great Symbols twain/do not advantage gain save in world of slain!/it is our lot to sail this crimson stream."[28] In *Mountain Wreath*, then, an important fusion took place: Orthodox Christianity was conceived as coterminous with Serbdom, and the moral imperative of fulfilling the national mission was reconciled with Christian morality.

The Vojvodina Serbs were greatly involved in the revitalization of the Kosovo legend because of their better educational status. Vojvodina Serbs were recruited for positions in the Serb bureaucracy. Ilija Garašanin, the leader of the Serb bureaucracy, was a Serbian by birth—who had, however, been schooled in Vojvodina.[29] Garašanin was the interior minister of Serbia in 1844 when he wrote his famous *Načertanije* (draft), a document that plays the same role in the articulation of Serb nationalism as Kolletis' (1844) speech in the Greek parliament.

Initially, Garašanin was in close contact with the Polish expatriate Prince Czartoryski and with Frantisek Zach, a Pan-Slav Czech. The original idea for the document came from Prince Adam Czartoryski, who was interested in using Balkan Slav nationalism as a counterforce against Russian and Habsburg expansionism (Despalatovic 1975, 155–7). Zach came to Belgrade in October 1843 and served as Czartoryski's permanent agent in Serbia. In the first weeks of 1844, after consultations with Garašanin, Zach drew up a draft outlining the role of Serbia as a future gathering point for the South Slavs. In January 1844 Zach wrote a letter to Ljudevit Gaj, the key theorist of the Illyrian movement, explaining his major ideas, but his proposals differed greatly from the platform of the Croatian National Party at the time. However, Gaj sent Stjepan Car in Belgrade to work on the Croatian side of the plan. Zach submitted his final draft to Garašanin in May 1844. In the next few months, Garašanin reworked the text and deleted all references to Croats.[30]

In *Načertanije*, the transformed Kosovo legend met its equivalent in public policy (Djordjevic 1991, 315). The South Slav idea became an extension of the Greater Serb program. The "Serb lands" named in *Načertanije* were Bosnia, Herzegovina, Montenegro, Kosovo; from the Habsburg territories, Srem, Bačka, and Banat were only briefly mentioned.[31] *Načertanije* set forth the goals of future Serb governments:

The Serb state must strive to expand and become stronger; its roots and foundation are firmly embedded in the Serb Empire of the thirteenth and fourteenth centuries and the glorious pageant of Serb history. Historically speaking, the Serb rulers, it may be remembered, began to assume the position held by the Greek Empire and almost succeeded in making an end of it, replacing the collapsed Eastern Roman Empire with a Serbian-Slavic one. The arrival of the Turks in the Balkans interrupted this change, and prevented it from taking place for a long time. But now, since the Turkish power is broken and destroyed, so to speak, this interrupted process must commence once more in the same spirit and again be undertaken in the knowledge of that right. . . . Such an enterprise would be endowed with inestimable importance and great prestige among the European cabinets, as well as in the eyes of its own people; for then we Serbs could appear before the world as the heirs of our illustrious forefathers, doing nothing that is new other than completing their work. Hence, our present will not be without a link to the past and will comprise one dependent, integrated, and systematic whole. Thus, the Serb idea and its national mission and existence will stand under the sacred law of history. . . . If we consider the rebirth of the Serb kingdom from these standpoints, then others will easily understand the South Slav idea and accept it with joy; for probably in no single European country is the memory of the historical past so vivid as among the Slavs of Turkey. . . . The Serbs were the first, of all the Slavs of Turkey, to struggle for their freedom. . . . Even now in many places . . . it is anticipated and expected that a great future is imminent for the Serbs, and it is this fact which has attracted the attention of Europe.[32]

The *Načertanije* also called for intelligence gathering in the neighboring lands. In his capacity as interior minister (1843–1852) and later as prime minister and foreign minister (1852–1853 and 1861–1867), Garašanin proceeded to establish a network of agents in Kosovo and Bosnia-Herzegovina. This network aimed at the organization of insurrections that would lead to the liberation of fellow Serbs (McKenzie 1982; 1988, 15). By the late 1840s Serb agitation was conducted in Kosovo, Metohija, and Novi Pazar. Garašanin also pushed the idea of a Serbo-Bulgarian state; accordingly, Serbs offered support to the Bulgarian clergy, printed Bulgarian books, and sent agents to assure them of Serb assistance.

Of course, Garašanin did not carry out all these activities by himself. During 1843–1844 Miloš Popović, editor of Serbia's official newspaper, *Srpske Novine* (Serb News), created a circle in Belgrade, welcomed Bosnian Franciscans dissatisfied with Habsburg rule, and provided a nucleus of dedicated national workers.[33] Garašanin and Aleksa Simić, Serbia's interior and foreign ministers, remained outside this circle but were kept closely informed of its activities and supplied monetary and other assistance from the Serb government. During 1844 émigré idealists, including some Illyrians, and some native Serbs created in Belgrade a secret nationalist society of South Slavs. According to Matija Ban, one of its leaders, the society's purpose was to broaden the views of Serbs from Serbia so that Serbia could lead South Slav peoples in their struggle for freedom and unity. By 1845 the society's membership had grown and Matija Ban reported that Prince Aleksandar Karadjordjević and the influential Serb military leader, Steven Kničanin, favored it. During 1848–1850 the Serb government paid 29 persons, including Ban, a total of 5,000 to 6,000 *talirs* for salaries, correspondence, and travel. Ban, a poet, publicist, professor, and politician, viewed Serbia as the future Piedmont of the South Slavs and was distressed that the Serbians' patriotism seemed limited to the principality alone.

## THE SERB LIBERALS AND ROMANTIC NATIONALISM

Although the conservative oligarchy of the Constitutionalists initiated the nationalist program, it was their opponents, the liberals, who popularized the goal of national unity. This popularization was slow when compared with the Greek experience. As late as the Eastern Crisis of 1875–1878 regionalism prevailed at the peasantry's level. When, following the Bosnian insurrection of 1875, the Serb Parliament considered going to war against the Ottoman Empire, a peasant deputy reportedly protested by saying "If we wrench Bosnia, my own field will not become any larger" (quoted in Djordjevic 1985, 309–11). The meager development of secular educational systems in the Habsburg lands and in the principality of Serbia was a major factor accounting for the slow nationalization of the peasantry. During the nineteenth century illiteracy was a major obstacle that had to be overcome in order to ensure the transformation of the peasantry's identity from a religious to a secular one. By 1866, only 4.2 percent of Serbia's population could read and by 1900 the figure grew only to 17 percent (Ekmečić 1991, 333; Jelavich 1990b, 40).[34]

The absence of a strong literary tradition and the predominance of the peasantry suggested that the manipulation of cultural markers would be more effective at the level of language rather than at the level of a certain historical tradition (as was the Greek case). By that time, in an article written in 1836 and published in 1849, Vuk Karadžić had defined as Serbs all those who spoke the *stokavian* dialect. Since the Croats spoke this dialect, Karadžić considered them Serbs; if they did not accept this designation, he said, they have no national name (Jelavich 1990a, 33–4; Banac 1984, 80). Karadžić held fast to his ideas and when, in 1856, Bogoslav Sulek, one of the leaders of the Croatian Illyrian movement, challenged his views, Karadžić reaffirmed his earlier statements. As early as 1811, Karadžić employed the word "nationalism" (*Nacionalismus*, not *narodnost*) to designate the direction of the Serb uprising (Petrovich 1988, 42). Karadžić's views had a lasting impact and were incorporated into Serb textbooks. Nowhere in the textbooks in use prior to 1910 were the Croats recognized as a separate nation (cf. Jelavich 1990b).

In the principality of Serbia, the rise of the liberals in the 1850s was the direct consequence of the emergence of a native educated class. While Serbia had fewer than a thousand pupils enrolled in its schools prior to 1830, the Constitutionalists' program of rapid modernization drastically expanded the scope of the educational system. By 1846–1847, according to the official records, there were 232 elementary schools, with 6,830 pupils enrolled (Karanovich 1995, 53). Two gymnasia were established in the 1830s and in 1838 Belgrade obtained a lyceum. In 1841 the lyceum obtained a faculty of law. Between 1836 and 1846 a seminary, two commercial schools, a technical school, a military academy, and a school of agriculture were also established.[35] With the development of education and the establishment of higher schools, it became possible in 1842 to organize the Serbian Literary Society (*Družstvo Srbske Slovesnosti*), the first learned society in Serbia (Karanovich 1995, 194–5). None of the society's initial members were natives of the principality, but, by the late 1840s, when Serbs abroad began returning to the principality, the society was able to enlarge its membership. The Society of Serb Youth was the first liberal organization that developed in the Serb principality. It was formed in 1847 by a group of lyceum students and the lyceum quickly turned into a meeting place for bright young Serbs. Its precursor was the 1845 youth organization Dušan's Regiment, founded by Matija Ban. The society published the first collection of student essays and poems in Serbia (Djordjevic 1970a, 105; Karanovich 1987, 146). Soon it became a champion of liberal and humanitarian ideas and a sharp critic of the regime.

Among its members was Vladimir Jovanović, the future leader of Serb liberals. In 1848–1849, groups of students in Belgrade allied themselves with the Vojvodina Serbs who were fighting for autonomy. The youth displayed both an aggressive nationalism and a strong discontent for the "German" bureaucracy of Serbia. During this period, the younger generation of students and literary figures took a decisive turn toward romanticism. Karadžić, who was almost forgotten during the 1840s, again became a central figure; with the aid of romanticism, his reformist linguistic program triumphed (Barac 1973, 124–5; Djordevic 1970a, 142–4). Romantic enthusiasm was accompanied by strong nationalist feelings. During the years 1848 and 1849, St. Vitus' Day (*Vidovdan*) began gaining prominence as a potential national holiday. The day coincided with the date of the Kosovo battle. St. Vitus, the legendary founder of the Serb Orthodox Church, was celebrated in the villages even in earlier centuries (Djordjevic 1990, 34–5). His cult was related to the Kosovo battle. Folk tales alleged that on that day the rivers turned red with the blood of the dead from the Kosovo battle. But the original cult received a strong boost from the growing Serb nationalism. The first celebration took place on 27 June 1851 when a group of young government employees organized a party commemorating Prince Lazar's supper on the eve of St. Vitus' Day (June 28).[36] Although ecclesiastical calendars marked St. Vitus Day as a holiday of only secondary importance, the date soon gained an almost mystical hold over the Serb populace. When in 1869, the Serb National Theater opened in Belgrade, the theme of St. Vitus was frequent in its plays. The Serb national anthem, introduced in 1872, was part of a musical (*Marko's Saber*) about the St. Vitus legend.

The 1848–1849 revolutions did not produce the results young romanticists desired. The establishment of Habsburg-controlled Serb Vojvodina in 1850 also signaled the repression of the more liberal intelligentsia in the Serb principality. In 1850 the Serb government suppressed *Sumadinka*, a new literary review established by the poet Ljubomir Nenadović, on the charge that it was a political rather than a literary publication; in 1851 the government abolished the liberal Society of Serb Youth (Stoianovich 1959, 254–5; Karanovich 1987, 147). In the 1850s, this emerging group of liberal students (led by Vladimir Jovanović, Jevrem Grujić, and Milovan Janković) became the champions of true (as opposed to fictional) constitutionalism. Their goal was to modernize the Serb state, both economically and politically. They became known as "Parisians" because many of them had been educated in Paris or espoused viewpoints associated with the 1848 Paris revolution. Their political program included national liberation; freedom of trade; freedom of the press, assembly, religion, and education; individual rights and security of property; better schools; and the building of adequate communication systems throughout the countryside.

In 1858, the Constitutionalists came into direct conflict with Prince Alexander Karadjordjević over his attempt to rival the council's authority. The stalemate that followed this conflict led the constitutionalists to favor the convocation of an assembly. Called on St. Andrew's Day, the assembly came to be known as the St. Andrew's Assembly. When the assembly was called, the liberals suggested that it become a true parliament through which the people would exercise their sovereignty (Stokes 1975, 18–21). These plans did not materialize. Despite their zeal and commitment to democracy, the liberals stood aloof from the peasantry and failed to establish permanent ties with the majority of the Serb population. The assembly called back into power Miloš Obrenović, who, however, died in less than a year. His son Mihailo succeeded him in 1860. Between 1860 and 1866, Prince Mihailo's government pursued its own nationalistic policy without making any concessions to the liberals.

Vladimir Jovanović, leader of the liberals at the time, soon found himself in exile. Jovanović's liberalism was partly inspired by French social thought, especially the writings of the French economist Bastiat, who emphasized social harmony as a necessary ingredient of social organization. The equivalent in the Serb context was Serb Orthodoxy and kinship loyalty; Jovanovic viewed both as preservers of national heritage (Stokes 1973, 135–7). Jovanović's liberalism was an attempt to reconcile individual interests with the general will. Assuming the leadership of the Serb nationalist movement in the 1860s, Jovanović employed nationalism as a vehicle to strengthen his own liberal program. While in exile, Jovanović published a number of critical newspapers abroad but his attempts did not meet with financial or political success.

The situation changed when the liberals became allied with student literary societies. In 1866, Jovanović suggested to the members of the Habsburg Serb student literary society Zora in Vienna, the formation of a larger cultural organization. The idea received enthusiastic support, and later the same year, 400 representatives of Serb youth from all Serb lands met in Novi Sad and founded the United Serb Youth (*Ujedinjena Omladina Srpska* or *Omladina*). Serb romanticists prevailed among its members (Stoianovich 1959, 258). Jovanović represented the *Omladina* as a vehicle of the nation while using it to legitimize his own political ideas. Jovanović's arguments drew their potency from the traditions of Orthodoxy and the strength of Serb kinship relations; he condemned individualism and suggested that the people found their realization in "brotherly consciousness" and a "harmonious spirit" (Stokes 1975, 93–5). During 1866–1868 the *Omladina* gained momentum among the youth. However, its liberal nature led to its persecution by Prince Mihailo; its most noticeable success was among the Vojvodina Serbs. Following Mihailo's assassination (1868), the liberals were gradually able to return to the principality of Serbia and some of them assumed high posts in civil service. The *Omladina* was finally dissolved in 1871 when the Hungarian authorities insisted that only Hungarian subjects could be members.

These efforts, however, established a permanent connection between Habsburg Serbs and the Serb principality. Serbia's policy in the 1860s and 1870s was to appease the Habsburgs in order to concentrate its efforts on liberating Serb territories under Ottoman rule. Although geopolitically sound, this strategy was rejected by Habsburg Serb liberals, who consistently demanded a more aggressive foreign policy. But the Vojvodina Serbs had practically no options in the post-1860 period other than supporting the Serb national program. Only Serbia could deliver them from Magyar nationalist policies in Vojvodina.

The liberal and secular orientation of Vojvodina Serbs does not negate the fact that Jovanović's liberalism borrowed heavily from Orthodox tradition. Jovanović's employment of the Orthodox idea of harmony in his own political program illustrates the redeployment of religious concepts into the political domain. By the 1880s this redeployment provided an important component in the Serb nationalist program; the 500th anniversary of the Kosovo battle (St. Vitus' Day, 28 June 1889) provided one of the best occasions to observe the close relationship of these concepts. The commemoration of the anniversary began with an outdoor service for the souls of those who had died at Kosovo, followed by a sermon, delivered by the metropolitan of the Serb church, which was inspired by the Kosovo tradition. The metropolitan concluded his remarks with a prayer beseeching Prince Lazar and the Kosovo martyrs to intercede with God to seek his help in restoring the Serb Empire and unifying the Serb nation (Emmert 1990, 129).

Over the 1850–1870 period, and also after the 1878 Habsburg occupation of Bosnia-Herzegovina, it was easier for Serbian claims to be put forward against the weak Ottoman Empire rather than the formidable Habsburg Empire. Serb intellectuals eagerly provided ammunition to this state-sponsored irredentism. Stojan Novaković, perhaps the most important Serb historian of the second half of the nineteenth century, rendered his support to the Serb nation-state, serving as a diplomat in a variety of posts and also becoming involved in Serb politics. Three times minister of education (1873, 1875, and 1880–1883), he authored 23 laws and 21 school curricula (Djordjevic 1988, 51–69; see also Jelavich 1990b). Novaković, who, among other things, changed his Christian name, Costa, to the more "Serbian" name Stojan, belonged to the romantic *Omladina* generation. As early as 1852 a Belgrade newspaper reported that "pure Serbian" was spoken in the region around Skopje (Banac 1984, 107). By 1866 Novaković recognized that the Serb linguistic claims to the Macedonian Slavs were weak compared to the Bulgarians' claims. Consequently, he urged the spread of Serb educational institutions in the region.

Indeed, the Serb government adopted in 1878 the *ekavian* dialect as the official language of the state in an indirect attempt to bring Serb official language closer to the spoken vernacular of the Macedonian Slavs (Poulton 1995, 63). Serb educational propaganda was intensified in the second half of the nineteenth century. Whereas in the eighteenth century only 2 Serb schools operated in the region, their number grew to close to 260 in the second half of the nineteenth century (Georgeoff 1973, 151–2). Their number fluctuated depending on the status of Serbo-Ottoman relations; for example, between 1860 and 1870, 83 schools were opened, but between 1874 and 1879, 84 schools were closed. The Serbo-Ottoman war of 1875 led to the closing of most of the newly established Serb schools. Serb propaganda reappeared in the 1880s with the founding of the St. Sava Society, with the expressed purpose of fostering Serbian educational, religious, and cultural activities in Ottoman European territories.

The Serb Orthodox Church also played a critical role in promoting the cultivation of Serb nationalism in the Habsburg territories (Dalmatia, Croatia-Slavonia, and, after 1878, Bosnia-Herzegovina). The issue that most clearly energized Croatian Serbs was the 1874 secularization of the educational system (Banac 1984, 92; Jelavich 1990b, 42–5). In earlier periods, education was controlled by the Catholic and Orthodox churches and, consequently, ethnic identity was safeguarded as part of the people's religious identity. The two identities should be viewed as intertwined: The definitions of "Croat" and "Serb" in earlier periods were coterminous with Catholic and Orthodox. The point was often made by Croat and Serb nationalists, who insisted that the Serbs were in reality Orthodox Croats or that the Croats were in reality Catholic Serbs.[37] The 1874 law aimed at the creation of social cohesion between Orthodox and Catholic so that the Orthodox Serbs, approximately 25 percent of the population in Croatia-Slavonia, would no longer be attracted to Serbia (Jelavich 1990b, 16). From 1874 to 1914 the Serb Patriarchate of Karlowitz and the Serb Church Congress persisted in their efforts to regain absolute control over the schools. Gradually, the Catholic clergy, although sympathetic to their efforts, began viewing their demands as a front for the creation of a Serb Orthodox "political-religious" community in Croatia-Slavonia. The Serb community supported the Habsburg governor Khuen-Hedervary and in 1888 it was rewarded with a revision of the 1874 law. Religious schools were reestablished, but the content of school text-books had to be approved by the government (Jelavich 1990b, 46–7). The 1888 law revived Serb Orthodox schools, but it exacerbated difficulties in Croat–Serb relations with Croat politicians of the Party of the Right characterizing it as forceful Serbianization of Croatian schools. In 1887 the Serb National Independent Party was formed in Croatia, asking for official recognition of a separate religious and linguistic Serb nationality (Dedijer et al. 1974, 385).

In Dalmatia, Serbs and Croats cooperated between 1860 and 1879; they were organized into a joint National Party advocating Yugoslavism and the union of Dalmatia with Croatia (Vucinich 1967, 23–25). The principal reason for this cooperation was that both Slavic populations were in conflict with the small but influential Italian minority. Croats and Serbs joined forces to overcome their underrepresentation in the Dalmatian Diet and by 1870 they were successful. The National Party won 25 seats in the Diet against the 16 seats of their principal opponents, the Autonomist Party. But this also marked the extent of their achievements. Serb–Croat cooperation was disrupted in the 1870s partly because of Austrian favoritism for the Catholics versus the Orthodox and partly because Serbs and Croats disagreed over the status of Bosnia-Herzegovina, each claiming the province for themselves. Finally, in Bosnia, the Catholic and Orthodox churches were revived during the second half of the nineteenth century and by the late 1860s there were 380 Catholic priests and at least 400 Orthodox clergy (Malcolm 1994, 126). Among them, there were a few individuals whose activities were not only religious but also political. For example, Teofil Petranović, a teacher at the Orthodox school of Sarajevo, formed a group and toured the villages teaching the Orthodox peasants to stop calling themselves *hriscjani* (the local term for Orthodox) and start calling themselves Serbs.

## CONCLUSIONS

Over the 1830–1880 period, both the principality of Serbia and the kingdom of Greece were able to develop into national centers for the Orthodox Slavic population of the Habsburg and Ottoman territories and for the Greek Orthodox population of the Ottoman lands. Greek nationalist efforts were more successful because of the more highly developed educational apparatus and the fact that the Greek Orthodox population was more urban than the Orthodox Slavic population.

Nevertheless, there is a remarkable similarity between the Greek and Serb cases. In both states, the discourse of nationhood provided the basic premises for the formation of local national identities. This discourse utilized the *redeployment of Orthodoxy* to transform religious into secular identities. First, this redeployment of Orthodoxy in the service of the nation-state was accomplished through the creation of independent national churches. National churches implied that membership in a particular church entailed the de facto endorsement of a particular national identity. Over the post-1870 period, this implicit understanding led the Balkan nations to fight a bitter struggle over the church affiliation of the Orthodox Christians in Ottoman Macedonia. Second, once an "imagined community" had been defined in terms of church affiliation, it was then connected with a particular territory conceived of as the national homeland of that particular nation. Garašanin's and Kolletis' actions in 1844 were the turning points for this process. From 1844 on, folklore, history, and literature were the instruments used to establish this emotional association. Both Greek and Serb intelligentsias put forward grandiose dreams that were far beyond their state's means. Both intelligentsias sought justification for irredentist policies in history and folklore. The intellectual careers of Paparrigopoulos and Novaković are examples of this trend. The symbolic manipulation of cultural markers such as language or folklore was a means to instill in the Balkan peoples a sense of belonging to a particular nation. In this manner, the "invented traditions" of the Balkan nations carried with them the seed of future ethnic conflict.

Of course, church affiliation did not represent the sole criterion for deciding the people's "nationality." Language as a main criterion for identifying their prospective nationals was also used by the Serb intelligentsia. This, in effect, complicated their claims further, because the Serbs defined the Croats or Bosnian Muslims as Catholic or Muslim Serbs, whereas no agreement could be reached regarding whether the Macedonian Slavs were in fact Serbs or Bulgarians. Schooling in Greek was also an important component of nation building in the Greek case; however, the use of *katharevusa*, or ancient Greek, by the Greek state undermined the utility of language as a cultural marker and led to the Greeks' highlighting religion as the most important cultural marker.

The intellectual edifice described in this chapter has had long-term consequences. In the twentieth century, it provided Greeks and Serbs with national ideologies that fostered ethnic homogenization. Moreover, during the post-1850 period, these intellectual currents were copied and adopted by the new national movements in Albania, Macedonia, and Bulgaria, which are discussed in chapter 5.

## NOTES

1. The Westernizers consisted mainly of the mercantile groups, settled throughout the Near East; the Phanariots (D. Ypsilantis, A. Mavrocordatos, T. Negris, and C. Karatzas) who came to the kingdom after the 1821 revolution; intellectuals from the Ionian islands; graduates of the European universities; and professionals (Petropulos 1968, 38, 41; Dimaras 1985, 330).

2. In the 1833–1835 period, the regency was responsible for creating a penal code and a civil code, modeled after the Bavarian code of 1813. On 11 July 1833 the state capital was moved from Nauplion to Athens. In the first regency (February 1833–July 1834), two of the regents, Maurer and Heidek, the "regency majority," routinely prevailed over the third regency member, Armansperg. In the second regency (August 1834–May 1835), Armansperg was in control and, although Otto came of age, he continued to rule until January 1837 because the king was away in Bavaria for a considerable time (Petropulos 1968, 157). Otto ruled as an autocrat until 1843.

3. For example, in 1837, in the official lectures given at the founding of Athens University, two speakers referred to the "conquering Macedonians." In 1841 Iakovos Rizos Nerulos, president of the newly founded Archaeological Society (1837) told his audience that "Byzantine history is almost coterminous [with] a long series of foolish . . . and shameful acts of violence . . . it is a shameful stigma of the utmost misery and exhaustion of the Hellenes" (quoted in Dimaras 1977, 394; translation mine). In a direct expression of the modernist spirit, Markos Renieris wrote in 1842 that the duty of the Greeks is to study and emulate Europe. This was the task prescribed by Adamantios Korais: Since the West inherited the wisdom of ancient Greece, the modern Greeks—by moving toward the West—were moving toward recapturing their own spiritual inheritance (Dimaras 1985, 339).

4. Born in 1780 in Thessaly, Oikonomos served in various posts in Smyrna and Constantinople. Initially a disciple of Korais, he grew conservative with age (Petropulos 1968, 294). In 1821 he fled to Odessa, where he read the commemoratory speech at the burial of Patriarch Gregorios V, a speech that soon became legendary. In 1822 he went to St. Petersburg for theological studies. Before returning to Greece, the Tsar offered him a 7,000-rubles-per-year pension (for a biographical sketch, see Frazee 1987, 173–9; Giannaras 1992, 281–8; on the opposite viewpoints regarding ecclesiastical affairs, see also Petropulos 1968, 189–92).

5. The Kairis affair was another major case in which the two sides clashed. The priest Theophilos Kairis, another significant Enlightenment figure, since 1835 had operated an orphanage on the island of Andros. Trained in Western universities in Pisa and Paris, Kairis was a follower of Korais. Under the influence of Auguste Comte, Kairis developed his own philosophical system (*theosophy*). By February and March 1839 the religious authorities began to investigate him and by September Patriarch Gregorios VI condemned theosophy as heretical and blasphemous. At the patriarch's request, the government sent armed forces to arrest Kairis; by 21 October, Kairis stood before the Holy Synod to answer the accusation of heresy. In his defense, Kairis suggested that he was prosecuted because of his attempt to educate the public. Despite his bold defense, he was excommunicated by the patriarch in December 1839. He was released and remained unrepentant until his death in 1866 (Frazee 1987, 187–91). Because Pharmakidis, a member of the Synod, initially supported Kairis, his conservative opponents fiercely attacked

him and were successful in removing him from his chair of theology at the university (he was given the modern Greek chair instead).

6. Skopetea (1988, 129). Some of the Westernizers were inspired by Protestant ideals; for example, the issue of whether priests should participate in the ecclesiastical synod was the subject of a heated debate because the inclusion of priests was concomitant with the Calvinist idea that the church ought to be governed by ministers, a thesis considered by the conservatives to be heretical and against Orthodox tradition (Frazee 1987, 185–7).

7. Dimakis (1991, 230). "They" were the Phanariots and other members of the state elite who drew the resentment of the indigenous warriors and local patricians. Mavrocordatos successfully suggested that the definition of the Greek citizen be separated from the eligibility for civil servant positions. His solution was approved by the assembly and provided the basis of further discussions on this issue.

8. Dimaras (1977, 407–10; 1986, 97) has pointed out that the Great Idea did not predate Kolletis' speech. According to Alexandros Soutsos, a contemporary observer, the slogan did not exist in 1840 (see also Skopetea 1988, 257–71). Strictly speaking, the indigenous Aristides Rentis predated Kolletis by giving a speech that also called for the liberation of the rest of the Greek counties (Dimakis 1991, 76–7). However, Kolletis' speech was the one that captured everyone's attention. Kolletis was more influential, an elder, the leader of a party, and a better speaker.

9. In 1864 the new king George I was given the title "king of the Hellenes" and not "king of Greece" as a means of expressing the unrealized hopes of national unification (Smith 1973, 3).

10. In 1851–1852, the Papoulakos movement exemplified this trend. Papoulakos was a butcher and pig trader who lived in the village Arbouna of Kalavrita. In 1842 he got sick, possibly of typhus, and after his recovery, he gave his property to his brothers, became a monk, and started traveling among the villages living off the peasants' offers and offering support to orphans and widows. Papoulakos condemned "Godless education" and taking oaths in public court (he considered it to be contrary to Orthodox tradition). He also viewed the foundation of the national Church as illegal; accused the English and Protestants of trying to destroy Orthodoxy; declared the Jews to be "scum"; called for the abolition of Athens University ("Devil's University") because, he said, it taught atheism; and, finally, addressed accusations against the king. He believed that he taught the "word of God"; the peasants viewed him as a holy man capable of performing miracles, and rallied around him. It became impossible to arrest him because of his large following and his arrest was accomplished in 1852 only through entrapment made possible by the bribery of one of his former followers (see Aroni-Tsichli 1989, 286–98).

11. See Politis (1984, 21–40) on the general European intellectual trends that aided the cultivation of folklore studies. Not surprisingly, Korais rigorously castigated the romantic turn as betrayal of classical standards and endorsement of humble passions (Dimaras 1985, 144–56), but other intellectuals, such as Ragavis, I. Zambelios, and A. Soutsos, were far less hostile to it.

12. Skopetea (1988, 172–3) and Veloudis (1982, 8–16). The first collection of Greek folk songs by Fauriel (1824–1825) did not gain an immediate response from within the Greek intelligentsia. Prior to 1821, only the Greek communities of the Habsburg Empire were sympathetic and knowledgeable about the work of Herder and they were inclined to pay more attention to folk tradition. This was in sharp contrast to Korais, whose approach had been molded by the French Enlightenment (see Politis 1984, 132–63).

13. In the 1830–1840 period, besides the memoirs of various warriors, there were only simple school textbooks without theoretical claims or any overall vision of history. They were typically translations from other Western European texts. During the 1830s, the last works of the Enlightenment tradition illustrated the gradual transition from the philosophical universalism of the Enlightenment to the romantic preoccupation with the people and the national past (Politis 1993, 36–7; Veloudis 1982, 20–1). For example, in his "Philosophical Treatise on the Progress and Fall of the Old Greece" (1839), Georgios Kozakis-Tipaldos constructed a philosophy of history structured around the concepts of "morality" and "nation" (for a discussion, see Argyropoulou 1989, 82–96). Tipaldos' division of Greek history into different periods is perhaps the first attempt to construct a genealogy of Greek historical continuity undertaken by a Greek author.

14. Spiridon Zambelios' viewpoint stands in sharp contrast to the views of his father, Ioannis Zambelios. Ioannis was a typical Enlightenment representative and viewed modern Greece as a revitalization of ancient Greece. This viewpoint was slightly modified later in his life, as the influence of romanticism became stronger. For a comparison between father and son, see Tambaki (1987, 31–45).

15. Herzfeld (1982, 55–71) and Politis (1993, 58–60). For an analysis of this legacy, see Danforth (1984). Despite the resurgence of interest in folk songs, most publications simply reproduced the material of earlier collections; in some cases, the folk songs were "rewritten" to suit the ideological purposes of the authors.

16. In 1866, in the introduction to *Papisa Ioanna*, Roidis mockingly defined the "Great Idea" as the liberation of Thessaly and Epirus alone. In 1877, Nikolaos Saripolos, in a dialogue between himself and King George, defined the Greek *irredenta* as including Crete, Thessaly, Epirus, Thrace, Macedonia, the Black Sea up to Trabzond, Asia Minor, the Aegean islands, and Cyprus. King George, however, replied that such a vision was extending the boundaries of Greece too far (quoted in Politis 1993, 63).

17. On criticisms from within the Greek kingdom, see Skopetea (1988, 347–60) and Politis (1993, 101–6). Politis (1993, 72) quotes Andreas Sigros writing in 1868 that the Greeks "lived through their imagination (*fantasia*)"—the word can be rendered as "imagination" or "fantasy" depending on the context. The implication is, of course, that nationalist delusions of grandeur were rampant in this period.

18. By 1885, the Greek kingdom had 2,400 university students. The student body was more numerous per capita than in most other European states. This high number was the result of the fact that Greeks from all over the eastern Mediterranean area attended Athens University. Between 1837 and 1877, 40.7 percent of all students went into law; 31.8 percent into medicine, and the rest into theology, philosophy, mathematics, or pharmaceutics (Tsoukalas 1987, 439). The major reason for the predominance of lawyers was the ability of the profession to be absorbed into the civil sector that remained throughout the nineteenth century the most stable of urban occupations.

19. On the rise of the demoticist movement, see Dimaras (1988, 353–71) and Jusdanis (1991, 70–8). Members of the demoticist movement, such as Kostis Palamas, were also ardent nationalists (see Augustinos 1977).

20. Tsoukalas (1987, 453). For an extensive overview of the societies in Anatolia, see Mamoni (1983, 63–114) and Augustinos (1992, 162–9) for a brief summary and analysis. For the proliferation of Greek nationalism in the Greek Orthodox communities in Pontos, Asia Minor, and Cyprus, see Kitromilides (1990b, 3–17).

21. In Thrace alone, the Society for the Propagation of the Greek Letters in the 1869–

1897 period financed 3 Greek schools, 21 girls' elementary schools, and 24 boys' elementary schools. See Belia (1988, 244–51) and Tsoukalas (1987, 456).

22. For an overview, see Petrovich (1976, 1:167–222). An estimated 94 percent of the 680,000 in the Serb principality were peasants. Most of them were free peasants living outside joint families (*zadruga*s) (Dedijer et al. 1974, 283).

23. By 1850, the principality of Serbia had almost as many Serbs as the Habsburg territories. During the 1850–1910 period this trend continued; in this period the principality's population increased by 1,965,165 while the population of Serbs under Hungarian rule increased by only 216,000 (Djordjevic 1967, 57).

24. Djordjevic (1991, 311). Jovan Sterija Popović's historical novels provide a good example of the importance of Kosovo as a major literary theme (see Holton and Mihailovoch 1988, 68–9).

25. For a biography of Njegoš, see Djilas' *Niegoš* (1966) and Barac (1973, 90–5). It is indicative of the high nationalist feelings of Njegoš that in 1846 he abandoned the wearing of the Turkish fez (hat) that was common in Ottoman society at the time.

26. See Holton and Mihailovich (1988, 144–56) and Djilas (1966, 335). Kosovo was not a fight (*bitka*) or battle (*boj*) but was an incessant (*neprestana*) conflict (Bogert 1991, 180).

27. Quoted in Ekmečić (1991, 335). The poem was originally published by Karadžić in 1823 and published in its final form in 1845.

28. Quoted in Djilas (1966, 339). Reprinted with permission of Harcourt Publishers and Aleksa Djilas. This decision to "sail this crimson stream" was not an easily justified one. Eastern Orthodoxy never produced a crusade mentality comparable to that of the Catholic West. Njegoš' hero, the legendary Bishop Danilo, has to struggle between his calling to the nation's cause and his Christian ethics. His final decision to "strike for the Cross! strike for the heroic name" (Djilas 1966, 342) is not celebrated. Instead, Danilo wails over the inevitability of massacring his opponents.

29. Ilija was born in 1812 in the *pashalik* of Belgrade (in Garasi). He studied in the Greek school of Semlin in Vojvodina and entered Prince Miloš' service in 1827 (McKenzie 1985, 10–15). Garašanin's rise to such a prominent position was mainly the result of close family relations between his father Milutin and Prince Miloš, as well as the general shortage of educated personnel.

30. The literature on *Načertanije* is voluminous. For overviews, see Zlatar (1979), Hehn (1975), and McKenzie (1985, 42–61). According to McKenzie (1985, 44) and Jelavich (1962a, 29–35), Garašanin's views reflected the aspirations of the bureaucratic elite to which he belonged.

31. The Serb government's military assistance to the 1848 Habsburg Serb revolt was part of Garašanin's policy. For further discussion on the relations among Vojvodina Serbs, the Habsburgs, and the Serb government, see McKenzie (1985, 94–112; 1994, 160).

32. Ilija Garašanin's *Načertanije* (1844), reprinted in Hehn (1975, 159–60).

33. This circle included Stevan Herkalović, a Croat residing in Belgrade from 1837; the Slovak Janko Safarik; Kovačević, a former Franciscan; Pavao Carlović, a Croat and colleague of the Illyrian leader Ljudevit Gaj; Zah, the Czech émigré; and Raja Damjanović, an official of Garašanin's interior ministry (McKenzie 1985, 63–9).

34. Literacy rates were four times higher in urban than in rural areas. Similarly, in Croatia, by 1880, 25 percent of the population was considered literate and by 1910, 52

percent of the population met the literacy criteria (Jelavich 1990b, 54). The low levels of literacy resulted in a relative absence of good historical works (Petrovich 1970).

35. Stoianovich (1959, 249). See Karanovich (1987 and 1995) for a detailed description. The lyceum copied the structure and curriculum of the German institutions. Emphasis was placed on providing Serbia with native educated graduates. The initial steps of the educational system were quite difficult because the government had to overcome the peasants' mistrust and unwillingness to send their children to school instead of using them for seasonal agricultural labor (for details, see Karanovich 1995, 62–3).

36. Ekmečić (1991, 336–8). The celebration caused an international incident because the Ottoman governor of Belgrade protested regarding the celebration's anti-Ottoman spirit. The Serb government was forced to take a cautious attitude, which lasted until 1878.

37. Jelavich (1967, 104). Some members of the Croat Sabor (parliament) suggested that there were no Serbs in Bosnia but only Orthodox Croats. On the significance of the Orthodox Church for the Serbs in Habsburg territory and the constant conflict with the Catholics, see Vucinich (1967, 34–43).

# 5

## The Latecomers: Nationalism in Bulgaria, Macedonia, and Albania

The main differences between the Greek and Serbian cases and the ones discussed in this chapter are the latter's belatedness and the lack of a state sponsor. While Serb and Greek nationalisms grew strong within the confines of their respective states, the movements in pre-1878 Bulgaria, Albania, and Macedonia lacked the backing of state power and the subsequent legitimacy such support would confer. Moreover, these movements were stimulated by and responded to the possibility of territorial expansion by the Greek and Serb nation-states. The need to respond to rival nationalisms led activists in Albania, Macedonia, and Bulgaria to pay less attention to fine elaborations of their national myths, and to put more emphasis in their ability to mobilize their local populations. Unfortunately for them, the peasantry did not display a national fervor comparable to that of the activists. The superimposition of national categories on the Balkan peasantry led to acute conflict among the rivals in the post-1878 European territory of the Ottoman state. As already discussed in chapter 4, the key mechanism used by Orthodox Balkan nationalists was the *redeployment of Orthodoxy* as a facet of the people's national identity. In the central zone of the Balkans, Serbs, Greeks, and Bulgarians contested this redeployment, and the use of religious markers was frequently situational. With this contested redeployment, national identity became a source of bitter rivalry in Macedonia and Albania.

### THE BULGARIAN INTELLIGENTSIA AND THE CHURCH STRUGGLE

Bulgarian nationalism was stimulated by the Ottoman reforms of the early nineteenth century (Shaw and Shaw 1977). First, the 1826 destruction of the janissaries removed a source of fiscal oppression and intimidation. Second, the 1832–1834 liquidation of the *sipahi* property offered the peasantry the opportunity to own their land (indeed, over 85 percent of the Bulgarian peasants did so). Third, the protection of trade, proclaimed by Mustafa III in 1773, and the organization of a regular army in the place of the janissary corps created the conditions for the emergence of small-scale manufacturing and mercantile activity (Nicoloff 1987, 14–5; McDermott 1962, 64–79; Genchev 1977, 27–30, 46; Tzvetkov 1993, 1:405–6; Palairet 1997, 50–60). In the course of the nineteenth century, merchants began to move outside the traditional guild structure and establish international commercial connections. Urbanization greatly enhanced this process: The town population of the Bulgarian lands was doubled in the first three quarters of the nineteenth century. The emergence of a merchant class provided an agent willing to finance intellectuals and an audience responsive to the intellectuals' call for national regeneration (Genchev 1977, 51–3; Meininger 1979, 78).

Whereas Bulgarian traders in the pre-1820 period were generally absorbed into the Greek *ethnie* or generally identified themselves as "Roman" (Greek Orthodox), in the 1820s and 1830s these rising merchant strata began to explore their Slavic identity.[1] This trend is acutely reflected in literary production: In the 1806–1830 period only 17 Bulgarian (mostly religious) books were published; the number rose dramatically in the post-1830 period. Between the 1830s and the 1870s, about 1,600 books were published (of which 467 were translations), a major part of them in the 1860s and 1870s. The list included 294 works of fiction, 276 scientific books, 432 textbooks, 303 religious books and 230 of other various genres (Genchev 1977, 64; 1981, 109).

With the ongoing secularization of Bulgarian cultural life, a group of Bulgarian clergymen and anti-Greek intellectuals (Neofit Bozveli, Ilarion Makariopolski, and Neofit Rilski) was able to achieve control of the Bulgarian national movement. This Bulgarian intelligentsia believed that the Bulgarians ought to withdraw from the Greek sphere of influence (Genchev 1977, 62). Their victory sealed the character of the Bulgarian nationalist movement, which soon began to oppose Grecophone cultural influences. It is indicative of the strong sentiments involved that a new term appeared (*Graecomani*) to denote Bulgarians who were acculturated into Hellenism (Meininger 1974, 76; Markova 1985, 41).

This turn of events was closely related to the economic exploitation of the peasantry by the high clergy of the Ecumenical Patriarchate. By the 1820s many Bulgarian peasants were paying to the Church twice what they were required to pay to the state.[2] By 1820 the inhabitants of Varna had unsuccessfully refused to pay dues to their Greek bishop, Metodi, who was notorious for his avarice. In 1825 a similar protest against the Greek bishop of Skopje also failed. In the 1820s and 1830s, further unrest in Vratsa, Samkov, Stara Zagora, Kazanluk, and Nova Zagora signaled peasant discontent with ecclesiastical fiscal oppression (Nicoloff 1987, 38; Crampton 1983, 10–12; Genchev 1977, 68–70). The chaotic situation of the Ottoman tax system during the mid-nineteenth century (and the subsequent fiscal oppression it invited) also fueled further peasant revolts in Niš (1841) and Vidin (1850).[3] By depicting the Ecumenical Patriarchate as an alien institution, the Bulgarian intelligentsia offered to the peasantry good ideological motives to resist Greek bishops and the fiscal oppression associated with them.[4]

Throughout the nineteenth century, Protestant and Catholic missionaries, the Constantinople immigrant Bulgarian community, the Bulgarian exiles in the Danubian principalities, and the Bulgarian communities in southern Russia (especially in Odessa) all seriously influenced the direction of the Bulgarian revival.[5] In the course of the century, Constantinople emerged as a national center for the Bulgarians; by the 1860s, the Bulgarian community there numbered 32,550 merchants, artisans, and laborers.

Protest against Greek bishops in the Bulgarian lands was galvanized by the contested replacement of bishop Ilarion of Turnovo.[6] When Ilarion passed away in 1838, he was replaced by the Greek bishop Panaretos. Panaretos' selection was strongly contested by the Bulgarian community, which called for Neofit Bozveli to be assigned to them. Their request was declined. The Patriarchate appointed another Neofit, a 25-year-old Greek clergyman, with Bozveli as his assistant. By the late 1840s additional protests against Greek bishops took place in Ruse, Ohrid, Serres, Lovech, Sofia, Samokov, Vidin, Turnovo, Leskovats, Svishtov, Vratsa, Tryavna, and Plovdiv (Philipopolis) (Crampton 1983, 10–12). In 1845, when Sultan Abdul Madjid convened the judicial council provided for by the 1839 *Hatt-i-sherif*, two of the Bulgarian members raised the issue of ecclesiastical autonomy. However, this protest came to a halt after the intervention of the Russian ambassador, who did not wish to see the Ottoman Orthodox Christians divided (Tzvetkov 1993, 1:418–9; Genchev 1977, 74; Nicoloff 1987, 27–30).

In his 1839 visit, the Bulgarian clergyman and educator Neofit Bozveli discussed his dream of building a Bulgarian Church in Constantinople with members of the Bulgarian community.[7] The idea received widespread support and the Bulgarian leadership begun discussing ways to obtain a permit to do so. In 1848 the Porte agreed to the foundation of a Bulgarian church. In 1849, Bozveli's dream was realized with the establishment of the Bulgarian church *Obshtina*, which was officially recognized as a legal representative of the Bulgarian people and became an advisory body for Bulgarian communities everywhere in the empire. In matters of doctrine and ecclesiastical justice the new church was to remain subject to the Patriarchate. In addition to being the home to the Bulgarian *Obshtina*, Constantinople gradually emerged as the place where most Bulgarian newspapers and journals were published. Throughout the 1850s, 10 Bulgarian magazines were published in the Ottoman capital, 1 in Smyrna, and 2 in Rustchuk. In the 1850s and 1860s a total of 66 Bulgarian newspapers and 34 periodicals were published either in the Ottoman Empire or abroad (Genchev 1977, 107). In addition to Constantinople, where 22 newspapers were published, the other major center was Bucharest, with 18 newspapers.[8]

Following the Crimean War (1853–1856), there was an upsurge in Bulgarian education. In the 1850s and 1860s Bulgarian students studied in Vienna, Paris, Prague, Belgrade, Zagreb, Bucharest, and Constantinople. Many of them returned to Bulgaria and became teachers. Of the Bulgarian intelligentsia, 40 percent got their higher education in Russia (Odessa, Kiev, Moscow, and St. Petersburg), 30 percent in France, and the remaining 30 percent in other European countries (mainly Germany, Austria, Greece, England, and Czechoslovakia) (Genchev 1981, 104). By 1876 there were 1,500 schools in Bulgaria. The Russian government assisted the work of the Russian Pan-Slavists in selecting young students and educating them in Russia. More than 200 young Bulgarians completed their education in Russia and later became prominent leaders in Bulgaria (Genchev 1977, 99–100; Nicoloff 1987, 61–71).

In 1856, Dragan Tsankov, a teacher (later, a newspaper editor) and two merchants, Kosta Marinov and Kosta Slavchev, established the Society for Bulgarian Literature (*Obshtina na bulgarskata knizhnina*), an association for the advancement of Bulgarian letters. Through a series of publications sponsored by this association—especially the *Bulgarian Papers (Bulgarski knizhitsi)*—Bulgarian authors were able to explore a wide variety of topics such as history, current church matters, political concerns, education, linguistics, folklore, poetry, and Slavic literature (Shashko 1974a, 10–16; Moser 1972, 58). In 1859 Tsankov began publishing his newspaper *Bulgariya* and in 1866 Petko R. Slavejkov, a poet and journalist, began publishing the weekly *Makedoniya* (published both in Greek and the local Macedonian Slav dialect printed with Greek letters). In 1867 the society sponsored the foundation of the St. Cyril and Methodius School, the most important of all Bulgarian schools. By 1871 the school had 80 students and 4 teachers. It was named after the brothers Cyril and Methodius, the two monks responsible for inventing the Cyrillic alphabet, whom Bulgarian nationalists declared to be Bulgarian nationals. In fact, the St. Cyril and Methodius Day was turned into an unofficial national holiday in the 1850s and 1860s.

The activities of the society were plagued by financial difficulties, mainly because of the lack of timely payments by its subscribers (Shashko 1974a, 15). The problem was endemic to most Bulgarian publications and journals during this period. Of all the publications, the *Constantinople Journal* was to last longest (from 1848 to 1862) and three other newspapers survived more than 5 years. However, the majority of the pre-1878 publications lasted less than a year (Meininger 1976, 22; Moser 1972, 50). This did not, however, discourage the young Bulgarian intelligentsia: in 1868 the Bulgarian charitable fraternity *Prosveshtenie* (Enlightenment) was established, with the goal of spreading education and national consciousness in Macedonia (Genchev 1977, 102). In 1866 a Bulgarian reading club was established in Constantinople and its example was soon imitated in provincial towns; by 1878, there were 186 reading clubs in existence (Shashko 1974a, 16; Nicoloff 1987, 72–8). In 1869, Vassil Stoyanov and Marin Drinov, two Bulgarian intellectuals who were already familiar with Czech cultural organizations, proceeded to form the Bulgarian Learned Society, a predecessor to the Bulgarian Academy of Sciences.[9]

In a study of 56 pre-1878 editors, Meininger (1974, 292–3) showed that these young intellectuals had an average age of 34; more than half of them had previous experience as teachers; and 16 percent of them became editors while they were students or recent graduates. The need for financial assistance led these young intellectuals to become protégés of older, established merchants and traders. This led to conflicts between the older and more conservative merchants and the young radicals. Bulgarian journalists criticized Bulgarians' lack of national self-awareness and some of them (such as Karavelov and Botev) even accused the Bulgarian merchants of pretensions to social superiority, snobbism, and pro-Greek sentiments (Meininger 1976, 22–8; Moser 1972, 81).

Bulgarian authors were generally influenced by Western European romanticism. But unlike their models, the Bulgarian romantics did not revolt against a classical tradition and turn toward subjective expression. Among them, nationalism and revolutionary enthusiasm prevailed.[10] Most of their publications were nationalist, with great emphasis placed on the glorification of medieval Bulgaria and its people. The trend characterized most of Bulgarian writing on history, art, and culture during the nineteenth and early twentieth centuries. Turning to folklore, language, and history, Bulgarian scholars followed the general tenor of (especially German) romanticism in seeking to provide an idealized vision of the past.[11] As with the Serbs, folk poetry provided the most explicit tie between the intelligentsia and the "people." Bulgarian epic folk poetry was similar to that of the the the Serbs—in fact, Karadžić included songs from Macedonia in his folk collection. Another cluster of oral folk poetry was the bandit songs (*haiduski pesni*) (Moser 1972, 87). Both categories of folk songs provided material for the romantic view of the "people's culture" as a depository of national consciousness. For some of their key works, great Bulgarian authors such as Rakovski, Karavelov, and Botev repeatedly seized on the image of the bandit as freedom fighter (for an overview, see Zarev 1977, 41–72). The deployment of Christian–Muslim conflict as a national—instead of religious—struggle marked the works of the first significant Bulgarian poet, Dobri Chintulov.[12]

Of the young Bulgarian intellectuals of the 1830–1880 period, the most ardent proponents of revolutionary activity were Georgi Rakovski, Vasil Levski, Hristo Botev, and Liuben Karavelov. Rakovski was an archetype of Bulgarian romantic. He declared Bulgarians to be the first and oldest inhabitants in Europe and argued that the Bulgarians had fought the Romans in antiquity, and were Christianized by St. Paul during his mission in Macedonia. Gavril Krustevich picked up on Rakovski's claim that the Huns were Bulgarians and in 1871 wrote an entire book on the subject (Petrovich 1982, 134; Zarev 1977, 16). The goal of this literature was to provide the rising Bulgarian nation with a glorious past. Just as Serbs and Greeks viewed the *haiduk*s and *klepht*s as fighters for national liberation, Georgi Rakovski's *Gorski patnik* (Forest traveler) appropriated Bulgarian bandits as exemplars of the people's constant struggle for emancipation.[13]

It is noteworthy, however, that this group of teachers, intellectuals, publicists, and revolutionaries was unable to successfully mobilize Bulgarian society toward revolutionary action. As discussed in Chapter 3, even during the 1860s,

Karavelov and Rakovski flirted with the idea of broader Balkan federation with Serbia.[14] Most attempts to stir a full-scale rebellion failed and leaders such as Vasil Levski and Hristo Botev died as a result of them.[15] The most successful of these uprisings occurred in April of 1876 and resulted in the massacre of many thousands of Bulgarians. The news of the Ottoman reprisals gained sympathy for the Bulgarian cause throughout Europe. But even in the 1876 April uprising, popular participation was uneven, with economically developed towns taking the lead.[16] This was partly the result of geography: Bulgarians lived side by side with sizable Turkish populations. But it was also partly the result of the economic prosperity enjoyed by Bulgarian merchants and traders. They displayed an aversion to violence because their prosperity would be seriously endangered by Ottoman reprisals. Moreover, the peasantry's lack of widespread participation in the 1876 April uprising was because of their relative prosperity and their widespread ownership of land (Meininger 1974, 17–8). Both factors inhibited peasant participation in the rebellions. Instead, the Bulgarian national movement had its major following among the more educated and urban strata. Since these strata were skeptical of violent means, the intellectuals' failure to produce a mass revolutionary movement is not surprising. This failure caused pervasive feelings of pessimism among some of them, in 1875 strong enough for Petko Slavejkov to write his poem *Ne sme narod* (We are no people) (Moser 1972, 57). In it, the poet categorically declares that the Bulgarians are just "carrion," whose reply to every question or suggestion is "I don't know" or "I can't."

For the emerging Bulgarian nationalist movement, the problem of defining the "Bulgarians" was troublesome because the "Bulgarian lands" (e.g., northern Bulgaria, Thrace, and Macedonia) were by no means inhabited by just one ethnic group. Jews and Greeks dominated in many cities, Gagauzes (Turkish-speaking Christians), Circassians, Turks, Pomaks (Bulgarian-speaking Muslims), Armenians, Gypsies, Hellenized Vlachs, Romanian-speaking Vlachs, and Catholic Bulgarians were all present in these territories. Even the *vilayet* of Danube (i.e., northern Bulgaria), where ethnic Bulgarians predominated, was ethnically diverse (Todorov 1969; Ashley 1985). The Bulgarian movement formed its center between 1821 and 1839 around the regional elites of the Stara Planina towns and from there it expanded outward to the rest of the Ottoman Balkan territory, providing a challenge to the Serb and Greek national centers of Belgrade and Athens (Ashley 1985, 42; Meininger 1974, 123). This region was the homeland of almost 50 percent of Bulgarian intellectuals during the 1835–1878 period. Of the 191 intellectuals studied by Meininger (1974, 124–6), 67.4 percent were born either in northern Bulgaria or in Stara Planina towns. Judging from their father's occupation, most of them came from a middle-class urban background: 22 percent of their fathers were large-scale businessmen, 19 percent were small-scale businessmen, and 12.4 percent were artisans.

For this nationalist intelligentsia, the issue of ecclesiastical autonomy rose from the desire to gain an institutional outlet for Bulgarian national organization within the context of the *millet* system. The movement also expressed a desire to overcome the "fusion" of the Bulgarians with Greeks and to assert Bulgarian national uniqueness—a trend most prominent in the peripheral regions of Macedonia, Adrianople, Thrace, the Black Sea coast and Dobrudja (Markova 1985, 41). The close connection between church autonomy and national self-assertion is revealed in a circular letter of 1851 from the Bulgarian community in Bucharest ending with the pregnant phrase, "Without a national Church there is no salvation" (quoted in Crampton 1983, 10–2).

In 1856, the Ottoman government's major reform act, the *Hatt-i-Humayun*, ordered *millet* reorganization, a move that paved the way for Bulgarian demands for an independent church. When the Grand Vizier Ali Pasha returned from the 1856 Paris Peace Conference, Bulgarian representatives filed a petition asking recognition of the Bulgarians as a separate people, different from the *Rum millet*. Their action illustrated the extent to which Ottoman Balkan society had changed during the eighteenth and nineteenth centuries. Whereas in the eighteenth century, the Ecumenical Patriarchate maintained that religion and not ethnicity was the major ascriptive criterion for Ottoman Orthodox Christians, the new Bulgarian movement shifted the definition of solidarity from a religious to an ethnic basis. The claim to a separate Bulgarian confessional organization was based on the premise of the existence of the Bulgarian nation (Markova 1985, 41). In itself this premise implied that only ethnic Greeks should be members of the *Rum millet*. The Patriarchate had just fought a bitter conflict over a similar trend with the state-sponsored Greek Church between 1830 and 1850—as discussed in Chapter 4. The new challenge further circumscribed the boundaries of patriarchal authority. Moreover, the Bulgarian crusade for a national church entailed a direct challenge to the whole Ottoman concept of administration, which identified nationality with religious confession.

The position of the Patriarchate was in many respects similar to that of the papacy and the medieval Roman Catholic Church. Theirs was a universal church that united the faithful in terms of religion alone. But, just as Protestantism challenged papal authority, Balkan nationalisms challenged not only the Great Church's authority, but also the whole conception that underlay the organization of the *millet* system. The Constantinople Society (*Obshtina*) requested all local branches (*obshtinas*) to send petitions to the Porte supporting their original request of Ali Pasha. In 1857, some 20 representatives from Bulgarian towns were assembled in Constantinople; together with 40 Bulgarians from the local community they addressed more than 60 petitions and requests to the Porte (Genchev 1977, 111). The Ottoman government, however, remained indifferent. Initially, Russian ambassador Novikov told the Bulgarians that he would not support their mission; however, the Russians, afraid of alienating the Bulgarian constituency, appealed to the Patriarchate. The Patriarchate responded in 1858 by making Ilarion Makariopolski bishop *in partibus* (without seat) of the Bulgarian Church in Constantinople and in 1859 the Ecumenical Patriarch laid the foundation stone of the new Bulgarian church. Bulgarian communities were also allowed to use

Slavic as the church language in regions such as Adrianople and Philipopolis (Nicoloff 1987, 40–41; Pundeff 1969, 113–5; Tzvetkov 1993, 2:439–52).

By October 1858 a religious council was convoked for dealing with church reforms. The Bulgarian representatives submitted a petition requesting that bishops be elected by the parishioners, that the bishops speak the language of their parishioners, and that their salaries be fixed and misappropriations of funds be stopped. When these demands were ignored, they requested the restoration of the Turnovo and Ohrid patriarchates and the right of people to elect their bishops, and refused to recognize the church debt to the Ottoman government (7,000,000 *piastres* at the time). The council concluded its sessions in February 1860. It categorically rejected the Bulgarian demands, declaring them incompatible with Church canons. The Bulgarian response to the assembly's decision was a major turning point of the Church question. On Easter Sunday 1860, Bishop Ilarion of Macariopolis, with the general approbation of the Bulgarian community, omitted the name of the Patriarch during the celebration of the liturgy and included instead that of the Sultan. This act meant that he no longer recognized the Patriarch as his spiritual chief. The Patriarchate excommunicated Ilarion and his supporters, including Bishop Paisius of Plovdiv (an Albanian) and Bishop Auxentius of Veles (Meininger 1970, 19–20) and successfully requested that the Ottoman government send them into exile.

The reaction of the Bulgarians to the events of Easter Sunday 1860 was swift. Thirty-three towns petitioned the Sultan expressing their solidarity with Ilarion, as did 734 merchants who were gathered at the Uzundjovo fair. During the 1860s many Bulgarians refused to pay taxes to the Patriarchate and the towns of Lovech, Samokov, Shumen, Preslav, and Vidin all refused to recognize the Bulgarian bishops who had been appointed by the Patriarch (Crampton 1983, 14). Still, the Bulgarian movement lacked Russian support of their goals. The Russian diplomats, following their traditional claim of being protectors of the Orthodox Christians, did not desire to fragment the Orthodox community. With Russian aid absent, the French aided the Bulgarian activist Dragan Tsankov and the pro-Catholic faction of the Bulgarian movement to institute a Catholic Bulgarian church (Nicoloff 1987, 45–50; McDermott 1962, 157–9; Tzvetkov 1993, 1:444–5). These plans turned out to be short-lived.[17] The Russian representatives intervened to secure their failure. Russian policy did not wish to see the Bulgarians moving outside the Orthodox faith since this would imply a significant loss of influence for Russia.

In 1864, when Count Ignatiev assumed the post of the Russian ambassador, Russian policy moved toward a reconciliation between Bulgarians and the Patriarchate (McDermott 1962, 161; Meininger 1970, 31–97). Ignatiev promoted the recognition of the Bulgarian Church by the Patriarchate (but not by the Sultan) and attempted to support fellow Slavs (and Russian foreign policy objectives) without breaking up the unity of the Eastern Church. Ignatiev enlisted the support of Bulgarian nationalists, but it was also among the most extreme nationalists that reaction against his attempts came. In 1867, Patriarch Gregorios

VI put forward a provisional plan suggesting a rapprochement. By that date, most appointed bishops had been expelled from the Bulgarian towns owing to the actions of the Bulgarian nationalists; thus, the Patriarchate had lost de facto control over the Bulgarian dioceses. The Patriarch's plan provided for a Bulgarian ecclesiastical territory extending from the Danube south to the Balkan mountains. The Bulgarians rejected the plan because it excluded Thrace and Macedonia. Then, the Grand Vizier Ali pasha developed a compromise plan recognizing ecclesiastical independence and the right of the Bulgarian population to have its own bishops, and in 1868 the Ottoman Council of Ministers approved a six-point program that permitted the Bulgarians to elect their own bishops and to retain the churches built at their own expense.

As a result of this decision, the ecclesiastical conflict between Greeks and Bulgarians intensified and the Ottoman government became an important player. The Ottomans manipulated the situation in order to divide the Balkan Christians and negate any future plans of Balkan cooperation (Markova 1983, 163). The plan worked, and until 1912 the Balkan states were unable to create a coalition among themselves to fight the empire. The "apple of discord" was Macedonia: Bulgarians claimed most of it (and most of Thrace) for themselves on the basis that the population was Bulgarian, whereas the Greeks viewed these claims as assaults on territories they considered to be rightfully theirs. When the Ottoman *firman* of 12 March 1870 officially established a Bulgarian Exarchate, it further complicated this situation. The *firman* limited the exarchate's jurisdiction to the Danubian Bulgaria (the area between Danube and Stara Planina mountain); however, it provided (Article 10) that the Exarchate could add additional dioceses if in a plebiscite two-thirds or more of the population voted to join it.[18] By 1878 the Bulgarian Exarchate included 18 dioceses with approximately 2,000,000 to 2,400,0000 people as its subjects (Markova 1988, 45–9). Although the initial phase of the Exarchate was short-lived (1870 to 1879), the organization imitated the patriarchal tendency to provide political support to the Ottoman administration. The newly born Exarchate considered requests for Bulgarian political independence to be extremely premature.

The Patriarchate summoned a council of Orthodox ecclesiastical leaders and— despite Ignatiev's plotting against an agreement—on 28 September 1872 the council members proclaimed the Bulgarian Church schismatic and all its adherents to be heretics. Surrender of Orthodoxy to ethnic nationalism was cited as the major reason for the proclamation of the schism (Meininger 1970, 189–90; Markova 1983, 162). From this point on, religious alliances became in effect national alliances; to be a follower of the Exarchate or the Patriarchate was to proclaim one's national identity. In the early 1870s Russian policy tacitly supported the Bulgarian Exarchate by influencing the Romanian and Serb Orthodox churches to adopt a favorable stand (Markova 1983, 69, 175–92). By 1873– 1874 the application of the infamous Article 10 became again the subject of diplomatic maneuvers; and Ignatiev unsuccessfully attempted once again to achieve a Greco-Bulgarian reconciliation. After the 1878 Berlin Treaty, the Exarchate lost authority in regions annexed to Romania and Serbia and a separate synod was set up in Sofia to govern the dioceses within the Bulgarian principality. Despite requests by the Patriarchate to move the seat of the Exarchate to the Bulgarian principality and restrict its authority to the principality, the Bulgarian Exarch continued to reside in Constantinople. Limited autonomy was offered to the Bulgarian bishoprics in Macedonia that continued to be administered by the Exarchate (Tzvetkov 1993, 1:519; Kolev 1991).

During the last quarter of the nineteenth century, Patriarch Joachim III repeatedly attempted to find a solution to the Bulgarian schism (Kofos 1984, 1986; Anagnostopoulou 1997, 422–44). The Patriarch's plans entailed the rejection of the "nationality principle" by the two sides—a viewpoint in accordance with the Church's eighteenth-century universalist orientation. But neither side could endorse such a viewpoint. It was not only that Bulgarian nationalists viewed the Exarchate as a means for their national self-assertion (Markova 1988, 49; Kofos 1984, 367). Greek nationalists from within the Greek kingdom—especially the Association for the Propagation of Greek Letters—adopted the view that the schism was beneficial to them because it allowed them to carry out nationalist propaganda presumably on behalf of the Patriarchate. By the early 1880s the association had in effect become the major vehicle for the Greek nationalist mobilization in Macedonia and Thrace (see Chapter 4). Its members, in close contact with the Greek consuls, were proceeding to organize a Greek resistance to the flow of Bulgarian nationalist propaganda. Reports from the consuls indicated that major complaints existed regarding the attitude of the majority of the bishops. In most cases the bishops refused to cede authority in matters traditionally under Church jurisdiction. Constantinos Paparrigopoulos expressed his desire that the Greek nationalists seize control of the ecclesiastical establishment (Kofos 1986, 110–1).

During the 1879–1884 period and also when he returned to the patriarchal seat in 1901, Patriarch Joachim III expressed a very different view. He considered that Greek policy was "irresponsible," that private individuals ought not be trusted with educational tasks, and that the clergy should keep control of the educational establishments. The Patriarch expressed the more ecumenical viewpoint that Church policy should not be subordinated to the interests of the Greek state. He called for the creation of a university in Constantinople so that the monopoly of the Athens university would be terminated and he attempted to bring nationalist organizations under his control. These schemes failed in Macedonia, where the Greek nationalists were successful in setting up their own network. The Patriarch succeeded mainly in Anatolia, Thrace, and Constantinople, where the benevolent society *Agapate Allilous* (founded in 1880) successfully countered the propaganda of the Association for the Propagation of Greek Letters (Kofos 1986, 113; Mamoni 1975, 106; 1988–1990, 218). The Patriarch's vision was closer to that of the Ottoman reformers of the *Tanzimat* period and collided with that of Greek and Bulgarian nationalisms.

Map 2
The Boundaries of the Bulgarian State According to the San Stefano Treaty
(1878)

## MACEDONIA: THE "APPLE OF DISCORD"

With the establishment of the principalities of Bulgaria and Eastern Romilia
in 1878 as well as with their unification in 1885, part of the Bulgarian nationalist
aspirations were satisfied. Still, Bulgarian nationalists aimed toward the acquisition of the lands granted to Bulgaria by the 1878 San Stefano Treaty—that is,
Ottoman Macedonia and Thrace (see Maps 2 and 3). "The San Stefano Treaty
became the *sui generis* metahistorical event in the development of Bulgarian
nationalism, a dream almost come true, and an *idée fixe* for decades to come"
(Todorova 1995, 77). The extent to which the annexation of Macedonia was
considered a future certainty is illustrated by the fact that Marin Drinov, one of
Bulgaria's most noted scholars and politicians, successfully bid for Sofia to
become the capital of the Bulgarian principality (Tzvetkov 1993, 1:521). Although Sofia had only 20,000 inhabitants at the time, he believed that the capital

**Map 3**
**Bulgaria and Macedonia after the Treaty of Berlin (1878)**

ought to be situated in a region in close contact and with good communications with Macedonia. "Macedonia" meant the three *vilayets* of Salonica, Monastir, and Kosovo. The region was not called "Macedonia" by the Ottomans and the name "Macedonia" gained currency with the ascent of rival nationalisms (Adanir 1984/85, 43–4; Wilkinson 1951).

During the Stambolov regime (1887–1894) the Bulgarian state used the Bulgarian Exarchate to foster the development of Bulgarian national identity in Macedonia and Thrace (Perry 1993). This strategy had limited official success: In July 1890 the Sultan issued permissions (*berats*) for Bulgarian bishops in Skopje and Ohrid, and in 1894 the metropolitans of Nevrokop and Veles also obtained their permissions (Kolev 1991, 44). This approach reflected the increasingly conservative attitude of the Exarchate leadership who were hostile to violence and preferred to work with peaceful means to gain peasant support (Markova 1988, 46–7; Poulton 1995, 51). However, the predominance of the clergy among the ranks of the intelligentsia was dwindling: By the 1870s teachers made up 50.5 percent of all intellectuals and the clergy took second place with 33.5 percent (Kolev 1991, 40). The Bulgarian movement benefited greatly by the disarray of the Greek side (Vakalopoulos 1988, 42–3, 263). Persistent conflicts occurred between Greek nationalist organizations and local bishops over the control of educational institutions. The venality of the metropolitans and the low quality of the clergy further added to the difficulties faced by the Greek nationalists. By the 1890s, the influence of the Patriarchate had declined in favor of the Bulgarian Exarchate and the Serb Church (Lange-Akhund 1998, 28–33).

The consolidation of a Bulgarian nation-state and calls for its territorial expansion directly threatened the Greek and Serb aspirations outlined in Chapter 4. Greek populations were scattered in mostly coastal areas and urban cities in the Ottoman Balkans. Macedonian towns such as Monastir (Bitola), Thracian cities such as Plovdiv (Philipopolis), or villages such as Arbanasi near Turnovo were predominantly Greek. In southern Macedonia in particular, there was no way of clearly drawing ethnic boundaries because Bulgarian, Greek, and Vlach communities were scattered throughout the region. The Greek claims received strong support from Grecophone Vlach populations in northwestern Macedonia (Vakalopoulos 1986, 56; Vermulen, 1984). Perhaps the only meaningful generalization pertained to the presence of a sizable Slavic majority in northern Macedonia and of a sizable Greek majority in the urban areas and in southern Macedonia, including coastal areas such as the Chalkidiki peninsula (Tzvetkov 1993, 1:442; Vakalopoulos 1986, 51–7). Between the northern and southern zones lay a wide region where population was mixed, with no clear majority and sometimes without even a clear notion of national identity. In this middle zone, Slavic-speaking populations predominated in numbers, while Greek speakers, being wealthier and more urban, predominated in influence (Vouri 1992, 47–58). Between 1830 (particularly after 1878) and 1912 the population of this intermediate territory shifted loyalties repeatedly depending on the success of particular national propagandas.[19]

The "apples of discord" for Balkan nationalists were, first, the Orthodox Slavic-speaking inhabitants of Ottoman Macedonia and, second, the bilinguals. During the nineteenth century, the increase in the Orthodox population of Ottoman Macedonia led many Macedonian Slavs to move into the urban regions. This population rivaled the established urban groups of Greeks, Vlachs, and Jews. These Slavic-speakers or Macedonian Slavs did not display a clear-cut support for any particular side (Lunt 1984, 108; Adanir 1984/85). Greeks claimed them because they were Orthodox; Serbs and Bulgarians declared them as their own on the basis of their Slavic language. Among at least some of the Slavic-speaking population, the word "Macedonia" slowly became a term colored with an ethnic as opposed to a purely regional significance. Among this avant-garde was Grigor Prlichev, whose poem "The Bandit," written in Greek, won a prize in a competition held in Athens in 1860. Although offered a scholarship, he turned down the offer and went in search of his own ethnic roots. He spent 5 months in Constantinople learning the "Slavic language" and returned to Ohrid with the intention of teaching it to the local population (Danforth 1995, 62–3). Needless to say, Prlichev ended up in prison because the local bishop opposed the use of any language other than Greek into the schools and churches. Prlichev's story illustrates not only the shifting identity of the local Slavic population but also the extent of bilingualism. Bilingualism was widespread among peddlers, merchants, and other people who frequently learned more than one language for professional reasons. For example, it was common practice to write Bulgarian commercial correspondence using the Greek alphabet (Todorova 1990).

For the first part of the nineteenth century, the Bulgarian church movement enjoyed the support of the Macedonian Slavs. In fact, in this period no clear distinction between a Slavic Macedonian and a Bulgarian intelligentsia is possible. The development of private schools teaching the Cyrillic alphabet was slow (1843 Prilep, 1859 Ohrid, 1868 Monastir) (Vouri 1992, 23–4; Friedman 1985, 33). Bulgarian nationalist activity in Ottoman Macedonia originated in 1845 when the Russian linguist Victor Grigorovic visited Macedonia and met the teachers Constantin and Dimitri Miladinov. Both were natives of western Macedonia and had received their education in Greek. Grigorovic had a considerable intellectual influence on Dimitri Miladinov, who abandoned his pro-Greek orientation and adopted a Bulgarian nationalist outlook. His ideological transformation is manifested in his signatures on various documents: He calls himself Miladinidis in 1840, Miladin in 1846, Miladinos in 1855, and Miladinov in 1857 (Tachiaos 1974, 33). The Miladinov brothers began teaching in Bulgarian and even published in Zagreb a folk song collection of Bulgarian Macedonian songs in 1861. The collection was published with the help of pro-Yugoslav bishop Strossmayer, to whom the book was dedicated. They were captured by the Ottomans, accused of working for the Roman Catholic Church, and imprisoned. While in prison, they died of typhus in 1862.

In the second half of the nineteenth century, Serbs, Greeks, and Bulgarians used educational and religious institutions to "convince" the local population that they belonged to the Serb, Greek, or Bulgarian nation. For example, in 1878 the Serb government adopted the *ekavian* dialect as the official language in an indirect attempt to bring the Serb language closer to the spoken vernacular of the Macedonian Slavs (Poulton 1995, 63). This strategy was a response to the fragmentation of the Bulgarian intelligentsia during the second half of the nineteenth century. The first literary Bulgarian figures wrote in western Macedonian-Bulgarian vernacular (Todorova 1990, 444). However, after 1850 the Stara Plannina towns became the nucleus of the national movement. This led to the gradual adoption of the eastern Bulgarian variant as the standard literary language. In 1836 Vasil Aprilov, the Bulgarian merchant who financed the first secular school in Bulgaria (1835), suggested that the eastern Bulgarian dialect be adopted as the basis of literary language. In the post-1856 period, the Society for Bulgarian Literature also promoted the eastern Bulgarian variant as the major literary language (Genchev 1977, 66; Shashko 1974a, 11; Friedman 1975, 90).

The western Bulgarian-Macedonian intelligentsia resented the victory of the eastern Bulgarian variant and between 1857 and 1880 16 textbooks were published in the western Bulgarian-Macedonian dialect. In the post-1878 period, the emerging Bulgarian educational system gradually codified the Bulgarian language, finally introducing the Drinov-Ivanchev orthography in 1899 (Todorova 1995, 77). Therefore, the Serb strategy aimed at increasing the gap between the two variants in order to incorporate the Macedonian Slavs into the Serb nation. When in 1891, Macedonian students in Bulgaria published a periodical (*Loza*) aiming at the creation of a Macedonian literary language, they soon discovered that "Macedonian separatism" was unwelcome. The journal was banned in 1892. In 1894, a new periodical, *Vardar*, which demanded linguistic autonomy for the Macedonian Slavs, appeared in Belgrade (Adanir 1992, 180).

While the Serbs proceeded to increase their nationalist and educational efforts in Macedonia, as discussed in Chapter 4, the Bulgarians and Greeks did much the same. By 1876 there were 350 Bulgarian schools in Macedonia alone and their number grew to 800 in 1900 for all Ottoman European territories (Georgeoff 1973, 153–5; Poulton 1995, 64–5). Before the Balkan wars of 1912–1913 the number of Bulgarian schools reached its peak: 1,141 schools operated with 1,884 teachers and 65,474 students. The Greek nationalist efforts received a boost only after the 1878 San Stefano Treaty. The realization of an immediate threat to their Macedonian *irredenta* led the Greeks to redefine their goals. The northern part of Ottoman Macedonia was "written off" and attention was concentrated in the middle and southern zones (Kofos 1980, 49, 52–3). Emphasis was put on education, and scholarships for study at the University of Athens were made available to local students. The Association for the Propagation of Greek Letters was initially in charge of these efforts. After 1881, a special governmental committee took over this task. By 1894 there were approximately 907 Greek schools with 1,245 teachers and 53,633 students (Vakalopoulos 1988, 157, 129–69; Vouri 1992). Suggestions by Macedonian Greeks to send armed bandits into the region were turned down by the Greek government. Greek guerrilla activity was initiated only after the 1903 Illinden uprising—to be discussed later on in this chapter.

Slowly the differentiation between Macedonian and Bulgarian intelligentsias led to calls for an autonomous or independent Macedonian state. In 1871, Petko Slavejkov wrote in his newspaper *Makedoniya* that those who called themselves *Macedonists* (*Makendisti*) were Macedonians and not Bulgarians (quoted in Slipijevic 1958, 116). By 1893 the Macedonian Question was complicated further with the foundation of the Internal Macedonian Revolutionary Organization (IMRO or VMRO) in Thessaloniki. Of the six founding members, four were teachers who had studied abroad, and three of them had participated in the publication of the journal *Loza*—discussed earlier (Lange-Akhund 1998, 36).[20]

The IMRO leadership's goal was an autonomous Macedonian state, possibly one that would be part of a broader Balkan federation. The organization created secret means of communication and established branches in the villages. Because of its initial small size (15 to 20 participants between 1893 and 1896) the group's existence remained unknown to Ottoman authorities until 1897 (Lange-Akhund 1998, 42–3).

In Bulgaria, Macedonian charitable clubs had been operating since the 1880s. They provided help to refugees from Macedonia and drew attention to their plight. In 1895 the Supreme Macedonian Committee was founded in Sofia. Soon, it developed strong ties with the IMRO leadership. Dominated by people with a military background, the committee viewed the IMRO as an instrument of Bulgarian policy, thus drawing sharp criticism from the more left-wing IMRO activists. Nevertheless, the IMRO maintained ties with the Bulgarian nationalists (Lang-Akhund 1998, 44–52; Adanir 1992, 179).

During the 1899–1903 period, the two groups cooperated with each other; their cooperation eventually culminated in the famous 1903 Illinden uprising. For a short period of time, the revolutionaries captured the city of Krusevo and declared Macedonian independence. However, the Ottoman forces acted promptly and crushed the revolt with swift force (for details, see Lange-Akhund 1998; Perry 1988). In the aftermath of the bloodshed caused by the revolt, Franz-Joseph of Austria-Hungary and Tsar Nicholas II of Russia met in Murzsteg and, with the support of the other European powers, imposed a program of reform on Macedonia.[21] The reform program introduced international representatives and military officers into Ottoman Macedonia. Their goal was to preserve the peace in the province by modernizing Ottoman administration. Not surprisingly, the program was viewed as a further humiliation by the Ottomans. Its implementation drew sharp criticism by the Ottoman officers, and it was one of the major reasons for the 1908 Young Turk revolution.

In 1903, simultaneously with the Illinden uprising, Krste Missirkov, a teacher and author from Macedonia, published his book *On Macedonian Matters* in Sofia. Missirkov claimed that the Macedonian Slavs had an identity separate from the Bulgarian one. Authorities in Sofia confiscated copies of the book. Following the failed 1903 Ilinden uprising, the Greek government decided to sponsor paramilitary activities in Ottoman Macedonia. The resulting Greek–Bulgarian paramilitary confrontation lasted until the 1908 Young Turk revolution (for a review, see Dakin 1966). The result of all this nationalist activity was that Ottoman Macedonia plunged into a prolonged period of anarchy, terrorism, and destruction from the 1890s forward. Thousands of people immigrated to the United States in a desperate attempt to find a better future (Gounaris 1989; Petkovski 1981). This chaotic situation provided the background against which the Young Turk military officers organized their 1908 movement, already described in Chapter 3.

## THE ALBANIAN NATIONAL MOVEMENT

The difficulties facing the Albanian national movement were considerable. First, the Albanians lived scattered throughout the western Balkans, and were divided by religion into Catholics, Muslims, and Orthodox. Because the Ottoman system operated on the basis of religion rather than ethnicity, it was difficult for them to find an institutional outlet for the expression of their national identity.[22] Second, Albanians were subdivided into two main groups, the Geghs of the northern part and the Tosks of the southern part. Moreover, among the highlanders of the Kosovo plateau and northern Albania, the persistence of a clan-based society did not allow for effective political mobilization. Albanian nationalism found considerable support in the central and southern parts of Albania. Some of its key speakers belonged to the dominant groups of conservative landowners and other members of the Ottoman elite. These groups were not favorably disposed toward radicalism and their actions were often prompted by their desire to protect their wealth and property from encroachment by Serbia and Greece.

The Albanian *Rilindja* (rebirth) period (1878–1912) refers to cultural mobilization for national self-assertion. Because AbdulHamid's government censored all forms of national expression, many works on Albanian issues were published in Bucharest, which hosted a large Albanian community (Ianovici 1971a; 1971b). Scores of Albanian intellectuals were educated in Greek schools. Consequently, many of them were favorably predisposed toward Greece, cooperated with Greeks, wrote literature, prose, and poetry in Greek, and advocated the use of the Greek alphabet for the Albanian language.[23]

The dominant figures of this period, the Frasheri brothers (Abdyl, Naim, and Sami), were schooled in the famous Zosimaia Greek School in Janina and worked for the Ottoman bureaucracy. In 1877 in Constantinople, the brothers founded the Central Committee for the Defense of the Rights of the Albanian People and the following year they participated in the League of Prizren. They were also responsible for extensive cultural mobilization, by founding societies, writing, and publishing.[24] Unlike their neighbors, however, in the Albanian case cultural mobilization followed the initial political mobilization. This was a reflection of the belatedness of the Albanian movement. For example, when the League of Prizren (1878) was formed, there was still no agreement among the intellectuals on a common Albanian alphabet. Each religious community (Catholic, Orthodox, Muslim) used a different alphabet (Latin, Greek, Ottoman Turkish). It was only in 1879 that Sami Frasheri devised a phonetic system relying primarily on Latin letters, with the addition of Greek and Cyrillic characters. However, the debate on a standardized Albanian alphabet persisted until 1900–1910.

The Albanian political movement was articulated over the 1878–1881 period, mainly as a reaction to the San Stefano Treaty.[25] The Serb army temporarily occupied parts of Kosovo. The realization that Kosovo might be annexed to Serbia prompted a coalition of conservative Muslim landowners and Albanian progressive intellectuals and bureaucrats who gathered in the city of Prizren in Kosovo. They protested the annexation of Albanian territory by Serbia or Greece and focused attention on the Albanian national question. National sentiments were strong in the views of the representatives of the southern part; these sentiments blended with the desire of northern leaders to exempt themselves from taxation and the draft (Jacques 1995, 258–60; Fischer 1995, 29; Vickers 1998, 44–5; Skendi 1967, 55–108; Malcolm 1998, 224–30). The Prizren League petitioned the Sultan to unite the *vilayets* of Janina, Monastir, Shkoder, and Kosovo into one political and administrative unit. In an effort to prevent Serb expansion, the league also contemplated a union between Greece and Albania (Pitouli-Kitsou 1997, 30). This idea persisted for some time, setting the stage for an ambiguous Greek–Albanian relationship of collaboration and competition.[26] On 8 May 1880 the league declared itself the autonomous provincial government of Albania. This action led to a reversal of the Ottoman tolerance of the league's actions. In 1881, the Ottoman forces reestablished control over Albanian territory and the league leaders were prosecuted or exiled.

In the post-1878 period, intellectuals, bureaucrats, and other elite members involved with the league of Prizren pursued Albanian cultural mobilization. This was a difficult task because of the Albanians' internal divisions, their low literacy rates, the Ottoman prohibition of nationalist activities, and competition from Greeks in the south. Although the results were meager, they indicated nationalism's success among the intelligentsia. Sami Frasheri's 1899 political manifesto *Albania—What Was It, What Is It and What Will Become of It? Reflections on Saving the Motherland from Perils Which Beset It* was the first monograph advocating an independent Albania, including proposals for education, public works, agriculture, industry, and an independent church (Elsie 1985, 1:246–8).

During the first decade of the twentieth century, Greek and Albanian educational societies competed with each other in the south. The Greek councils' reports indicate that the primarily religious identity of the Orthodox Christians in the region did not readily translate into support for the Greek side. On the contrary, the use of the Albanian language facilitated the development of Albanian national identity (Pitouli-Kitsou 1997, 94–104). Although the Ecumenical Patriarchate issued in September 1908 a decree suggesting that the Christian population preserve its amicable relations with the Muslims, Greek–Albanian rivalry persisted. The Albanians sought to establish schools taught in their own language. This was resisted by the Ottomans, as well as, by the Patriarchate, which was threatened with loss of its educational monopoly (Elsie 1985, 1:282–3).

In addition to dealing with the strong Greek cultural presence, the Albanian nationalists had to face the gradual expansion of the Serb sphere of influence in Kosovo. In 1893 the first Serb bookshop opened in Pristina (Vickers 1998,

57). The joint efforts of the Serb and Montenegrin governments also led to the consecration of a Serb, Archyncellus Dionisije Ptetrović, to the Raska-Prizren bishopric (1896–1900). Following the Serb government's directions, the new bishop reorganized educational and religious institutions, opened new schools, renewed the teaching staff, and united the Serb activists (Batakovic 1992, 132).

Still, however slowly, the Albanians were able to found their own schools. Petro Nini Luarasi was the first teacher who taught Albanian in the south. With the financial assistance of Nikola Naco, Luarasi was able to found several schools between 1883 and 1886. In 1887, he was excommunicated by Kyrilos, the metropolitan of Korytsa. The first officially recognized Albanian school was opened in Korytsa in 1887 (for details, see Jacques 1995, 290–5). In the 1880s and 1890s there was a proliferation of Albanian journalism and publishing. The first Albanian weekly, *Pellasgos*, appeared in 1860–1861 in Lamia (central Greece) and was published in both Greek and Albanian (Jacques 1995, 298; Elsie 1985, 1:304). Also, the official Turkish-language publication of the *vilayet* of Shkoder, *Ishkodra*, was taken over by the League of Prizren in 1879 to 1880. During the same period, in Athens, Anastasios Kulluriotis began publishing a weekly newspaper, *I Foni tis Alvanias*, in both Greek and Albanian and using the Greek alphabet for both languages. The first scholarly review of Albanian studies, the journal *Drita* (Light) appeared in 1884 with Sami Frasheri as its director (Jacques 1995, 290). As in the Greek, Serb, and Bulgarian cases, considerable effort was expended in recovering and recording the Albanian oral folk tradition (Elsie 1985, 1:292–304).

A decisive factor in the success of the Albanian cultural revival was the interest of Italy and the Habsburg monarchy, who were determined to prevent the expansion of Greece and Serbia into the western Balkans (Skendi 1967, 238–86). Specifically, the Italians founded schools, consultancies, and commercial agencies as a means of increasing their influence, thereby helping to expose many Albanians to Western ideas (for details, see Fischer 1985; Skendi 1967, 215–37). In addition, Albanian intellectuals and bureaucrats participated extensively in the Young Turk movement during the pre-1908 period. Indeed, the participation of Albanian troops in the 1908 revolution contributed significantly to its success. The news that the revolution was supported by Albanian forces, considered to be the most loyal to the Sultan, made Sultan AbdulHamid willing to surrender his power to the Young Turks.

On November 1908, an Albanian congress was held in Monastir in Ottoman Macedonia with the purpose of improving Frasheri's initial alphabet. However, two currents emerged, one favoring the Latin alphabet and another favoring Arabic script. The congress did provide a further improvement on Frasheri's alphabet, but did not settle the issue completely; consequently, the use of different alphabets persisted (Jacques 1995, 308; Vickers 1998, 64–5; and Elsie 1985, 1:242–3 for details). The Latin Albanian alphabet caused the strong reaction of the Young Turks as well as that of the Orthodox metropolitan of Skopje, who signed a decree for the suppression of this "alien script" (Malcolm

1998, 243). The Organization of Ottoman Serbs, founded in Skopje after 1908, also joined in this campaign. On the Albanian side, leadership in linguistic and cultural matters did not come from the northerners and Kosovo Albanians, but rather from the southerners, as well as the Albanians of Ottoman Macedonia.

The Albanian declaration of independence was the work of Ismail Kemal, the son of a wealthy Muslim landowner from the city of Vlora. Kemal studied in the Zosimaia School of Janina and became an Ottoman bureaucrat. He participated in the Young Turk movement of the early 1900s, but his relationship with them deteriorated after the 1908 revolution (Fischer 1995, 31–2). In 1907 Ismail Kemal concluded an agreement with the Greek government of premier G. Theotokis. The agreement signaled the abandonment of the Greek position of absorbing Albanians into Hellenism and the acceptance of an independent Albanian state (Pitouli-Kitsou 1997, 48–56). Secret agreements pledged the support of Greek cultural societies for the introduction of the Albanian language into Greek schools. The agreement was never fully implemented because Albanian nationalists in the south opposed territorial concessions to the Greeks. However, the Greek state was interested in preserving its influence among the Orthodox Christians of the south.

The Young Turks' centralization policies in the post-1908 period quickly alienated the Albanians and led to a series of revolts over the 1908–1911 period (Jacques 1995, 262–73; Malcolm 1998, 239–44). Kosovo Albanians viewed the Ottomans' efforts to impose the draft and tax collection as an infringement on their traditional self-government. These local demands led to calls for regional autonomy with minimal interference from the Ottoman government. In 1912 Hasan Bey of Pristina led another revolt in Kosovo. It quickly drew the participation of almost 45,000 Albanians and forced the Ottomans to the 18 August 1912 granting of Albanian autonomy. Most of the fighting took place in the northern part of the country and in Kosovo, where the centralization policies of the Young Turks were particularly resented by the local clan leaders. The turmoil led to an estimated 150,000 people's fleeing Kosovo, including close to 100,000 Serbs (Vickers 1998, 70–2; Malcolm 1998, 245–50). The Albanian paramilitary groups involved in these uprisings received the support of Serb societies such as the infamous *Ujedinjenje ili Smrt* group (discussed in Chapter 6). In 1912 the Serb government offered the Albanians a guarantee of freedom of religion; use of their language in education, courts, and local administration; and a separate Albanian assembly to deal with religious, educational, and legal matters (Mikic 1987, 170). The agreement was conditional on the Albanians' acceptance of Serb rule, and was rejected by the Kosovo Albanians. On the eve of the Balkan wars, national identity was being gradually molded among Kosovo Albanians. Still, resistance to Serbia owed much to a combination of religious conservativism among those loyal to the empire, and to the newly born Albanian national identity.

The ongoing revolts brought the Albanian issue to the attention of the Great Powers. Russia, the Habsburgs, and Italy began a protracted process of negotiation and boundary drawing. This provided an additional impetus for Serb participation in the Balkan wars of 1912–1913. Following the Balkan wars and the disastrous defeat of the Ottoman forces, Ismail Kemal arrived in the city of Vlora on a ship provided by the Habsburgs. There, he convened an assembly of 83 notables, who, on 28 November 1912 proclaimed Albanian independence (Fischer 1995, 33). Although his movement was overlooked by all parties, the long-standing desire of Italy and the Habsburgs to prevent Serb and Greek expansion into Albanian territory encouraged the formation of a state.

The young and inexperienced Prince William of Wied was selected as a prince for Albania, but he served a scant 6 months before leaving Albania in September 1914. During World War I, most of the Albanian state's territory was occupied militarily by Greek and Serb forces. Ahmed Zogu, a local notable, was gradually able to assert his authority over most of the country and by 1922 he took control of the state itself (Fischer 1984). Albanian independence was further secured in the treaties following World War I, although the new state continued to have territorial disputes with Serbia (later Yugoslavia) in the north and with Greece in the south. These developments (and the post-1918 Serb–Albanian confrontation in Kosovo) are discussed at length in Chapter 7.

## CONCLUSIONS

The national movements in Bulgaria, Albania, and Macedonia illustrate the gradual fragmentation of the Eastern Orthodox cultural universe of the Ottoman period. As I have described in Chapter 2, the origins of this process date as far back as the 1821 revolution. It is not accidental that the targets of the three movements reviewed in this chapter included both the Ottoman government and the Ecumenical Patriarchate. Cultural revivals had to face not only Ottoman hostility but also ecclesiastical disapproval. Although Bulgarian, Albanian, and Macedonian nationalists accused the Patriarchate of being an agent of Greek hegemony, their claims cannot be taken at face value. Unfortunately, a great deal of contemporary scholarship routinely accepts the mistaken assumption that the Church and Greek nationalists were simply different faces of the same coin. Yet the Patriarchate followed consistently a policy of preserving a Greek-speaking but largely prenational community of believers. As I have discussed in Chapter 4, the Patriarchate opposed the independence of the Greek Church and was equally opposed to surrendering its control of the educational system in Ottoman territories, even when the contenders were Greek nationalists. Consequently, the rise of national movements in the nineteenth-century Balkans must be interpreted as a corollary of the secularization of cultural life. This secularization was far more pronounced among the intelligentsia than among the Balkan peasantry in Albania, Bulgaria, and Macedonia. In attempting to use religious markers toward the pursuit of their secular nation-building process, the Balkan intelligentsias employed the discourse of *nationhood* as a means of transforming the preexisting religious ties into national ones.

Substantively, the Bulgarian cultural revival is the clearest example of this trend. From the 1830s forward, Bulgarian nationalism developed as a result of the emergence of a group of Bulgarian traders and merchants who were more numerous than in earlier times. This group provided the material support for the Bulgarian intelligentsia, a group of young authors, writers, poets, and publicists. This national awakening received considerable inspiration from the Grecophone institutions operating on the peninsula in the pre-1830 period. Gradually, as young Bulgarians witnessed the success of the Greek revolution and became more familiar with the Western ideas of freedom, progress, and liberty, they began to resent their subordinate position in the empire's social system. Thus, the Bulgarian intelligentsia sought to assert itself by fighting a dual battle: against the Ottomans for national liberation, and against the Patriarchate and Grecophone cultural superiority. The best vehicle for gaining recognition as an autonomous "imagined community" was the existing system. The church struggle was in effect a national struggle. Despite the fact that language was taken to signify membership in the Bulgarian nation, it was church affiliation that served as the political indicator of this membership. In this sense, the Bulgarian Exarchate allowed for the open assertion of Bulgarian nationalism. Membership in the Exarchate was also used to signify a pro-Bulgarian orientation among the Balkan Slavs after 1878 and illustrated the triumph of ethnic nationalism over the *millet* system. In this regard, Bulgarian nationalism was similar to the post-1830 Greek and Serb state-sponsored nationalisms.

The Bulgarian case illustrates that the *redeployment of Orthodoxy* as a facet of the people's national identity cannot be satisfactorily explained as a by-product of state centralization, for, simply, the Bulgarians lacked a state before 1878. Over the post-1870 period, the implicit understanding that church affiliation was a de facto signifier of "nationality" led the Balkan nations to fight a bitter struggle over the church affiliation of the Orthodox Christians in Ottoman Macedonia.

The nationalist movements in the Balkan central regions of Macedonia and Albania were belated and strongly influenced by the impact of Greek, Serb, and Bulgarian nationalisms. In Ottoman Macedonia, the IMRO developed the notion that the region should become autonomous or independent, and this notion fostered the development of a distinct Slavic Macedonian identity. However, the ethnic mixture of Ottoman Macedonia, IMRO's limited appeal, and the persistent efforts of Greeks, Serbs, and Bulgarians in the region did not allow the widespread proliferation of a separate Macedonian identity. In this regard, IMRO's difficulties were not unique. The Albanian movement experienced similar difficulties because of the internal fragmentation of the Albanians into different religions, clans, and regional identities. In the Albanian case, the application of nationhood was quite problematic because religious affiliation, the main cultural marker of the empire, divided rather than united the Albanians. In both the Albanian and Macedonian cases, the development of a national identity was hindered by the latecomer status of the two movements. These movements had to compete with the older and more established movements of Serbia, Greece, and post-1878 Bulgaria. As their articulation proceeded slowly into the twentieth century, these movements gained momentum and gradually matured. However, they did not play a major role in the Balkan wars and World War I. Consequently, the problems associated with the Macedonian and Albanian "national questions" persisted well into the interwar period.

## NOTES

1. The period between 1762 and 1878 is known as the Bulgarian national revival or national "renaissance" period (Georgeoff 1982; Genchev 1977; Georgiev 1978, 239–40). Its traditional starting point is the writing of Father Paisi's *SlavoBulgarian History* (1762). But Paisi's work was appreciated during the nineteenth century. Between 1800 and 1869, when Marin Drinov published his preliminary study on the origins of the Bulgarians, most of Bulgarian historiography consisted largely of copying either Paisi's work or Rajić's multivolume *History of the Various Slavic Peoples* (1794–1795) (Petrovich 1970, 303). Moser (1972, 40) divides the Bulgarian "renaissance" into three segments: from 1762 to 1825, from 1825 to 1856, and from 1856 to 1878.

2. This financial burden was the consequence of the Ottoman practice of *peshkesi*, that is, obligatory gifts of a subordinate to his superior. Every new Patriarch had to pay such a gift, leading to an increase in the Church's debt. By 1730 the debt was estimated to be 100,769 *piastres*; it reached 1.5 million by 1821 (Runicman 1991, 10–15). The practice was not limited to the upper layers of the hierarchy. The local bishops paid a similar "gift" in order to secure their appointment, and attempted to reimburse themselves from their parishioners.

3. Although a diffuse desire for liberation and hopes for Serb participation were also present in the Vidin revolt, the two movements registered mainly peasant discontent over taxation (Pinson 1975, 103–46; McDermott 1962, 170–2). Bulgarian historiography considers them to be nationalist revolts or at least revolts inspired both by material factors and nationalist aspirations (Genchev 1977, 80–8; Tzvetkov 1993, 1:433–4; Kuzmanov 1981, 61–7).

4. In 1839, the young Bulgarian intellectual Georgi S. Rakovski wrote that the Greek bishops were "annihilators of faith and enlightenment." According to Rakovski, the high clergy was afraid of Bulgarian "enlightenment" because "when this happens, then [they] ... will have to leave us alone, and will no longer be able to milk our poor Bulgarians as sheep" (quoted in Dimof 1974, 180). Similar sentiments were echoed in Neofit Bozveli's *Lament of Poor Mother Bulgaria*, written in the mid-1840s and printed in 1874 (Moser 1972, 49).

5. Tomiak (1985, 34–7). For an overview, see Pundeff (1969, 99–110). On Bulgarians in the Danubian principalities in particular, see Velichi (1970, 1979); on the Constantinople community, see Nicoloff (1987, 20).

6. Bishop Ilarion was one of the protectors of the rising Bulgarian intelligentsia. Ironically, Bulgarian nationalists, who were determined to portray all Greeks in a negative light, later on reinterpreted his legacy. For a discussion of his legacy, see Boulaki-Zissi (1976).

154 • Nationalism, Globalization, and Orthodoxy

7. Neofit Bozveli (1785–1848) was a native of Kotel. He studied at the Hilendar Monastery at Mt. Athos where he worked in the monastery's library. As a result of his nationalist activities he was arrested in 1841 but escaped a few years later and resumed his agitation. He was arrested and tortured to death in June 1848 (Moser 1972, 48).

8. In 1835 Bulgarian educator Rilski published in Bucharest his *Tables for Mutual Instruction* and his *Bulgarian Grammar*. The same year Bozveli published his *Slaveno-bolgarskoe detovodstvo za malkite deca*, a miscellany incorporating instruction in good manners, arithmetic, Church Slavonic grammar, geography, and so on. (Moser 1972, 47–8). The first Bulgarian newspaper was published in 1846 in Leipzig by Ivan Andreev Bogorov, a native of Karlovo, who had studied at the Greek school in Kurucheshme on the Bosporus. Bogorov studied chemistry in Leipzig (1845–1847); during his studies he published the *Bulgarian Eagle*. Two years later he was the owner of a printing shop in Constantinople where he printed the *Constantinople Journal* (Nicoloff 1987, 25). In Smyrna from 1844 to 1846 Kostantin Fotinov published the first Bulgarian periodical, *Philology*, with the aid of the missionaries of the Evangelical Association (Nicoloff 1987, 31–3; Genchev 1977, 66; Moser 1972, 50).

9. The society opened in Galata in Constantinople on 25 September 1869, but soon it was moved to Braila in Romania, where a prosperous and less conservative Bulgarian community existed. Marin Drinov, the best Bulgarian historian at the time, became the society's first president. In 1878, the society's seat was moved to the Bulgarian capital, Sofia, and in 1911 the association was renamed Bulgarian Academy of Sciences (Hristov 1988).

10. "Influenced by romantic nationalism's need for a foil, Bulgar intellectuals of the 1830s began to impart a strong anti-Greek character to their writings and oratory" (Meininger 1974, 74–5). See also Zarev (1977, 14–15). For an overview and critique of Bulgarian nationalist biases in art, culture, and history see Kiel (1985, 1–55). Also, Bulgarian authors were influenced extensively by Grecophone literary production (Alexieva 1993; Georgiev 1978, 239; Genchev 1981, 100).

11. For example, in the 1840s Petko Slavejkov traveled throughout Bulgaria and collected about 15,000 proverbs (Moser 1972, 84). Dobri Voinikov published his *Kratska bulgarska istoriia* in 1861, Konstantin Fotinov published his *Tsarstvenik ili Istoriia bolgarskaia* in 1844 in Bucharest, and Dragan Tsankov published the textbook *Bulgarsjka istoriia* in 1866 (Petrovich 1982, 134). In 1860 in Belgrade S. Verkovich published his work the *Popular Songs of the Macedonian Bulgars*. Other works included Liuben Karavelov's folklore collection, *Monuments of the Mode of Life of the Bulgarian People*, which was published in 1861 in Moscow, and Naiden Gerov's Bulgarian dictionary, which was first published in 1845 (Genchev 1977, 107; Pundeff 1969, 108; Moser 1972, 85; Nicoloff 1987, 79–94).

12. In his "rebel songs," Chintulov called for the overthrow of Ottoman rule with lyrics such as "arise, arise young hero of the Balkans/awaken from your deep sleep/and lead the Bulgarians/against the Ottoman people" (quoted in Moser 1972, 52) For Chintulov, the conflict between Bulgarians and the Ottoman Empire was a manifestation of the holy war of Christendom against Islam.

13. Moser (1972, 67–8) The poem assumed for Bulgarian literature a position similar to that of Njegoš' *Mountain Wrath*. Rakovski's writings represented the high point of Bulgarian nationalism (see Genchev 1977, 121–4, about his revolutionary activities). For Rakovski, the Phanariots were "by nature and trade . . . engaged in slander, lies, thievery, luxury, and prostitution" and the Bulgarians "must give a good thought to what kind of

human-faced beasts they have to deal with . . . and must wipe them out from the face of Bulgaria by whatever means possible" (quoted in Dimof 1974, 187–8). Rakovski had a similar negative view of the Catholics and Protestants and viewed them as undermining the unity of the Bulgarian nation.

14. In their efforts to win some type of autonomy, in 1867, conservative merchants proposed to the Porte the creation of a dual monarchy—similar to that of post-1867 Austro-Hungary—with Abdulaziz as Sultan both of the empire and Tsar of Bulgaria. The Porte paid no attention to this plan (Davison 1963, 155–6; Shashko 1974b, 143; Stavrianos 1944, 89). See also McDermott (1962, 193) and for Rakovski in particular, see Trajkov (1984).

15. For an overview of the failed insurrections of the early 1870s and the 1876 uprising, see Genchev (1977, 121–74), McDermott (1962, 188–275), and Nicoloff (1987, 131–57). For a biography of the most prominent of the revolutionaries, Vasil Levski, see McDermott (1986).

16. For the Bulgarian participation in the 1876 April uprising see Meininger (1977, 250–61; also 1979, 73–104) and McDermott (1962, 274). Meininger's perspective is highly valuable in understanding the scope of the Bulgarian uprisings.

17. In 1859 the Bulgarian inhabitants of the city of Kukush in southern Macedonia refused the appointment of a new bishop and with the help of the French consul in Thessaloniki they broke relations with the Patriarchate and consummated an act of union with the Catholic Church. The Patriarchate dispatched the Bulgarian activist bishop Ilarion Makariopolski to undo the conversion of Kukush into Catholicism. Ilarion was successful and, after Paterni Zografski was appointed as the new bishop, Kukush returned to the Orthodox faith. Since 1859, with the aid of the French and Austrian embassies, the pro-Catholic Uniat movement had gained momentum. In 1860 the Pope even ordained Josif Sokoloski as archbishop of the Bulgarian Catholic Church (Genchev 1977, 114). In the 1860s, Protestant missionaries organized Bulgarian communities in Constantinople, Plovdiv, Saloniki, Bitola, Stara Zagora, and Bansko.

18. Nicoloff (1987, 50–3), Meininger (1970, 129–30), and McDermott (1962, 162–7). On the plebiscites, see Genchev (1977, 117), Tzvetkov (1993, 1:486), and Kolev (1991, 42). Additional regions occasionally joined the church council; for example, the 1871 church council was attended by representatives from 22 eparchies and the Nevrokop region—although some of them were still formally under patriarchal jurisdiction. Initially the Exarchate included 16 dioceses. Plebiscites held in contested territories (Skopje and Ohrid) in 1874 produced results in favor of the Exarchate; this led to the Ottomans' confirmation of the appointment of Bulgarian bishops in the two towns.

19. Vakalopoulos (1988, 40–1). See Gounaris (1996) for further discussion on the interplay among class, ethnicity, religion, and support for a particular side. Most foreign observers confirmed that for the majority of the peasantry it was confessional rather than national identity that was the most significant cultural marker. For some characteristic statements, see Vermulen (1984), Kofos (1964, 12–3, 24), and Georgeoff (1973).

20. Originally, the organization was an offshoot of the Bulgarian national movement and its earliest statute (dating from 1896) refers only to the "Bulgarian population" and stipulates that only a Bulgarian could become a member. By 1902 such qualifications were dropped and the organization begun assuming a more separatist stand (Adanir 1992, 172–3). For further discussion of the historiography on this subject, see Lange-Akhund (1998, 38–9).

21. The nine articles of the agreement are reproduced in Lange-Akhund (1998, 142–3).

22. This point is made in almost all publications on Albanian nationalism (e.g., Skendi 1967 and 1980). In the nineteenth century, the Greek historian Constantinos Paparrigo-poulos considered the Albanians a "race" that could be acculturated into Hellenism. His viewpoint was greatly influenced by the considerable Albanian contribution to the Greek War of Independence (1821–1828). However, during the nineteenth century, the collapse of the *Rum millet* system entailed the secularization of identity and allowed Albanians to reconceptualize their political position within the empire. In fact, in 1878 the Albanian Jani Vreto had to publish an entire book (*Apologia*) in Greek to make the case for Albanian distinctiveness (Elsie 1985, 1:250–2; for similar cases, see 253–6).

23. See Elsie (1985, I; 1991) for examples of individual cases. The Albanian language was used among the Catholics in the northern part of the country, but the educational network was underdeveloped. In 1878, there were only two Roman Catholic schools in Shkoder (Pollo and Puto 1981, 115).

24. In addition to the work of the Frasheri brothers, literary production and cultural mobilization occurred among the Albanians of Italy, the Roman Catholics of the north, and the Albanian immigrants to the United States (see Elsie 1985, I; Jacques 1995, 277–308).

25. In the pre-1878 period, there were various projects for an Albanian state or principality, developed mainly among émigré communities. See Malcolm (1998, 218–9) and Jacques (1995) for further discussion.

26. The Greco-Albanian National Coalition was founded in 1899 to promote a dual state under the Greek king, but with extensive autonomy in areas other than foreign affairs and the military (Pitouli-Kitsou 1997, 52–4).

# 6

## The Articulation of Irredentism in Balkan Politics, 1880–1920

In the last two chapters, I discussed the articulation of nationhood as a normative standard in the nineteenth-century Balkans. Although the basic tenets of the discourse of nationhood were established during this period, it would be a mistake to think that this process came to a halt. Cultural reproduction is an ongoing process. Therefore, the ideological elaboration of nationhood continued well into the twentieth century.

In this chapter, I examine the articulation of irredentism in the domestic politics of Greece, Serbia, and Bulgaria over the 1880–1920 period. Critics consider Balkan irredentism a force that diverted valuable resources from modernization; opposing voices point to the considerable achievements of the Balkan states in their nation and state building (for example, Mishkova 1995). The terms of the debate between these groups, however, are not adequately clarified, and this leads to a conceptual ambiguity that perpetuates the inconclusiveness of the debate. In its broadest sense, nationalism may come in both ethnic- and civic-oriented varieties, a feature making it a concept considerably broader than *irredentism*, that is, the vision of national integration or national unification common to the Balkan national societies of the second half of the nineteenth century. Conducting the discussion about the Balkan states in terms of nationalism instead of irredentism entails a level of abstraction that obscures a simple point, namely, that not all nationalists were in favor of irredentist claims. Examples are the cases of Athanasios Souliotis and Ioannes Dragoumis—or that of Georgi Rakovski, discussed in Chapter 3.

In addition, in the debate about the Balkan road to modernity the arrow of causality is often seen as flying along the path of irredentism's contribution to modernization. The relationship ought to be reversed. The substantive issue should not be whether irredentism was a positive or negative element in the modernization of the Balkan national societies, for this narrow political ideology is in fact an expression of modernity itself. Irredentism is conceptually impossible without nation-states that assume the role of national homelands for a particular people (Brubaker 1996, 13–22, 55–76). It is therefore necessary to narrow the scope of the inquiry. Because of the complexity of nationalism, I have restricted the scope of my discussion in this chapter to the *political artic-ulation* of irredentism in the political culture of the Balkan nation-states from 1880 to 1920. This restriction does not disregard the importance of intellectuals in providing the intellectual edifice for Balkan irredentism. But ideas alone are never sufficient, and the decisive factor in their success or failure is the existence of *political constituencies* that will endorse or oppose particular ideological viewpoints.

My analysis focuses on the key political constituencies of the Balkan nation-states and on the social factors responsible for their emergence. My goal is to show that underdevelopment in conjunction with the class structure of the Balkan nation-states, and their statism promoted the consolidation of political constituencies that favored irredentism. That is, the creation of an independent freeholding peasantry in Greece, Serbia, and Bulgaria, coupled with the peasantry's ability to influence electoral results, led the Balkan elites to employ the state as a mechanism of fiscal extraction and income redistribution toward the state-dependent urban strata. From 1880 to 1920, it was the urban strata that favored irredentism, with the military corps at the forefront. In fact, when it became necessary to mobilize the peasantry in order to accomplish the urban strata's national missions, it was plain that the peasantry's support for irredentism came with a steep price, when it existed at all.

## FREEHOLDING PEASANTRY AND UNDERDEVELOPMENT

Underdevelopment is a common feature of all the Balkan nation-states (Romania, Serbia, Greece, and Bulgaria). Their "backwardness" is a topic of heated discussion;[1] for our purposes, the social and political consequences of under-development are important. The traditional line of argument suggests that if modernization of a country is going to occur, urban elites need to develop a strategy (either democratic or authoritarian) that will allow them to appropriate agricultural surplus for the benefit of the industrial sector (Moore 1966). Of course, this generalization pertains to those cases in which such modernization has been implemented. It is not historical destiny. It is entirely possible that regional elites might not be able to develop such a successful strategy. For example, Romania's nineteenth-century political oligarchy did not lead to successful economic development. By contrast, the parliamentary rule established at an early stage in Greece, Serbia, and Bulgaria made it inherently difficult to follow an unpopular developmental strategy (Mouzelis 1986). The simultaneous coexistence of economic underdevelopment and freeholding peasantry in these states, in combination with the peasantry's (relatively unrestrained) ability to participate in politics, led to the consolidation of the peasantry as an important political constituency.

Let us review each state's historical trajectory in some detail. During the period from 1860 to 1910 the peasantry was the largest social group in Greece, Serbia, and Bulgaria. In each state, the peasantry was gradually able to appropriate the land, thereby preventing the consolidation of a large-scale landowning class. After 1832, most of the land in the kingdom of Greece came under the nominal control of the state. The small landholders did not buy the land from the state. They practiced land usurpation, a strategy effectively fostered by the lack of a land register and by the application of the Byzantine principle of land appropriation, which awarded landownership after 30 years of occupancy. The final solution of the land question was initiated by the 1871 reform plan. Between 1871 and 1911, 357,217 title deeds were issued, transferring a total of 2,850,000 *stemmas* of land to private hands (Tsoukalas 1987, 71–84; Mouzelis 1978, 15; McGrew 1985, 213; Vergopoulos 1975). The growing importance of the peasantry as a political constituency is revealed in the gradual shift of the tax burden: The urban population contributed only 2.79 percent of state revenue in 1852–1854, but the percentage rose to 10.89 percent by 1871–1873, 23.94 percent by 1892–1894, and 48.12 percent by 1910–1912. Unpopular peasant taxation was replaced by indirect taxation (sales taxes, value-added taxes, etc.), which rose from 29.9 percent of state revenue in 1833–1835 to 53.69 percent in 1871–1873, and 80.23 percent in 1910–1912 (Dertilis 1993, 25–31). Indirect taxation shifted the tax burden to the lower-income urban classes—who had to buy a whole range of peasantry-produced goods.

A similar social pattern developed in Serbia. In 1835 and 1836, Prince Miloš, in his effort to curb the power of rival local prelates, enacted legislation that legalized possession of forests and fields by village communities and established a baseline of protected landholding that was not subject to confiscation by moneylenders. Codified in the 1838 constitution, this legislation effectively prohibited local prelates from becoming large landowners.[2] The result was the creation of a free peasant landholding class. In 1836, 90 percent of the population were peasants, and by 1900, 84 percent of the population still worked in agriculture. The importance of the peasantry as a political constituency gradually led to a shift in the tax burden similar to that in the Greek case. In 1865 there were more than 21,000 urban dwellers who paid direct taxes; there were nearly 200,000 such taxpayers in the rural areas (McClellan 1964, 25; Palairet 1979, 719–40). However, after 1880, both Prince Milan's administration (1880–1889) and the subsequent Radical cabinets shifted this burden to the city dwellers; until the 1880s urban taxation had been slight (probably less than 5%), but in the period preceding World War I it rose steadily to reach 17 percent by 1911.

A similar social pattern is observed in post-1878 Bulgaria, but the situation was less favorable for the Bulgarian peasantry. Following the departure of the

Ottoman *ciftlik* estate owners and many of the Turkish peasants, the Bulgarian peasantry took over a considerable portion of their land. By 1897, 49 percent of the land and 87.3 percent of all farms consisted of small holdings (up to 10 hectares). However, the Bulgarian peasant was forced to buy the land and this resulted in a rapid increase in land prices. Since credit was not available, the peasantry fell victim to usurers, whose high interest rates (often as much 150 percent annually) ruined a great many of these buyers of former Ottoman lands (Berov 1979, 106; Tomasevich 1955, 39–48). Despite this important difference, the joint result of land redistribution and usurpation in Serbia, Greece, and Bulgaria was a more or less equitable distribution of resources and the consolidation of a freeholding peasantry.

Reacting to this socioeconomic pattern, the Balkan states fostered the development of agricultural exports in an attempt to accumulate capital. Throughout the period from 1860 to 1910, this strategy worked for brief periods of time but, with the rise of protectionism and international competition at the turn of the nineteenth century, it failed to produce visible results (Lampe and Jackson 1982, 175–92; Stoianovich 1994, 212–22). Consequently, the creation of a peasant smallholding class did not improve the peasants' lot. The result was not agricultural modernization, but the preservation of traditional methods of land cultivation.

## THE URBAN SECTOR, STATE LEGITIMACY, AND NATIONALISM

The underdevelopment of the urban sector in the Balkan nation-states is closely related to the absence of industrial development during the nineteenth century. Only on the eve of the twentieth century did a few industrial stirrings appear. The ability of the Balkan states to use tariffs and other economic strategies to enhance their economic development was hindered by a series of international agreements (Crampton 1983, 215–25; Berend and Ranki 1974, 75–89, 140–50, 166–8; Dertilis 1977; Palairet, 1997). Consequently, the urban settlements of the Balkan states assumed a petit bourgeois nature. In addition, throughout the nineteenth century, many of the traditional commercial urban centers declined steadily in favor of the local capitals or other new urban settlements associated with the local nation-states. The old economic unity of the Balkan peninsula was fragmented, and a new socio-spatial distribution emerged that reflected the slow formation of national societies. The creation of the new states resulted in slower urbanization and relative economic decline, both of which were the inevitable consequences of the region's disassociation from the empire (see Palairet, 1997 for details).

The gradual growth of the urban population in the Balkan states is shown in Table 8. Table 7 provides an account of the urban population with special reference to the prominent role reserved for the new capitals. It is plain to see that the new capitals (Athens, Sofia, Belgrade) served as focal points for urbanization. Table 8 provides an illustration of the spread of urbanization throughout

**Table 7**
**Populations of the Balkan Nation-States**

| YEAR | Total Population | Urban Population | % | Population of Capital |
|------|------|------|------|------|
| Serbia | | | | Belgrade |
| 1815 | 450,000 | -- | -- | 2,500 (1820) |
| 1839 | 800,000 | 50,000 | 6.25 | 12,900 (1838) |
| 1848 | 826,000 | 53,000 | 6.4 | 18,600 |
| 1866 | 1,216,000 | 116,000 | 9.5 | 25,000 |
| 1874 | 1,353,000 | 138,700 | 10.2 | |
| 1884 | 1,902,000 | 236,000 | 12.4 | |
| 1890 | 2,185,000 | 286,000 | 13.1 | 54,000 |
| 1900 | 2,529,000 | 351,000 | 13.9 | 70,000 |
| Bulgaria | | | | Sofia |
| 1881 | 2,007,919 | 336,102 | 16.7 | 20,000 |
| 1888-9 | 3,154,375 | 611,250 | 19.3 | 45,000 |
| 1900 | 3,744,000 | 745,560 | 19.9 | 67,000 |
| 1910 | 4,337,513 | 829,522 | 19.1 | 103,000 |
| Greece | | | | Athens |
| 1828 | 753,400 | -- | | 14,000 (1836) |
| 1856 | 1,062,627 | 277,748 | 26 | 30,969 |
| 1879 | 1,679,470 | 367,494 | 22 | 65,499 |
| 1889 | 2,187,000 | 486,915 | 22,22 | 114,355 |
| 1907 | 2,631,952 | 628,000 | 24 | 175,430 |

*Source*: Yerolympos (1996, 17).

the Balkan nation-states. It includes counts of urban settlements with 2,000 inhabitants or more, and therefore, it allows for an estimate of the extent of urbanization.

Despite the numerical discrepancies between the two tables, the slow level of urbanization is plain to see. The only exception is Serbia, but Serbia began with

**Table 8**
**Proportion of Urban Population in the Balkan States, Nineteenth Century**[a]

| Year & Region | Towns | Percentage of Population |
|---|---|---|
| Northern Bulgaria | | |
| 1866 | 39 | 15.3-18.4 |
| 1880 | 45 | 17.2 |
| 1892 | 50 | 19.2 |
| 1900 | 53 | 18.3 |
| 1910 | 53 | 18.8 |
| Eastern Romilia | | |
| 1884 | 23 | 22.4 |
| 1892 | 24 | 23.7 |
| 1900 | 24 | 23.4 |
| 1910 | 25 | 21.7 |
| Serbia | | |
| 1834 | 7 | 4.1 |
| 1863 | 19 | 7.0 |
| 1874 | 22 | 8.4 |
| 1890 | 36 | 11.6 |
| 1900 | 39 | 12.0 |
| 1910 | 40 | 10.8 |
| Greece | | |
| 1853 | 23 | 15.5 |
| 1861 | 24 | 16.8 |
| 1879 | 32 | 18.5 |

[a]Counts all towns with 2,000 or more inhabitants. It is possible that even in these towns, a number of people were involved in agriculture.

*Source*: Palairet (1997, 26).

only 4% of the population living in urban settlements. Therefore, the defining characteristic of urban life in nineteenth century Balkans was the reconfiguration of the urban patterns. The new urban formations remained political and administrative structures, similar to their Ottoman counterparts in the earlier centuries. However, they were operating as instruments that facilitated the Europeanization of the Balkan states and the creation of distinct national societies (Castellan 1980; Yerolympos 1996; Jelavich 1983, 2:45–50). Their political and administrative nature is revealed in their occupational patterns, which were dominated by civil servants, professionals (lawyers, doctors, etc.), traders, artisans, shopkeepers, and small-scale investors. Athens, Belgrade, and Sofia illustrate this pattern (Lampe 1979; Berov 1979; Tsoukalas 1981; Sanders 1980). In Belgrade, public employees and their families constituted more than 22 percent of the households from 1895 to 1902. In Sofia in 1905, they constituted 25.5 percent of the total population. Although 1 in 4 of Sofia's working citizens was a bureaucrat, in the rest of the country the figure was 1 in 12.

In all three Balkan states, the civil service was a significant sector of the economy. This feature reflected the dominant role of the state in "society." The state did not stand apart or in contrast to "society"; on the contrary, the state facilitated the birth of the Balkan national societies (Sotirelis 1991, 95–6). In summary, then, there were two main sectors in these emerging Balkan national societies: (1) a class of small-scale independent land cultivators, and (2) the various employees of the public sector and other petit bourgeois professionals. The creation of a freeholding peasantry meant that capital accumulation could not take place through "pure" economic mechanisms. For the new elites of the Balkan nation-states the inevitable choice was to use the state as a fiscal mechanism. State resources were widely used for the funding of public-sector positions. These positions in turn were used for political patronage, providing the material means for the integration of broad segments of the population into the emerging national societies.

In Greece, over the course of the nineteenth century, the prelates took advantage of the fiscal dependency of the peasantry to create a system of political patronage. A number of political "families" (tzakia) became, in effect, the dominant oligarchy of the Greek kingdom. Their power base changed over time; from landowners with an immediate relationship to the peasantry, they evolved, especially after 1870, into a class of politicians offering state employment in exchange for votes. From 1843 to 1878, 57 percent of the political leaders and 77.5 percent of the ministers belonged to one of these "families," and from 1878 to 1910, these numbers were 91.7 percent and 58.3 percent, respectively (Legg 1969, 306; see also Tsoukalas 1987, 219, and Lyrintzis 1991, 140, 169).

Regardless of whether this group is viewed as a political oligarchy or as a state bourgeoisie, it successfully used the state to dominate Greek political life.[3] Since no other occupational category existed with the numerical strength or the symbolic prestige of the civil service, state employment became one of the standard ways to close the gap between the peasant and urban worlds. The public sector was divided into two main categories: the well-paid tenured employees and those who were in fact part of the institutional structure of the state itself, and the adjunct or temporary employees, who received small salaries and could be dismissed at any time. With each change of government, the old temporary employees were dismissed and new ones were hired (Tsoukalas 1981, 125, 134–7; 1987, 136).

The same system (known here as partisanstvo) was established in Bulgaria. By 1878–1879, there were a mere 2,121 native Bulgarian administrators; between 1880 and 1900 the expansion of state services raised the number to 20,000. In order to attract able men to the civil service, high salaries were offered. Within a few years, the attractive salaries created high expectations among educated men, many of whom simply refused any form of employment other than civil service posts. The parties' obligation to provide their leading supporters with employment was the first priority of any new ministry. As in nineteenth-century Greece, already existing employees were dismissed and the

party cadres were appointed to a variety of positions, becoming regional pre-
fects, mayors, village and town officials, and even policemen (Crampton 1983,
214, 159–60; Nikolova 1990; Konstantinova 1995). Elections became a facade
as "almost every new government managed to obtain the majority it needed
through violence, machinations, and administrative, military and police outrage"
(Grancarov 1982, 43). Moreover, popular participation in the elections was low,
and it was only in 1902 that participation in urban areas exceeded 50 percent
(Konstantinova 1995, 21–7). Subsequently, elections were more even-handed in
urban areas, while in rural regions governmental "influence" counted heavily
toward the final outcome. In her concluding remarks to her study of the Bulgarian political system during the 1879–1946 period, Konstantinova (1995, 106)
writes that "the pre-election terror and the lack of information led to the formation of a group of voters always supporting the government." The wide
swings in the electoral support for particular political parties observed in the
Bulgarian politics of the first half of the twentieth century should be attributed
to these mechanisms of coercion and violence.

Contrary to the Greek (and Bulgarian) use of the civil service for political
patronage, in Serbia the bureaucracy evolved, at least for while, into a state elite.
The key difference between the Greek and the Serbian bureaucracies concerned
their size: In 1842, Serbia's civil servants numbered only 1,151, whereas in
Greece there were 8,865 civil servants in 1853 (Tsoukalas 1981, 96). Under the
Constitutionalists' regime (1842–1858), the distinction between Serbian state
employees and peasants was exaggerated: State employees enjoyed written provisions as to their rights, privileges, and restrictions; they could not be dismissed
without cause; they were given titles and uniforms; they were required to be
clean shaven; and they could not engage in trade or other private pursuits (Dragnich, 1978; McClelllan 1964, 20–5; Djordjevic 1970a, 95–6). It is indicative of
the attraction of civil service posts that, during the 1870s, many among the
Serbian Liberals (who were fierce critics of the Serbian regime in the 1860s)
did not hesitate to compromise their lofty ideals in exchange for civil service
posts. Under these conditions, state employment became popular as a means of
achieving a stable sinecure. However, Serbia lacked adequate numbers of educated personnel: By 1857 there were only 11,461 males and 959 females at-
tending school in the principality and in 1858 the entire principality had only
200 graduates (Karanovich 1987).

To summarize, it is clear that in the Balkan nation-states, the simultaneous
pursuit of state building and nation building entailed considerable tensions between the urban and rural sectors. These tensions were not simply problems of
a belated effort at nation building (cf. Mishkova 1995) alone; the two processes
were intertwined. The state, acting as a collective representation of society,
performed all the activities that led to national unification (Bourdieu 1994). The
rapid expansion of the Balkan bureaucracies was not natural, not a simple, organic, national evolution, although the "appeal to the nation" makes them appear
useful and necessary. On the contrary, this expansion of the bureaucracy is an

indicator of something more purposeful, of the making of distinct national societies.

These national societies were initially formed around the new urban settings and then began encroaching on the countryside. In so doing, they carried with them not only the physical power of the state (Max Weber's monopoly of violence) but also its symbolic power. This symbolic power was predicated in the identification of the "people" with the "nation," on whose behalf the actions of the state were taken. As already discussed in the two preceding chapters, over the course of the nineteenth century, the Balkan intelligentsia were instrumental in producing a series of irredentist visions for the three nation-states. This was typical of the broader European pattern of the time (Mann 1993, 588). These irredentist visions provided the local states with a mission to accomplish, hence offering legitimacy to the local bureaucracies and their urban clientele. In the countryside, Balkan nation building skillfully used church affiliation (in Ottoman Macedonia) and the educational system to achieve the nationalization of the peasantry. This process was slow in part because of the fact that illiteracy rates remained high during the nineteenth century. In 1866, only 4.2 percent of Serbia's population could read (Jelavich 1990b, 54). Male literacy in the kingdom of Greece was 12.5 percent in 1840 and 21.62 percent in 1870; female literacy for 1870 was 6.3 percent (Tsoukalas 1987, 393). In 1881–1884 the aggregate literacy rates for all ethnic groups in Bulgaria were 5 percent for males and 1.5 percent for females (Mishkova 1994, 86).

Therefore, after 1880, the gradual end of the "oligarchic parliamentary rule" (cf. Mouzelis 1986) and the active participation of the peasantry in political life generated a new problem: The Balkan state elites and the urban groups had to persuade their newly formed national societies to pursue their "national missions," but the bulk of those societies were illiterate.

## THE ARTICULATION OF IRREDENTISM: A BRIEF OVERVIEW

From 1880 to 1920, the promotion of the Greek, Serbian, and Bulgarian national missions owed much to the local urban (and mostly state-dependent) strata. These nationalist agendas faced the hostility of the peasantry but were aggressively pursued by the Balkan military corps. The contrasting attitudes of the two groups reveal the articulation of irredentism as a phenomenon associated with the modernization of the local national societies. Of course, throughout Europe in the nineteenth century, proponents of nationalism were found everywhere among groups of people whose livelihood depended on the state (Mann 1993, 733–4).

The only peculiarity that the socioeconomic patterns of Greece, Serbia, and Bulgaria reveal is that state-dependent strata were particularly numerous in these states. Public-sector employment figures for Bulgaria were 27,989 for 1904 and 49,683 for 1911 (Directorate de la statistique, 1908; 1918). For Greece, the total number of public-sector employees was 23,187 in 1870, rising to 31,001 in 1879 and to 33,027 in 1889 (Tsoukalas 1987, 185–7). These numbers include people who worked for central or local government, the army, and other categories of state-dependent employees. The overwhelming majority of the employees were males, and one should consider the numbers as representing families and not single individuals.

These strata fueled their countries' pursuit of irredentism. Irredentism provided them with a powerful and globally legitimate ideology. In the three Balkan states, the rise of military officers into an important constituency was closely connected to the organization of the armed forces into more substantial and sophisticated entities (Djordjevic 1982). In fact, military officers coming from upwardly mobile strata were in the forefront of the national agenda. This phenomenon reflected the professionalization of the Balkan armies after 1870; in the Balkan war of 1912, Greece, Serbia, and Bulgaria mobilized approximately 725,000 soldiers. Greek officers initiated the 1909 military coup; their Serbian counterparts were responsible for the 1903 coup in their own country and the assassination of the last Obrenović.

In the Greek case, the military academy was radically reformed after the 1870s and pursued the task of military training in a newly rigorous manner. This was simultaneous with the establishment of universal conscription (between 1879 and 1882), resulting in a standing army of 30,000. Between 1872 and 1895 the size of the Greek officer corps increased more than 240 percent, from 700 to 1,800; during the same period officers (mostly academy graduates) constituted 7 percent to 15 percent of the deputies in parliament. At the turn of the century academy graduates became the vanguard of military corporatism (Varda 1980–1982; Veremis 1997, 33–8, 44–5). Military officers accounted for 80 percent of the membership in the (later infamous) National Society, the nationalist organization that led Greece to a disastrous defeat in the 1897 Greek–Turkish war (Yianoulopoulos 1999, 3–82). From 1903 to 1908, many among the officers were involved in guerrilla warfare in Macedonia. The 1908 Young Turk revolution put an end to their semi-official missions.

In less than a month after the revolution, on 13 August 1908, Greek officers formerly involved in guerrilla warfare formed the Panhellenic Organization under the leadership of Colonel Panagiotis Danglis (Veremis 1982; Gounaris 1986; Papacosma 1977). A Military League of officers affiliated with this association prompted the 1909 coup. Their complaints blended professional demands with nationalist rhetoric; support for irredentism also aided the status of the army. By 1910, unable to formulate a coherent political program, the league brought the Cretan politician Eleutherios Venizelos to Athens.[4] In 1910–1911 Venizelos organized the Liberal Party and led it to the highly successful 1911 elections, in which the party dominated the parliament (300 of 362 seats) (Kitsikis 1973, 222; Mavrocordatos 1983b, 68). Venizelos began a multifaceted program of political and economic modernization that spanned the 1911–1935 period.

Similarly, the pre-1903 buildup of the Serbian officer corps owed much to its reorganization. The regular territorial army was organized in 1883, after the disastrous war of 1875 with the Ottoman Empire. When former prince Milan returned to Serbia during the reign of his son, Alexander (1893–1903), he took command of the army and increased the number of military units fourfold; this led to an increase in the officer corps. Training at the military academy was shortened from 4 to 2 years. Simultaneously, the ministry of education reduced the number of high schools and many senior pupils, especially those of poorer families, had no alternative but to join the army, if they sought any kind of professional career (Dedijer 1966, 84). Among this group of officers, the pro-Habsburg policy of the Obrenović dynasty was greatly resented. This situation resulted in the 1903 coup, Alexander's assassination, and the restoration of the Karadjordjević dynasty. In the aftermath of the 1903 coup, the military enjoyed a growing influence in Serbian political life. In the first months after the coup, officer conspirators held 4 of 10 cabinet posts and many top military and government positions. Among them, the young colonel Dragutin Dimitrijević-Apis gradually became an increasingly influential figure. This brought him inevitably into conflict with the Radical party leadership, which considered him a dangerous and irresponsible competitor for power.[5]

Whereas the Serbian and Greek militaries became visible agents in politics, the Bulgarian military found in Prince Ferdinand an ally and protector, and therefore was less visible as an independent political force.[6] Ferdinand began encouraging a following among the monarchists in the army during the Stambolov (1887–1894) regime. To remedy Ferdinand's initial lack of popularity among the military officers, prime minister Stambolov reorganized and modernized the army in 1888. The armed forces' size increased by 50 percent thus opening avenues for the promotion of officers and reducing the likelihood of discontent.

After 1896, Ferdinand began to handpick the minister of war, and as a rule of thumb the minister was a general on familiar terms with the prince (Grancarov 1982, 42; Perry 1993, 136). Under Ferdinand's regime, foreign loans were extensively used to buy armaments, and this strategy contributed to a 70.42 percent increase in Bulgaria's foreign debt in the 1901–1912 period (Crampton 1983, 393). The trend increased in the period prior to the Balkan wars of 1912–1913. On the eve of those wars, the Bulgarian army numbered 87,150. The growing militarization was accompanied by an increase in the gap between the officers' corps (a well-paid and privileged group) and the Bulgarian peasantry. Increased borrowing was accompanied by increased taxation, therefore providing justification for the Agrarian Party's critique of Ferdinand's policy, discussed later in this chapter.

According to Lange-Akhund (1998, 44), in late nineteenth-century Bulgaria, 430 out of a total of 1,289 officers (including reservists) originated in Ottoman Macedonia. Maurice Paleologue, foreign representative in Sofia, wrote in 1908 that the army believed itself to be capable of playing a decisive role in conquering the Bulgarian *irredenta*, and was eager to do so (quoted in Constant 1980, 208). Nevertheless, contrary to the bellicose attitude of these officers and the Macedonian lobby, Prince Ferdinand was content to use diplomatic intrigue to achieve, first and foremost, full independence for Bulgaria and the title of king for himself. Ferdinand accomplished both in 1908, taking advantage of the Young Turk revolution. Between 1896 and 1903 Ferdinand even attempted to gain some control over the Macedonian lobby, especially the Sofia-based Supreme Committee (discussed in Chapter 5). However, his hold was always tentative and the two wings of the Macedonian lobby (the Supremacists and the IMRO) were never brought under his control (Crampton 1983, 271–85).

As this brief overview illustrates, military officers found a variety of ways to shape political developments in the three countries. However, the rise of irredentism did not receive the endorsement of the peasantry. Perhaps the best known case is that of Bulgaria, where the urban strata and the political–military establishment brought the country to the two Balkan wars and World War I. In so doing they became the main targets of the Bulgarian Agrarians, who took a strong antimilitarist stand. In the 1900s, the Bulgarian Agrarian National Union (BANU), under the leadership of Alexander Stamboliski, gradually emerged as one of the most important political parties in Bulgaria. The party opposed Ferdinand's usurpation of the title of Tsar in 1908, setting the stage for a confrontation between BANU and the king. Because full independence amounted to a loss of the Exarchate's privileged position in Ottoman Macedonia, loss of favored status vis-à-vis Ottoman customs, and loss of access to the Ottoman markets, BANU sharply criticized the move and its deputies refused to recognize Ferdinand's title of Tsar (Bell 1977, 91). From then on, Stamboliski became the most consistent voice opposing the regime and the military expeditions under preparation.

In the years 1914 and 1915, Ferdinand and Stamboliski clashed over the issue of Bulgaria's entrance into World War I. Ferdinand was in favor of entering the war, whereas Stamboliski favored neutrality. When, on 4 September 1915, Ferdinand announced his decision to enter the war to the opposition leaders, Stamboliski threatened that BANU would become an instrument of vengeance for his ill-guided policies. The two leaders quarreled publicly with each other, each claiming to represent the true interests of Bulgaria.[7] A few days later, Stamboliski prepared a pamphlet calling on the people, especially the soldiers, not to take part in the war. On September 10, the police raided the Agrarian press. Stamboliski was put on trial in a military court, which sentenced him to death. Ferdinand was impressed by the protests of the opposition and commuted his sentence to life in prison. Stamboliski remained in prison for most of the duration of the war.

By October 1915, Bulgaria entered the war. By 1916 Bulgaria had effectively conquered most of its *irredenta* in Macedonia and Thrace. However, in 1916, the entrance of Romania into the war and the Allied advances in Macedonia (where the Serbs retook Monastir) demonstrated that the war was not going to end soon and was most likely to continue for some time (Crampton 1983, 450). The continuation of the war led to a deterioration in living conditions. The mood of the public turned increasingly sour. The costs of the war were staggering: By 1918 900,000 men, or 40 percent of Bulgaria's male population, had been conscripted. The army suffered 300,000 casualties, of which 100,000 were killed.[8] Clothing, food supplies, and ammunition were scarce. When the Allied troops rolled up the Bulgarian front on September 18, army discipline broke down as several thousand soldiers decided they had had enough and, like their 1917 Russian counterparts, voted for peace with their feet (Rothschild 1959, 76–7; Palmer 1965, 207–22). The military collapse paved the way for the Agrarians' eventual rise to power in 1918–1919 and their 3-year administration (1920–1923).

In Serbia, the confrontation was expressed in the conflicts between the Serb Radical government and the military officers. Between 1880 and 1903 the Serb Radical Party gradually emerged as the main representative political organization for the Serb peasantry.[9] By 1874, Nikola Pašić had emerged as the key organizer and leader of the Radical Party. When in 1881 the Radicals were registered as a legal party organization, scores of volunteers participated in taking their message to the peasantry. To the illiterate peasant, the Radicals appeared to be an agent that bridged the gap between his own universe and the alien world of the city. Thousands of peasants joined the party; by 1883 membership amounted to 60,000, with 60,000 more unofficially affiliated (Djordjevic 1970a, 226; Stokes 1990, 232). By 1881, the Radicals had established their own newspaper and issued a proclamation blending the visions of greater Serbia and Yugoslavia, moving away from their initial federalism toward a more nationalist position. In their 1882 first national congress, Pašić was elected leader of the party without any opposition and maintained this position (with brief interruptions) until his death in 1926. Gradually, in the post-1880 period, the Radical Party's social profile became more diverse.[10] From a peasant party with only a few intellectuals, it was transformed into a party that attracted some native intellectuals, provincial merchants, and rich peasants.

Throughout the 1880s, the Radicals' ascent was accompanied by internal strife with (prince and later king) Milan. Milan abdicated in 1889 in favor of his son Alexander, but political intrigue persisted. In 1893 Alexander, with the aid of military officers faithful to his father, executed a royal coup and attempted to govern by himself. Alexander called Milan back to Serbia and father and son proceeded to govern together.[11] In 1897, Alexander inaugurated a personal autocratic regime with Milan as army chief. In 1898 he abolished all political parties and transformed the assembly into an obedient instrument. Overall, during the 1893–1903 period, Alexander carried out four state coups, abrogated three constitutions, and named and dismissed 12 cabinets (McKenzie 1991, 55). In 1900, Alexander announced his intention to marry his mistress, Draga Masina, an older woman he had met at his mother's court. Draga had been a mistress to many people in her life, and the announcement dismayed everybody, including Milan. The royal wedding provided the impetus for the 1903 coup, Alexander's assassination, and the restoration of the Karadjordjević dynasty.

After 1903, the Serb Radicals, under Pašić's leadership, became Serbia's main government party. The Serb Radical government attempted to shake the country's political-economic dependency on Austria-Hungary. The result was the "Pig War" of 1906–1911, during which Austria-Hungary closed its borders to Serbian pork, the most important export of the agricultural Serbian economy. From 1906 forward, Serbia found new ways of exporting livestock, plums, and grains, thus increasing the Radical party's popularity among exporters, peasants, and manufacturers. The "Pig War" helped promote domestic industrial growth. From 1900 to 1910, the number of industrial enterprises increased from 153 to 465, and the value of industrial production increased sevenfold. Austria-Hungary—which previously had controlled 90 percent of Serbian trade—controlled only 30 percent of it afterward (Dedijer et al. 1974, 429; Vucinich 1968, 235; Dragnich 1974, 64).

However, this kind of economic nationalism did not imply an endorsement of the most radical plans advocated by the officer corps. In early twentieth-century Serbia, such plans entailed the unification of all "Serb lands" (including Montenegro, Bosnia, and Croatia) under Serbian leadership (Petrovich 1976, 2: 607). In 1904, Serb organizations were formed in Macedonia, and guerrilla bands were formed and led by Serb officers. Following the failure to gain any meaningful compensations for the 1908 annexation of Bosnia-Herzegovina by Austria-Hungary, two organizations were formed: *Narodna Odbrana* (National Defense) and *Ujedinjenje ili Smrt* (Unification or Death).[12] *Narodna Odbrana* aimed at registering Serb protests against the annexation and at organizing volunteer troops to be sent to Bosnia. Within a month, 220 local committees had sprung up spontaneously in towns and villages throughout the country and 5,000 volunteers registered with them. After Austrian demands to curtail *Narodna Odbrana*'s reach in 1909, the Serb government was forced to disavow it, and *Narodna Odbrana* concentrated on cultural activities. By 1911–1912, *Narodna Odbrana* had established ties with the other major society, *Ujedinjenje ili Smrt*, and the two became parallel in action and overlapping in membership.

Their interlocking leadership gave the impression that the *Odbrana* was indeed involved in violent revolutionary activity (McKenzie 1995, 44), but this was the prerogative of the group *Ujedinjenje ili Smrt*, informally known as the Black Hand. This secret society was formed in 1910, with a membership pool of military officers and intellectuals. Its original goal was to coordinate Serb guerrilla bands in Macedonia, but its long-term goal was to bring about Serb unification. By 1911, court members, assembly deputies, journalists, diplomats, and the government knew of its existence. Already involved in the 1903 coup, Dragutin Dimitrijevic ("Apis") soon became the focal point of the new secret society. Fearful of the lack of official control over the society's actions, the Radical Party government sought to distance official Serbia from its actions. This internal rift was temporarily suspended during the two Balkan wars. However, by 1913, the occupation of northern Macedonia by Serbian forces resulted in an acute political–military conflict regarding the administration of the newly acquired territories, with the military insisting that it should assume all authority

(Dedijer et al. 1974, 243, 470; Dragnich 1974, 74–7; Djordjevic 1970a, 378–9; McKenzie 1989, 67–86, 105–22, 137; 1995, 43–6). As will be discussed in Chapter 7, it was the Apis group that, contrary to the will of the Radical government, offered assistance to the Young Bosnians who plotted the assassination of Archduke Ferdinand in Sarajevo. Apis viewed the archduke as a threat to greater Serbian nationalism because of Ferdinand's endorsement of trialism (an Austrian–Hungarian–South Slavic federation). If the archduke's plans were to prove viable, Serbian irredentism toward Bosnia and Vojvodina would be fatally frustrated.

In the Serbian case, the rift between the military and the civilian authorities was never expressed in public; in Greece, a similar type of conflict achieved momentous proportions as it became a central feature of the Greek national schism. As in Serbia, significant shifts in the structure of the military corps after 1909 promoted irredentism. The creation of the permanent reserve officer corps, members of which received promotions only in time of war, created a military constituency.[13]

The Greek national schism was expressed in the post-1915 period as a conflict between King Constantine and Premier Eleutherios Venizelos over the question of Greece's entrance into World War I.[14] The king was in favor of neutrality (with his sympathies on the Central Powers' side); the premier was in favor of entering the war on the side of the Entente. It was more than a personal conflict; the two leaders expressed political and social coalitions with very different perspectives. When the Entente began the Dardanelles expedition in 1915, a wave of enthusiasm swayed the Greek public, offering to Venizelos a golden opportunity to ally Greece with the Entente. In two successive councils, the king and the prime minister failed to agree on the proper course of action and the prime minister resigned (Leon 1974, 1, 22–32; Smith 1973, 49–50). In the new elections of 13 June 1915 the Liberal Party won a clear majority with 185 seats; the opposition won 122 (Leon 1974, 208; Ventiris 1970, 2:61). Consequently, a new Liberal cabinet was formed. Nevertheless, it was becoming evident that the state had indeed two governments: an elected official one under Venizelos and a shadowy informal one under the Crown.

Following Bulgaria's partial military mobilization on 21 September 1915, Venizelos called for a mobilization of the Greek armed forces. By a June 1913 military convention, Greece was obliged to aid Serbia if Serbia was attacked by Bulgaria provided that Serbia would put 150,000 troops on the field (Palmer 1965, 19). After the Bulgarian mobilization, the Serbian government telegraphed an appeal for 150,000 French and British troops—exactly the number specified by the 1913 Greek–Serb treaty (Palmer 1965, 32–3). It was evident that if Bulgaria attacked Serbia and Serbia fulfilled the treaty's letter and called for Greek assistance, Greece would be involved in the war. Although a Greek mobilization was finally ordered, the gap between king and prime minister became increasingly impossible to bridge. The mobilization also signaled the beginning of a wavering public opinion, especially among the peasantry, which constituted two-thirds of the armed forces. In the meantime, after two more weeks of painful negotiations, it became plain that the king and Venizelos could not agree. Despite attempts to break the Liberal Party, Venizelos succeeded in getting a confidence vote that called upon the king to enter the war (Ventiris 1970, 2:64). Following this vote and given the king's opposition to such a policy, Venizelos resigned for a second time. Five days before his resignation, Venizelos invited Allied troops to Thessaloniki (Vournas 1977, 177). The troops landed on October 5, putting the new anti-Venizelist cabinet in a difficult position.

Once more, the king proceeded to dissolve the parliament and call for new elections. Venizelos deemed the dissolution of the parliament unconstitutional and called for a boycott of the new elections by his followers.[15] In the December 19 elections, only 230,000 citizens voted, whereas in the previous elections the number had been 730,000 (the boycott was especially successful in the post-1913 "new lands").[16] In the spring of 1916, the new royalist government concluded an agreement with Germany and Bulgaria that called for the two powers to occupy various posts in Eastern Macedonia, including Fort Roupel.

The Entente powers were quick in reacting. On 7 June 1916 the Entente forces began a partial blockade of the Greek coast and by 8 June 1916 the Entente asked for the demobilization of the Greek army (Leon 1974, 362–9). Under pressure from the Entente, the anti-Venizelist government did not hesitate to use the police and the mob to terrorize the Athens' Venizelists. The demobilization of the army was executed over the summer of 1916 and led to the formation of Reservists' Leagues, dominated by anti-Venizelist sentiments. The leagues soon numbered close to 200,000 members. Under the guidance of the General Staff (and the assistant commander of the General Staff, Ioannis Metaxas, in particular), the Reservists developed into a formidable anti-Venizelist weapon. They spread throughout the country south of Macedonia and became full-fledged paramilitary organizations, terrorizing countryside and town until 1920 (see Mavrocordatos 1996).[17]

By late May 1916, while the Greek army was demobilized and the national schism was gradually consolidated, the anti-Venizelist Greek government surrendered Fort Roupel (in eastern Macedonia) to the Bulgarian–German forces. The surrender was part of an agreement with Germany, which allowed for the temporary occupation of military fortifications in eastern Macedonia by mixed Bulgarian–German forces in exchange for the return of these territories after the end of the war. Civilian Greek authority was to be maintained in these areas.[18] The Venizelists considered Roupel's surrender treacherous; they viewed it as a willful surrender of Greek fortifications to Greece's main enemy, Bulgaria. The gradual advancement of Bulgarian forces into Greek Macedonia led to harassment of the Greek population by irregular bands. By the end of August, the populations of the cities of Drama and Serres began to flee toward the port of Kavala in fear of these paramilitary bands. In the end, the whole Fourth Army Corps was surrendered to the Bulgarians, who proceeded to occupy the port of Kavala and all of eastern Macedonia. This shocked the Athens government, which was completely unprepared for such a turn.

The waves of refugees, the alarm caused by these actions among the Greek Macedonians, and the fear that the rest of Greek Macedonia would have the same fate provided the incentive for a new nationalist coup. In August 1916 in Thessaloniki, followers of the Liberal Party founded a Committee of National Defense. The initiative belonged to local Greek Macedonians who were worried about a possible Bulgarian offensive. Soon they were joined by other Venizelists and the Cretan National Guard (Palmer 1965, 95–7). In September 1916, under French protection, Venizelos left Athens for Crete, where he announced the formation of a provisional government and pledged to fight on the side of the Entente. He then proceeded to Thessaloniki, where he joined the officers of the National Defense.

Greece split into two parts: the post-1912 "New Lands" under Venizelos and the pre-1881 "Old Greece" under King Constantine. The national schism thus became a territorial one. Venizelos' coup was met with enthusiasm in the post–1913, New Lands (Crete, Macedonia, and Epirus), whereas the (pre-1881) Old Greece remained indifferent or even hostile to it. When the provisional government of Venizelos, Danglis, and Koundouriotis declared itself allied with the Entente and officially entered the war, the Athens regime reacted with indignation (Ventiris 1970, 2:255). On the side of the king stood the old political oligarchy of pre-1912 Greece, which was displaced by the 1909 coup, and Venizelos' Liberal Party. They were supported by the majority of Greek yeomen, peasantry, and petit bourgeois strata of pre-1912 Greece. On the side of the premier were the populations of the new territories of post-1913 Greece (Crete, Epirus, and the Greeks of Macedonia)—regions where the Greek population felt they owed loyalty to Venizelos.

The only major peasant constituency for Venizelos came from the landless peasants of Thessaly. In 1881, following the incorporation of Thessaly into the Greek state, the Ottoman landowners had sold their land to approximately 40 rich Ottoman Greek families, who organized them into plantations. These holdings included 350 villages with a total of at least 11,000 families.[19] By 1910 a bloody peasant uprising in Killerer had raised the issue of land reform. Peasant support for the Venizelists was conditional on their support for land appropriation. This agreement finally yielded results: From 1917 onward, Venizelist—as well as post-1920—governments carried out extensive land redistribution plans.

In the years 1916 and 1917, the Entente forces kept pressuring the Athens government to step down and King Constantine to abdicate. Finally, on 12 June 1917, Constantine agreed to leave Greece and his second son, Alexander, assumed his duties as king.[20] On 26 June 1917, Venizelos returned to Athens, and 2 days later he assumed his duties as prime minister. Venizelos resurrected the 13 June 1915, chamber (which, henceforth, became known as "the Lazarus" chamber) and proceeded to govern—essentially as a dictator—for the next 3 years. Because of his efforts, the Greek army eventually intervened in the war on the Entente side.

## NATIONALISM AND THE BALKAN PEASANTRY

During the nineteenth and early twentieth centuries, the characteristic feature of socioeconomic patterns in Greece, Serbia, and Bulgaria was the sharp juxtaposition between urban and rural sectors. The urban sector was dominated by the state—which was the mechanism used for both nation building and state building in these newly created national societies. This social pattern was the product of the creation of a freeholding peasantry, of underdevelopment, and of statism. In Greece and Serbia the peasantry's political importance led to a taxation policy favorable toward them. As elsewhere in Europe, the state-dependent strata offered support to nationalist ideologies. These strata were numerous in the Balkan states, and had no other urban social group to oppose them. The local political elites used the state bureaucracy for patronage purposes. The local intelligentsia developed irredentist visions that legitimized the local states' project of nation building, and, consequently, the growth of the local bureaucracies.

In all three Balkan states, the peasantry played a key role in national politics. The immediate question of the relationship between irredentism and the peasantry has, however, a rather simple answer: In none of the three states was the peasantry a motivating factor for nationalist mobilization. The peasantry had to be coached and indoctrinated to irredentism. However, to do so in the face of widespread peasant illiteracy was impossible. The national societies of the Balkan states centered around the urban world, a world alien to the peasantry, who looked on it with mistrust or with outright hostility. To gain peasant support required providing the peasantry with ideal or material incentives for a particular party platform.

Against the peasant world stood the urban world of the Balkan states. It centered around the state and middle-class groups of small-scale merchants, professionals, artisans, and shopkeepers. The central role of the state in Balkan national societies meant that bureaucracy and civil service were privileged occupations, benefiting from the symbolic prestige and omnipresence of the state in social life. The manner in which the Balkan bureaucracies were organized varied from state to state. In Greece, the bureaucracy was organized on the basis of a "spoils system" of patronage and clientelism that guaranteed widespread popular support. In Serbia, the opposite was the case: The bureaucracy became a privileged minority ruling over the majority of the population. This was the outcome of the failure of the Serb prelates to successfully challenge Prince Miloš' authority. In Bulgaria, the bureaucracy combined Greek-style extensive patronage with the heavy-handed manner of the Serb bureaucracy.

In all three states, the native freeholding peasantry did not endorse irredentism. The peasantry of pre-1881 Greece, the Bulgarian peasantry, and the Serb peasantry all displayed a rather negative attitude vis-à-vis irredentism. In practice, only during the 1880–1920 period did the peasantry enter into politics as an *active* political force. The participation of the peasantry was a sign of national integration but it also raised the question of peasant support for irredentism. During this period, the peasantry was not among the groups associated with irredentism. Its political parties most often quarreled with the officer corps, which was the group most closely associated with irredentism. In itself, this conflict illustrates the close connection between statism and irredentism. Irredentism was the consequence of state-sponsored strategies of modernization; the more "modernized" the local societies became, the more numerous state-dependent strata became.[21] The post–World War II communist regimes in Yugoslavia and Bulgaria exaggerated this already existing trend. Similarly, throughout modern Greek history, the public sector has been the major employer among the urban population.

Nevertheless, during the 1880–1920 period, both the Bulgarian peasantry and the Greek peasantry of Old Greece took an antinationalist stand. The Greek Liberals could count only on Greece's urban strata, the population of the New Lands where memories of Ottoman rule were alive, and the landless peasants of Thessaly for support. In the end, it was not enough, and the anti-Venizelist forces carried the day. Contrary to the situation in Greece, the urban and military establishment of Bulgaria was successful in bringing the country into the two Balkan wars and World War I. However, it failed to deliver results that would improve the peasantry's condition. Instead, the peasantry was squeezed to raise funds for the military, and in the end, the peasantry gave up, offering massive support for BANU and its antimilitaristic platform. The Serb peasantry gained its property guarantees early in the nineteenth century. Contrary to the Greek and Bulgarian experiences, the ascent of the Serb Radical Party represented more of a struggle against the Obrenović dynasty rather than a struggle over foreign policy. The Radical Party policy of taxing the urban rather than the peasant population prevented peasant discontent from becoming explosive. As a result, urban and nationalist politics never captivated the rural population. The Balkan wars of 1912–1913 were swift victories, and World War I was fought mainly as a defensive war.

To gain popular support, the Greek Liberals had to promise massive land redistribution; the Serb Radicals and BANU had to cater to the peasant hostility toward the urban world and promise an improvement of social conditions in the countryside. These were clear financial incentives and were unrelated to nationalism. Indeed, the strength of regional ties prevented the articulation of nation-wide goals; in the 1915 Greek national schism, Greece split into two parts, a clear manifestation of the lack of national integration (Mavrocordatos 1983a). In Bulgaria, the Macedonians and the Bulgarian peasants fought a similar conflict, albeit not one that was regional, at least to the extent of the Greek case. For the majority of the Balkan population, then, nationalism would reach the popular level only in the twentieth century, with the coming of mass literacy and mass media.

## NOTES

1. The extensive debate on the Balkan underdevelopment and its causes falls beyond the scope of this book. For an overview of some of these debates, see the essays in

Chirot (1989). See also Lampe and Jackson (1982), Palairet (1997), and Berend and Ranki (1974) for further discussion.

2. Castellan (1991, 415), Djordjevic (1970a, 83–4), and Tomasevich (1955, 39–41, 180–92). The inviolability of a certain portion of peasant land was further strengthened by the Civil Procedure Act of 1860 and by the protected minimum homestead legislation of 1873. See Lampe and Jackson (1982, 114–6) and Petrovich (1976, 2:374).

3. Tsoukalas (1978, 1987) views this group as a state bourgeoisie. Dertilis (1977, 156) suggests that the lack of class-consciousness indicates they were more akin to a political oligarchy. For critiques of both approaches, see Lyrintzis (1991) and Sotirelis (1991, 93–8).

4. Although the debate about whether the coup was a bourgeois revolution or not has been a lively one, the movement appears to have presented the generalized discontent of various strata of the population. Ventiris (1970, 1:17–46) suggested that 1909 was a bourgeois revolution. By contrast, Vournas (1977, 7–8) believed that the Greek society of the time lacked the deep class cleavages necessary for the emergence of class politics. Dertilis (1977, 202–20) and, to some extent, Vournas (1977) suggested that the 1909 regime change was the outcome of a broad social coalition. Mavrocordatos (1983b, 121–4) suggested that 1909 turned into a bourgeois movement after Venizelos' involvement with it. See Smith (1973, 10–11) and Ventiris (1970, I) for biographical notes of Venizelos' pre-1910 activities.

5. McKenzie (1982; 1989, 58–61). Against the Apis faction stood a group of older officers, prominent under the Obrenović dynasty, who were deeply resentful of the conspirators' actions. In 1903 and 1905 they attempted counterconspiracies that were put down forcefully; this led to extensive purges of the officer corps.

6. This attitude stands in sharp contrast to the active involvement of military officers in Bulgarian political life during the reign of Bulgaria's first ruler, Prince Alexander of Battenberg. For a discussion of the military's involvement in politics during Alexander's regime, see Durman (1987).

7. See Bell (1977, 118–21) and Constant (1980, 301) on the confrontation between Ferdinand and Stamboliski. Despite Ferdinand's elated announcement of Bulgaria's entrance into the war, the Bulgarian public was not jubilant about the war, and some incidents of mutiny were reported during the first days of the mobilization (Constant 1980, 304; Crampton 1983, 447–9).

8. Bell (1977, 122–3). For a general review of the war's impact, see Crampton (1983, 472–510). According to Constant (1980, 309), the publication of President Wilson's Fourteen Points and his additional Four Principles further demoralized the army. The Bulgarian soldier implicitly believed that after the war, national self-determination would prevail, and hence, the Bulgarian character of Macedonia would be acknowledged. The United States had not, in fact, declared war to Bulgaria and the American minister in Sofia arranged for Wilson's speeches to be translated and widely distributed throughout the country.

9. Its intellectual origins are to be found in Svetovar Marković's combination of peasant traditionalism and socialism (McClellan 1964, 77–8; Stokes 1990, 52; Petrovich 1976, 2:377). Marković wished to maintain the traditional egalitarian style of Serbian life. The slogan launched by Marković and adopted by the Serb Radical Party was *samouprava* (i.e., self-government). It meant the right of the people to elect local government officials and thus to participate directly in the government of their locale.

10. On their 1881 program, see Stokes (1990, 197), and on Pašić's 1882 election, see

Dragnich (1978, 63). On the Radicals' 1880s gradual transformation, see Djordjevic (1970a, 226) and Petrovich (1976, 2:447–8).

11. On Alexander's regime, see Djordjevic (1970a, 255–64), Petrovich (1976, 2:463–9), Dragnich (1974, 44–58), and especially, on the 1903 coup, McKenzie (1991, 55–76).

12. On guerrilla bands in Macedonia, see McKenzie (1982, 334). On the growth of the National Defense, see McKenzie (1982, 334) and Djordjevic (1970a, 353). On the post-1909 restructuring of its activities, see Dedijer (1966, 608).

13. The percentage of academy graduates in relation to the total number of officers dropped from 29 percent in 1909 to 14 percent in 1914 (Veremis 1997, 36–7). The reserve officers met the contempt of the academy officers, who never accepted them as equals.

14. For narratives of the national schism, see Leon (1974), Vournas (1977), and Ventiris (1970). Leon's is perhaps the best study of the 1914–1917 period. For a novel interpretation of Venizelos' charisma, as well as for further literature on Venizelos, see Mazower (1992).

15. Although Venizelos was probably correct on the legal aspects of this issue, his position was also the result of political calculation: Almost 400,000 men were in the army and Venizelos estimated that approximately 75 percent of them were his followers. Because the army could not vote, his chances in the new elections were slim. In addition, the erosion of Liberal support among the peasantry further diminished the Liberals' chances.

16. Leon (1974, 309) and Ventiris (1970, 2:89). During 1915 and consistently throughout the interwar period, the Liberal Party enjoyed remarkable popularity among the Greeks in Macedonia, Crete, Epirus, and Thrace. It is worth noting that the Jews of Thessaloniki and the Turks and Slavs of Macedonia were hostile to the party because they correctly understood the implications of its irredentist policies. This group was allied with the majority of the peasantry and the old political establishment in the Old Greece (cf. Mavrocordatos, 1983b, esp. 226–72).

17. In reaction to the Reservists' Leagues, the Venizelists organized their own league (July 14) but their efforts to develop regional branches failed due to harassment and persecution by the authorities (Ventiris 1970, 2:60; Leon 1974, 376).

18. Vournas (1977, 179–80). For a detailed description of the events, see Ventiris (1970, 2:110–29). On the Fourth Army Corps' surrender and Kavala's occupation, see Ventiris (1970, 2:178–9) and Leon (1974, 400).

19. See Arseniou (1994, 24, 240–5), Leon (1974, 374–6), and Vournas (1977, 55–72). The total amount of land redistributed prior to and after 1917 involved a total of 3,000 estates, approximately 40 percent of the country's arable land, and 310,000 peasant families (Mavrocordatos 1983b, 159; Arseniou 1994, 258–67).

20. Smith (1973, 59) and Leon (1974, 487). The king went into exile, where he attempted to organize a plot for his return. He asked for the aid of the German government but did not receive it. The German government had sided with the Bulgarians, promising them territorial compensation in Macedonia in exchange for their entering the war on the Central Powers' side. Hence, King Constantine's plans did not meet a receptive audience (for an overview, see Leontaritis 1990, 81–115; also see Veremis 1980a, 568, for a brief summary).

21. For example, in 1941, when the Bulgarian state attempted for a third time to realize the dream of a "San Stefano" Bulgaria, its civil servants numbered 130,000; with their families they numbered 650,000 people, a third of the urban population (Stoianovich 1994, 212).

# 7

# The Consequences of Modernity: National Homogenization and the Minority Question

Serbia should hold at all costs and in all circumstances to the Yugoslav program. She should never justify the fatal insinuation that it would suffice to enlarge Serbia with as many provinces as possible. . . . The *entire* Triune Kingdom [of Croatia] ought to be united with Serbia. For it would certainly be unnecessary to point out to Your Royal Highness that if Croatia became an independent state alongside Serbia, the situation of the latter would be still less favorable than before the war; for in that case, the two sister nations would be enemies; in place of the idea of the national unity of all Serbs, Croats, and Slovenes in a single state, we would have an acute conflict between two opposing Slav programs; and in view of the impossibility of drawing any territorial line of separation between Serbs and Croats, each of the two states—the new Serbia and the new Croatia—would be torn apart from one end to the other by two rival irredentisms—the Catholics and Muslims of enlarged Serbia looking to Zagreb, and the Orthodox of Dalmatia looking to Belgrade.

> R. W. Seton-Watson in a letter to Prince Regent Alexander of Serbia, 17 September 1915, quoted in Rusinow 1995, 305–6

Nothing, I venture to say, is more likely to disturb the peace of the world than the treatment which might, in certain circumstances be meted out to the minorities.

> U.S. president Woodrow Wilson, quoted in Robinson 1943, 10

The post–World War I reconstruction of the political map in Eastern Europe was a monumental change in the pattern of regional political organization. By

1920 the Ottoman, Habsburg, and Russian empires had disappeared and a completely new geopolitical configuration had emerged. Still, Eastern Europe included three times the number of ethnic groups and nationalities of Western Europe. Moreover, according to past imperial policies, the peoples had been frequently intermixed with each other, thereby producing a mosaic that could not possibly conform to national boundaries (Pearson 1983). However, in the expanding and consolidating international system of nation-states, there was little room left for different political solutions (McNeill 1985; Mayall 1990). On the contrary, "minority peoples were anomalies within the nation-state, and were perceived as elements which weakened and divided it" (Musgrave 1997, 10).

Still, the boundaries established after World War I enjoyed considerable longevity. With minor exceptions, these boundaries remained the same during most of the twentieth century (see Map 4). This does not mean that the boundaries were not contested. On the contrary, during World War II, Bulgaria occupied a considerable part of its Macedonian *irredenta* as well as Western Thrace, while the so-called independent State of Croatia occupied most of Bosnia-Herzegovina, and the Italian and German forces shared in the occupation of Serbia, Macedonia, and Greece. However, none of the aforementioned territorial changes survived World War II, and in its aftermath, the continental boundaries of the Balkan nation-states returned to the pre–World War II lines.

The Balkan system of nation-states that emerged from the Balkan wars of 1912–1913 and the subsequent World War I (1914–1918) formed a political field in which the issues of national minorities and national homogenization shaped intrastate and interstate relations (Brubaker 1995). No state among them was able to incorporate all of its potential nationals in its own territory. Indeed, the problems posed by the incomplete nature of "national liberation" were common throughout Eastern Europe. The resolution of these issues was the first major test for the twentieth-century international system of nation-states.[1] However, the League of Nations was unable to deal effectively with these issues, and this led to the collapse of the interwar system and paved the way for World War II. Among the key factors for this failure was the differential adaptation of the principle of self-determination from the U.S. and Western European context to the Eastern European mosaic of ethnic groups and nationalities. Early segments of this principle were proclaimed by the Bolsheviks in the aftermath of the October 1917 revolution. The principle was later on explicitly formulated by U.S. president Woodrow Wilson, but not without a twist that was to be the source of major problems in the interwar period. Wilson initially connected self-determination to democratic self-government, but his statements were reinterpreted by Eastern European nationalists in terms of their own concept of self-determination, entailing the formation of its own nation-state by each ethnic group (Musgrave 1997, 17–24). This selective incorporation of self-determination reflects the different normative contexts in the U.S. versus the Eastern European context. In the discourse of citizenship, self-determination as

**Map 4**
**The Boundaries of the Balkan Nation-States after World War I**

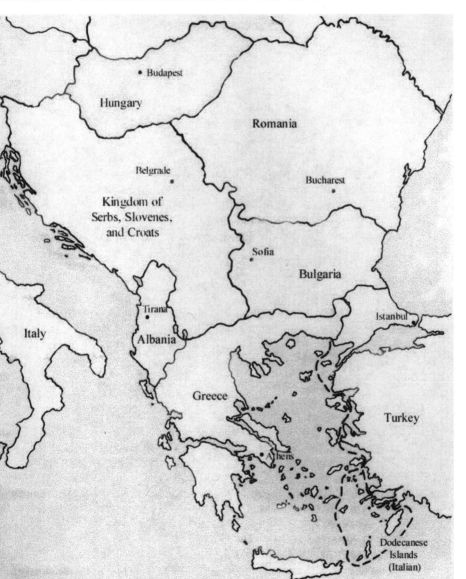

a political principle was connected to democracy and inclusion; within the discourse of nationhood, self-determination provided legitimacy for the nationalist goals of the ethnic groups in the Eastern European empires.

Furthermore, completion of the nation-building process entailed centralization and homogenization. Both projects were an extension of state-sponsored strategies of modernization (cf. Giddens 1985) aiming to Europeanize the Balkans. The issue of ethnic heterogeneity in the Balkans became a problem for state administrators and international committees, whose goal was to construct nationally homogeneous imagined communities. As discussed in Chapters 4 and 5, the historical traditions, public institutions, national histories, and literature of the Balkan nations strongly emphasized nationhood rather than citizenship as the basic component of their national identities. Therefore, the pursuit of centralization and homogenization entailed a clash with the local cultures of various minority groups. Rival nation-states did not hesitate to lay claims to such minorities, thereby adding oil to the fire.

Keeping these general issues in mind, in this chapter I discuss the way the "national question" was dealt with in the interwar Balkans. In the following, I concentrate on those minorities that were claimed by more than one of the Balkan nation-states. These were not the only minority groups in the region, but they were the most numerous and most important ones for interstate relations and public policy.[2]

## THE UNMIXING OF PEOPLES AND THE END OF THE EMPIRE

From the Balkan wars of 1912 to 1913 until the Greek–Turkish population exchange of 1923, the demographic and political map of the Balkan peninsula experienced drastic changes that altered the human geography of the region. The Balkan wars were followed by extensive population movements. In 1912 a part of the Ottoman Muslim population—roughly around 100,000—fled before the armies of the Balkan countries. Following the second Balkan war, 15,000 Bulgarians followed the Bulgarian army in its retreat and 10,000 Greeks fled the parts of the region granted to Bulgaria. Approximately 70,000 Greeks emigrated from western Thrace, which was occupied by Bulgaria; 48,570 Muslims from the same region emigrated to Ottoman Turkey; and 46,764 Bulgarians left eastern Thrace for Bulgaria (Ladas 1932, 15).

The trend intensified after World War I and led to extensive population transfers aiming to separate peoples according to ethnic, linguistic, and religious criteria. The two regions most acutely affected were Macedonia and Anatolia. The former was divided among the Balkan states (Serbia, Bulgaria, and Greece) and the latter became the homeland of the emerging Turkish nation. Both regions experienced extensive and often forced population exchanges—a practice that came to be known in the 1990s as "ethnic cleansing". Still, this ethnic cleansing was considered legitimate at the time, and was sanctioned by an array of international treaties.

Macedonia was divided among Greece, Bulgaria, and Serbia (the post-1917 kingdom of Serbs, Slovenes, and Croats). Because of the ethnic intermixing of peoples in the region, the division was not uniformly accepted, and interstate rivalry over the region persisted during the interwar period. Bulgaria's efforts to conquer the greater part of former Ottoman Macedonia were frustrated both in the Balkan wars and in World War I. In the aftermath of World War I, Greece and Bulgaria agreed on a mutual population exchange during which approximately 30,000 Greeks left Bulgaria and 53,000 Bulgarians left Greece (Pentzopoulos 1962, 60). The Macedonian separatist organization IMRO opposed the implementation of the exchange because it would weaken claims to the Greek-held part of Macedonia (Barker 1950, 30). Consequently, those under IMRO influence chose to remain in the country. By far the most important development in Greek Macedonia was the departure of the Muslim population and the resettlement of Greek Orthodox refugees from Anatolia. With the 1923 Greek–Turkish population exchange agreement, 354,647 Muslims left Greece and 339,094 Greeks arrived in Greek Macedonia from Anatolia (Pentzopoulos 1962, 69, 107; Ladas 1932). The result was a complete change in the ethnic composition of Greek Macedonia. By 1928 Greeks accounted for 88.8 percent of the population in Greek Macedonia, totally altering the pre-1913 mixture of ethnic groups and nationalities (Pentzopoulos 1962, 127–37).

The other region that experienced dramatic demographic changes was Anatolia. In this case, the change was produced by the collision between Greek and Turkish nationalisms in the 1910s and 1920s. In the course of this conflict, Greece and Turkey were transformed into presumably homogeneous nation-states. In the aftermath of the 1912–1913 Balkan wars, there was a twofold shift in the Young Turks' ideological orientation: In the field of state policy, liberalism gave way to a statist-corporatist policy; in the ideological field, strong influences of Pan-Turanism or Pan-Turkism slowly transformed cultural Ottomanism into Turkish nationalism. The rise of statism was facilitated by the realization that political independence was impossible to achieve without real economic independence (Zurcher 1984, 56).[3] Given the absence of an indigenous Muslim middle class, CUP policies did not have a clientele: A Muslim "bourgeoisie" would need to be created if the goal of saving the state was to be accomplished. Only such a class could provide support for their policies. Such a class existed but was Orthodox (Armenian and Greek) Christian, not Muslim. The problem was to displace the Orthodox and put Muslims in their place.

Pan-Turkism received its impetus from migrant Turkish intellectuals from Russia whose aim was to liberate all other Turks suffering under foreign yoke. They were rapidly accepted by Ottoman Turks as equals; prominent immigrants, such as Gasprinsky, Akcura, and Agaoglu, were co-opted into Young Turk or other circles (Landau 1981, 34). In 1904, the Tartar Yusuf Akcura published in Cairo an article arguing that the interests of the three main groups of the empire (Muslim Turks, non-Turk Muslims, and non-Muslims) did not coincide. According to him, the recognition of the nationalist claims of Arabs and Christians was inevitable; therefore, the Turks should relinquish the empire and become a Turkish nation (Kitsikis 1990, 97–9; Kushner 1977, 5).

After 1908, Pan-Turkists began to organize in the Ottoman Empire in a series of cultural organizations that attracted a large number of intellectuals. Akcura left Russia for Turkey in 1908. He began teaching Turkish political theory at various institutions in Constantinople and was a founder of or at least a very active member in a large number of Pan-Turkist societies. In 1908 he founded the Turkish Association (Turk Dernegi), the first Turkish nationalist organization. In addition to writing a number of books and articles, his outstanding efforts during his 6-year term as editor of the journal *Turk Yurdu* made the periodical not only a leading journal of Pan-Turk propaganda but also gave it a prestige that led some of the foremost Turkish intellectuals of the time to contribute to it (Arai 1992, 58–65, 96–7; Landau 1981, 41–2). By 1913, Akcura publicly criticized the concept of "political and administrative Tanzimatism," which he judged harmful to Ottoman Turks. By then he had been joined by other intellectuals (e.g., Ziya Gokalp), who argued against the *Tanzimat* and political Ottomanism. Their writings in this period formulated a new ethnic ideal that rejected the political or cultural "fusion of the elements" (i.e., Ottomanism) in favor of an ethnically defined Turkish identity.

The Turkish nationalist societies enjoyed widespread popularity; one of them, the Turk Ocagi (Hearth of the Turks), was founded in 1911 at the military medical school and by 1914 had 16 hearths in the Ottoman Empire with a total of 3,000 or more members; by 1920, its membership was close to 30,000 (Landan 1981, 41; Alp 1917, 33–42; Arai 1992, 68–73). During the 1908 to 1913 period, Pan-Turkism was gradually becoming the major political platform. The bone of contention for the rising Turkish nationalism was the charge of being essentially anti-Islamic; nationalism destroyed the brotherly feeling toward other Muslims. Throughout the 1910s, nationalist writers grouped around the journal *Genc Kalemler* argued that their new orientation was not condemned by the Koran. The journal's leading figures met in a CUP club almost every day and argued about literature and philosophy. By 1911 to 1913, linguistic arguments about the simplification of the Turkish language were intrinsically linked with the issue of a Turkish—as opposed to an Ottoman—identity. The intellectuals' strong populism put them in favor of the spoken language, a choice that reflected not only the Young Turks' literary taste but also their lower-class origins. The influence of this intellectual evolution was reflected in the CUP agenda (Arai 1992, 24–46; Landau 1981, 48).

The losses of the Balkan wars and the apparent failure of Ottomanism reinforced support for the Pan-Turk option.[4] The combination of Pan-Turkism and statism was manifest in the changing attitude of the CUP toward the minority population. The goal of the new CUP policies was to establish control of the economy by the Turkish ethnic group (Ahmad 1980, 342–3). During the 1908–1918 period, government officials collaborated with local merchants, traders, or rural notables to set up a series of new companies that were to undertake major commercial functions in Anatolia. To counter the dominant role of the Greek and Armenian communities, they strongly encouraged the "Turkish" character of commercial establishments; buying from a Turk instead of a Greek or Armenian became a matter of patriotism.

To implement this policy the Young Turks began a policy of intimidation and deportation in Anatolia, where most of the Christian population lived. In 1909, the unionists coordinated a commercial boycott of Ottoman Greek commerce aimed at punishing Athens for supporting Crete's declaration of union with Greece.[5] The aim of the boycott was also to raise political and national consciousness among the Turks and, over time, this factor became more important than the original aim, because the Committee became aware of the need for a "national economy" and a Turkish bourgeoisie (Ahmad 1982, 414). More pressure was applied to the Ottoman Greek community when in 1909 Greece annexed the islands of Lesvos and Chios and when Greece annexed western Thrace after the second Balkan war (1913) (Alp 1917, 50–1). By the end of 1913, more Muslim refugees flooded into the empire. The harassment of the Muslims in the newly conquered territories made the Unionists opt for a population exchange between the Muslims of the Balkan states and the Ottoman Greeks of the empire (Ergil 1975, 62; Ventiris 1970, 1:191–4). Treaties between Bulgaria and Turkey in 1913 and between Greece and the Ottoman Empire in 1915 attempted to bring about population exchanges; but World War I interrupted these plans (Smith 1973, 31–3; Pentzopoulos 1962, 54–5).

During the 1914–1918 period, the harassment of the Ottoman Greek minority took the form of open economic and paramilitary warfare. A total of 481,109 persons were deported into the interior of Anatolia in the four years of the war; even after the 1919 armistice, the expulsions continued, being directed this time against the Greeks of the Black Sea and Trebzond areas (Pentzopoulos 1962, 57). Paramilitary bands were formed among the Muslim refugees and the reign of terror against the Ottoman Greek minority continued until 1916. The Unionist government asked all foreign firms to fire their Greek employees and hire Turks instead. Under the leadership of Enver pasha and Celal Bey, a "special organization" was formed to "nationalize" western Anatolia. In 1914, approximately 130,000 Greeks were forced to leave for Greece or the Aegean islands from the rich suburbs of Smyrna, the main commercial center of western Anatolia and home to a majority of the Ottoman Greek population (Ergil 1975, 63).

The final solution of the minority question took place with the Greek Anatolian venture in the 1921–1922 period. The attempt to conquer Anatolia failed miserably and resulted in the 1922 Asia Minor debacle. The Greek failure also constituted the high point of the Turkish war of national independence (1919–1922), begun under the leadership of Mustafa Kemal, who became known as Kemal Ataturk, the founder of modern Turkey.[6] The Turkish victory led to the practical disappearance of the Greek Orthodox presence in Anatolia.[7] The overwhelming majority of the Ottoman Greek population in Anatolia fled their homes after the collapse of the Greek Army in 1922. In the 1923 Lausanne treaty, the Greek and Turkish governments agreed on the compulsory exchange of the Muslim minority in Macedonia and the remaining Ottoman Greek population of Anatolia. The result of the "ethnic cleansing" of the Ottoman Greek (and Armenian) populations was the successful homogenization of the Republic of Turkey. (At the time, the Kurds of eastern Anatolia did not represent a major threat).

The major exception in the Greek–Turkish population exchange concerned the approximately 300,000 Greeks of Constantinople and the Muslims and Turks of Western Thrace. The Constantinople Greeks were exempted from the population exchange after some pressure by the Western powers who were concerned that this could hurt their commercial interests. But the exodus of the Greek minority was unavoidable: Their numbers declined to about 100,000 in 1927 (Alexandris 1983, 87). The remaining population was subjected to further state pressure to homogenize within the emerging Turkish Republic. The minority and the patriarchate became pawns in Greek–Turkish relations (see Alexandris 1983 for a review). Indeed, the Turkish Republic of the post-1920 period undertook a whole series of specific policies designed to marginalize the minorities (Poulton 1997a, 114–29; Salamone 1989a and b). These policies aimed at reducing the ethnic heterogeneity of Anatolia and acculturating various Turkish ethnic groups (Tatars, Circassians, Lazes, etc.) into a single Turkish nation.

After the Greek state annexed western Thrace in 1920, it estimated the Muslim and Turkish population to be 84,000, 20 percent of whom were Muslim Pomaks (Milios 1997, 302–3). As with the Muslim and Turkish minority in Bulgaria (discussed later), a key issue concerned the status of Muslim educational institutions. The first mention of this issue was in the Greek–Turkish treaty of 1913. The Treaty of Lausanne in 1923 further codified the minority's status and over the next three decades the Greek state gradually attempted to introduce the teaching of the Greek language into the minority's schools (Baltsiotis 1997, 318–21).

## THE MINORITY QUESTION IN THE SOUTHERN BALKANS

Although Macedonia and Anatolia were thus cleansed of ethnically undesirable populations, the problems posed by the pursuit of homogenization, nation formation, and state building were far from resolved. The problem of ethnic heterogeneity persisted internally in the Balkan states, even in Macedonia, which was the site of extensive population transfers.

In the aftermath of the population exchanges, a total of approximately 200,000 to 400,000 Slavic speakers resided in Greek Macedonia, located almost exclusively in the northwestern region (Koliopoulos 1994; for a discussion of the ambiguities of various estimates, see Mihailides 1998). For the Greek state, this was a "Slavophone Greek" population, that is, Slavic-speaking, but Greek in terms of its national identity. This proclamation owed much to the desire to minimize the appeal of Bulgarian protests in international forums in the interwar period, and it influenced greatly the official Greek line on the issue. In this region, the assimilationist policy of the Greek state was compounded by the conflict between local Slavs and the often Turkish-speaking Greek refugees who settled in the region. The conflict typically involved possession of homes and agricultural lands. The state's support of refugees contributed significantly to the delegitimization of the state in the eyes of the local Slavic population (Koliopoulos 1994, 45). The state administrators' view of the situation was strongly colored by the persistent effort to thwart Bulgarian propaganda (and revisionism) among the Slavic population. Their reports differentiated groups on the basis of their loyalty to the state, rather than on purely ethnic criteria (Karakasidou 2000).[8]

During the interwar period, the IMRO, previously the champion of Macedonian autonomy, faced a disastrous situation. Macedonia was then divided into three regions, each controlled by a nation-state eager to consolidate that control. The organization was fragmented repeatedly during the interwar period, and two main factions developed. First, a conservative wing became a powerful player in interwar Bulgarian politics, actively participating in the 1923 coup and the assassination of Bulgarian prime minister Alexander Stamboliski (Banac 1984, 321–3). From 1919 to 1934 the organization conducted paramilitary warfare in Serb-controlled Vardar Macedonia. Until 1934, this Bulgarian IMRO remained a potent political force in Bulgarian life, and practically a state within a state in the Pirin region (Koystantinora, 1995, 107). Its open irredentism found a constituency among the 220,000 refugees from Macedonia and Thrace who flooded into Bulgaria in 1918 (Lampe 1996, 152–3). In 1934, the Zveno, a group of military officers, overthrew the government in an attempt to "restore order" from the admittedly ineffective parliamentary regime. Virtually its first act was to arrest the IMRO leadership, putting an end to its regime of intimidation and terrorism.

Second, a left-wing IMRO faction developed mainly in the Serb-held and Greek-held regions of the divided Macedonia. The consolidation of an international Communist organization (i.e., the Comintern) in the 1920s led to some failed attempts by the Communists to use the Macedonian issue as a political weapon. In the 1920 Yugoslav parliamentary elections, 25 percent of the total Communist vote came from Macedonia. But participation was low (only 55%), mainly because the pro-Bulgarian IMRO organized a boycott against the elections (Lampe 1996, 140). In the following years, the Communists attempted to enlist the pro-IMRO sympathies of the population in their cause. In the context of this attempt, in 1924 the Comintern recognized a separate Macedonian nationality. Still, the Comintern's suggestion that all Balkan Communist parties adopt a platform of a "united Macedonia" was rejected by the Bulgarian and Greek Communist parties (Papapanagiotou 1992). Despite this rejection, their conservative opponents within the two states accused the two parties of plotting against the nation; this led to the prosecution of the two Communist parties in

Bulgaria and Greece. By the 1930s, Slavic-speaking Communist sympathizers were viewed by the Greek state as separatists (Karakasidou 1993b). Throughout the interwar period, the Slavic Macedonian population in Greek Macedonia was subjected to an intensive acculturation campaign by the Greek state (Momiroski 1993; Carabot 1997; Karakasidou 1993a, 2000; Pribichevich 1982; Poulton 1989). When the Metaxas dictatorship came into office in 1936, Greek official policy took a turn toward harsh suppression of the Slavic Macedonian language and culture. The Slavic population in Vardar Macedonia was also exposed to a similar assimilation campaign by the Serb authorities. The official viewpoint declared Vardar Macedonia to be southern Serbia. During the initial Serb occupation (1913–1915) and after the return of the region to the Serb-controlled kingdom of Serbs, Slovenes, and Croats, the Serb authorities expelled the Bulgarian Exarchist clergy and teachers, removed all Bulgarian signs and books, and dissolved all Bulgarian cultural associations. In addition, approximately 4,200 Serb families settled in the region by 1940 (Banac 1984, 318–9). The populations' subsequent resentment was registered in the growing support for the Yugoslav Communists. Yet, even as late as 1941, the population of Skopje celebrated the occupation of this part of Yugoslavia by Bulgarian forces.

In addition to Macedonian Slavs, the Albanians were a major ethnic group divided by the new boundaries. The Serb (and later Yugoslav) state occupied Kosovo, the brethren of Serb nationalism.[9] Still, the region was populated mostly by Albanians and had, as a matter of fact, hosted the League of Prizren, the initial organization of the Albanian movement—discussed in Chapter 5. In the 1921 census, out of 436,929 inhabitants in Kosovo, there were 280,440 Albanian speakers, of whom 72.6 percent were Muslims, 26 percent Orthodox, and 1.4 percent Catholics (Vickers 1998, 95). Consequently, the stage was set for an Albanian–Serb confrontation. The *kachak* movement, actively assisted by Italy, challenged Serb rule as early as 1918. In late 1918, the movement's leaders Azem Bjeta and his wife, Shote, commanded almost 2,000 fighters and 100,000 adherents (Banac 1984, 302–5). The movement was brought under control only in 1922, with the help of Ahmed Zogu, Albanian minister of the interior at the time. The Serb-controlled government employed Wrangelite White Russian troops to assist Zogu in overthrowing the Fan Noli government in 1924. In return, Zogu assisted in the suppression of the *kachak* so that he could disarm the Albanian bands in the northern part of the country and consolidate his own rule. Zogu eventually turned to Italy for assistance and, with Italian encouragement, he declared himself king of Albania in 1928.

The pacification of Kosovo was completed by 1924 but this signaled only the beginning of the Serb–Albanian confrontation. As did the Greeks of the mid-nineteenth century, the Serb intelligentsia did not acknowledge that the Albanians possessed a national identity. They viewed them as "savages" or "criminal interlopers" who lived in the wild and preyed on innocents (Banac 1984, 293–5). Simultaneously, they developed the thesis that many of them were initially

Serbs who had been converted to Islam. They spoke of *arnautaši* (Albanized Serbs) in order to "reclassify" the Albanians as Serbs.[10] With the return of Serbian troops in 1918 all Albanian schools were closed down and the authorities tried to assimilate Albanian children by allowing only Serb education. In addition to the manipulation of ethnic labels, the Serb-controlled government moved poor Serb families into the region as a means of increasing the Serb minority. The colonization program of 1922 to 1929 and 1933 to 1938 included the settlement of 10,877 families on 120,672 hectares of land. Support for the colonists and the appropriation of land on their behalf naturally inflamed hostility between Serbs and Albanians. In an effort to increase the gap separating the Kosovar Albanians from those in the Albanian state, the post-1929 Serb administration deported more than 100,000 Albanians, Turks, and Muslims from Kosovo and Macedonia into Turkey.[11]

While the Albanians in Kosovo were thus the targets of an assimilation campaign, the newly created Albanian state had its own minority issues in the south. The boundaries of the Albanian state were discussed as early as 1913 but they were finalized by an international commission only in 1920 (Vickers 1995, 78–93). In its final reincarnation, the boundary line between Greece and Albania fell short of the maximalist Greek claims, leaving a strip of land on the Albanian side. This ill-defined territory, inhabited by a Greek Orthodox minority, was destined to become "northern Epirus," an object of territorial dispute between Greece and Albania for most of the twentieth century.[12] When Albania entered the League of Nations (1920) it recognized the international minority treaties regime. However, the Albanian state recognized the existence of a mere 15,000 Greek Orthodox Christians in the south, a figure that was far from the Greek claims. The Greek side routinely exaggerated the Greek minorities' numerical strength by counting as Greeks practically all Orthodox Albanians and Vlachs. On the other hand, Albanian official policy sought to separate the Vlachs from the Greeks by providing them with education in Romanian-language schools.

The institution of the Albanian state led to efforts to establish an independent state church, thereby allowing the Albanian side to reduce the influence of Greek language in the south. In 1923 legislation was introduced that excluded priests who were not Albanian citizens, did not speak the Albanian language, and were not of Albanian origin. During the interwar period, the Albanian state viewed Greek education as a potential threat to its territorial integrity. Consequently, the state took a negative view of Greek-language schools and a positive view of Romanian-language schools. When Albania institutionalized the prohibition against "foreign" schools in 1934 the Greek minority (with the help of the Greek state) brought the issue to the World Court of Hague which ruled in 1935 in favor of the minority.[13]

The final boundary demarcation between Greece and Albania also left approximately 20,000 Muslim Albanians (Chams) in Greece.[14] Many of them were local landlords and resented the land appropriation plans undertaken during the interwar period. During this period Italy and Albania repeatedly raised the

Chams' issue. More than 20 protests were filed with the League of Nations concerning violations of the Chams' rights (Divani 1997, 181–2). During World War II, the majority of Chams sided with the Axis forces and terrorized the local Greek population. This fueled resentment by the Greeks, and in the aftermath of World War II, the Chams had to flee to Albania.

Bulgaria's nation-building efforts exemplify the application of nationhood as the determining criterion for membership in the nation. Using the territorial definition of the Bulgarian state as a starting point, the commonly held assertion was that the population of the state had to be (or be made into) "Bulgarian," which meant they ought to be Eastern Orthodox in religion and Bulgarian-speaking in language. As the discussion in Chapter 5 has shown, however, the Bulgarian state included a variety of peoples who did not conform to this ideal. To deal with this discrepancy between ideology and reality, coercion, intimidation, and legislation were used to force those deemed undesirable to leave the state or to acculturate into the Bulgarian nation. In some instances, such as that of the Turkish-speaking Christians (Gagauzes) of the Black Sea coast, the people were simply declared to be Bulgarian. In other cases, such as that of the Greek urban population, the assimilation campaign led either to emigration or to acculturation. Over the post-1880 period, the Greek population declined in all Bulgarian cities, falling from 53,028 in 1880–1884 to 9,601 in 1934 (Crampton 1989, 71, 56; Karpat 1989, 3). The approximately 50,000 Bulgarian Catholics were also subject to pressure and persecution. Of all these groups, the most numerous was the Muslim minority.

In 1876 there were 1,130,000 Bulgarians and 1,120,000 Turkish Muslims in the Danube province (Simsir 1988, 4). The Muslim population was (and still is) divided into four main groups: the Turks, by far the largest group; the Pomaks, converts to Islam who have retained their customs and language; the Tatars, who arrived in the mid-nineteenth century as refugees from Crimea, and the Gypsies (Roma). The Turkish and Muslim populations were extensively affected by the establishment of the Bulgarian principality (1878) and its expansion into Ottoman territory. Thousands of Muslims fled during the 1877–1878 Russo-Turkish war. The immigration wave persisted in the following years. Between 1878 and 1912, 350,000 Turks immigrated into the Ottoman empire; 101,507 immigrated into Turkey between 1923 and 1933, and 97,181 between 1934 and 1939 (Eminov 1997, 79). The departure of the Turks was facilitated by legislation enacting property taxation and by an 1879 law prohibiting the cultivation of rice, a staple of their diet. Moreover, the realization that the restoration of Ottoman power was not a viable option contributed to persistent emigration. The growth of the Bulgarian state and the influx of refugees also affected demographic trends. The Bulgarian population increased from 2,000,000 in 1880 to 4,300,000 in 1910 and 7,000,000 in 1956. In contrast, the Muslim population (with an overwhelming majority of Turks) grew slightly from 676,212 in 1887 to 821,298 in 1934. Consequently, the Turks' proportion fell from 26 percent of the population in 1878 to 14 percent in 1900 (Simsir 1988, 5; Crampton 1989, 42–50).

Between 1877 and 1886 the Turkish minority experienced massive immigration, plunder, usurpation of their property, and demolition of their schools and religious establishments. The minority recovered during the 1886–1894 period. By the 1894–1895 school year, there were a total of 1,300 minority schools in Bulgaria with 1,516 teachers and 72,582 students (Simsir 1988, 22). The minority had to face the attitudes of Bulgarian nationalists who wished to see their schools shut down and the minority assimilated into mainstream Bulgarian culture or simply leaving the country.

However, Turkish and Muslim minority rights were guaranteed in a series of conventions signed by the Bulgarian state in 1878, 1909, and 1919. Consequently, the state undertook specific actions to protect minority rights and to reassure the continuation of their educational and religious institutions. Simultaneously, the state centralized these institutions by creating a religious hierarchy with the Sofia-based *mufti* as the supreme religious leader, and by bringing private minority schools under state regulation and control. From the state's viewpoint, these actions were aimed at severing the ties between Muslims and the Ottoman state (later, Turkey), thereby affirming state sovereignty. Predictably, there was not always sufficient goodwill on both sides, and complaints about regulations and their implementation were raised by the minority (for reviews, see Eminov 1997; Crampton 1989; Sismir 1988).

Over the interwar period, the minority gradually adjusted to its new situation, and began efforts to organize itself as a political lobby in Bulgarian politics. These efforts indicated a gradual socialization into the Bulgarian political body. However, Bulgarian political life did not favor such an accommodation. Although the short-lived Agrarian government (1919–1923) was favorably disposed toward the minority, Bulgarian nationalists continued to view the minority with suspicion. The Turkish National Congress of 1929 raised once again the key issues of schools, religious institutions, and cultural societies. In the late 1920s, the minority adopted the new Turkish (Latin) alphabet, instead of the old Arabic one. Because the new alphabet was instituted by Kemal Ataturk in Turkey, Bulgarian nationalists viewed this action with great suspicion. The state reaction was to gradually suppress the minority's educational institutions. The number of Turkish schools declined from 1,712 in 1921–1922 to 949 in 1928–1929 (Simsir 1988, 112). The military junta that came to power in 1934 closed down more Turkish schools and by the end of 1944 only 377 schools remained open. In addition, *wakf* property was expropriated, Turkish newspapers were closed down, and Turkish intellectuals were sent into exile (Eminov 1997, 49; Simsir 1988, 114–25).

## THE MAKING AND UNMAKING OF THE FIRST YUGOSLAVIA

The collapse of post–World War II Yugoslavia has been variously interpreted as a repetition of the problems that plagued the so-called first Yugoslavia.[15] However, the problems of the first Yugoslavia were similar to the difficulties that doomed proposals for interethnic and multicultural citizenship in the nineteenth century (reviewed in Chapter 3). The revitalization of the Yugoslav movement on the eve of the twentieth century coincided with the return of Alexander Karadjordjević to the Serb throne in 1903 and the ascent of Serbia as the chief challenger to Habsburg rule.

Yugoslavism emerged from the intellectuals' efforts to find a formula for South Slav unification (Gross 1977, 634–8). In Croatia and Dalmatia, rising middle strata were disappointed over the Habsburgs' refusal to grant autonomy to their South Slav subjects. Consequently, they sought new ways to advance their interests. Their political representatives were responsible for reorienting the course of their national movements. In 1905 a Croatian and Serb coalition was formed in Dalmatia and Croatia-Slavonia and in 1906 this coalition won the Croat elections (Djordjevic 1970a, 322–3). The coalition was led by Ante Trumbić and Frano Supilo, young Croat intellectuals who were convinced that the Croats could no longer survive in the Habsburg Empire and should find their future in a South Slav state. These leaders supported an agenda of "Croat–Serb oneness" (*narodno jedinstvo*), that is, the proposition that the Croats and Serbs were—or were becoming—one people with two names (Banac 1984, 96–8).

This emerging Yugoslav movement carried with it the seeds of a future conflict. It was never clarified how the "fusion" of the South Slav "tribes" would take place and it was easy to misinterpret greater Serbian nationalism as simply Yugoslavism. In turn, the Habsburg Serbs were themselves divided into greater Serb nationalists and those looking to Serbia as the creator of a Yugoslav state in which Serbs, Croats, and Slovenes would be separate and equal (Rusinow 1995, 358). For the first group, the Yugoslav solution was frequently cast in terms of fulfilling the idea of greater Serbia. The second group's ideology was almost identical to the ideology of *narodno jedinstvo* advocated by the young Croat intelligentsia.

Bosnia-Herzegovina came under Habsburg administration in 1878.[16] Conscious of the Serb and Croat nationalists' appeal to the region, the Habsburgs sought to cultivate a separate Bosnian (*Bosnjak*) nationality that could unite the population across religious lines and weaken the nationalist claims of Serbs and Croats in the area (Vucinich 1967, 28; Donia 1981, 17–9; Malcolm 1994, 137–44). The Orthodox, Catholic, and Muslim religious associations were brought under the direct authority of the Habsburg emperor in an effort to thwart their use for nationalist purposes. In particular, the Habsburg authorities prohibited the use of religious books published abroad (e.g., in Russia and Serbia), and controlled the appointment of higher and lower clergy. Their general aim was to isolate the Catholic and Orthodox Christian communities from their potential national homelands.

Even though the Ottoman government used the term "Bosnian" to designate all of Bosnia's inhabitants, the only people who traditionally had called themselves Bosnians (*Bosnjanci*) were the Muslims (Friedman 1996, 33–47; Malcolm 1994, 145–7; Vucinich 1967, 30). The term expressed their strong regionalism and their sense of difference vis-à-vis the Ottoman Turks. Nevertheless, the

Bosnian Muslim elites identified themselves with the Ottoman state, mainly because the state guaranteed their land possessions in Bosnia and protected their privileged position in society. After 1879, the Habsburgs administratively separated the community of the Bosnian Muslims from the rest of the Ottoman Muslims. They reorganized the Muslim religious establishments (*wakfs*) and redirected funds from them toward a reformed Muslim educational system. Their actions caused the resentment of the local Muslim elites whose wealth and power was largely based on their control over the *wakfs*. Their resistance movement led to petitions for religious and cultural autonomy (Burg 1983, 6–9; for overviews, see Friedman 1996, 57–67; Donia 1981).

By 1906 the Muslims had formed the Muslim National Organization (MNO), which claimed to represent the entire Muslim population but was, in fact, dominated by Muslim elites.[17] After the 1908 annexation of Bosnia-Herzegovina into the Habsburg Empire, the emperor issued a statute for the autonomous administration of Islamic religious affairs in 1909. In addition to safeguarding their control over the religious establishments, the other major concern of the Muslim elites was protecting their extensive landholdings. According to the 1910 census, the population of Bosnia was 43.49 percent Orthodox, 32.25 percent Muslim, and 19.28 percent Catholic. The majority of the serfs were Orthodox, but the majority of the landowners were Muslims (Jelavich 1967, 104; Dedijer et al. 1974, 367). In 1908 the Muslims allied themselves with the Serbian National Organization (itself founded in 1907) because both of them desired an end to Habsburg rule. However, after the 1908 annexation and the creation of a parliament, the MNO shifted alliances (Donia 1981, 169–94; Friedman 1996, 70–6). A peasant uprising in 1910 was seen as instigated by Serbs. But the Muslim landowners dominant on the MNO's executive committee were determined to prevent a compulsory end to feudal peasant obligations. In 1911 the MNO joined a coalition with the Croatian Catholic Organization founded in 1910 by Archbishop Stadler. In the 1920s, the MNO was superseded by the Yugoslav Muslim Organization and became representative of the more urban, professional groups, mainly because the power of the clerics and the landowners was undermined by increasing modernization and land redistribution plans (Friedman 1996, 96–101; Lampe 1996, 132).

The movement to secure religious, cultural, and educational autonomy resulted in a heightened awareness among the Muslim elites of their status as Muslims rather than as Turks. The period of Habsburg rule saw a dramatic expansion of the secular, cultural-educational bases of the Bosnian Muslim community. Numerous cultural societies, reading clubs, and economic and political organizations were established by Muslims. Ironically, this Muslim identity was itself the by-product of the secularization policies pursued by the Habsburgs. This transformation led to a secularization of the earlier religious differences (Burg 1983, 12; Friedman 1996, 75).

In Bosnia, the Habsburgs banned all kinds of associations and, consequently, all cultural activities had to take place in secrecy. Known as the Young Bosnians, an intelligentsia of peasant origins emerged at the turn of the century. These young men endorsed modernism, the right to self-determination, and anti-Habsburg sentiments. Some of them were Serb nationalists; others were Yugoslav federalists. Secret societies flourished among them, although many of them had cultural rather than revolutionary pursuits (Dedijer 1966, 177–83; Djordjevic 1970a, 391–3; Dedijer et al. 1974, 463–4). After the 1908 annexation of Bosnia to the Habsburg Empire, the Young Bosnians' frustration over the Habsburg attempts to prevent Yugoslav unification led to a more aggressive course of action. The Habsburgs announced a new constitution in 1910, but it provided for restrictive franchise limited to a small segment of the population. The majority of the people—who were working in the local *ciftliks*—did not participate and were not allowed to own land. In 1910 alone, more than 13,500 peasants were forced to leave their land because of default in payment of taxes to the state and the landowners (Dedijer et al. 1974, 448–50).

The conservative nature of the MNO and the desire of the Serb and Croat mainstream parties to gain its support led to a general unwillingness to deal with the vexing "peasant question." It fueled the resentment of the rising Young Bosnian intelligentsia, which opted for more radical ways of achieving social justice. Terrorism became part of their repertoire.[18] A revolutionary ideology with strong undertones of socialism and anarchism, the long-standing tradition of Balkan banditry, and their view of the Habsburgs as tyrants, justified these actions in the eyes of the Young Bosnians. Although the Young Bosnians employed revolutionary terrorism and cooperated with Serb nationalist organizations (such as the "Unification or Death" group, discussed in Chapter 6), they aimed toward the creation of a federal state for all South Slavs. In fact, among their ranks, there were not only Serbs but also Muslims and Croats (Dedijer 1966, 114). It was in this context that the fateful 1914 Sarajevo assassination of Archduke Ferdinand by the Young Bosnian Serb Gavrilo Princip took place. Following the assassination, Austria-Hungary declared war on Serbia. As the European system of alliances came into effect, the conflict was soon transformed into World War I.

During World War I, support for Yugoslav unification came from the Yugoslav Committee, founded by émigré leaders (Supilo, Trumbić, and Mestrović) from the South Slav Habsburg lands (Stokes 1980b, 51–72; Petrovich 1976, 2:626–49; Djordjevic 1970a, 404–10; Dedijer et al. 1974, 496–8; Banac 1984, 214–25; Lederer 1969, 428–32). The Yugoslav Committee and the Serb government did not always have amicable relations: for example, the committee desired to organize separate military units while the Serb government wanted these units to become part of the Serb army. The vexing question of implementing a power-sharing agreement that would allow for peaceful coexistence between Serbs and Croats was emerging at the time. In fact, Yugoslavism represented a diplomatic solution through which the actual problems that the unification entailed could be avoided rather than dealt with. Seton-Watson's quotation at the beginning of this chapter illustrates the vicissitudes of the debates on Yugoslavism. Indeed, these difficulties were never fully resolved, and the diplomats were forced to proceed without having a clear-cut and substantive agreement on the nature of the new state. In the 20 July 1917 Corfu declaration, all sides agreed to the establishment of the kingdom of Serbs, Croats, and Slovenes under the Karadjordjević dynasty. By 1918 the new state was rapidly becoming a reality, as the war was ending.

The questions that plagued the early negotiations between Serbs and Croats, however, had not been resolved. Whereas the Serb government viewed the question of Yugoslavia as an expansion of Serbia into Habsburg lands, the Habsburg Slavs (especially Croats) viewed the issue in terms of a federation of independent and sovereign units (Zlatar 1997; Lederer 1969, 432). This fundamental issue would plague the new state during the interwar period.[19] During the 1920s, it was impossible to reconcile the views of the Croat movement (represented by Radić's Croat Peasant Party), who proposed decentralization or federalism, with the views of the Serb government (represented by Pašić's Radical Party), who opted for centralization. After the 1920 elections, the two sides were unable to agree on a constitution. Pašić used his parliamentary majority and political skill to pass the so-called Vidovdan Constitution in 1920 (proclaimed on St. Vitus' Day, the Serb national holiday). The constitution centralized power in the hands of the central government in Belgrade and was immediately resisted by the non-Serb minorities, most vocally by the Croats.

This was just the beginning of the infamous "national question." In practical terms, the new state could not be governed without cooperation between Serbs and Croats. In 1921 only 39 percent of the population was Serb (including the Montenegrins). The Croats amounted to 23.9 percent, the Slovenes were 8.5 percent, and the Bosnian Muslims were 6.3 percent, followed by smaller groups of Macedonian Slavs, Germans, Albanians, Hungarians, Turks, Romanians, and Italians.[20] Throughout the interwar period, interethnic cooperation was not forthcoming, and this was the primary reason for the gradual delegitimization of the state. The expansion of a Serb-dominated bureaucracy (172,000 by 1928) contributed to the perception of Serb domination (Lampe 1996, 130).[21] The interwar governments redistributed approximately 10 percent of the country's arable land, effectively putting an end to the large landowning regimes of the Ottoman period (Lampe 1996, 146–7). The central government also attempted to unify the economic and political frameworks of the parts of the new kingdom.

Although the economic record was relatively positive, it was the national question that haunted the kingdom of Serbs, Slovenes, and Croats. The persistent failure to construct a viable political coalition plagued the state in the 1921–1928 period. The failure was because of the resistance of Croats and other non-Serb groups to accept the centralized structure of the new state. Passions were greatly inflamed in the process, and eventually culminated in the 1928 shooting of Croat Peasant Party's leader Stjepan Radić in the floor of the parliament. By 1929, King Aleksandar, frustrated with the parliament's inability to implement effective centralization, carried out a coup and assumed direct control of the government until his 1934 assassination. On this occasion, the name of the state was changed to Yugoslavia from Kingdom of Serbs, Slovenes, and Croats. New provinces were constructed, allegedly based on purely geographic criteria, to bring about Yugoslav unity. The provinces allowed Serbs a lion's share in administration; this was widely viewed as a Serb ploy for domination. Furthermore, the 1931 census illustrated this policy of centralization and homogenization. The census included a single "Serbo-Croat" nationality, thereby constructing a facade of homogeneity, with 77 percent of the population recorded as Serbo-Croat (Pearson 1983, 152). In 1934 the king was assassinated by IRMO terrorists and this signaled the beginning of a downward spiral for the first Yugoslavia. In 1939, a belated attempt at reconciliation between Croats and Serbs created a large and autonomous Croatian province, yet without providing the Serbs of Croatia with a similar province (Rusinow 1995, 377). Perhaps such a compromise could have prevented the disintegration of the state; however, the Axis invasion of April 1941 rendered it a moot issue. The "first Yugoslavia" was ended.

## POLITICAL REVISIONISM AND WORLD WAR II

In the first decades of the twentieth century, two main routes were available for the political reconstruction of southeastern Europe. The first route was that of major compulsory population transfers, a strategy applied to Macedonia and Anatolia, the heartlands of the Ottoman Empire. This strategy, known as ethnic cleansing in the 1990s, resulted from the collusion among Greek, Bulgarian, and Turkish nationalisms in the first three decades of the twentieth century. Needless to say, it failed to produce homogeneity even in Anatolia and Macedonia. In the southern Balkans, this strategy was applied only to a limited degree and the minority question plagued interstate relations in Bulgaria, Greece, and Albania. The application of nationhood as a guiding principle for centralization and state building contributed significantly to the marginalization of minority groups.

The second main route to the problem of national homogenization was the creation of a common state to house peoples of different ethnicities, religions, and cultural backgrounds. Although this option was never implemented in the southern Balkans, it was successfully pursued in the South Slav lands. The creation of the Kingdom of Serbs, Slovenes, and Croats (1917) was a skillful attempt to manage ethnic heterogeneity within the boundaries of a single state, thereby avoiding bitter territorial disputes among them. Seton-Watson's quotation in the beginning of this chapter is a good illustration of the diplomats' urgent desire to support Yugoslavism as a conflict-resolution strategy. However, the so-called first Yugoslavia faced all the problems that had plagued the pursuit of interethnic and transnational citizenship in the nineteenth century. The chronic legitimization crisis of its institutions contributed to the state's swift disintegration in the 1940s.

The statist policies of cultural assimilation pursued by the Balkan states and the actions undertaken by them to facilitate national homogenization must be placed in the context of the European, indeed international, trends of the interwar period. The end of World War I and the proclamation of the principle of self-determination legitimized nationalist projects throughout Eastern and Central Europe, thereby paving the way for state intervention. In the 1920 Paris Peace Conference and the League of Nations, the Allies were careful in excluding their own territories from the application of the principle. Specifically, the treaty provisions that emerged from the Paris Peace Conference were twofold. First, the enemy states of Austria, Hungary, Bulgaria, and Turkey signed minority provisions as a part of the peace treaties. Second, the allied states created or enlarged by the conference (i.e., Poland, Czechoslovakia, Romania, Yugoslavia, and Greece) signed separate treaties safeguarding minority rights (for a complete listing, see Thornberry 1991, 41; Musgrave 1997, 41). As part of the international minorities treaties regime, in 1921 the League of Nations established a procedure according to which minorities could petition a special commission regarding their treatment. However, the minorities did not have the right to come before the council itself, and it was up to the council to decide the merit of the individual petition. Consequently, "within time, most minorities saw the League not as a judge but as a policeman, far less concerned with justice than the maintenance of law and order" (Pearson 1983, 143).

According to the "minorities treaties regime," the subgroups that became parts of larger nation-states were not defined as people of the nation-state within which they lived but, rather, as national minorities. That is, they had no right to seek union with their own nation-state, but they were, nevertheless, entitled to maintain their separate ethnic identities through guarantees of certain linguistic, cultural, and religious rights (Musgrave 1997, 39; Thornberry 1991, 44–52). In 1930 and 1931 the league received 204 petitions, but by 1938 to 1939 the number dropped to 4. The minority states viewed the treaties as violations of their sovereignty. They were further concerned that the continued separation of the ethnic minorities would undermine their loyalty to the state. Moreover, the World War I losers (Germany, Austria, Hungary, and Bulgaria) claimed that the application of self-determination was one-sided and that many of their nationals had been separated from them because the Peace Conference ruled against them in an arbitrary manner (Musgrave 1997, 55–9). As a result, the viability of the system was undermined by both sides. The rise of Nazism and fascism in the interwar period further contributed to the delegitimization of the international regime, setting the stage for the violent confrontations of World War II.

The situation may be formulated in terms of Hirschman's (1970) famous choice between exit and voice. Minorities can either attempt to exit their state or they can attempt to gain a voice within the political system. If the minority is loyal to the state, it tends to opt for participation, whereas if loyalty is low the minority might attempt to exit the state through succession. Loyalty, however, was quite problematic in the Balkan context. Local national identities were established through the discourse of nationhood, thereby a priori excluding the possibility of accommodating cultural difference within the boundaries of a single imagined community. During the interwar period, this conundrum cast its long shadow over Balkan politics. From the Serb–Croat confrontation to the minority issues in the southern Balkans, politicians and administrators were not able to develop formulas conducive to successful state building. The main problem, of course, was the influence of nationhood in state policy. The discourse of nationhood marginalized the minorities, thereby effectively restraining the possibility of their successful incorporation into the national political body. The use of terms such as "Slavophone Greeks" (for the Slavic Macedonians in Greece) and "*arnautaši*" for the Albanians in Kosovo aptly illustrates the manner in which administrators and intellectuals attempted to make reality conform to their preconceived notions.

Moreover, the lack of international universalistic standards and the preoccupation with national minorities fostered the view that repressive state policies toward minorities were acceptable. The entire system eventually became unstable, especially after the Great Depression (1929) and the rise of Italian fascism and German national socialism. With these developments, political revisionism came fully into the political agenda of European politics, thereby leading eventually to World War II. The Balkan system of states was greatly influenced by these trends.

In the aftermath of the Balkan wars and World War I, nationalism lost its mass appeal for Bulgarians. The dominant intellectual genre of the interwar period was "folk psychology," for example, academic writing set to prove the distinctiveness of the Bulgarian soul through the centuries. The genre is indicative of the reflective mood of the intelligentsia in the aftermath of World War I. But the humiliating defeats of the Balkan wars and World War I fostered resentment against the post–World War I treaties. Right-wing and nationalist associations proliferated, eventually leading Bulgarian policy toward revisionism. Some of them espoused racist and fascist ideologies (Todorova 1995, 84). Revisionism found its expression in the production of numerous works on the Bulgarian *irredenta* (mainly Macedonia) and the memoranda protesting the treatment of the Bulgarian population in Greece and Serbia (for an overview, see Gounaris and Mihailidis 2000). Political revisionism triumphed during World War II. Bulgaria entered into the war on the side of the Axis forces and occupied its *irredenta* in Serb and Greek Macedonia as well as western Thrace. In both places, the Bulgarian state carried out a repressive acculturation campaign. The gains were indeed short-lived, as eventually Bulgarian forces had to withdraw at the end of the war. The occupation intensified anti-Bulgarian sentiments among the population and was promptly exploited by the anti-Communist forces in Greece.

Following the Nazi invasion of Yugoslavia in April 1941 the state ceased to exist. In Croatia, the Nazis supported the establishment of a Nazi regime through the Ustase party of Ante Pavelic. The so-called Independent State of Croatia

(known as NDH by its Croatian initials) included Bosnia-Herzegovina, but excluded parts of Dalmatia and its islands, annexed by Italy. The state carried out
extensive ethnic cleansing in its territories, killing or violently converting Serbs
to Catholicism. The regime also set up an extermination camp at Jasenovac
and killed hundreds of thousands of people in both Croatia and Bosnia-
Herzegovina.[22] The ultimate beneficiaries were the Communists, who, under
Tito's leadership, were able to gain considerable support in the South Slav lands,
eventually building a social basis broad enough to reconstitute Yugoslavia as a
federation under their control.

## NOTES

1. The International Red Cross and the 1864 and 1868 Geneva Conventions introduced the concept of international consensus. International peace conferences were convened in The Hague in 1899 and 1907 and a Permanent Court of Arbitration was
established.

2. For example, the Jews of the Balkan states were not part of the national rivalries
of the region. Eventually, most of the Jewish population fell victim to the Holocaust.
The most spectacular example of the Jewish disappearance is provided by the city of
Thessaloniki. When the city came to Greece in 1913, 39 percent of its 158,000 inhabitants
were Jewish (Therborn 1995b, 45). In 1943 the Nazis deported the city's Jews to concentration camps. Very few survived and, consequently, Thessaloniki, a cosmopolitan
city with a heterogeneous population for most of its history, became completely Greek.

3. During the 1908–1912 period the Young Turks initially followed a policy of economic liberalism. However, their attempts to negotiate loans and to abolish the capitulations met the rejection of Western governments (Ahmad 1969, 75–81; Ergil 1975, 54–7).

4. On 19 May 1914, Halil Bey, an influential CUP member, urged his compatriots
to remind themselves and future generations of the responsibility to "redeem" the
Empire's lost territories (Alp 1917, 21–3; Landau 1981, 47, 50; Arnakis 1960, 31). Three
of the most important CUP policy makers in this period, Enver, Talat, and Cemal, were
favorably disposed toward Pan-Turkism. The adoption of Turkish nationalism by the
CUP had a devastating effect on the Ottoman Christians, who lost all faith in reform.
According to contemporary observer N. Batzaria, the Turkification of the Christians was
doomed to fail because the Turks were economically weak, educationally disadvantaged,
and lacked a strong middle class (Karpat 1975, 293).

5. Following the Cretan uprising of 1896–1899, Crete became an autonomous principality under Constantine, the heir to the Greek throne. The prince collided with Eleutherios Venizelos, a local Cretan politician who played an instrumental role in the Cretan
uprising. Constantine eventually left the island, and Venizelos assumed control of the
government. Cretan desire for unification posed a serious political problem in Greek–
Ottoman relations during the 1899–1911 period. In the aftermath of the 1909 coup,
Venizelos was invited in the kingdom of Greece, where he assumed the prime minister's
position. He founded the Liberal Party, won the 1911 elections, and led Greece in the
1912–1913 Balkan wars.

6. Despite the institutional rift between the republic and the empire, there was considerable substantive continuity between the two: 85 percent of the civil servants and 93

percent of the empire's staff officers retained their positions in the republic (Rustow 1981, 73).

7. The Armenian Genocide belongs to this period. Because the Armenian case is beyond the scope of this book it is not discussed here. For an introduction to Armenian history and politics, as well as a general overview, see the collected essays in Hovannisian (1997).

8. The plight of the Slavic-speaking minority is illustrated by their pleas not to have separate educational institutions. Under the treaties regime, the Greek government decided to issue a primer (Abecedar) for use in the Slavic community. Minority protests against its use highlighted the minority's desire not to be considered different from the rest of the population. This desire was directly linked to worry that such a difference would intensify their unequal treatment by the authorities. For a discussion, see Mihalidis (1996). The Abecedar primer is considered hard evidence by the Macedonian side that the Greek state recognized the existence of a Macedonian population within its boundaries.

9. Considerable fighting, killing, and destruction took place during the Balkan wars and World War I (Mikic 1987; Vickers 1998; Banac 1984, 298). Approximately 16,000 Albanians fought alongside the Ottoman forces. Serb reprisals were also extensive. Approximately 20,000 to 25,000 Albanians were killed in Kosovo (Malcolm 1998, 254, 257). The Serb army marched through Kosovo in its 1915 retreat to the Adriatic, and almost 100,000 of them perished in the process.

10. The first writer to claim that all northern Albanians (Geghs) were Albanized Serbs was Miloš Milojević. In 1872 he presented his argument in the Serb Royal Academy but was rebutted by Stojan Novaković. Spiridon Gopčević, the "father of Serbian political geography," followed the same logic and declared all Albanians to be Serbs (Malcolm 1998, 199). His work greatly influenced the Serb geographer Jovan Cvijić (1918, 343–55).

11. Vickers (1998, 105–20; see also Banac 1984, 301–3) puts the figure at some 200,000 to 300,000. Malcolm (1998, 286) estimates the figure to be between 90,000 and 150,000.

12. By 1911 the Greek government's internal reports estimated that the approximately 220,000 Orthodox Albanian Christians of the provinces of Shkoder, Janina, and Monastir had a Greek "national consciousness" (Pitouli-Kitsou 1997, 87–94). In 1913 a Greek insurrection to the south raised the issue of autonomy for the Greek minority. In 1920 to 1921 further clashes between Albanian nationalists and the Greek minority raised the issue of educational and ecclesiastical protection (Vickers 1995, 98–9).

13. The court's decision allowed the minority to keep its educational institutions. However, the decision was never implemented. During World War II, Romanian-language schools were opened whereas Greek-language schools were closed down (Kostelancik 1996; Divani 1997, 186–9).

14. Initially, the Chams were to be part of the Greek–Turkish exchange of population but the Albanian state asked for their exemption because of their Albanian origin (Michalopoulos 1986).

15. Generations of scholars have surrendered to the notion of Yugoslavia as an inevitable reality. With Yugoslav disintegration, opinions suddenly moved the other way around, emphasizing "age-old hatred" as the root of its collapse. Twentieth-century Yugoslav historiography remains a contested field, mainly because political partisanship has spilled over into academic debate (see Lampe 1996, 4–6).

16. Donia (1981, 14–16). Between 1882 and 1903, it was administered by Benjamin von Kallay. Kallay and his Austrian contemporaries believed that the Ottoman system was responsible for chaos and anarchy, and considered it his duty to bring order, end brigandage, and replace arbitrary rule with the "rule of law."

17. In addition to the MNO, Serb and Croat nationalists attempted to gain the support of the Bosnian Muslims. Although cases of individual Muslims who supported one side or the other exist, the Muslims as a group did not provide full-scale support for either side (Friedman 1996, 66–9).

18. Assassination attempts were made against Emperor Francis Joseph in 1910, General Marijan Varesanin (the head of Bosnia-Herzegovina) in 1910, the Croatian *Ban* (governor) Slavko Cuvaj (twice in 1912), the new Croatian *Ban* Baron Ivo Skerleć in 1913, and Archduke Salavdor and *Ban* Skerleć again in 1913 (Dedijer et al. 1974, 465–6).

19. For extensive discussions, see Banac (1984), Djilas (1991), and Rusinow (1995). Despite the government's attitude, the majority of Belgrade intellectuals were opposed to grounding all authority in the state and the church (Lampe 1996, 188–90).

20. The 1921 statistics are reported in Lampe (1996, 129). World War I undermined the demographic predominance of Serbs among South Slavs. Serbia lost as many as a million people in the war, thereby losing almost an entire generation of males (almost 25% of its total population). Had this not been the case, Pearson (1983, 159) argues, the Yugoslav minorities would have been more conciliatory toward the Serbs.

21. The successive cabinets and political manipulations during the interwar period are too extensive and inconsequential to be reviewed here in detail. There has been a lively debate in the literature regarding the blame for the failure of the first Yugoslavia. See Banac (1984) for a pro-Croatian viewpoint and Dragnich (1983) for an attempt to exonerate the Serb side (and prime minister and Radical Party leader Nikola Pašić in particular). The interpretation adopted here is close to the balanced and nuanced perspective of Lampe (1996).

22. The number of people killed has been endlessly debated by the experts (see Rusinow 1995, 380 for further discussion). I have avoided debating the issue at length here, mainly because the magnitude of the figures has become an area of Serbo-Croatian intellectual dispute in the 1980s and 1990s. However, it is almost certain that at least 300,000 died as a result of ethnic cleansing.

# 8

# The Balkans in a Global Age

[T]he new Europe, like interwar Europe, confronts a potentially explosive—
and in some cases actually explosive—dynamic interplay between a set of
new or newly reconfigured *nationalizing states*, ethnically heterogeneous yet
conceived as nation-states, whose dominant elites promote (to varying degrees) the language, culture, demographic position, economic flourishing,
and political hegemony of the nominally state-bearing nation; the substantial, self-conscious, and (to varying degrees) organized and politically alienated *national minorities* in those states, whose leaders demand cultural or
territorial autonomy and resist actual or perceived policies or processes of
assimilation or discrimination; and the *external national "homelands"* of
the minorities, whose elites (again to varying degrees) closely monitor the
situation of their co-ethnics in the new states, vigorously protest alleged
violations of their rights, and assert the right, even the obligation, to defend
their interests.

[Emphasis in original] Brubaker 1995, 108–10

The collapse of Yugoslavia in the 1990s has been the topic of extensive academic discussion; an extensive body of literature provides a more than adequate
treatment of the recent events.[1] Therefore, in this final chapter, I will be less
concerned with a detailed narrative of the Yugoslav case (or other less publicized
cases), and more interested in contextualizing regional developments in the light
of global trends. The previous chapters addressed the export of the nation-state
model to the Balkan peninsula and its recontextualization in the light of local
peculiarities. The post-1945 period has been described as the period of contem-

porary globalization (Held et al. 1999). Its decisive difference from the modern era of globalization (1830–1945) is the contextualization and reconfiguration of modernization projects, as well as the growing influence of worldwide institutions on local societies.

In the first section of this chapter, I discuss the way in which the post-1945 trends in the international division of labor and global politics have affected the region. These new trends have increased the socioeconomic and institutional gap between the Balkans and Western Europe. In turn, this growing gap has had serious consequences for the image of the Balkans in the international scene. Public policy has been greatly influenced by popular perception. Consequently, my discussion focuses on the differential perception of central-eastern and southeastern Europe in public discourse in the 1980s and 1990s. The unequal treatment of these regions and the marginalization of southeastern Europe are acutely reflected in the inward, ethnocentric perspectives dominant in local historiography and, more specifically, in history textbooks. In sharp contrast to Western Europe, such texts continue to operate with nineteenth- and early twentieth-century perspectives, thereby contributing to ethnic stereotypes about neighboring nations. With these general long-term trends in mind, I conclude with a brief overview of the "minority question" in the Balkan nation-states during the 1945–1990 period.

## ECONOMIC DECLINE AND NATIONALIST RESURGENCE

The division of Europe into a Western and Eastern bloc acutely affected the status of the Balkans in the post-1945 period. With Greece and Turkey in the Western camp and the rest of the Balkans in the Communist bloc, interstate relations were deeply affected by the Cold War. Moreover, the frontier character of the peninsula was strengthened by the peculiar position of Tito's Yugoslavia. Simultaneously Communist and nonaligned, the second Yugoslavia was a buffer zone between the West and the East. Under these political divisions lie more deeply entrenched features and tendencies concerning the relationship between the region and the global trends of the second half of the twentieth century.

To analyze this situation, it is necessary to have a bird's-eye view of global developments. Like their Latin American counterparts, the Balkan states failed to "catch up" with the developed countries during both the nineteenth and twentieth centuries. Although by the late 1970s they were no longer agricultural societies, their urban sector failed to become competitive in the world market. Indeed, their external debt grew rapidly in the post-1950 period (Stoianovich 1994, 212–5, 223–5; see also Wallden 1996). Table 9 provides an illustration of the growing inequality between the Balkans and the advanced industrialized societies of Western Europe and North America over the 1860–1970 period.

Of course, this performance must be put into the larger European context. The redrawing of the European boundaries in the post–World War II and post-1989 periods has been strongly influenced by the demographic and economic

**Table 9**
**Real GNP per Capita in 1960 U.S.$**

| COUNTRY | 1860 | 1913 | 1929 | 1950 | 1960 | 1970 |
|---|---|---|---|---|---|---|
| US | 550 | 1,350 | 1,775 | 2,415 | 2,800 | 3,605 |
| UK | 600 | 1,070 | 1,160 | 1,400 | 1,780 | 2,225 |
| Germany (West) | 345 | 775 | 900 | 995 | 1,790 | 2,705 |
| France | 380 | 670 | 890 | 1,055 | 1,500 | 2,535 |
| Bulgaria | 215 | 285 | 340 | 420 | 725 | 1,380 |
| Yugoslavia | 225 | 300 | 370 | 360 | 610 | 1,035 |
| Greece | 235 | 335 | 405 | 410 | 635 | 1,255 |
| Romania | 215 | 370 | 365 | 360 | 575 | 1,060 |

*Source*: Bairoch (1981, 10). Data adjusted for geographical boundaries.

trends of the western and southeastern European regions. The southern, Mediterranean border of Europe has become economically most clearly demarcated. For example, in 1950 the combined gross domestic product (GDP) per capita of Egypt, Morocco, and Turkey was 80 percent that of Portugal, one of the poorest European countries. By 1988, this proportion was only 49 percent, and this is indicative of the growing economic discrepancies between the northern and southern parts of the Mediterranean (Therborn 1995a, 35; Tovias 1994). Consequently, although the Balkans have failed to catch up to Western European standards, they have also avoided slipping into Third World levels.[2]

In this respect, their performance is typical of other developing regions. However, the Balkans were also negatively affected by the "information revolution" of the post-1960 period. The information revolution fosters the rise of a "network society" (Castells 1996), where human interaction and association are reshaped by information technology. In the postindustrial network societies of Western Europe and North America, information becomes absorbed into the fabric of diverse social, economic, and cultural activities. A comparison of intercontinental clusters of mass consumption in 1938 and 1989–1990 reveals that the countries of southeastern Europe (Albania, Greece, Bulgaria, Romania, and Yugoslavia) have remained within the lowest consumption cluster (reported in Therborn 1995a, 144). Consequently, Balkan societies have been less affected by mass media and culture industries. Their lack of engagement in the global circuits of mass consumption increases their sociocultural and economic distance from the societies of Western Europe and North America.[3] The absence of common reference points and a shared frame of reference leads to cross-cultural misunderstandings, whereby actions undertaken within the Balkan context are recontextualized in the Western context, and vice versa.

Castells (1998) suggests that the growing inequalities of the Global Age entail a polarization between the advanced, postindustrial, communication-intensive regions of the First World, and the marginalized, communication-deficient regions of what he calls the Fourth World. The Balkans provide another example of such a polarization. Although Greece and Yugoslavia enjoyed brief periods of spectacular growth in the 1960s and 1970s, respectively, their economies declined significantly in the 1980s. The gradual consolidation of international trading blocs (European Union [EU], United States, South Asia) further marginalized the region. Soaring unemployment rates and the proliferation of the underground economy characterized the Balkan countries throughout the 1980s (Bookman 1994, 75–87). The statism of the local economies has further contributed to economic failure. In the 1980s, the Yugoslav experience was indicative of this trend; the local managerial elites of the republics were caught in a situation of decreasing economic performance. Their inability to arrive at compromise solutions was the outcome of their desire to protect the locally based clientele of largely inefficient state enterprises (Rusinow 1985, 131–65; Woodward 1995, 47–81). The subsequent rise of Slobodan Milosevic, discussed later in this chapter, provided an ideological dimension to this initially regional conflict over economic resources.

The post-1989 period initiated a new circle of decline because the wars, economic sanctions, and the problem of transitioning to a capitalist economic system contributed to a significant decline in socioeconomic indicators (Danopoulos and Ianeva 1999). The reversal of these conditions will undoubtedly be gradual. The necessity of a Marshall-style plan for the region has been pointed out repeatedly by recent commentaries along with the fact that Serbia cannot be excluded from such a plan. In the long run, the post-1989 proliferation of small states in the region is likely to increase the need for regional cooperation. The new economic zone currently under construction in the region centers on Greece, the poorest of the EU countries, yet the wealthiest state in the Balkans.

Table 10 offers a glimpse of regional socioeconomic conditions.

In the post-1989 period Greek investment in the Black Sea and Balkan countries increased substantially. For example, Greek exports to Albania increased from $12.2 million in 1991 to $221 million in 1994; those to Bulgaria increased from $87.8 million in 1991 to $446 million in 1994 (Giannaris 1996, 58). The consolidation of a new economic zone is largely incomplete, mainly because cooperation among the countries remains troublesome. Their national rivalries are among the key factors preventing greater regional cooperation (Larrabee 1994). The same reason keeps foreign investment away. Therefore, although economic decline potentially fosters ethnic tensions, economic development requires regional stability.

## THE IMAGE OF THE BALKANS IN THE NEW WORLD ORDER

Global economic restructuring has led to a reorganization of labor within large corporations, with extensive headquarters located in advanced industrial coun-

**Table 10**
**Key Indicators of the Balkan States, 1994**

| Country | Population (millions) | GNP per capita in $US | Average Annual Inflation 1980-92 |
|---|---|---|---|
| Albania | 3.3 | 1,290 | n.a. |
| Bulgaria | 8.5 | 1,330 | 11.7 |
| Greece | 10.3 | 7,290 | 17.7 |
| Romania | 22.7 | 1,130 | 13.1 |
| Turkey | 58.5 | 1,980 | 46.3 |
| Yugoslavia (former) | 23.9 | 3,060 | 123 |

*Source*: Giannaris (1996, 112).

tries while the actual plants are relocated in the global periphery (Sassen 1996, 6–20; Lash and Urry 1994). This reorganization leads to the growing need for transnational legal regimes to foster common sets of global rules as a means of ensuring the standardization of legal codes on a global basis (Held 1995). The circulation of goods has been accompanied by the circulation of people— amounting to about 120 million immigrants worldwide. Indeed, the challenges posed by the new post-1945 immigration are closely connected with the shift toward the global accountability of the state (Sassen 1996, 59–100; Esman 1992).

The nation-state is gradually reconceptualized as an agent responsible for the human rights of every person within its territory (Jacobson 1996), and this provides an area for minority and immigrant groups to participate in the state's political body. Such participation is possible even when the immigrants do not have formal membership in the state (Mitchell and Russell 1996; Soysal 1994). Therefore, protection of minorities becomes a topic of global significance, because a significant percentage of conflicts involves issues of minority rights (Gurr 1993; Peerce 1997). This strategy grew out of the desire of the World War II victors to avoid the disasters of the post–World War I situation. The growing realization that international standards had to be applied in a uniform manner if they were to be respected worldwide provided the impetus for a series of international treaties, culminating in the Helsinki accords of the 1970s (Musgrave 1997). The dramatic increase in international organizations has been well documented (McGrew and Lewis 1992; McNeely 1995). These organizations have offered a variety of constituencies the opportunity to bypass the state and appeal directly to an international audience. The marked trend toward uniform international patterns (Meyer 1995) is an important new constraint on state action and a de facto limitation of state sovereignty.

This globewide trend owes much to the post-1960 rise of multiculturalism in

Western democracies (the United States, Canada, and Australia). Multicultur-alism has been a new means of incorporating unassimilated citizens into their own nations (Taylor 1992). Although contested even in the West, the worldwide institutionalization of multiculturalism has meant that ethnicity has become in-creasingly decoupled from citizenship. The post–World War II, UN-sponsored trend toward the standardization of human rights on a global basis offered an opportunity to extend this tendency into the international domain, thus turning it into a late twentieth-century "standard of civilization" (Gong 1984) according to which peripheral societies are judged. The unresolved issues surrounding the minorities' issues and the national rivalries in the Balkans have been subse-quently received and interpreted with new lenses, radically different from those of the interwar period.

Interstate treaties and the further elaboration of a legal system of rights, duties, and responsibilities have largely driven the post–World War II institutional de-velopment of the EC/EU. The expansion of EU membership into east-central and southeastern Europe raises the possibility of successful accommodation be-tween the cultural, legal, and economic frameworks of these countries and the EU's post-1945 legal tradition (Delanty 1995; Judt 1996). Perhaps the best in-dicator of such difficulties is the constitutional nationalism exemplified in the constitutions of the former Yugoslav republics (Hayden 1992b). A majority of the new constitutions draw legal distinctions among citizens, privileging the members of a specific imagined community (Slovene, Croat, Macedonian) against those citizens who do not identify with them.

Given these radically conflicting trajectories, the successful incorporation of southeastern Europe into the EU becomes a politically laden topic. It is quite clear that if "Europe" could be defined by excluding the Balkan nation-states, the EU would not have to become entangled in the Balkan web of nationality, ethnicity, and interstate rivalry. Indeed, there is a long tradition of Orientalist thought on the Balkans.[4] Over the past two centuries, the consolidation of the term "Balkan" in Western discourse was closely related to its political, cultural, and ideological overtones (Skopetea 1992, 17–92). The term itself lacks preci-sion and does not represent a concrete geographical territory. In Western Eu-ropean discourse it surfaced in 1808 when the German geographer Johan August Zeune first employed the word *Balkanhalbinsel* (Balkan peninsula).[5] In 1831 Major George Thomas Keppel published a book titled *Narrative of a Journey across the Balkans*, but it was only after the middle of the nineteenth century that the term gained currency (Stoianovich 1994, 1; Carter 1977, 7). By the early twentieth century the terms "Balkan" and "Balkanization" had achieved their pejorative connotation. Subsequently, they were reconnected to the original geographic territory. Rebecca West's classic *Black Lamb and Grey Falcon* (1941) provides a particularly useful illustration of the "dark" and "violent" nature of the Balkans as represented in Western discourse.

In the 1980s and 1990s, the social sciences have provided ample ammunition for a neo-Orientalist view of the region. The analysis of post-1500 European regional development has emphasized the instrumental role of a central core of Western European cities located along the Rhine. This "city belt" dates back to the 843 Kingdom of Lothar. Over the post-1945 period, the network of core postindustrial countries closely corresponds to the earlier city belt (Therborn 1995a, 184; Rokkan and Urwin 1983, 43). If expanded to include industrial and postindustrial regions, the net result is a socioeconomic boundary that roughly corresponds to the division of Europe into Orthodox and Catholic–Protestant sections. Of course, the religious schism of Christianity into an eastern and a western part goes farther back, to 1054, if not even earlier. Nevertheless, the convergence between socioeconomic inequality and religious affiliation has led to the tempting suggestion that "Europe" ought to mean the more developed, Catholic and Protestant Europe (see, for example, Gemerek 1996; Delanty 1995, 48–58).

Originally echoed by Milan Kundera in his 1984 article in the *New York Review of Books*, this notion has provided the backdrop for a debate on the meaning, boundaries, and political significance of Central Europe (Schopflin and Wood 1989; Gaubard 1991). In depicting the Soviets as annihilators of all cultural production, Kundera elaborated on a long tradition of Russophobia, a genre dominant in Eastern Europe. In the late 1980s, this intellectual genre led to the gradual formation of the clumsy term "East Central Europe," defined as the former Communist Catholic and Protestant countries (Poland, Czechoslovakia, Hungary, and Slovenia). The ultimate goal of this cultural and political project was the inclusion of these countries in the expanding EU and NATO. These goals were largely realized in the 1990s.

As an offshoot of this political and cultural project, the poorer countries of southeastern Europe have been excluded from fast-track EU membership. The same ideology that justified the inclusion of the northern Eastern European countries has also been employed to justify the exclusion of southeastern Europe. The ideological edifice has been most clearly articulated in Huntington's "clash of civilizations" thesis (1993, 1996).[6] Specifically, Huntington fused the socioeconomic and cultural boundaries into a single European boundary, whereby the Eastern Orthodox countries are excluded from membership in European "civilization" and are considered to have a Slavo-Orthodox civilization of their own.

In the 1990s, a series of commentators and journalists (e.g., Kaplan 1992; Kennan 1993) have echoed this theme, greatly contributing to a distorted image of the region. Ironically, the nationalist mobilizations in 1990s Yugoslavia attempted to transform this image into a reality (Sluga 1998; Salecl 1994). The success of nationalist visions in the region, however, should not be attributed solely to the ability of local intellectuals to provide narratives that justify exclusion and animosity. Such narratives become powerful because the local cultural traditions and educational institutions provided an elaborate ethnocentric template tilting the intellectual field in favor of nationalist thought.

## THE PRODUCTION OF INTOLERANCE: TEACHING ETHNOCENTRISM

Ethnocentrism and nationalistic stereotypes influenced the evolution of the "national question" in the 1990s. Although global post-1945 trends empowered minorities to achieve protection from discrimination and unequal treatment, the situation is different in the Balkans, where heterogeneity is viewed negatively, as a potential threat to the integrity of the nation. In fact, reliable counts of minorities in the Balkans are extremely difficult to obtain (for example, see Roudometof 1996b). The reasons are twofold. On the one hand, the local states desire to minimize the official appearance of ethnic fragmentation. On the other hand, the interplay between religious and ethnic identity blurs the lines dividing minority populations. For example, the dividing line between Pomaks and Turks is hazy, as is the line between Orthodox Albanians and ethnic Greeks or—in the cases of Bulgaria and the Republic of Macedonia—between Gypsies and Turks. In these cases, religion establishes a more important link than language, a feature that testifies to the extent that the modern Balkan nations trace their origins to the disintegration of the *millet* system of the Ottoman Empire. Hence, the consolidation of "national minorities" operates through the identification of some of these "intermediate" groups with one or another "national" minority (or majority). The presence of an external national homeland is an important factor determining the consolidation of a group as a "national minority." Minority groups that lack a highly visible external homeland—the Gypsies, for example—do not pose visible threats for the states' regional security.[7]

Whereas the Balkan states have tried to minimize the numerical strength of minority groups in their dealings with the international community, internal debates frequently raise the specter of the minorities' high demographic rates. These high rates are routinely interpreted as a potential threat to the nation. For example, over the post–World War II period Albanians in Serbia (Kosovo) had a higher birth rate than Serbs and this resulted in their increase from 67.2 percent of the Kosovo population in the 1961 census to 77.4 percent in 1981 and nearly 90 percent in 1991. Even when one calculates the Albanian population using the total population of Serbia as the baseline, one finds that the Albanian population increased from 14 percent in 1981 to 17.2 percent in 1991. During the post–World War II period, there was considerable Slav emigration from the province because of economic considerations. Serbs have alleged that this emigration was the result of Albanian terrorism but outside observers blame poor economic conditions. Serbs willing to leave sold their lands to Albanians (often in hard currency earned by Albanian workers in the West).

A higher birth rate has also helped the Albanians of the People's Republic of Macedonia to increase their proportional share from 19.8 percent in 1981 to 21.0 percent in 1991 (Cviic 1991, 67; Petrovic 1992). In Bosnia-Herzegovina, the Muslim population increased from 39.5 percent in 1981 to 43.7 percent in 1991. In Bulgaria a similar trend is observed: According to the preliminary results of the most recent census (4–14 December 1992), the population decreased at a 5.3 percent rate compared to the previous nationwide census of 1985. Although emigration was a significant factor in this decline, the demographic trends show a very low birth rate for the Slavic population accompanied by high birth rates for Turks, Gypsies, and Pomaks (Nikolaev 1992; Poulton et al. 1989, 9–10).

To inquire into the reasons behind the (semi-)official view of the minorities as "aliens" to a nation's "soil" it is necessary to take into account the educational mechanisms responsible for the production and proliferation of stereotypes. As the different nationalist agendas of the Balkan nation-states gradually became enshrined in regional historical discourse, they inevitably found their way into songs, schoolbooks, and local traditions. Consequently, the "invented traditions" of the nineteenth-century Balkan nation-states are today routinely enacted in public lectures, national holidays, official histories, and other forms of "banal nationalism" (Billig 1995). The collective memory constructed by the daily production of such national "commemorations" (Gills 1994) is one of the main obstacles to finding mutually acceptable solutions to most of the disputes of the region.

This is a huge topic, worthy of separate investigation in its own right. For our purposes, however, it is sufficient to highlight the function of school textbooks in providing inaccurate images of the Other. Jelavich's (1990b) pioneer study of pre-1914 Yugoslav textbooks has illustrated the one-sided and ethnocentric nature of the textbooks and their contribution to distorted images of other nations. These images influenced popular perception, thereby significantly contributing to the impossibility of compromise between rivals. Although the history textbooks of the kingdom of Yugoslavia downplayed Serb–Croat antagonism, they devoted two-thirds of their curriculum to the coverage of Serbian history, a feature deeply resented by non-Serbs (Dimic and Alimpic 1996). Moreover, the textbooks offered an idealized view of Yugoslav unification, state formation, and the Serb dynasty.

In other states the situation was worse. As early as 1926, Dimitris Glinos, one of the modernizing intellectuals of the interwar period, conducted a survey of 90 Greek books—79 of which were school textbooks covering the 1914–1926 period. Glinos lamented the texts' ethnocentrism and pointed out the tendency to transform recent conflicts into transhistorical struggles. In doing so, the textbooks contributed to the construction of stereotypes alienating the Balkan peoples from each other (Iliou 1993).

In post–World War II Yugoslavia, textbooks conformed to the political slogans of self-management and "brotherhood and unity" (*bratstvo i jedinstvo*). The constant repetition of these slogans, however, rendered them meaningless for educational purposes. The influence of communist ideology on history writing was considerable, yet this did not lead to an explicit treatment of past disputes. On the contrary, interethnic rivalry was viewed as a "bourgeois" feature that was said to have disappeared under communism (Hopken 1996).

In sharp contrast to post–World War II Western Europe, the educational institutions and textbooks of the Balkan states were not cleansed of nationalistic propaganda and ethnocentric stereotypes. In most of the Yugoslav republics, the failure to address the "national question" in a fair and open manner encouraged the proliferation of historical revisionism in the 1980s and 1990s. In the post-1990 period, history education was renationalized, providing the ideological infrastructure for the armed conflicts of the period. Although Serbian textbooks provide the paradigmatic case for this tendency, post-1989 Macedonian and Bulgarian textbooks provide additional evidence for a regional ethnocentric cultural turn.

Macedonian textbooks issued in the years 1992 and 1993 contributed to resurgent irredentism in the new republic. The textbooks drew a distinction between geographic-ethnic borders (*geograftsko-etnitska granitsa*) and state boundaries (Kofos 1994, 14). The latter were confined to the state's current borders, whereas the former included parts of Bulgarian and Greek Macedonia. The textbooks constructed a particularly negative image of the neighboring countries. In her study of these textbooks, Vouri (1996b, 199) counts 43 negative (versus 2 positive and 7 neutral) references for Bulgaria, 30 negative (versus 5 positive and 11 neutral) references for Greece, 20 negative (versus 2 positive and neutral) references for Serbia, and 10 negative (versus 2 positive and 8 neutral) references for Albania.

The 1991–1992 Bulgarian history textbooks also provide a distorted image of neighboring countries and peoples. In the textbooks, Greeks are presented as having political, religious, and military power, which they use to exploit and subordinate the Bulgarian people. Of the themes specifically mentioned in the history textbooks, the "national unification of the Bulgarian areas" remains a dominant one. In the 1992 textbooks it was mentioned 70 times versus only 30 for the 1991 textbooks. Other themes include "Greece's denationalization policy," mentioned 24 times in 1991 and 20 times in 1992, and "Greece's territorial expansion pursuits," mentioned 42 times in 1991 and 34 times in 1992 (Vouri 1996a, 70).

Moreover, history textbooks provide selective interpretation of their histories. Greek textbooks attribute the success of the 1821 Greek revolution to the heroic deeds of the revolutionaries; Turkish textbooks attribute the revolution's success to Great Power interference. Macedonian and Albanian textbooks trace their people's national liberation efforts back to the 1821 revolution, thereby legitimizing these two latecomer nations (Katsoulakos and Tsantinis 1994; Roudometof 1996a, 263). Key events of recent Balkan history are presented in a highly ethnocentric manner. For example, the 1912–1913 Balkan wars receive a highly selective treatment in the Greek, Macedonian, Serb, and Bulgarian textbooks (Belia 1993; Vouri 1993). Generally speaking, the wars are presented from nationalistic perspectives. The nation's suffering is exalted and "injustices" are pointed out. The rest of the Balkan states are blamed and the nation is assumed to bear no responsibility for the turn of events. Good deeds are generally reserved for one's nation and bad deeds are the work of others.

In the 1990s, extensive qualitative and quantitative research has provided ample evidence of ethnocentrism in the Greek educational system.[8] Mirroring their Balkan counterparts, the basic themes of Greek schoolbooks revolve around the concepts of continuity, preservation, homogeneity, resistance, and superiority. National identity is viewed as transcendental and continuous from antiquity to the present. The West is viewed as a threatening presence and neighboring countries become targets for exalting Greek superiority. Such stereotypes are also reflected in the public's attitudes. For example, a survey conducted in 1995–1996 in Greek Macedonia found that 64.6 percent of the respondents "disliked" (Slavic) Macedonians and 54.2 percent "disliked" the Muslims (or Turks) of western Thrace (Mihalopoulou et al. 1998, 201). Like the Bulgarians or the Serbs, the Greeks appear to have been unfairly treated in key historical moments (Dragona 1997, 84–5; Hopken 1996). The growing socioeconomic gap between the Balkans and the West is contextualized as a threat to national identity (Dragona 1997, 87–9). Technological progress is viewed as an element alienating people from their own identity, and ultimately threatening national authenticity.

In almost all Balkan countries, the Ottoman legacy is viewed as purely negative. Students are led to believe that the Ottomans conquered the Balkans by force, violently converted Orthodox Christians into Muslims, and lacked any claim to civilization.[9] These images account for the negative attitudes of Serbs, Bulgarians, and Greeks vis-à-vis Turkey. Entrenched as they are in public discourse and everyday life, these attitudes inevitably become major obstacles to conflict resolution and contribute to the negative image of Muslim minorities in the Balkan states. For example, in a 1992 survey a reported 83.8 percent of the Bulgarian public considered the Turks to be "religious fanatics," and, subsequently, refused to marry them (80.8%) or even to be friends with them (38.7%) (Hopken 1997, 77).

## THE DOWNWARD SPIRAL: YUGOSLAVIA 1950–1990

The socioeconomic decline of the region and the gradual rift between local cultural traditions and evolving global trends in human rights and state policy contributed significantly to the post-1945 downward spiral into an "ethnic revival." Of course, this "revival" was such only for outsiders. In reality, the national question never disappeared from regional politics. But the Cold War helped contain and temporarily suppress these issues. Consequently, regional problems were dealt with as security concerns on a case-by-case basis, without any overall perspective on their nature and cause. This selectivity and post hoc treatment has not allowed for the development of long-term strategies for regional stability.

The most deceptive case was the so-called second Yugoslavia. Resurrected by Tito's partisans, the new Yugoslav state again proclaimed the principle of "brotherhood and unity" as a means to move beyond the legacy of World War II. In practical terms, the partisans allowed for the open affirmation of local national and ethnic identities, thereby offering a "voice" to those excluded from participation in interwar Yugoslavia (Shoup 1968; Woodward 1995). This strategy duplicated the Soviet solution to the national question. The Communist regime was successful in employing the party apparatus to prevent nationalist tensions among the republics. Moreover, the establishment of a federal structure offered at least a minimal recognition for the independent political entities representing the major "nations" of the federal Yugoslavia. Thus, although Croatia, Slovenia, Serbia, Macedonia, and Bosnia-Herzegovina were not sovereign states, the federal structure provided at least a space where concerns over autonomy—conceived mainly as independence from Serb domination—could be articulated. Therefore, the federal structure was an important vehicle for defusing nationalist aspirations.

During the 1960s, however, these issues again became threatening. Under the leadership of Rankovic, Serbianization policies were put in place in Kosovo, Bosnia-Herzegovina, and Vojvodina. This caused the reaction of the other national groups and led to a series of frictions during the 1966–1972 period (Ramet 1992; Rusinow 1977; Cohen 1993). Largely in response to this situation, the 1974 constitution attempted to further weaken the federal structure by significantly expanding the autonomy of the provinces of Vojvodina and Kosovo. The autonomy of the provinces was first established in 1947 but the 1974 constitutional expansion of this autonomy was seen as a carving up of the Serb territory and served as the first basis for future grievances (Ramet 1992, 73–8; Dragnich 1989). In addition, the new constitution recognized the Muslims as one of the sovereign nations in Bosnia; this provided the legal basis for the development of national identification on the basis of religious difference (Rusinow 1982). This was to a considerable extent a movement to accommodate the rising Muslim nationalism during the 1969–1971 period. In light of the fact that Serbs and Croats had advanced nationalist theories claiming the Muslim inhabitants as their own, the assertion of a new national group offered—at least for some time— the opportunity for a "consociational" model of democracy to advance in Bosnia.

The recognition of Kosovo's autonomous status led to a proliferation of nationalist activity that took the form of organizations, literature, and so on throughout its territory (Malcolm 1998; Vickers 1998). In 1981, Albanian nationalism expressed itself in a series of demonstrations, arson, and terrorist activities. The University of Pristina—with a population of approximately 37,000 students—was the principal site of the nationalist activity. Through the blatant use of military force, the Yugoslav armed forces crushed the rebellion. By no means, however, did this repression put an end to nationalist activity. Throughout the 1980s several underground organizations were uncovered and, during the 1981–1987 period, the local authorities brought criminal charges against 5,200 Kosovo Albanians (Ramet 1992, 195–8).

Until the mid-1980s, Yugoslavia appeared to be stable because the threat to centralization was coming from "peripheral" republics and not from the center (Serbia). In fact, the possibility of fragmentation remained rather remote given the control of the Communist Party over the federal apparatus and its commitment to the federal idea. This was to change with the appearance of the new leader of Serb Communists, Slobodan Milosevic, in the political scene. But Milosevic did not operate in a vacuum. Through the 1970s and 1980s economic conditions worsened, causing a widening of the economic gap between the country's rich northern provinces and the south (Rusinow 1988). Concomitant with it was the legitimization crisis of the Communist regime. Milosevic offered a way out to the Communist elites by endorsing the Serb Orthodox Church and becoming the leader of Serb nationalism (Ramet 1992, 225–30; Glenny 1992).

Prior to his ascent to power, the Serb case against the Titoist arrangement was spelled out in the draft memorandum prepared in 1985 by a working group of the Serbian Academy of Sciences under the chairmanship of Antonije Isakovic, one of the country's prominent writers. The Serb complaints against the government argued for discriminatory policy vis-à-vis Serbia in the economic field; for the partition of Serbia proper into three parts under the 1974 constitution (Serbia proper and the autonomous provinces of Vojvodina and Kosovo); and for the allegedly anti-Serb policy pursued in Kosovo by Albanian "separatists" (Cviic 1991, 65). In January 1986, 200 prominent Belgrade intellectuals signed a petition accusing the authorities of committing national treason and "genocide" against the Serb minority in Kosovo (Poulton 1991, 19). The intensification of nationalist feelings with respect to the Kosovo Serbs was also greatly facilitated by the attitude of the Serb Orthodox Church. The Church added a religious element to the conflict because it had allied itself with those opposing the Serb "genocide" in the province (Ramet 1999, 99–116).

Milosevic exploited the Albanian "threat," building popular support for the Communist Party. In the spring of 1987 Milosevic paid a visit to the province to take part in the celebration of the 1389 Kosovo battle. Milosevic played out the national themes with reference to the contemporary situation. He promised Kosovo Serbs that "nobody would ever beat them again." Within a few months, he used their alleged suffering to attack the previous leadership in Serbia and carried out a purge throughout Serbia that resulted in the consolidation of his position. In October 1987, more federal police units were dispatched to Kosovo. Milosevic orchestrated a number of protests and demonstrations that led to the fall of the local governments in Vojvodina and Montenegro (in 1988 and 1989), bringing these regions under the control of his followers.

In Kosovo, a general strike in February 1989 led to military suppression that crushed the Albanian protests within a week with 24 deaths reported. On 23 March 1989 Kosovo's Assembly, ringed by Yugoslav army tanks, gave its consent to the constitutional changes demanded by Belgrade (Cviic 1991, 67–8). On 28 March 1989 Serbia's Assembly adopted these changes, giving the Serb authorities in Belgrade control over Kosovo's police, courts, and territorial defense (a similar strategy was followed in Vojvodina) (Roudometof 1996b). All of these procedures raised Milosevic's popularity to unprecedented heights and resulted in his reelection as president of Serbia in December 1990. Milosevic appeared to be the protector of all Serbs in Yugoslavia.

The Kosovo affair—and to a lesser extent the similar developments in Montenegro and Vojvodina—acted as warnings for Croatia and Slovenia that the Serb program of "centralized democratization" meant the return of Serb supremacy. As pluralism within and outside the Communist Party lines came to the forefront of politics during the late 1980s, politicians in both countries used the national question as a means to attract votes. In addition, the federal government's intention to revise the federal constitution to produce a different arrangement among the republics gave the republics the pretext they were looking for in order to exit the federation.

The major event that led to the official collapse of the second Yugoslavia was the Slovenian crisis of 1989 (Hayden 1992a; Cohen 1993, 177–81; Andrejevich 1990a; Ramet 1992, 221). Slovenia's desire to break its ties with the federation was heightened by the increasingly centralized and nationalist policies of Serb president Slobodan Milosevic. The Slovenes preferred a loose confederation, whereas the Serbs opted for a centralized federation. The difference between the two sides and the Slovenian insistence on rejecting a compromise led to the crisis of 1989–1990. There are no significant national minorities within the Slovenian territory, but this affair was of great strategic importance because it provided a model for the Croatian attempt to break ties with the Yugoslav federation. The Slovenian route for establishing independence was to amend the republic's constitution in a way inconsistent with the guidelines of the federal structure. The crisis was intensified when, following the elections of 1990, the victorious nationalist coalition of five parties (DEMOS) pursued a strategy of debating the options of confederation or complete succession. The Serb government reacted by cutting the commercial ties with the republic, an action that forced the option of "exit" for the Slovenes and hurt the remainder of Yugoslavia more than Slovenia (Andrejevich 1990b). On 2 July 1990 Slovenia declared its "sovereignty," setting the stage for similar developments in Croatia and Kosovo.

Following the Slovenian declaration, Croatia was quick to follow the same route. During the first multiparty elections in April and May 1990, the right-wing, nationalist party of Franjo Tudjman emerged as the winner. The party promised to break its ties with the old arrangement but the way this would take place remained open. Tudjman's victory was seen as a return to World War II Croatian nationalism and raised fears among the Croatian Serbs regarding their future in the new state. A number of actions undertaken by the new government confirmed these fears. The new regime attempted to balance the nonproportional character of most civil service positions through the hiring of Croats and the firing of Serbs; this only intensified the feeling of persecution among Croatian Serbs. In addition, the Croatian constitution was amended in order to provide for the adoption of the traditional Croatian symbols—a coat of arms, flag, and national anthem—as the official insignia of the republic. The Latin script was also adopted as the official alphabet (Cohen 1993, 131). The new ethnic symbolisms emphasized the explicit ethnic character of the proposed new state. The adoption of the old (World War II) nationalist symbols by the new regime acted as a reminder to a large portion of the Serb minority of the horrible events that occurred during the establishment of the Croat fascist regime. Fear acted as a stimulus leading to the mobilization of the local Serb community around a nationalist program.

On 1 August 1990, Croatian Serbs in the Knin area east of the Adriatic staged an armed rebellion, conducted their own referendum on the issue of autonomy, and proclaimed themselves an autonomous region (the so-called Krajina republic). Supported openly by the Belgrade regime, the Croatian Serbs proclaimed themselves to be "the Serbian region of Krajina in Croatia" on 4 January 1991 and a part of Serbia in March 1991 (Poulton 1991, 27; Cviic 1991, 73–4; Glenny 1992, Ch. 1). During the second half of 1990 a stalemate was reached with the two northern republics and Serbia (with Montenegro) between peace and war. Finally, on 25 June 1991 the two republics seceded, setting the stage for the Serbo-Croatian war. For a short time hostilities took place in Slovenia but soon the war was focused between Croatia and Serbia.

In Bosnia-Herzegovina, the democratization process intensified the ethnic rivalries among the three minority groups (Muslims, Croats, and Serbs). Muslim nationalism appeared officially during the 1968–1971 period. Following the establishment of the Yugoslav federation in 1944, the Yugoslav Communists had promoted the development of regionalism as a means for preventing rival nationalisms from rising and reinforcing the necessity of a federal structure. But the Muslim nation was not institutionalized until the late 1960s because of the negative image of Muslims within the party, the lack of strong local national consciousness, and the threat that a Muslim national consciousness would be usurped by clerical and bourgeois elements (Rusinow 1982, 4).

It was only in January 1968 that the Muslims officially became a nation. According to the regime's official position, the new nation was not constructed; rather, its status was simply affirmed. Emphasis was placed on the secular identity of the Muslims in an effort to overcome the religious character of the new national affiliation. Consequently, a revisionist Bosnian historiography emerged claiming the Muslims as a Bosnian nation. Within the newly designated Bosnian group the conflict between clericalists (advocates of Islam as the primary source of Bosnian distinctiveness) and Westernizers persisted throughout the 1970s. Transcending these two poles, a third, "bourgeois-nationalist," line of *Bosnjastvo* (Bosnianism) emerged claiming for Bosnian Muslims the status of another South Slav nation, equal to those of the Croats and Serbs.

Of these groups, the clericalists were suspected of attempting to convert the newly formulated Bosnian identity to Islam. This led to their prosecution by the local authorities. A number of Muslim nationalists were prosecuted, including Alija Izetbegovic, who was later to become president of the republic. The so-called Sarajevo Muslims were accused of attempting to establish an Islamic state based on the religious identity of the Muslim community. In 1983 Izetbegovic received a 14-year sentence (of which he served almost 6 years) for his writing of the 1970 Islamic declaration. The prosecution claimed that the declaration called for the establishment of a fundamentalist regime in Bosnia, a claim that was rejected by the supporters of the Muslim group. Although it is undeniable that the group espoused a more activist religious role, it is doubtful that they represented a genuine fundamentalist revival (Poulton 1991, 42–4; Ramet 1992, 177–86; Andrejevich 1991). Rather, the clericalists were successful in mobilizing the religious element of the population toward a nationalism that aimed to create a new nation from the existing religious identity.

Beginning with the 1971 census "Muslim" ceased to be a purely religious identification and became an ethnic category. Thus, the road was paved for the construction of a national identity from a religious identity. Muslim nationalists espoused the theory that the Muslims were neither Croats nor Serbs but rather of Turkish origin. In the following years, the theme of Muslim hegemonism became a focal point for rallying Serb and Macedonian nationalists in Bosnia, Serbia, Kosovo, and Macedonia.

In the crisis of 1989–1990 Bosnia's political parties were organized along ethnic lines. The few attempts to create parties that would transcend ethnicity failed. In fact, the leader of the Yugoslav-oriented Serbian Democratic Party attributed the failure of the federal-oriented party to the Serbs' preference for ethnically oriented organizations (Cohen 1993, 146). Izetbegovic's party, representing mainly the Muslim element, attempted to negotiate a middle-range position between the Serbs and the Croats. However, Serb nationalism was seen as more dangerous than Croat nationalism. Although Serb nationalism was not welcomed, Izetbegovic attempted to promote—with Macedonian president Gligorov—the idea of a broader Yugoslav confederation. The proposed solutions did not work, however, and in a televised address on 16 March 1991, Milosevic announced that Serbia could not continue to recognize the Yugoslav federation. By spring 1991 all attempts had failed and after 19 July 1991, the Yugoslav Army departed from Slovenia—where no significant Serb minority existed—thus directing attention to Croatia (and Bosnia). In connection with these events the threat of war in Bosnia was first raised.

Bosnia remained calm until October 1991, although at the same time the Serbo-Croatian war was taking place. Then, the Croats and Muslims in the government coalition declared their intention to secede and, correspondingly, to hold a referendum on the issue. There was no consensus, however, regarding whether voting would take place within each ethnic group or whether a "one man one vote" approach should be followed. The Bosnian Serbs' anxiety over their future was heightened in February 1992 when the plans for the referendum were announced and the Muslim–Croatian leadership adopted the "one man one vote" solution. Fear of exclusion from the political process pushed the Serbs to boycott the referendum. Bosnian Serb officials in cooperation with the Yugoslav Army started preparations for hostilities. On 1 March 1992, when gunmen fired on members of a Serb wedding party at Serajevo, the signal was given: Within hours, barricades were erected and soon the fighting spread to the rest of the republic (Cohen 1993, 237).

## THE REST OF THE BALKANS

The creation of the second Yugoslavia carried with it an important change in the politics of the Macedonian Question.[10] During World War II, the Yugoslav Communists were successful in obtaining the support of the majority of the population in Yugoslav Macedonia (Shoup 1968, 144–83). This success was largely because of their willingness to endorse the concept of an independent Macedonian nation, a goal initially proclaimed by the pre–World War I IMRO.[11] Soon after the 1944 proclamation of the People's Republic of Macedonia, Yugoslav and Bulgarian Communists attempted the conversion of pre-1913 Macedonia into a single unit (for details, see Palmer and King 1971; King 1973; Kofos 1964). The plan called for the construction of a broader South Slav federation, which would have included Bulgaria. The plan failed when Bulgarian and Yugoslav Communists disagreed over the status of Bulgaria in the federation, that is, whether it would be an equal partner to the whole of Yugoslavia or simply another republic. The 1948 rift between Tito and Stalin made all future plans for such a goal a practical impossibility.

Still, for a period of time, the inhabitants of the Bulgarian part of Macedonia (known as Pirin Macedonia) were officially classified as Macedonians (Korobar 1987). This classification was the result of swift "persuasion" by local Communist cadres (Nikolov 2000). It remained in use for some time after the Tito–Stalin rift. In April 1956 the Bulgarian Communist Party reversed its policy and decided to withdraw its recognition of a separate Macedonian nationality, even though the December 1956 census showed the presence of 187,789 Macedonians (Cviic 1991, 39–40). By 1960 the official record ceased to have a separate entry for Macedonians.

During the 1941–1943 period, German, Bulgarian, and Communist propaganda also influenced the Slavic Macedonian population in northwestern Greek Macedonia (for details, see Koliopoulos 1994). Consequently, as the occupation forces withdrew from the region, the Communists were able to attract the Slavic population by forming separate units—*Slovenomakedonski Narodno Oslobodi-telen Front* (SNOF)—and promising equal treatment to the Slavic minority.[12] The Slav Macedonians fought alongside the Greek Communists during the Greek civil war (1944–1949), causing serious discomfort and embarrassment for the Greek Communist Party. The party had promised equal rights to the Slavic Macedonians but could not support the creation of a separate Macedonian state that would include segments of Greek Macedonia, because this would cause an upheaval among the local Greek population. The victory of the pro-Western nationalist forces in the Greek civil war restored the pre–World War II boundaries. However, the situation was not completely resolved because some of the Macedonian Slavs fled with the remnants of the Communist forces into Yugoslav Macedonia, while others chose to remain in the region. After 1945, large numbers of Macedonian Slavs emigrated to Canada, Australia, the United States, and other Western countries, giving rise to a Macedonian diaspora. This diaspora was instrumental in post-1945 Macedonian nation building (Danforth 1995).

The population transfers, policy changes, warfare, and emigration were accompanied by an intense post-1945 nation-building effort within the People's Republic of Macedonia. Macedonian nation building fused the ideology of IMRO with that of the Yugoslav Communists by proclaiming the creation of the Macedonian Republic to be equivalent to a second Illinden, analogous to the original 1903 failed uprising (Brown 2000; Poulton 1995). In accordance with the Balkan tradition of manipulating religion for nationalist purposes, in 1967 the Yugoslav Communists proclaimed the creation of a separate Macedonian Church.[13] In addition, Macedonia's history was rewritten to provide the new (Slavic) Macedonian nation a glorious history similar to that of Greece and Bulgaria. According to the post-1945 Macedonian narrative, the Macedonians are a nation inhabiting geographic Macedonia since 600–700 A.D., when Slavs first appeared in the Balkans (Mojzov 1979; Tashkovski 1976; Apostolski et al. 1979). A significant part of what Bulgarians considered to be their own medieval history, including the reign of Tsar Samuil, was appropriated into Macedonian history. In addition, it has been suggested that the Macedonian nation was instrumental in developing, first among the Slavic peoples, a written language and alphabet, namely, the Cyrillic alphabet.

From this viewpoint, the 1913 partition of Macedonia was a national catastrophe that divided Macedonians among the conquering nations of Bulgaria, Serbia, and Greece. All three neighboring nations were viewed as enemies trying to "convince" Macedonians to assimilate into the Serb, Greek, or Bulgarian nations, although heavy emphasis was placed on Bulgarian irredentism and the desire to create a Greater Bulgaria, inclusive of Macedonian territory (Hristov 1971; Katardzhiev 1973; Lape 1973). This viewpoint caused significant difficulties in post-1945 political relations among Yugoslavia, Greece, and Bulgaria.[14] The 1990s collapse of the second Yugoslavia set the stage for the eventual disassociation of the Macedonian state from the Yugoslav federation. However, throughout the 1990s, international recognition was hindered by the persistent efforts of the Greek state. For official Greece, "Macedonia" is a name that belongs to the Greek historical tradition. Greece has refused to recognize the Republic of Macedonia, setting off a cultural, ideological, and diplomatic struggle over the republic's name (for further discussion, see Roudometof 1996a; Danforth 1995).

The Macedonian saga aptly demonstrates that the Yugoslav crises of the

1990s should not be considered a Yugoslav peculiarity. Indeed, these crises are a manifestation of the broader regional issues of nationality, ethnicity, and minority rights. Perhaps the best publicized case is that of Cyprus. Cyprus was originally part of the Ottoman Empire but came under British rule in the late nineteenth century. As was the case in other parts of the empire, Greek nationalism spread gradually into the island, facilitating the transformation of the Greek Orthodox religious identity into a secular Greek Cypriot identity (Kitromilides 1979). By the mid-1950s the Greek Cypriots undertook armed struggle against the British, demanding the island's union with Greece. Because there was also a sizable Muslim Turkish minority on Cyprus, the problem of the island's self-determination became an area of yet another Greek–Turkish confrontation. In the 1950s, the Cyprus issue led to a deterioration of the relations between the two countries. Turkish pogroms against the Greek minority in Istanbul further shrank the Greek population of the city to a mere 3,000 people (Alexandris 1983). The island eventually became an independent state in the 1960s, but this did not resolve the issue of the Turkish minority's status in the new state. Like the Krajina Serbs in the 1990s, the Turkish Cypriots never felt sufficiently included in the new republic. Relations between the two communities continued to be troublesome. In 1974, when the Greek junta cooperated with Greek Cypriot officers to overthrow the Cypriot government and declare the island's union with Greece, Turkey sent in its troops to occupy 40 percent of the island's territory. This territory became a ghostly republic, recognized by Turkey alone.[15]

The 1974 Turkish invasion of Cyprus sent shock waves across the other Orthodox countries in the region. The state most acutely affected was Bulgaria, mainly because of its sizable Turkish and Muslim minorities in southeastern Bulgaria. In the post-1945 period, the Bulgarian Communist regime attempted to "modernize" the Muslims' traditional lifestyle by liquidating autonomous cultural institutions and organizing state-controlled associations.[16] The Cyprus affair provided the impetus for a more pronounced shift in Bulgarian policy. Fearful of repetition of the Cyprus experience on Bulgaria's own soil, the Bulgarian state developed a policy of negating Turkish minority identity (Neuremberg 1997, 5–6). By 1975 most Turkish schools, newspapers, and journals were closed down. By 1984 the Bulgarian Communists had reinterpreted history to disassociate the Turks from Turkey. Accordingly, there were no Turks in Bulgaria, just "Turkified Bulgarians" who had been forcibly Islamicized and Turkified during Ottoman rule.

From 1985 to 1989 the Bulgarian state attempted to make reality conform to this official fiction by carrying out an assimilation campaign aiming to forcibly acculturate the Turks and other Muslims into Christian Bulgarian culture (Roudometof 1996b; Karpat 1990; Poulton 1991). The campaign entailed imposed changes of names from Muslim to Christian and issuing new identification papers to the minority. For those who avoided the change, the local bureaucracy denied the validity of their old papers. In effect, this created serious problems in all dealings with the state. The free operation of religious institutions was restricted and speaking Turkish was prohibited.

The campaign was met with sporadic small-scale protests by the Turks. By 1989 a Turkish civil rights group was formed and mass protest started, including huger strikes, demonstrations and so on. As a result the authorities increased their pressure and began expelling a number of Turks—mainly activists in the beginning—to Turkey. Soon this took the form of an exodus, with at least 60,000 refugees crossing the border during the first half of the year. By late August the number climbed to 300,000. The collapse of the Communist regime in 1990 and the democratization of the Bulgarian political system also resulted in a defusion of the ethnic crisis. On 29 December 1989 the Bulgarian government revoked the assimilation campaign. A number of the refugees returned, discovering that in many cases government officials and local people had taken advantage of their absence to sell movable and immovable property for profit. During the summer of 1990, the central authorities instructed the local government to make efforts to resettle the returning group. Muslims continued to suffer from public discrimination in housing, education, and health care, but the gradual liberalization of political life resulted in a general improvement in human rights for the minority group. In October 1990 the first Islamic institute teaching Muslim culture was founded in Sofia, and in February 1991 the first Turkish-language newspaper appeared.

The attempt to reverse the assimilation policy did not go unopposed. Organized by local nationalists in the city of Karbzhali on 31 December 1989, the Committee for the Defense of National Interests called for a plebiscite on the government's decision. By 4 January 1990 demonstrations opposing the reversal of this policy had been reported in Sofia, Plovdiv, Haskovo, Pleven, Shumen, Ruse, Targovishte, Sliven, and other places. Attempting to defuse the situation, the government brought both sides together in a Social Council of Citizens. The council voiced its demand for guarantees of Bulgaria's "national interest and security." It recommended that separatist and autonomist organizations be banned and conceded to Bulgarian nationalist opinion by calling for the banning of public displays of the Turkish flag and confirming Bulgarian as the only official language. Subsequently, on 15 January 1990, the Bulgarian National Assembly approved a declaration reiterating the main points agreed on by the council (Ashley 1990). There were two major reasons for this intense backlash: the fact that many individuals had profited through the selling of the Turks' property and were afraid of their return, and the fear that the minority would be given political and cultural rights and a type of autonomy that would be the first step toward the carving up of Bulgarian territory.

Throughout the 1990s, the situation gradually improved, although ethnic tensions have persisted. Soon after the collapse of the Communist regime, the Muslim minority organized itself into the Movement of Rights and Freedoms (or DPS). The movement eventually mutated into a political party, thanks to tacit support by the former Communist, Bulgarian Socialist Party (BSP). Despite an official ban on electoral participation for organizations based on religious and ethnic platforms, the Muslim minority's political party did survive throughout the 1990s and has secured its participation in Bulgarian politics. (For a review of the party's trajectory in the 1990s, see Ilchev, 2000, 249–63.)

Greeks have repeatedly expressed similar fears with regard to the Muslim and Turkish minority in western Thrace. Since the 1920s, an estimated 250,000 Muslims left western Thrace for Turkey. The minority's numerical strength has not been diminished, but its composition has changed as the rate of Pomaks increased to 30 percent of all Muslims (Poulton 1997a). During the late 1980s and early 1990s the vocal protests of the minority's representatives were frequently viewed as a front for a Turkish-sponsored agenda of autonomy and possibly, separatism (cf. Tsikelikis and Christopoulos 1997). The conservative Greek government of the 1990–1993 period attempted to improve the status of the minority by ending discriminatory practices against the minority in the public sector and by attempting to develop this economically underdeveloped region (western Thrace). As is the case with other Muslim groups in the Balkans, the gradual modernization of local society fosters a shift from a religious ("Muslim") identity to a national or ethnic ("Turk") identity. This shift is most pronounced among the Muslim Pomaks and has led to Greek efforts to carve out an ethnic Pomak identity. However, these efforts have not been successful, at least thus far.

In the 1990s, the minority issue also played a role in Greek–Albanian relations. During World War II the Greek Army had temporarily occupied southern Albania or northern Epirus (see Chapter 7). Officially, Greece maintained a state of war with Albania until 1987. During the Communist regime's rule the Greek minority was isolated and subjected to harsh repression by the authorities, especially with respect to religious practices. By the mid-1980s the regime's attitude had softened and relatives could visit their compatriots on the other side of the border. In the 1990s, the collapse of the Communist regime led to the immigration of approximately 300,000 Albanians into Greece. The large number of these illegal immigrants restructured Greek–Albanian relations, because both sides realized their mutual benefit from cooperation.

Following the collapse of the Communist regime and the first free elections in Albania, the Greek minority was organized into the Omonia party and attempted to compete in the elections. This did not go unopposed; the ministry of justice attempted to restrict parties that organized themselves on an "ethnic" basis. Omonia was successful in electing five deputies to the new Albanian Parliament. Following this electoral success a law was passed barring the formation of parties based on ethnicity (Pettifer 2000, 175–7).

In 1993, the political situation deteriorated when Albanian authorities forced the newly appointed archbishop Anastasios of the Albanian Orthodox Church to leave the country on the grounds of his alleged "nationalist propaganda" against the Albanian state.[17] The Archbishop's deportation was accompanied by widespread ethnic violence targeting the Greek Orthodox minority, carried out with the toleration or participation of the local authorities. The minority rallied behind the Archbishop, whereas the Albanian authorities treated the situation as a nationalist provocation. On the other side of the border, the Greek authorities were quick to react. In the days following the Archbishop's deportation, some 5,000 Albanians were deported to Albania. Given the inadequate control of the border, there was little doubt that most of them would be back within a few days, but the purpose of these actions was to "remind" Albania of its financial dependence on the income coming from Albanian workers in Greece. In an interview in the Greek journal *Economic Review* (19 August 1993) Greek premier Costas Mitsotakis made clear that Albania could not afford to react to the deportations of Albanians from Greece because its weak economy made the state dependent on remittances from Albanians in Greece. In the aftermath of this affair, the Greek premier declared that the status of the Greek minority in southern Albania (or northern Epirus) should be equated with that of the Albanian population in Kosovo, and if autonomy was to be given to them, the same should apply to the Greeks in Albania. The post-1993 socialist governments have abandoned this approach and relations between the two states have improved.

Of crucial importance to the restructuring of Greek-Albanian relations was the Greek government's swift persecution of the Northern Epirus Liberation Front (MAVI), which in 1994 and 1995 was accused of orchestrating attacks on Albanian military posts and personnel. But the position of the minority is not determined solely by the Greek state's actions or foreign policy. Equally important is the interplay among Albanian domestic politics, the Albanian tribal division between Ghegs and Tosks, and religious affiliation. All these factors shaped the Greek minority's position in the 1990s and will undoubtedly continue to do so in the future. (For a review, see Pettifer, 2000.)

## CONCLUDING REMARKS

This brief overview of the minority issue in the post-1945 period is not an exhaustive account and is limited to those minorities claimed by an external national homeland. Nevertheless, it clearly illustrates the importance of the minority issue for the region at large. Roger Brubaker's quotation at the beginning of this chapter highlights the extent to which contemporary problems with regard to minorities in the region bear a close similarity to the problems of the interwar period. It would be a mistake, however, to view the current situation as a simple extension of the pre–World War II regional disputes. Far from a "recycling" of past concerns, the post-1989 situation has been greatly influenced by post-1945 global trends in economy, society, and culture.

During the post-1945 period, both declining economic performance and the articulation of global transnational rules for the international system of states have contributed to increased ethnic tension. Although the role of economic decline has been quite important in fostering ethnic competition in the 1980s

**Map 5**
**The Post-Yugoslav New States, 1990–2000**

*Source*: U.S. Central Intelligence Agency 1996.

Yugoslavia, I believe it would be a mistake to attribute ethnic tensions solely to economic factors. The transformation of economic grievances into more cultural and political nationalist rivalries has been greatly facilitated by the dominant role of nationhood in local national cultures. This is most clearly revealed in the ethnocentrism that still prevails in local educational systems.

Consequently, minority groups are not considered legitimate members of the local nations. The inclusion of minority groups in local societies is perhaps the most important challenge for the future development of civil society in the region. The wars of the 1990s have been a major step backward in this regard. International intervention in Bosnia and in Kosovo has been interpreted by both majority and minority populations as an undue infringement on state sovereignty, designed to offer statehood to Bosnian Muslims and Kosovo

Albanians. The fragmentation of Yugoslavia and the new states born out of the former republics is illustrated in Map 5. The creation of all these small states could be a force fostering regional peace and stability, provided that their creation would signal the end of national rivalries in the region. However, these rivalries do not stem from the need to make geography conform to the patterns of ethnic dispersion. On the contrary, they are products of the cultural logic of regional nation-state building. In this regard, the post–World War II international trends toward establishment of a global regime of human rights adds ammunition to the local nationalists' dreams and desires. In the aftermath of the 1999 Kosovo crisis, the lesson seems to be that the international community is willing to offer support to minority groups fighting for autonomy. The list of such groups includes the Macedonian Albanians, the Bulgarian Muslims and Turks, and the Greek Turks. It is almost certain that activists within these groups will contemplate taking such an action in the future. The most decisive way to prevent such action is building up civic ties that would transcend the principle of nationhood. Indeed, this strategy is a necessary requirement for future entrance into the EU. Whether this will be the case remains to be seen. Needless to say, however, dealing with the minority issue is a major prerequisite for developing stable interstate cooperation and eventually attracting badly needed foreign capital investment to the region.

The role of Turkey as a benevolent protector for local Muslim minorities further complicates the picture. The Orthodox nations of the region have built their self-image against the image of Ottoman Turkey as a ruthless suppressor of their national self-determination. Turkey's influence is viewed as little less than an expression of revisionism, aiming to reclaim the lands of the former Ottoman Empire.

## NOTES

1. For examples, see Cohen (1993), Glenny (1992), Rezun (1995), and Ramet (1992, 1999). Policy-making and security analysts have also debated the national rivalries of the Balkan states. However, their analyses tend to reify state action, thus preventing an examination of the production of national rivalries. See, for example, Johnsen (1993), Brown (1992), and the essays in Shoup (1990). For a critical response, see Wheeler (1996).

2. During the post-1945 period, Europe has become more integrated, mainly owing to economic development and modernization. The differences between Eastern and Western Europe persisted, and convergence among EU countries occurred largely prior to their entrance into the union (Therborn 1995a, 195–96). The effects of EU membership on poor countries have been limited. Ireland's GDP per capita was 61.4 percent of EC-12 in 1972, and it rose to 67.3 percent in 1990. Greece's GDP was 58.2 percent of the EC average in 1980 and 53 percent in 1990.

3. It is indicative of the region's economic marginalization that there are very few regional economic studies of the Balkans. This is partly a reflection of the Cold War. The Communist countries of the Balkans were grouped with the other Eastern European

economies, whereas Greece, an EC and NATO member, was grouped with the Western European countries. These classifications reflected the Cold War mentality of the 1950–1990 period, and they are likely to be revised in the foreseeable future.

4. See Todorova (1994; 1997), Bakic-Hayden and Hayden (1992), and Bakic-Hayden (1995). Although in agreement with regard to the Balkans' distorted image in the West, Todorova (1997, 19) argues that "Balkanism" is a discourse distinct from Orientalism (cf. Said 1978).

5. At least until 1827, the region was commonly called the "Hellenic peninsula," "Byzantine peninsula," "Thrace," "Roman peninsula," "Illyrian peninsula," or "Greek peninsula" (Todorova 1994, 463; Wilkinson 1951).

6. The ideological exclusion of the Balkans from a community of shared values and norms provides the context for emotional detachment from the passions involved or what Mestrovic (1996) calls "post-emotionalism." For Mestrovic, post-emotionalism is responsible for the weak Western response to the Balkan conflicts of the 1990s.

7. A considerable number of Gypsies lives in Bulgaria. Because the majority of them are Muslim, they could be identified with the "Turkish" or "Muslim" minority groups if such an identification was perceived as desirable. In 1993, FYROM's Roma (Gypsy) political party addressed a letter to the UN calling for a separate nation. In addition, some Muslim Roma, apparently desiring to disassociate themselves from the Turks, formed an association proclaiming Egypt as their historical homeland and asking recognition as "Egyptians." For all practical purposes, invoking "Egypt" as an external homeland is an attempt to increase Roma's public voice. For discussions, see Troxel (1992), Poulton (1991, 90–3), and Ilchev and Perry (1993).

8. Frangoudakis and Dragona (1997). The project is based on an analysis of textbooks, as well as interviews with teachers. The massive nature of the project does not allow a detailed description of the specifics, and consequently, my discussion simply highlights some key aspects of the overall tendencies. The evidence suggests a twist in Todorova's (1997, 43–5) account of the Greeks' view of the Balkans. Increasingly, Greeks distance themselves from the Balkans in an effort to avoid precisely the stereotypes Todorova analyzes in her brilliant book.

9. While teaching a class of Serbs, Macedonians, Greeks, and Albanians at the American College of Thessaloniki in 1998, I asked them whether they attributed the spread of Islam to violence and forced conversion. Despite the information provided in their textbook, nearly all students responded that this was indeed the case. The students doubted the reliability and accuracy of their "American textbook" and preferred to rely on the knowledge they had accumulated in their elementary and high school years.

10. This section draws heavily on Roudometof (1996a). For further discussion, see Danforth (1995), Roudometof (2000b), and Pettifer (1999).

11. The 1943 "Report of the Organizing Committee of the Anti-Fascist Assembly of National Liberation of Macedonia" (ASNOM) declared that "the fighting Piedmont of Macedonia has fiercely proclaimed that it will not stint on support or sacrifice for the liberation of the other two segments of our nation and for the general unification of the entire Macedonian people." The manifesto issued by ASNOM's first section also explicitly stated its hope for the "unification of the whole Macedonian people" (quoted in Kondis et al. 1993, 36).

12. According to Koliopoulos (1994), the participation of the local peasants in the war was determined by their proximity to the partisans. Where the peasants were vulnerable to partisan attacks, they tended to join the guerrilla forces. Not all the Slavs

supported the Communist or occupation forces. Some of them enlisted in the right-wing partisan forces (Karakasidou 1993a, 463).

13. For details, see Alexander (1979, 280–8). The proclamation met the strong resistance of the Serb Orthodox Church. Its sister Orthodox churches did not recognize the Macedonian Church because its independence was not achieved according to Orthodox tradition. It is indeed quite ironic that even a Communist regime had to employ Orthodoxy as a state religion to foster its nation-building efforts.

14. In the 1960s, the Bulgarian state bitterly protested the designation of medieval monuments as "Macedonian" (Rusinow 1968). The Bulgarian Academy of Sciences published a volume of archival documents (1978) in an effort to publicly repudiate the Macedonian claims that the inhabitants of the region did not call themselves Bulgarians in medieval times. A similar Greek publication appeared in 1992 (Koliopoulos and Chasiotis 1992).

15. For further discussion on rapprochement between Turkish and Greek Cypriot communities, as well as additional literature on the Cyprus issue, see the collected essays in Calotychos (1998).

16. In addition, in 1950–1951 some 140,000 Turks were expelled into Turkey. This emigration wave grew out of the Turkish minority's anxieties over the 1946 nationalization of Turkish schools and the confiscation of the minority's private property. Emigration was strictly controlled by the Communist regime, thereby preventing large numbers of Turks from immigrating to Turkey (for details, see Simsir 1988, 145–70).

17. In this context, it is important to note that the boundaries differentiating Orthodox Albanians from Greeks are unclear. Many members of the Greek minority have only an elementary knowledge of Greek and look to the Orthodox Church as the basic marker for their own cultural differentiation from the rest of the population. Therefore, an emphasis on the "Greek" character of the Albanian Orthodox Church can be seen as an attempt to "acculturate" members of the Albanian Orthodox community into Hellenism (Roudometof 1996b).

# Conclusions

This book has shown that current or future ethnic conflicts are directly linked to national rivalries generated by the reorganization of southeastern Europe according to the model of the nation-state. The adoption of the nation-state model by the Balkan peoples is a manifestation of their modernity, not their "backwardness." The post-1989 Yugoslav crises are a specific manifestation of these broader regional patterns. The dynamics of the "national question" in the former Yugoslavia are similar to those of the less publicized cases of Bulgaria, Macedonia, and Albania (or the better known case of Cyprus). Because of the historical factors outlined in this book, this reorganization led to the elevation of nationhood into the foundational principle in regional nation formation. Consequently, discrimination against minorities has been legitimized by reference to cultural difference. Therefore, the recurrent phenomenon of ethnic conflict in the region is not due to "tribalism" but to the nation-states' specific historical paths to modernity.

In order to describe the Balkans' route to modernity, I have used in this book a conceptualization of globalization as a world-historical process. My inquiry was organized into the three main historical periods of globalization: the early modern phase (1500–1830), the modern period (1830–1945), and the contemporary period (1945–present). In considering the early modern period of globalization, I focused on the gradual articulation of the Balkans as a geopolitical configuration distinct from the Near East, that is, the territory of the Ottoman world-empire. Consequently, the first two chapters of the book were devoted to an analysis of the Balkan national revolutions. To capture the complexity of nationalism, I performed a multidimensional analysis of these revolutions. Following Mann's (1986) image of "society" as consisting of overlapping power networks, I conceptualized Ottoman society as a combination of socioeconomic, politico-military, and cultural-ideological networks. In the first two chapters I inquired into the changes within these networks and their contribution to the outbreak of the Balkan revolutions.

The emergence of nationalism in the Balkans has been linked to the growing contacts between the Ottoman world-empire and the emerging European world-economy. However, the conventional thesis that the Balkan revolutions were associated with the empire's eighteenth-century economic incorporation into the capitalist world-economy is not fully substantiated by the historical record. The socioeconomic contacts between Western Europe and the Ottoman Empire date back to the sixteenth and seventeenth centuries' involvement of Western powers in eastern Mediterranean trade. The Ottoman world-empire was only gradually drawn into the European world-economy. Slowly, the geopolitical and economic competition among the Western powers influenced the place of Ottoman Christians. During the eighteenth century a Greek Orthodox Balkan merchant class gradually came into existence. This was a stratum relatively wealthy and open to communication and cross-cultural contact with Western Europe.

Prior to the emergence of this stratum, Greek Orthodox Christians were fully incorporated into the empire's social and cultural universe. In accordance with both Islamic custom and *raison d'état*, Ottoman rulers organized all non-Muslims under their respective religious leaders. Thus, Jews, Catholics, and Orthodox Christians became incorporated into the empire within their own confessional associations (*millet*s). The dominant *millet* in the Ottoman Balkans was the *Rum millet*. Within the *Rum millet*, the Ecumenical Patriarchate of Constantinople became the central political and religious authority. The formerly political identity of the Roman subject became under Ottoman rule confined to the religious-political identity of the *Rum millet*. Its members called themselves "Christians" or "Romans"; Western Europeans referred to them as "Greeks" (Greek Orthodox). Millenarianism provided the major ideological orientation of the Ottoman Greek Orthodox elites, that is, the high clergy and the Phanariot princes who administered the Danubian principalities between 1711 and 1821. According to this view, the destruction of the Orthodox Roman Empire was God's punishment for the sins of the Christians.

During the seventeenth and eighteenth centuries, the politico-military reorganization of the Ottoman administration led to the creation of Muslim and Orthodox Christian provincial administrative elites. The attempts by the central bureaucracy to reassert central authority over the local overlords (*ayan*s) provided the context for the Serb and Greek revolutions. In the Danubian principalities (i.e., Moldavia and Wallachia), where a Christian landowning class (boyars) had emerged over the course of the 1400–1800 period, Vladimirescu's movement of 1821 was an attempt to eliminate the oppression of the peasantry by the local landowning class. Unlike the case in the Danubian principalities, no such important socioeconomic cleavage existed in Serbia and southern

Greece. In these two areas, the local Christian prelates were not landowners and were not afraid (as were the Wallachian boyars) that the peasant movement would threaten their own position. Therefore, they joined the peasantry in revolt. These movements were further fueled by the presence of Christian bandits, a by-product of authority decentralization.

Although these factors account for the local variations of the particular movements, we must still account for the ideology of these revolutions. Specifically, if the research agenda is limited to structural factors alone it is not possible to differentiate between the Serb and Greek revolts, nor is it possible to account for their differential reception by the European public. Serbs fought for many years but their cause did not stir any visible support in the European public nor did such support lead to great power intervention. Both happened in the Greek case. To understand these differences it is necessary to specify the interpretative models employed by Western Europeans in dealing with the peoples of southeastern Europe.

The impact of cross-cultural contacts with Western Europe raises the question of the relationship among Enlightenment influences, secularization, and the articulation of national ideologies. The presence of a nationalist ideology in the Serb case is a belated phenomenon that owes much to the Serb communities of the Habsburg Empire. It was not present in the early stages of the 1804 Serb uprising. In the principalities, the goal of "liberation" was different for boyars and peasants and this discrepancy did not allow for a sustained movement to occur. The peasantry desired the overthrow of the boyars, whereas the lower boyars desired the overthrow of the Phanariot princes and the usurpation of administrative power for themselves.

Within the Ottoman Balkans, the Enlightenment's impact must be related to the urban literate strata. In most cases (with the exception of the boyar class) these strata were Hellenized, Grecophone, or Greek. In fact, the ideological domination of the Orthodox *millet* by the Orthodox clergy was predicated on the identification of "Greek" (*Rum*) with Orthodoxy. During the second half of the eighteenth century, a new Balkan intelligentsia emerged, supported by Greek Orthodox Balkan merchants. This intelligentsia was predominantly Grecophone and aimed at the diffusion of "enlightened reason" in the empire. The growing secularization and the influence of the French revolution led to articulation of a new secular identity: Hellenism. For liberal intellectuals such as Korais, Moisiodax, and Velenstinlis, *Hellenism* represented the secular facet of the *Rum millet*.

During the late eighteenth and early nineteenth centuries, the Church fought against this new ideology, which undermined its position. However, Hellenism was enough to provide for a new secular orientation among urban groups, merchants, and intellectuals. The strong influence of the Western European obsession with classical antiquity led to the revitalization of a secular Hellenic identity. Secret societies were formed and plans for a Balkan Orthodox uprising were made. In 1821 this effort produced the Wallachian movement and the

Greek revolution. The liberal plans for a democratic Balkan federation were never implemented because the revolutions were soon determined by the local forces and not by a general plan. The result of this attempt, however, was to articulate clearly the Greek ethnic community (*ethnie*) as a nation. It became impossible to maintain the links among class position, status, and "Greek" (*Rum*) identity.

During the modern period of globalization (1830–1945), there was a growing realization throughout southeastern Europe of the need for a political reorganization. In Wallachia and Moldavia, there was a growing political and cultural mobilization resulting from the transplantation of Romanian national ideology from Transylvania into the two principalities. From the 1820s forward, a rising Bulgarian merchant class began to organize its own educational apparatus; this led eventually to the emergence of a Bulgarian nationalist intelligentsia and the nationalist claims that accompanied it. Both developments were offshoots of the transference of Enlightenment ideas into the Balkans; they were influenced by the earlier Grecophone Balkan Enlightenment. In the Serb case, the organization of the autonomous principality of Serbia (1830) led to the slow physical concentration of the Serb population in the new region.

These developments indicated that the confessional mode of social organization (the *millet* system), dominant within the Ottoman Empire for almost four centuries, was becoming increasingly outdated. The search for new models, largely adopted from the Western European and American experience, was a pervasive characteristic of nineteenth-century Balkan social life. These models are best understood as *discourses*, that is, modes of organization, thinking, and mentality. The conceptual choices available to the Balkan peoples entailed the selection of either *nationhood* or *citizenship* as their models for the political reorganization of the peninsula. The first choice postulated the organization of ethnically homogeneous nation-states by suggesting that each ethnic group or community should have their own state; the second choice postulated some type of institutional arrangement that would allow the ethnically heterogeneous population of the Ottoman Balkans to continue living together.

The attempt to institutionalize citizenship in the region took two distinct routes. First, there was an attempt to organize a political system based on transnational citizenship, that is, acknowledging the existence of different nations but uniting them into a federal union. The project carried echoes of American federalism. The ethnic intermixing and the cultural syncretism of the region facilitated its adoption in the Balkans. The Balkan federalists and the Yugoslav movement aimed specifically at an institutional arrangement that would include peoples of different faiths and ethnicities in national communities. The federal project was not successful because the geopolitical rivalry among the emerging national centers of Belgrade, Athens, Bucharest, and, later on, Sofia prevented its implementation. State elites would have their authority curtailed in such an arrangement; this was contrary to their interests. Federalism was pursued as a tactical option, as an opportunity that was promoted insofar as it aided a particular state's or movement's goals.

Similarly, Yugoslavism was a predominantly intellectual movement promoted by some Habsburg Serbs and many among the Croatian intelligentsia. During the nineteenth century, Yugoslavism's ascent was fostered by the weakness of the Croat national movement, which lacked strong popular support and the ability to counter Magyar or Habsburg domination. It was also a response to the uncomfortable reality that many of the lands claimed by the Croat nationalists were inhabited by large numbers of Serbs. In the early twentieth century a rising Croat intelligentsia of mostly middle-class background was able to form coalitions with local Serbs and promote Yugoslavism. Their visions materialized after World War I with the creation of the kingdom of Serbs, Croats, and Slovenes.

Although the contrasting interests of state elites plagued federal plans, the other major attempt to institutionalize citizenship involved the construction of interethnic citizenship, a political identity that would include both the Muslim and non-Muslim communities of the empire. From 1839 forward, the Ottoman bureaucratic elites attempted to develop the concept of *Ottomanism* as a means to build bonds of social solidarity among their subjects that could transcend religious or ethnic differences. The problem of this effort was the growing economic gap between Muslims and Orthodox Christians. During the nineteenth century, the economic incorporation of the Ottoman world-empire into the world-economy benefited the Ottoman Orthodox commercial communities who served as intermediaries between Western firms and Ottoman markets. Their rise was slow in the earlier centuries, when chronic economic insecurity for long-distance trade and the Ottoman capitulations made Orthodox merchants the beneficiaries of Western commercial ties. The nineteenth century gave new impetus to this trend. Greek Orthodox communities became mostly urban, professional, and involved in world trade. Their dreams called for a reconstitution of the empire as a new Byzantium, a multiethnic state where political liberalism would allow them to exert their influence beyond their status as *reaya* (subject). Political liberalism found support among Ottoman statesmen and led to the abortive effort to establish a constitutional monarchy in 1876. The plan failed when Muslim traditionalists protested the abandonment of Islamic principles and Sultan AdbulHamid manipulated the situation so as to rule as an absolute monarch until 1908.

Under his reign the dissident Young Turk movement grew. It was divided into multiple factions, but with two main groups dominating the agenda: a liberal wing calling for political liberalism which was supported by the Ottoman minorities, and a more nationalistic wing calling for a revitalization of Turkish identity. This second wing was more successful in the long run. In the post-1890s period, Ottoman Muslim intellectuals reevaluated their Turkish heritage and increasingly called for a Turkish as opposed to an Ottoman identity. After the 1908 revolution, the Young Turks became the dominant political force.

Although widespread promises were made to the Ottoman minorities, the Young Turks were in favor of *cultural* as opposed to *political* Ottomanism. Their goal was to acculturate the minorities into a common culture—not to grant them equal status as minorities. The choice was, to use contemporary vocabulary, between assimilation or multiculturalism. The Young Turks promoted assimilation, whereas the Ottoman minorities opted for multiculturalism. The Young Turk assimilatory policies after 1908 were greatly resented, and provided the Balkan states with a rationale to unite against the Ottomans. By 1913, the Balkan states had defeated the Ottomans in the 1912–1913 Balkan wars and conquered most of the peninsula for themselves. Still, there remained the problem of Ottoman minorities in Anatolia (mainly Ottoman Greeks and Armenians). The Young Turks gradually came to view these groups as obstacles to state modernization. The Young Turks promoted economic nationalism and began a campaign of terror against the minorities in an effort to undermine their class position and create a national bourgeoisie. In the 1920s the Greek attempt to conquer Anatolia ended in disaster and the Ottoman Greek population fled to Greece. The major difficulty in promoting a Greco-Turkish project was the sharp discrepancy between status and class. Ottoman Greeks were becoming increasingly prosperous while the Ottoman Muslim population was impoverished. Political liberalism would further the interests of the wealthy urban Ottoman Greek communities against the predominantly Muslim state bureaucracy and army.

The specific factors outlined in the preceding paragraphs led to the failure of transnational and interethnic citizenship to provide for a normative standard in the emerging Balkan national societies. Consequently, the discourse of *nationhood* gradually became the dominant one. Indeed, the promotion of irredentism by the Balkan states during the nineteenth century was one of the factors that inhibited the success of Ottomanism. Between 1830 and 1880 a romantic Balkan nationalist intelligentsia shaped the Greek, Serb, and Bulgarian version of the "nation" through such devices as historical narrative, religious symbolism, the reinterpretation of folklore, or the writing of nationalist literature and poetry. In their collective reinterpretation of the "nation," the Balkan intelligentsia developed grandiose irredentist dreams that gradually brought the Balkan states into conflict with one another. Cultural romanticism, the dominant literary genre in nineteenth-century Europe, shaped Balkan national narratives (Castellan 1985). Accordingly, the Serbs dreamed of the reconstitution of Tsar Dusan's medieval empire; the Bulgarians dreamed of the reconstruction of the medieval Bulgarian empire; and the Greeks, the resurrection of the Byzantine Empire. Keeping pace with European romanticism, these empires were thought of as national states and not as imperial nonnational formations.

Underneath this process of nation building was the long-term process of secularization of southeastern Europe. The process began with the Grecophone Balkan Enlightenment of the late eighteenth century. With the articulation of the Greek *ethnie* as a secular nation, there was a powerful example for other Balkan activists to emulate. Given the predominance of religious ties in the

Balkan Orthodox population, it is not surprising that for Balkan nationalists the first step was to manipulate religious institutions in order to transform these ties into national ones (Castellan 1984). This choice was dictated by the widespread illiteracy of the Balkan peasantry: The shortest route for nation building was to shift the meaning of church affiliation and turn it into an equivalent of national affiliation. The effective means through which this transformation was accomplished was the institution of separate national churches. Since the Ecumenical Patriarchate was an agent of conservatism and because the eighteenth-century liberal alternative to the Eastern Orthodox commonwealth did not materialize, national churches provided a means of organizing Orthodox Balkan *ethnies* according to European models.

The new churches (Greece, 1832; Serbia, 1832; and the Bulgarian Exarchate in 1870) provided a medium through which the traditional ties of Orthodox Balkan peoples could be severed and new national ties constructed. The establishment of the Bulgarian Exarchate represented the fragmentation of Eastern Orthodox universalism in its most visible and dramatic manner. The Greek–Bulgarian ecclesiastical schism represented the recognition of a major shift in the nature of church affiliation, with national secular identity gaining the upper hand against the religious identity of the *Rum millet*. During the late nineteenth and early twentieth century the Patriarchate became identified with Greek irredentism; this resulted in the total collapse of the earlier organizational structure. Membership in a church became the equivalent to membership in a nation. The Patriarchate was a rather reluctant agent in this process, but it was constrained by the rising Greek and Bulgarian nationalisms and the continuing process of secularization.

While church affiliation became the domain of nationalists, religious symbolism was redeployed as national symbolism, thus facilitating the *redeployment of Orthodoxy* as part of the Balkan peoples' national identity. The battle of Kosovo, St. Vitus' Day, Annunciation Day, the St. Cyril and St. Methodius' Day—all of which had initially religious connotations—were reinterpreted as national symbols of the emerging Greek, Serb, and Bulgarian nations. The political cleavage between Christians and Muslims was reinterpreted as a national cleavage between "oppressed" Balkan peoples and Ottoman "oppressors." The use of poetry, prose, and journalism for nation building further contributed to this process.

Education provided the means through which the Orthodox Balkan peasantry was socialized into the emerging Serb, Greek, and Bulgarian "imagined communities." Secular schools taught not only literacy but also national identity. The association between education and national identity was well understood and explicitly promoted by the Balkan nationalists. However, the use of nationalist rhetoric in the educational system exacerbated the animosity among the Balkan peoples. In Ottoman Macedonia, education was one of the main areas of competition among Serb, Bulgarian, and Greek nationalist organizations. Education not only provided for the socialization of the peasantry in each respective national group; it also provided for the legitimization of irredentist claims on behalf of these nation-states.

Although similar in content, the nationalist mobilizations of the Greeks and Serbs, and those of the Bulgarians (in the pre-1878 period), Macedonians, and Albanians are significantly different. The former were able to use a state for their own nation-building process; the latter were excluded from state power. Moreover, the lands of Macedonians and Albanians were targets of territorial expansion by neighboring states. In both cases, the influence of rival propagandas, as well as low literacy levels, did not allow the formation of strong nationalist movements.

The close association between "state" and "society" in the region further facilitated the promotion of the discourse of nationhood. Local societies grew within state boundaries and were practically forged out of the body of the state. The Ottoman Balkans provide a model of social organization that illustrates the *constitutive role of the state* in the making of "national societies" (Weber 1976). In the nineteenth-century Balkans, the Ottoman legacy of corporatism gained new strength through the dominance of civil service as a major occupation in the urban areas. Literacy, state service, and nationalism combined into a whole. Irredentism facilitated the consolidation of national societies and, thus, the prestige of state elites. In Greece, Bulgaria, and Serbia the local state elites used the state as a depository for patronage systems. Under these circumstances, liberalism was paid lip service; liberal policies were almost never implemented and foreign loans were used to build up the military arsenal rather than to pursue development plans.

Although Balkan nation building skillfully used church affiliation and the educational system to gain peasant support, the problem of peasant illiteracy implied that a more direct approach was necessary. In fact, during the nineteenth century the Balkan states did not hesitate to use organized banditry and paramilitary militias as "agents" of their national propaganda. Among these specialists of violence, the Balkan military corps was instrumental in fostering the rise of irredentism in the post-1880 period. Greek officers initiated the 1909 military coup; their Serb counterparts were responsible for the 1903 coup and the assassination of the last Obrenović. In both countries the officers became the voice of irredentism. The Bulgarian military found in Tsar Ferdinand an ally and therefore it was less visible as an independent political agent. Similar processes were observed within the Ottoman military. It was among the officers' corps in Macedonia that the Young Turk movement found recruits and key members of the post-1908 scene came from the ranks of the military.

By 1912–1913, the Balkan nation-states were able to expel the Ottoman Empire from Europe. But their mutually competing nationalist claims were not satisfied, nor could they possibly be satisfied. Simply put, the ethnic intermixing of peoples operated against the logic of ethnic homogenization. Following the wars of 1912 to 1918, then, the Balkan nation-states became locked in a political struggle for successful national integration. The result was acute political conflict—a phenomenon that reappeared in the post-1989 period. The local nation-states were committed to a policy of ethnic homogenization, that is, a policy of realizing the postulates of the discourse of nationhood within each national society. Indeed, this policy was pursued throughout Europe in the post-1917 period. In southeastern Europe, the exclusion of minorities from the national "imagined community" was given a *cultural* justification: Muslim Pomaks, Bosnian Muslims, Macedonian Slavs, and a host of others were not viewed as "genuine" members of the Bulgarian, Serb, or Greek nations. The invention of such terms as "Slavophone Greeks" and *arnautasi* to describe Slavic Macedonians and Kosovo Albanians is indicative of the dominant mentality of the time.

In interwar Yugoslavia, a similar issue surfaced in the discussion concerning the position of non-Serbs (especially Croats). The Serb administration proceeded to "nationalize" the Macedonian Slavic population, and deported Kosovo Albanians to Turkey. Finally, the ethnic intermixing between Croats and Serbs in Croatia-Slavonia, Bosnia-Herzegovina, and Dalmatia only further fueled resentment of a Serb-dominated Yugoslavia. The elites of the Serb state viewed Yugoslavia as an extension of Serbia: Serbia was to be the Piedmont of the South Slavs. Their claim to power was contested by the Croat elites who envisioned Yugoslavia as a confederation of equal nations. The conflict between these two perspectives was to plague the state for most of the twentieth century.

For the Balkans at large, the existence of rival nation-states committed to a policy of support for their "national minorities" significantly contributed to ethnic polarization. In effect, the discourse of nationhood entailed the assumption of *external national homelands* for these minorities and indicated that their rights could be sufficiently protected only by the inclusion of the territories they inhabited in their prospective nation-states (Brubaker 1996). The most dramatic consequences of this cultural logic are to be found in the unresolved tensions surrounding the "national question" during the twentieth century. Specifically, Bulgaria contested Macedonia three times over the course of the twentieth century (1913, 1915–1917, and 1940–1944) and lost each time. Greece twice (1913, 1940) contested northern Epirus (southern Albania), with its sizable Greek Orthodox minority. It also laid claim to the island of Cyprus in the post-1950 period; this gave rise to a bitter Greek–Turkish dispute. Large segments of Albanians remained "unredeemed" in Yugoslavia, and the Macedonian Slavs contested the occupation of Greek Macedonia by Greece during the 1944–1949 period. Bosnia remained a bitter object of Croat–Serb dispute for most of the twentieth century, as well.

In the post-1945 period of contemporary globalization, the Balkans experienced a temporary suspension of these conflicts, mainly because of the strong bipolarism of the Cold War. Two new factors were introduced into the global scene during the post-1945 period. First, the inequality between advanced, industrialized societies and developing countries was exacerbated. Second, the trend toward international human rights regulations radically reconfigured state sovereignty. Both factors influenced the Balkan nation-states. First, the economic decline of the region has been one of the factors for the popularity of nationalist rhetoric in the region. Second, the consolidation and reproduction of ethnocentric stereotypes put regional cultures at odds with international standards for human rights and equality. This is acutely reflected in the proliferation of nationalistic stereotypes in the school history textbooks of the Balkan states.

The combination of these two factors helps account for the return of the national question in the post-1989 period. The end of Communist rule in Eastern Europe in 1989 offered the opportunity for a revitalization of these rivalries. The "new world order" did not entail an explicit institutional arrangement for the region; in this case, the hard-won "freedom" only meant the return of the pre-1950 rivalries to the political agenda. The articulation of the discourse of nationhood has been an embattled process in southeastern Europe, and has been ongoing since the nineteenth century. The adoption of nationhood by the Balkan nation-states entailed their transformation into agents that contribute to ethnic and national rivalries. Consequently, the recurrent problems of ethnic conflict in the region are a systemic outcome of the regional pattern of nation formation.

It is indeed ironic that one of the unintended consequences of the discourse of nationhood is chronic ethnic conflict in the region. Because these dynamics operate throughout the region, interesting and revealing contradictions follow. For example, the Serbs are willing to suppress the Albanians' rights in Kosovo while fighting on behalf of the Serbs' rights to self-determination in Croatia and Bosnia. Albanians complain about the suppression of their rights in Kosovo and FYROM while they do the same to the Greek Orthodox minority in southern Albania. Greece complains about these violations while it denies the existence of Macedonian and Turkish minorities within the state's boundaries. The Macedonian state (FYROM) complains about the suppression of fellow Macedonians in Bulgaria and Greece while it carries out a similar policy against its Albanian minority.

Moreover, the process of Balkan state formation privileged the redeployment of Eastern Orthodoxy as a facet of local national identities. By and large, the Muslim population of the Balkans failed to develop a national identity comparable to that of its Christian counterpart. Being mostly in a position of privilege and also because of their relative isolation from the West, the Muslim communities were rather passive recipients of social changes. In the course of the twentieth century, these groups found themselves surrounded by Christian majorities and living in nation-states that tend to emphasize ethnic and religious identity as the major component of membership in each nation. Asserting their "cultural rights" is not a simple matter because the shadow of "Turkish rule" has marked the Balkans to such an extent that the incorporation of a Muslim element into the local societies is difficult. These Muslim minorities have provided excellent scapegoats for ex-Communists turned nationalists.

This book has helped overthrow some established myths about the rise of nationalism in southeastern Europe. First, the historiographic interpretations that view Orthodox Christians locked in a constant conflict with Muslims, a conflict between two "civilizations" or "ways of life," are the product of native Balkan nineteenth-century historiography, a historiography the goal of which was to promote nation building. Indeed, the promotion of the discourse of nationhood was a sign of the Balkan nation-states' claim to be part of the modern world of Europe. The subsequent logic of ethnic homogenization was the direct product of the reception within Ottoman Balkan society of the Western concepts of "nation" and of secular forms of social organization. Over the past two centuries, the economic, political, and cultural interactions between the Ottoman world-empire and the Western European world-economy have dramatically transformed practically all parameters of social life. Indeed, this transformation led to the "making of the Balkans" as a distinct geopolitical region. This structural and cultural transformation illustrates both the critical impact of Western modernity in developing regions and the cultural specificity of regional routes to modernity. Thus, the "making of the Balkans" demonstrates the significance of globalization as a world-historical process.

Second, nationalism played a key role in the articulation of the "Balkans" as a concrete geopolitical configuration. Throughout the nineteenth century, nationalism was an expression of the Balkan nations' claim to modernity and of their desire to "catch up" with Western European "civilization." During the nineteenth century, both statecraft and nation building in the region were determined by the strong influence of Western organizational models, and the attempt to transplant these models into a social context that had been developed along vastly different historical trajectories (Stokes 1987, 73–4; Daskalov 1997). Ironically, the megalomania of the Balkan nation-states, all of them possessed by "anachronistic" imperial visions out of proportion to their size, was an expression of their peculiar internal connection with the West (Skopetea 1992, 105). Such visions were the product of their efforts to mimic Western history in their own national genealogies, and their attempts to participate in it through their irredentist projects.

Therefore, in sharp contrast to Todorova (1996), I would argue that the Balkans are *not* the Ottomans' legacy. On the contrary, the "making of the Balkans" was the consequence of the adoption and selective appropriation of Western ideas into the European part of the Ottoman Empire. The process led to a reversal of the normative hierarchy dominant in the Anglo-American world. It is nationhood rather than citizenship that comes first in the Balkans. This makes the region's politics seem "odd" or "backward" to U.S. policy makers and journalists, and this impression leads to arguments about "ancient ethnic hatred" or primordial ethnic conflict (Johnsen 1993, 60–1). In exorcising the Balkans, Western commentators exorcise principles of ethnic difference they consider illegitimate in their own societies. The Balkans, then, are an area of domestic ideological contestation in the U.S. and Western Europe.

Although the Cold War has helped contain visible manifestations of these ethnic rivalries for a period of time, these problems continue to plague the region. They will continue to do so until a major event or long-term force shifts the general foundations of Balkan political culture. This situation is not unique to the Balkans: France, Germany, and most of Western Europe were locked into a similar situation until 1945. With the end of World War II, French and German political elites decided to cooperate instead of rivaling each other; this decision led to the eventual founding of the European Community. Could such an international organization provide for a long-term solution for the Balkans as well? It could, but it would require a cultural reversal leading to the decisive institutionalization of the discourse of citizenship. It is therefore clear that the region's basic problem for the next century concerns the local states' ability to develop stable regional cooperation and a shared system of rules for dealing with their ethnic heterogeneity. The "unmixing" of peoples has been one of the most unfortunate results of the nation-state model in the region. In an era of radical reconfiguration of state sovereignty, the Balkan states must reconceptualize their traditions of state-centered nationalism. The region's rich history of cultural variety and coexistence offers a powerful reservoir for such a conceptualization. The twenty-first century will be the testing ground for the region's efforts to adjust to the brave new world of the "Information Age."

# Bibliographical Note

Although I have tried to provide an extensive discussion of the historical events in the region, I should point out that this book is not a history of the Balkans. For a general introduction to the region's history, there are a number of regional histories covering the past 500 years. Among them, I need to make special reference to the works of L. S. Stavrianos, Charles and Barbara Jelavich, and Georges Castellan, all of them cited in this book's reference section. The Balkans have also attracted the interest of world historians. Arnold Toynbee, William H. McNeill, and L. S. Stavrianos have all written monographs and histories about the region.

Historical knowledge on the Balkans is closely tied to the relative scarcity of archival sources. The researcher will find no organized archival collections dating back six or seven centuries. Moreover, the decentralized nature of Ottoman administration meant that archives were all too often kept locally. Over the past two centuries, the process of data collection has been further complicated by warfare. Therefore, some primary sources have been lost and others are still collecting dust in attics. Nevertheless, there is an extensive literature on the region, but most of it is located in the libraries of North America and Western Europe.

This book is a *sociological history* of nationalism in the region, and therefore, it covers a variety of fields. The coverage of the literature could not possibly be comprehensive. The subject of nationalism is related to an enormous literature on economics, cultural and intellectual history, politics, anthropology, sociology, and other subfields.

The economic and social history of the Ottoman Empire is an extensive field of inquiry. Perhaps the best summary of the current state of affairs, as well as a useful guide to the literature, is the *Social and Economic History of the Ottoman Empire* (1994). With regard to the Balkans, special mention should be reserved for the articles and books by Traian Stoianovich, whose work is simply unmatched in the field. Nikolai Todorov's *Balkan City* (1986) also deserves special mention, because it is the most thorough monograph on urbanization. In the field of economic history John Lampe and Marvin Jackson's (1982) *Balkan Economic History* is the best book I am aware of. Also, Michael Palairet's *The Balkan Economies ca 1800–1914* (1997) provides an excellent, novel interpretation of the nineteenth-century Balkan economy, especially with regard to the South Slav lands and Bulgaria. Palairet's central argument is that the Balkans were relatively prosperous under the Ottomans and their disassociation from the Ottoman Empire led to further economic decline. Although his line of argument goes against the conventional line of interpretation, it is nevertheless an interpretation worthy of further consideration. Palairet questions the standard assumption of world-system literature, that is, that the Ottoman Empire was incorporated into the world-economy and that this incorporation led to a steady economic decline. On this issue, it is worth comparing D. Quataert's *Ottoman Manufacturing in the Age of the Industrial Revolution* (Cambridge: Cambridge University Press, 1993) to the analyses produced by world-system theorists, such as Kasaba and Wallerstein.

In the fields of cultural and intellectual history, one must take special notice of the contribution of K. Th. Dimaras, whose volumes provide by far the best guide to the complexities of Balkan intellectual life during the eighteenth and nineteenth centuries. In numerous publications, cited in the reference section, Paschalis M. Kitromilides has elaborated a complex, intellectually stimulating, and quite sophisticated analysis of the Enlightenment's impact in the region. The transformation of religious into secular identity is also a central theme in the works of Georges Castellan.

In the field of nineteenth-century South Slavic historiography, the articles and books by Dimitrije Djordjevic and Gale Stokes stand out as particularly important, especially with regard to Serbian history. For the first Yugoslavia, Ivo Banac's *National Question* provides an almost indispensable guide. Lampe's *Yugoslavia as History* offers by far the most comprehensive treatment of twentieth-century Yugoslav history, an account of particular importance given the author's attention to social and economic factors. With regard to Tito's Yugoslavia, the most comprehensive books belong to Stephan Pavlowich, Dennison Rusinow and Sabrina P. Ramet.

This book is based primarily on a survey of post-1960 secondary sources, mainly in English, Greek, and French. It draws on literature from the humanities, history, cultural studies, and social sciences. I believe I have covered most of the secondary literature, but I cannot claim that the bibliographical search has been exhaustive. My intention has been to write a book that makes a theoretical and substantive contribution to a number of ongoing debates, not to provide a general bibliographical survey.

Consequently, my approach has focused on the comparison and critical evaluation of North American literature and native Balkan historiographical research. Arguments and interpretations from these publications have been cross-checked and discussed in the text or the footnotes. Of crucial importance is the combination of the Greek historiographical research of the last 30 years with the research published in North America and Western Europe. In the post–World War II period, considerable resources were invested in researching the Communist states in the Balkans, and consequently, a wealth of research was produced. Because research results were rarely compared with the Greek historiography, many (but not all) regional analyses have a tendency to be incomplete or misleading. My intention in this book has been to balance research agendas and to provide an even-handed account of Balkan nationalisms. Of the Greek literature, most of the "new" post-1960s monographs in economic, cultural, and social history were used (for a literature review, see Kitroeff 1989).

The text is based heavily on secondary sources, a choice of necessity because of the scope of the subject and the long time period. Secondary historical sources on the Balkans can be classified into three broad categories: first, North American and Western European literature, written predominantly in English and French; second, native journals, annual serials, and proceedings of regional conferences; and third, native histories and specialized monographs, written in the local languages. My search was restricted mostly to the first two of these three categories. A considerable number of native Balkan publications are in French, which served as the main language of scientific communication for many decades. For example, Stoianovich (1974, 90) reported that in the First International Congress of Balkan Studies held in Sofia (26 August–1 September 1966) more than two-thirds of the papers and comments were in French—although no speaker was of French nationality.

The on-line *American Bibliography of Slavic and East European Studies* (University of Illinois, Urbana) was used as a starting point for the accumulation of the literature. It was supplemented by consulting the book version of the *Bibliography*. Supplementary bibliographical information was gathered from various regional bibliographical guides. A "snowballing" technique was used to find additional publications.

In addition to general bibliographical guides, I surveyed a series of journals published in North America, Great Britain, Greece, Bulgaria, Serbia, and Romania. The journals surveyed and their abbreviations are listed at the end of this note. Of course not *all* journals covering regional and national histories were surveyed. The choice was dictated by the specialization of particular journals in specific historical periods and eras. Serials focusing on medieval history, for example, were excluded. Relevant material from these journals that addressed the post-1800 period was reviewed. The review was restricted to the post-1960 journal issues (with few exceptions). Only the material cited in the book is listed in the references. I should stress that this is only a part of the material actually reviewed.

Statistics and other "hard data" are subjects of extensive debate among local historians. The principal reason for this "battle of the numbers" is the attempt by various sides to produce "evidence" of their particular beliefs by systematically manipulating statistical information. This problem still plagues contemporary research. I have attempted to be as careful as possible in the use of statistical data. But I have no doubt that various sides will have their own objections to particular numbers. Thus, I urge the reader to be mindful of this issue.

Proceedings of regional and interstate conferences were also surveyed. Due to the frequent duplication of substantive information in the various conference presentations, attention was paid to the substance of various communications. Earlier publications whose subject was covered in greater detail by the same author's later publications were disregarded. As with the journal survey, not all the sources reviewed are cited in the book.

I have attempted to cover this literature as comprehensively as possible, to be critical and not to accept or adapt the ideological viewpoints of the various authors, and to avoid becoming a victim of political or academic partisanship. The secondary literature is full of nationalistic biases. I have surveyed the literature carefully and sought to critically evaluate and double-check the information provided in various publications.

Transliteration of names and places for a region where several different languages and alphabets are in use is a difficult task. For some languages (such as Greek), no standard method of transliteration exists. Moreover, different sources use different methods of transliteration. These difficulties are further compounded by the challenge of standard-izing the name for a particular city or place. For example, Thessaloniki is also frequently referred to as Saloniki, Salonik, or Salonica. I have tried to be as consistent as possible throughout the text. Nevertheless, I have retained the original orthography and spelling of names and places in quotations as well as in the bibliography.

The fundamental guide used was the name index in Barbara Jelavich's *History of the Balkans* (1983). With regard to the Slavic languages, words have been rendered into English according to the transliteration systems of the Library of Congress. In the bib-liography, English and French sources are cited in these languages. Greek sources are cited in English, and their original language of publication is indicated by (G).

Where a Greek edition of a particular book was used, this is indicated by the words [Greek edition] next to the book's title. In the case of reprints of original works or collections of various publications the choice of referencing was dictated by the useful-ness of providing full citation. For some Grecophone collections and reprints of material previously available elsewhere (such as Asdrachas, Dimaras, Gedeon, and Angelou), only the reference of the compilation volume is given. Finally, because the text contains numerous references to specific areas and provinces in the region, I need to briefly address some issues of geography. The text is accompanied by a few maps, which I believe help the reader to grasp the Balkan terrain. Although the Yugoslav wars of the 1990s helped the international audience to gain familiarity with the region's geography, I am acutely aware that knowledge of the region's geography should not be treated as a given. Therefore, readers who would like to gain better insight into the region's geog-raphy are advised to access the Perry-Castañeda Library Map Collection of the University of Texas–Austin. The Collection has an extraordinarily rich collection of maps of the Balkans, both contemporary and historical. Of particular value are the ethnographic maps of the former Yugoslavia. Because of cost and space considerations, I have refrained from reproducing these maps in the text. These can be accessed on line at http://www.lib.utexas.edu/Libs/PCL/Map collection/Map collection.html.

# References

## LIST OF JOURNALS AND ABBREVIATIONS

| Journals | Abbreviations |
|---|---|
| *Balkan Studies* | *BS* |
| *Balkanica* | |
| *Balkanistica* | |
| *Bulgarian Historical Review* | *BHR* |
| *International Journal of Turkish Studies* | *IJTS* |
| *Canadian Review of Studies in Nationalism* | *CRSN* |
| *Comparative Studies in Society and History* | *CSSH* |
| *East European Quarterly* | *EEQ* |
| *East European Politics and Societies* | *EEPS* |
| *Etudes Balkaniques* | *EB* |
| *Etudes Historiques* | *EH* |
| *Istorika [Historica]* | |
| *International Journal of Middle Eastern Studies* | *IJMES* |
| *Journal of Modern Greek Studies* | *JMGS* |
| *Journal of the Hellenic Diaspora* | *JHD* |
| *Middle Eastern Studies* | *MES* |
| *Deltion tis Istorikis kai Ethnologikis Etairias tis Ellados [Review of the Historical and Ethnological Society of Greece]* | *DIEE* |

*Deltion tou Kentrou Mikrasiatikon Spoudon [Review of the Center*   DKMS
*for Asia Minor Studies]*
*Revue Nouvelles d'Histoire*
*Revue des Etudes de Sud-est Européennes*      RESE
*Serbian Studies*
*Slavic Review*
*Southeastern Europe*      SE
*Studia Albanica*

Abercrombie, N., S. Hill, and B. S. Turner. 1980. *The Dominant Ideology Thesis*. London: Allen and Unwin.

Abou-El-Haj, Rifa'at 'Ali. 1991. *Formation of the Modern State: The Ottoman Empire, Sixteenth to Eighteenth Centuries*. Albany: State University of New York Press.

Abu-Lughod, J. 1989. *Before European Hegemony: The World System, A.D. 1250–1350*. New York: Oxford University Press.

Adanir, F. 1984/85. "The Macedonian Question: The Socioeconomic Reality and Problems of Its Historiographic Interpretation." *IJTS* 3(1):43–64.

———. 1989. "Tradition and Rural Change in Southeastern Europe during Ottoman Rule." *The Origins of Backwardness in Eastern Europe*, edited by D. Chirot, 131–75. Berkeley: University of California Press.

———. 1992. "The Macedonians in the Ottoman Empire 1878–1912." In *The Formation of National Elites: Comparative Studies on Governments and Non-dominant Ethnic Groups in Europe, 1850–1940*, edited by A. Kappeler, Vol. 6, 161–92. New York: New York University Press.

Adler, P. 1974a. "Notes on the Beginnings of Modern Serbian Literature: The Kurzbeck Press in Vienna and Its Successors." *SE* 1(1):34–45.

———. 1974b. "Why Did Illyrianism Fail?" *Balkanistica* 1:95–103.

———. 1979. "Nation and Nationalism among the Serbs of Hungary, 1790–1870." *EEQ* 13(3):271–85.

Ahmad, F. 1969. *The Young Turks: The Committee of Union and Progress in Turkish Politics, 1908–1914*. Oxford: Clarendon Press.

———. 1980. "Vanguard of a Nascent Bourgeoisie: The Social and Economic Policy of the Young Turks, 1908–1918." In *Social and Economic History of Turkey, 1071–1920*, edited by O. Okyar and H. Inalcik, 329–50. Ankara: Meteksan Ltd.

———. 1982. "Unionist Relations with the Greek, Armenian, and Jewish Communities of the Ottoman Empire, 1908–1914." In *Christians and Jews in the Ottoman Empire*, edited by B. Braude and B. Lewis, Vol. 1, 401–34. New York: Holmes and Meier.

Ahrweiler, H. 1988. *L'Ideologie Politique de l'Empire Byzantin* [Greek edition]. Athens: Psichogios.

Albrow, M. 1997. *The Global Age*. Stanford: Stanford University Press.

Alexander, J. C. 1985. *Brigandage and Public Order in the Morea, 1685–1806*. Athens: Imago.

Alexander, S. 1979. *Church and State in Yugoslavia since 1945*. Cambridge: Cambridge University Press.

Alexandris, A. 1980. "The Greeks in the Service of the Ottoman Empire." *DIEE* 32:365–404 (G).

———. 1983. *The Greek Minority of Istanbul and Greek–Turkish Relations, 1918–1974*. Athens: Center for Asia Minor Studies. 1983.

Alexieva, A. 1993. *Les Oeuvres en prose traduites du Grec a l'epoque du reveil national Bulgare*. Thessaloniki: Institute for Balkan Studies.

Allardyce, G. 1990. "Toward World History: American Historians and the Coming of the World History Course." *Journal of World History* 1:(1):23–76.

Alp, T. 1917. *The Turkish and PanTurkish Ideal* [Greek edition, 1992]. Athens: Armenian Horizons.

Alter, P. 1989. *Nationalism*. London: Edward Arnold.

Anagnostopoulou, S. 1997. *Asia Minor 19th Century–1919: The Greek-Orthodox Communities, from Rum Millet to the Greek Nation*. Athens: Ellinika Grammata (G).

Anderson, B. R. 1991. *Imagined Communities: Reflections on the Origin and Spread of Nationalism*. London: Verso.

Andoniadou-Bibikou, E. 1979. "Villages desertes en Greece. Un blian provisoire." In *The Economic Structure of the Balkan Countries (15th–19th Centuries)*, edited by S. Asdrachas, 195–259. Athens: Melissa (G).

Andrejevich, M. 1990a. "The Dispute between Serbia and Slovenia." *Report on Eastern Europe*, 19 January, 23–6.

———. 1990b. "Slovenia Heading toward Independence." *Report on Eastern Europe*, 30 March, 36–40.

———. 1991. "Moslem Leader Elected President of Bosnia and Herzegovina." *Report on Eastern Europe*, 10 January, 30–32.

Angelopoulos, A. 1983. "The Archdioceses of Ahris and Pec on the Basis of Patriarchical Acta Edited by K. Delikanos (17th/18th Centuries)." *BS* 24 (2):337–42.

Angelou, A. 1988. *Of Enlightenment*. Athens: Ermis (G).

Anonymous. 1789/1977. "The Anonymous of 1789." Reprinted in *Modern Greek Enlightenment*, by K. T. Dimaras, 412–60. Athens: Ermis (G).

Anonymous. 1798. *Fraternal Teaching*. Constantinople [authorship attributed to Patriarch Anthimus of Jerusalem, see Clogg, 1969].

Anonymous. 1806/1980. *Hellenic Nomarchy*. Athens: Kalvos (G).

Apostolski, M., D. Zografski, A. Stoyanaski, and G. Todorovski, eds. 1979. *A History of the Macedonian People*. Skopje: Macedonian Review.

Appadurai, A. 1996. *Modernity at Large: Cultural Dimensions of Globalization*. Minneapolis: University of Minnesota Press.

Arai, M. 1992. *Turkish Nationalism in the Young Turk Era*. Leiden: E. J. Brill.

Argyropoulos, R. D. 1984. "Nicolas Piccolos et la philosophie neohellenique." *BS* 25 (2):235–42.

———. 1989. "Georgios Kozakis-Tipaldos between Enlightenment and Romanticism." *DIEE* 32:81–92 (G).

Armstrong, J. A. 1982. *Nations before Nationalism*. Chapel Hill: University of North Carolina Press.

Arnakis, G. 1960. "Turanism: An Aspect of Turkish Nationalism." *BS* 1 (1):19–32.

———. 1963. "The Role of Religion in the Development of Balkan Nationalism." In *The Balkans in Transition*, edited by C. Jelavich and B. Jelavich, 115–44. Berkeley: University of California Press.

———. 1969. *The Near East in Modern Times*. Vol. 1, *The Ottoman Empire and the Balkan States to 1900*. Austin, Tex.: Pemberton Press.

Aroni-Tsichi, A. 1989. *Peasant Revolts in Old Greece, 1833–1881.* Athens: Papazisi (G).

Arrighi, G. 1994. *The Long Twentieth Century.* London: Verso.

———. 1998a. "Capitalism and the Modern World-System: Rethinking the Non-debates of the 1970s." *Review* 21(1):113–29.

———. 1998b. "Globalization and the Rise of East Asia." *International Sociology* 13(1): 59–77.

Arseniou, L. A. 1994. *The Epic of the Thessaly Peasants and their Insurrections, 1881–1993.* Trikala: FILOS (G).

Arsh, G. 1994. *Albania and Epirus in the Late 18th and Early 19th Centuries* [Greek edition]. Athens: Gutenberg.

Asdrachas, S. 1988a. *Economy and Mentalities.* Athens: Ermis (G).

———. 1988b. *Greek Society and Economy in the 18th and 19th Centuries.* Athens: Ermis (G).

Ashley, S. 1985. "Minority Populations and the Nationalist Process in the Bulgarian Lands (1821–1876)." In *Proceedings of Anglo-Bulgarian Symposium,* London, July 1982, edited by L. Collins, 41–64. Vol. 1, *History.* London: School of Slavonic and East European Studies.

———. 1990. "Bulgaria: Ethnic under during January." *Report on Eastern Europe,* 9 February, 4–11.

Augustinos, G. 1977. *Consciousness and History: Nationalist Critics of Greek Society, 1897–1914.* Boulder, Colo.: East European Quarterly.

———. 1992. *The Greeks of Asia Minor: Confession, Community, and Ethnicity in the Nineteenth Century.* Kent, Ohio: Kent State University Press.

Augustinos, O. 1994. *French Odysseys: Greece in French Travel Literature from the Renaissance to the Romantic Era.* Baltimore: Johns Hopkins University Press.

Axford, B. 1995. *The Global System.* Oxford: Polity Press.

Baggally, J. W. 1936. *Greek Historical Folksongs: The Klephtic Ballads in Relation to Greek History (1715–1821).* Chicago: Argonaut.

Bairoch, P. 1981. "The Main Trends in National Economic Disparities Since the Industrial Revolution." In *Disparities in Economic Development Since the Industrial Revolution,* edited by P. Bairoch and M. Levy-Leboyer, 3–17. New York: St. Martin's Press.

Bakic-Hayden, M. 1995. "Nesting Orientalisms: The Case of Former Yugoslavia." *Slavic Review* 54(4):917–31.

Bakic-Hayden, M., and R. M. Hayden. 1992. "Orientalist Variations on the Theme 'Balkan's: Symbolic Geography in Recent Yugoslav Cultural Politics." *Slavic Review* 51(1):1–15.

Baltsiotis, L. M. 1997. "Greek Governance and Minority Education in Thrace." In *The Minority Issue in Greece. A Contribution from the Social Sciences,* edited by K. Tsikelidis and D. Christopoulos, 315–48. Athens: Kritiki (G).

Banac, I. 1981. "The Role of Vojvodina in Karadjordje's Revolution." *Sudost-Forschungen* 40:31–61.

———. 1984. *The National Question in Yugoslavia: Origins, History, Politics.* Ithaca, N.Y.: Cornell University Press.

Barac, A. 1973. *A History of Yugoslav Literature.* Ann Arbor: Michigan Slavic Publications.

Barber, B. 1995. *Jihad vs. McWorld: How Globalism and Tribalism Are Reshaping the World.* New York: Ballantine.

Barkan, O. L. 1975. "The Price Revolution of the Sixteenth Century: A Turning Point in the Economic History of the Near East." *IJMES* 6:3–28.

Barker, E. 1950. *Macedonia: Its Place in Balkan Power Politics*. London: Royal Institute of International Affairs.

Barkey, K. 1994. *Bandits and Bureaucrats. The Ottoman Route to State Centralization*. Ithaca, N.Y.: Cornell University Press.

Barth, F. 1969. "Introduction." In *Ethnic Groups and Boundaries: The Social Organization of Cultural Difference*, edited by F. Barth, 9–38. Boston: Little, Brown.

Barthélemy, J. 1843 [1788]. *Voyage du jeune Anacharsis en Grèce vers le mileu du Ive siècle avant l'ere vulgaire*, 2 vols. Paris: Didier.

Bartl, P. 1984. "Kossova and Macedonia as Reflected in Ecclesiastical Reports." In *Studies on Kosova*, edited by A. Pipa and S. Repishti, 23–40. Boulder, Colo.: East European Monographs.

Batakovic, D. 1992. *The Kosovo Chronicles*. Beogrand: Pluto.

Batalden, S. K. 1982. *Catherine II's Greek Prelate. Eugenios Voulgaris in Russia, 1771–1806*. Boulder, Colo.: East European Monographs.

Beck, U. 2000. *What is Globalization?* Oxford: Basil Blackwell.

Beck, U., S. Lash, and A. Giddens. 1994. *Reflexive Modernization: Politics, Tradition, and Aesthetics in Modern Social Order*. Cambridge: Polity.

Belia, E. D. 1988. "The Educational Policy of the Greek State towards Thrace, 1869–1910." In *The Historical, Archaeological, and Folklore Research for Thrace*, 243–68. Thessaloniki: Institute for Balkan Studies (G).

———. 1993. "The Balkan Wars in History Textbooks." In *Greece of the Balkan Wars, 1910–1914*, 279–98. Athens: ELIA (G).

Bell, J. D. 1977. *Peasants in Power: Alexander Stamboliski and the Bulgarian Agrarian National Union, 1899–1923*. Princeton N.J.: Princeton University Press.

Bencomo, C., and E. Colla. 1993. "Area Studies, Multiculturalism, and the Problems of Expert Knowledge." *Bad Subjects*, 5 (May).

Bendix, R. 1978. *Kings or People: Power and the Mandate to Rule*. Berkeley: University of California Press.

Bentley, J. H. 1996. "Cross-Cultural Interaction and Periodization in World History." *American Historical Review* 101(3):749–70.

Bereciatru, G. J. 1994. *Decline of the Nation-State*. Reno: University of Nevada Press.

Berend, I. T., and G. Ranki. 1974. *Economic Development in East-Central Europe in the 19th and 20th Centuries*. New York: Columbia University Press.

Bergesen, A. 1995. "Let's Be Frank about World History." In Sanderson (1995), 195–205.

Berindei, D. 1973. *L'année revolutionnaire 1821 dans les pays roumains*. Bucharest: Editions à l'Academie de la République Socialiste de Roumanie.

———. 1979. "The Rumanian Armed Forces in the 18th and 19th Centuries." In *War and Society in East Central Europe*. Vol. 1, *Special Topics and Generalizations on the 18th and 19th Centuries*, edited by B. K. Kiraly and G. E. Rothenberg. 215–47. New York: Columbia University Press.

Berkes, N. 1964. *The Development of Secularism in Turkey*. Montreal: McGill University Press.

Berlin, I. 1981. *Against the Current*. New York: Viking Press.

Beron, P. 1824. *Vukvar s razlichni poucheniya, sobrani ot Petar H. Berovicha za bol-*

*garskite uchilishta. Napechaia sia sas pomoshta g. Antonova Ioannichova.* Brasov: Romania.

Berov, L. 1979. "Changes in the Social Structure of the Urban Population in Bulgaria from 1878 to 1912." *SE* 5(2):105–20.

Billig, M. 1995. *Banal Nationalism.* London: Sage.

Black, C. E. 1943. *The Establishment of Constitutional Government in Bulgaria.* Princeton, N.J.: Princeton University Press.

Bloch, M. 1961. *Feudal Society,* 2 vols. Chicago: University of Chicago Press.

Blok, A. 1974a. *The Mafia of a Sicilian Village, 1860–1960.* New York: Harper and Row.

———. 1974b. "The Peasant and the Brigand: Social Banditry Reconsidered." *CSSH* 14:494–503.

Bogert, R. 1991. "Paradigm of Defeat or Victory? The Kosovo Myth versus the Kosovo Covenant in Fiction." In *Kosovo: Legacy of Medieval Battle,* edited by W. S. Vucinich and T. A. Emmert, 73–88. Minneapolis: University of Minnesota Press.

Boissin, H. 1970. "Les Lumières et la conscience nationale en Albanie." In *Les Lumières et la formation de la conscience nationale chez les peuples du Sub-Est européen,* 43–46. Bucharest: Association Internationale d'Etudes du Sub-Est Européen.

Bookman, M. Z. 1994. *Economic Decline and Nationalism in the Balkans.* New York: St. Martin's Press.

Borsi-Kalman, B. 1991. *Hungarian Exiles and the Romanian National Movement.* Boulder, Colo.: East European Monographs.

Botzaris, N. 1962. *Visions Balkaniques dans la Préparation de la Révolution Grecque (1789–1821).* Geneve: Librarie E. Droz.

Bouchard, J. 1982. "Nikolas Mavrocordatos et l'aube des Lumières." *RESE* 20(2):237–46.

Boulaki-Zissi, C. 1976. "Ilarion of Tarnovo and the Renaissance in Bulgaria during the First Decade of the 19th Century." *BS* 17(1):123–30.

Boura, K. 1983. "The Parliamentary Elections in the Ottoman Empire: The Greek Deputies, 1908–1918." *DKMS* 4:69–86 (G).

Bourdieu, P. 1977. *Outline of a Theory of Practice.* Cambridge: Cambridge University Press.

———. 1984. *Distinction.* Harvard: Harvard University Press.

———. 1994. "Rethinking the State: Genesis and Structure of the Bureaucratic Field." *Sociological Theory* 12(1): 1–18.

Brad-Chisacof, L. 1988. "The Language of Tudor Vladimirescu's and Alexander Hypsilanti's Revolutionary Proclamations." *RESE* 26(1):35–42.

Brass, P. 1985. "Ethnic Groups and the State." In *Ethnic Groups and the State,* edited by P. Brass, 1–56. New York: Barnes and Noble.

Braude, B. 1982. "Foundational Myths of the Millet System." In *Christians and Jews in the Ottoman Empire, Vol. 1,* edited by B. Braude and B. Lewis 69–88. New York: Holmes and Meier.

Braudel, F. 1972. *The Mediterranean and the Mediterranean World in the Age of Philip II,* 2 vols. New York: Harper and Row.

Brown, J. F. 1992. *Nationalism, Democracy, and Security in the Balkans.* Brookfield, Vt.: Dartmouth Publishers.

Brown, K. 2000. "A Rising to Count On: Illinden between Politics and History in Post-Yugoslav Macedonia." In Roudometof (2000b), 143–72.

Brubaker, R. 1992. *Citizenship and Nationhood in France and Germany.* Cambridge: Harvard University Press.

———. 1995. "National Minorities, Nationalizing States, and External National Homelands in the New Europe." *Daedalus* 22(2):107–32.

———. 1996. *Nationalism Reframed: Nationhood and the National Question in the New Europe.* Cambridge: Cambridge University Press.

Brummett, P. J. 1994. *Ottoman Seapower and Levantine Diplomacy in the Age of Discovery.* Albany: State University of New York Press.

Bryer, A. 1965. "The Great Idea." *History Today* (March):159–68.

Burg, S. L. 1983. *The Political Integration of Yugoslavia's Muslims: Determinants of Success and Failure.* Pittsburgh, Pa.: Carl Beck Papers in Russian and East European Studies.

Byrnes, R. F., ed. 1976. *Communal Families in the Balkans: The Zadruga.* Essays by Philip E. Mosely and Essays in His Honor. South Bend, Ind. and London: University of Notre Dame.

Calotychos, V., ed. 1998. *Cyprus and Its People: Nation, Identity, and Experience in an Unimaginable Community.* Boulder, Colo.: Westview Press.

Camariano, N. 1965. "Les Relations de Tudor Vladimirescu avec l'*Heteria* avant la Révolution de 1821." *BS* 6(1):139–64.

Camariano-Coran, A. 1974. *Les Academies Princières de Bucarest et de Jassy et leurs professeurs.* Thessaloniki: Institute for Balkan Studies.

———. 1975. "Le Role de la Revue 'Logios Ermis' de vienne dans les relations culturelles internationales au XIXe siècle." *RESE* 13(4):549–58.

Carabot, P. 1997. "The Politics of Integration and Assimilation vis-à-vis the Slavo-Macedonian Minority of Inter-war Greece: From Parliamentary Inertia to Metaxist Repression." In *Ourselves and Others: The Development of a Greek Macedonian Identity Since 1912,* edited by P. Mackridge and E. Yiannakakis, 59–78. Oxford: Berg.

Carter, F. W. 1977. "Introduction to the Balkan Scene." In *An Historical Geography of the Balkans,* edited by F. W. Carter, 1–24. New York: Academic Press.

Castellan, G. 1967. *Le Vie Quotidienne en Serbie au seuil de l'independance 1815–1839.* Paris: Hachette.

———. 1980. "Les fonctions culturelles de la ville du Sub-Est Européen XVIIIe–XXe siècles." *EB* 4:27–39.

———. 1984. "Facteur religieux et identité nationale deans les Balkans aux XIXe–XXe siècles," *Revue Historique* 27(1):135–51.

———. 1985. "Le romantisme historique: Une des sources de l'ideologie des Etats Balkaniques aux XIXe et XXe siècles." *EH* 3(1):187–203.

———. 1988. " 'Les Balkans face à la Révolution Française.' Idées nouvelles et sociétés traditionnelles: Problèmes méthodologiques," *EB* (3):7–10.

———. 1989. *A History of the Romanians.* Boulder, Colo.: East European Monographs.

———. 1991. *Histoire des Balkans* [Greek edition]. Athens: Govostis.

Castells, M. 1996–1998. *The Information Age,* 3 vols. Oxford: Basil Blackwell.

Cernovodeanu, P. 1986. "Mobility and Traditionalism: The Evolution of the Boyar Class in the Romanian Principalities in the 18th Century." *RESE* 24(3):249–57.

Chaconas, S. G. 1942. *Adamantios Korais: A Study in Greek Nationalism.* New York: Columbia University Press.

Chasiotis, I. K. 1993. *Overview of the History of Modern Greek Diaspora.* Thessaloniki: Vanias (G).

Chateaubriand, F. 1811. *Itinéraire de Paris à Jérusalem et de Jérusalem à Paris: En allant par le Grèce et revenant par l'Egypre, la Barbarie et l'Espagne.* Paris: Le Normant.

Chatterjee, P. 1986. *Nationalist Thought and the Colonial World.* Minneapolis: University of Minnesota Press.

Chirot, D. 1976. *Social Change in a Peripheral Society: The Making of a Balkan Colony.* New York: Academic Press.

Chirot, D., ed. 1989. *The Origins of Backwardness in Eastern Europe.* Berkeley: University of California Press.

Chirot, D., and K. Barkey. 1984. "States in Search of Legitimacy: Was There Nationalism in the Balkans of the Early Nineteenth Century?" In *Current Issues and Research in Macrosociology,* edited by G. Lenski, 30–46. Leiden: E. J. Brill.

Clark, E. C. 1974. "The Ottoman Industrial Revolution." *IJME* (5)1:65–76.

Clark, J. F. 1954. "Father Paisi and Bulgarian History." In *Teachers of History: Essays in Honor of Laurence Bradford Packard,* edited by H. S. Hughes, 258–83. Ithaca N.Y.: Cornell University Press.

Clark, R. P. 1997. *The Global Imperative: An Interpretative History of the Spread of Humankind.* Boulder, Colo.: Westview Press.

Clogg, R. 1969. "The *Dhidhaskalia Patriki* (1798): An Orthodox Reaction to French Revolutionary Propaganda." *MES* 5 (2—May):87–115.

———. 1976. "Anti-Clericalism in Pre-Independence Greece, 1750–1821." In *The Orthodox Churches and the West,* edited by D. Baker, 257–76. Oxford: Basil Blackwell.

———. 1980. "Elite and Popular Culture in Greece under Turkish Rule." In *Hellenic Perspectives: Essays in the History of Greece,* edited by J. T. A. Koumoulides, 107–44. Lanham, Md.: University Press of America.

———. 1981. "The Greek Merchantile Bourgeoisie: 'Progressive' or 'reactionary'?" In *Balkan Society in the Age of Greek Independence,* edited by R. Clogg, 63–84. London: Macmillan.

———. 1982. "The Greek Millet in the Ottoman Empire." In *Christians and Jews in the Ottoman Empire,* Vol. 1, edited by B. Braude and B. Lewis, 185–208. New York: Holmes and Meier.

———. 1985. "Sense of the Past in Pre-Independence Greece." In *Culture and Nationalism in Nineteenth-Century Eastern Europe,* edited by R. Sussex and J. C. Eade, 7–31. Columbus, Ohio: Slavica.

———. 1988. "The Byzantine Legacy in the Modern Greek World: The Megali Idea." In *The Byzantine Legacy in Eastern Europe,* edited by L. Clucas, 253–81. Boulder, Colo.: East European Quarterly.

Cohen, L. J. 1993. *Broken Bonds: The Disintegration of Yugoslavia.* Boulder, Colo.: Westview Press.

Connor, W. 1993. "Beyond Reason: The Nature of the Ethno-national Bond." *Ethnic and Racial Studies* 16: 373–89.

———. 1994. *Ethnonationalism: The Quest for Understanding.* Princeton, N.J.: Princeton University Press.

Constant, S. 1980. *Foxy Ferdinand, Tsar of Bulgaria.* New York: Franklin Watts.

Constantine, D. 1984. *Early Greek Travelers and the Hellenic Ideal*. Cambridge: Cambridge University Press.

Constantiniu, F. 1984. "Tudor Vladimirescu's Revolutionary Army." In *War and Society in East Central Europe*. Vol. IV, *East Central European Society and War in the Era of Revolutions, 1775–1856*, edited by B. K. Kiraly, 230–45. New York: Columbia University Press.

Constantinu, F., and S. Papacostea. 1972. "Les Reforms des Premiers Phanariotes en Moldavie et en Walachie: Essai d'interpretation." *BS* 13(1):89–118.

Crampton, R. J. 1981. "Bulgarian Society in the Early 19th century." In *Balkan Society in the Age of Greek Independence*, edited by R. Clogg, 157–204. London: Macmillan.

———. 1983. *Bulgaria 1878–1918: A History*. New York: East European Monographs.

———. 1989. "The Turks in Bulgaria, 1878–1944." *IJTS* 4(2):43–78.

Cunningham, A. 1978. "The Philhellenes, Canning, and Greek Independence." *MES* 14(2):151–81.

Cvetkova, B. A. 1975. "To the Prehistory of the Tanzimat (An Unknown Ottoman Political Treatise of the Eighteenth Century)." *EH* 7:133–46.

———. 1977. "Problemes du regime ottoman dans les Balkans du seizeme au dix-huitieme siecle." In *Studies in Eighteenth Century Islamic History*, edited by T. Naff and R. Owen, 165–83. Carbondale: Southern Illinois University Press.

———. 1979a. "L'evolution du regime feodal turc de la fin du XVIe jusqu' au milieu du XVIIIe siecle." In *The Economic Structure of the Balkan Countries (15th–19th centuries)*, edited by S. Asdrachas, 89–112. Athens: Melissa (G).

———. 1979b. "Typical Features of the Ottoman Social and Economic Structure in South-Eastern Europe during the 14th to the 16th Centuries." *EH* 9:129–49.

———. 1982. "The Bulgarian Haiduk Movement in the 15th–18th centuries." In *War and Society in East Central Europe*. Vol. II, *East Central European Society and War in the Pre-Revolutionary Eighteenth Century*, edited by G. E. Rothenberg, B. K. Kiraly, and P. F. Sugar, 301–38. New York: Columbia University Press.

Cviic C. 1991. *Remaking the Balkans*. London: Royal Institute of International Affairs.

Cvijic, J. 1918. *La Peninsule Balkanique*. Paris: Librairie Armand Colin.

Dakin, D. 1955. *British and American Philhellenes during the War of Greek Independence, 1821–1833*. Thessaloniki: Institute for Balkan Studies.

———. 1966. *The Greek Struggle for Macedonia*. Thessaloniki: Institute for Balkan Studies.

Danforth, L. 1984. "The Ideological Context of the Search for Continuities in Modern Greek Culture." *JMGS* 2(1):53–86.

———. 1995. *The Macedonian Conflict: Ethnic Nationalism in a Transnational World*. Princeton, N.J.: Princeton University Press.

Daniilidis, D. 1934. *Modern Greek Society and Economy*. Athens: n.p. (G).

Danilevskii, N. IA. 1869 [1966]. *Rosiia I Evropa: Vstupiel'naia stat'ia lu.Ivaska*. New York: Johnson Reprints.

Danopoulos, C., and E. Ianeva. 1999. "Poverty in the Balkans and the Issue of Reconstruction: Bulgaria and Yugoslavia Compared." *Journal of Southern Europe and the Balkans* 1(2):185–99.

Danova, N. 1980. "Les Bulgares vus par les intellectuels grecs a la fin du xviiie et au debut du xixe siecles." In *Greek-Bulgarian Cultural and Political Relations from* the mid-15th to the mid-19th Centuries, 157–67. Thessaloniki: Institute for Balkan Studies (G).

Daskalakis, A. B. 1979. *The Revolutionary Plans and Martyrdom of Rigas Velenstinlis*. Athens: E. G. Vagionaki (G).

Daskalakis, A. D. 1937. *Rhigas Velestinlis: La Revolution Francaise et les Preludes de l'independance Hellenique*. Paris: n.p.

Daskalov, R. 1997. "Ideas about, and Reaction to Modernization in the Balkans." *EEQ* 31(2):141–80.

Davison, R. H. 1954. "Turkish Attitudes concerning Christian-Muslim Equality in the Nineteenth Century." *American Historical Review* 59(3, April):844–64.

———. 1963. *Reform in the Ottoman Empire, 1856–1876*. New York: Gordian Press.

———. 1968. "The Advent of the Principle of Representation in the Government of the Ottoman Empire." In *Beginnings of Modernization in the Middle East: The Nineteenth Century*, edited by W. R. Polk and R. L. Chambers, 93–108. Chicago: University of Chicago Press.

Dedijer, V. 1966. *The Road to Sarajevo*. New York: Simon and Schuster.

Dedijer, V., I. Bozic, S. Cirkovic, and M. Ekmecic. 1974. *History of Yugoslavia*. New York: McGraw-Hill.

Delanty, G. 1995. *Inventing Europe: Idea, Identity, Reality*. New York: St. Martin's Press.

Deletant, D. 1981. "Rumanian Society in the Danubian Principalities." *Balkan Society in the Age of Greek Independence*, edited by R. Clogg, 229–48. London: Macmillan.

———. 1991. *Studies in Romanian History*. Bucharest: Editura Enciclopedia.

Deringil, S. 1991. "Legitimacy Structures in the Ottoman State: The Reign of Abdul-Hamid II (1876–1909)." *IJMES* 23:345–59.

Dertilis G. 1977. *Social Transformation and Military Intervention, 1880–1909*. Athens: Exantas (G).

———. 1993. *Productive or Unproductive? Taxation and Authority in the Modern Greek State*. Athens: Alexandria (G).

Despalatovic, E. M. 1975. *Ljudevit Gaj and the Illyrian Movement*. Boulder, Colo.: East European Quarterly.

Devereux, R. 1963. *The First Ottoman Constitutional Period: A Study of the Midhat Constitution and Parliament*. Baltimore, Md.: Johns Hopkins University Press.

Dimakis, I. 1991. *The Constitutional Change of 1843 and the Issue of Autochnonous and Heterochnonous*. Athens: Themelio (G).

Dimaras, K. Th. 1970. "L'apport de l'Aifklarung au development de la conscience neo-hellenicque." In *Les Lumieres et la formation de la conscience nationale chez les peuples du Sub-Est europeen*, 53–72. Bucharest: Association Internationale d'Etudes du Sub-Est Européen.

———. 1975. "The Enlightenment's Shape." In *History of the Greek Nation*, Vol. 11, 328–59. Athens: Ekdotiki (G).

———. 1977. *Modern Greek Enlightenment*. Athens: Ermis (G).

———. 1985. *Modern Greek Romanticism*. Athens: Ermis (G).

———. 1986. *Konstantinos Paparrigopoulos*. Athens: National Bank of Greece (G).

———. 1988. *History of Greek Literature*. Athens: Ikaros (G).

Dimic, Lj., and D. Alimpic. 1996. "Stereotypes in History Textbooks in the Kingdom of Yugoslavia." In *Oil On Fire? Textbooks, Stereotypes, and Violence in South-*

*eastern Europe*, edited by W. Hopken, 89–98. Hannover, Germany: Verlag Hahn-sche Buchhandlung.

Dimitrakopoulos, F. 1996. *Byzantium and the Modern Greek Intelligentsia in the Middle of the 19th Century*. Athens: Kastaniotis (G).

Dimof, A. G. 1974. "Georgi S. Rakovski in the Struggle for the Reestablishment of the Bulgarian Church." *EEQ* 7(2):177–202.

Directorate Generale de la statistique, Royame de Bulgarie. 1918. *Statistique des fonctionnaires et employes pres les administrations de l'etat et des administrations electorales vers l'l-er avril 1911*. Sofia: Imprimerie de l'Etat.

Directorate de la statistique, Principaute de Bulgarie. 1908. *Resultats du Reconsement des foctionnaires et employes d'etat, execute de 1-er juin, 1904*. Sofia: Imprimerie Balkan.

Divani, L. 1997. "The Consequences of the League of Nation's Minority Regime in Greece: The Foreign Office Perspective." In *The Minority Issue in Greece. A Contribution from the Social Sciences*, edited by K. Tsikelidis and D. Christo-poulos, 171–204. Athens: Kritiki (G).

Djilas, A. 1991. *The Contested Country*. Cambridge: Harvard University Press.

Djilas, M. 1966. *Njegos*. Introduced and translated by M. B. Petrovich. New York: Harcourt, Brace and World.

Djordjevic, D. 1963. "La Societe 'L'Alliance Des Peuples des Balkans' en Serbie en 1890–1891." *BS* 4(1): 137–54.

———. 1965. *Revolutions nationales des peuples balkaniques, 1804–1914*. Belgrade: Institute of History.

———. 1967. "The Serbs as an Integrating and Disintegrating Factor." *Austrian History Yearbook*, Vol. 3, Pt. 2: 48–82.

———. 1970a. *History of Serbia, 1804–1918*. Thessaloniki: Institute for Balkan Studies (G).

———. 1970b. "Projects for the Federation of South-East Europe in the 1860s and 1870s." *Balkanica* 2:119–46.

———. 1975. "Balkan versus European Enlightenment: Parallelism and Dissonances." *EEQ* 9(4): 487–97.

———. 1980. "Yugoslav Unity in the Nineteenth Century." In *The Creation of Yugoslavia, 1914–1918*, edited by D. Djordjevic, 1–18. Santa Barbara, Calif.: Clio.

———. 1982. "The Role of the Military in the Balkans in the Nineteenth Century." In *Der Berliner Kongress von 1878: Die politik der Grossmachte und die probleme der Modernisierung in Sudosteuropa in der zweiten Halftedes 19 Jahrhunderts*, edited by von R. Melville and Hans-Jurgen Schroder, 317–47. Wiesbaden: Steiner.

———. 1985. "The Serbian Peasant in the 1876 War." In *War and Society in East Central Europe. Vol. XVII, Insurrections, Wars, and the Eastern Crisis in the 1870s*, edited by B. K. Kiraly and G. Stokes, 305–18. Boulder, Colo.: Social Science Monographs.

———. 1988. "Stojan Novakovic: Historian, Politician, Diplomat." In *Historians as Nation-Builders. Central and Southeast Europe*, edited by D. Deletant and H. Hanak, 51–69. London: Macmillan.

———. 1990. "The Role of St. Vitus Day in modern Serbian History." *Serbian Studies* 5(3): 33–40.

———. 1991. "The Tradition of Kosovo in the Formation of Modern Serbian Statehood in the Nineteenth Century." In *Kosovo: Legacy of Medieval Battle*, edited by W. S. Vucinich and T. A. Emmert, 309–30. Minneapolis: University of Minnesota.

Donia, R. J. 1981. *Islam under the Double Eagle: The Muslims of Bosnia and Herzegovina, 1878–1914*. Boulder, Colo.: East European Monographs.

Dragnich, A. 1974. *Serbia, Nikola Pasic and Yugoslavia*. New Brunswick, N.J.: Rutgers University Press.

———. 1978. *The Development of Parliamentary Government in Serbia*. Boulder, Colo.: East European Quarterly.

———. 1983. *The First Yugoslavia*. Stanford, Calif.: Hoover Institution Press.

———. 1989. "The Rise and Fall of Yugoslavia: The Omen of the Upsurge of Serbian Nationalism." *EEQ* 26(2): 183–98.

Dragona, Th. 1997. "When National Identity Is Threatened: Psychological Strategies of Coping." In *"What's Our Motherland?" Ethnocentrism in Education*, edited by Th. Dragona and A. Frangoudakis, 72–105. Athens: Alexandria (G).

Durman, K. 1987. *Lost Illusions: Russian Policies towards Bulgaria in 1877–1877*. Stockholm: Almqvist and Wilksell International.

Dusserl, E. 1998. "Beyond Eurocentrism: The World-System and the Limits of Modernity." In *The Cultures of Globalization*, edited by F. Jameson and M. Miyoshi, 3–31. Durham, N. C.: Duke University Press.

Dutu, A. 1967. "National and European Consciousness in the Romanian Enlightenment." *Studies on Voltaire and 18th Century* 55: 463–79.

———. 1973. "Tradition and Innovation in the Rumanian Enlightenment." In *Rumanian Studies*, Vol. 2, 1971–1972, 104–119. Leiden: E. J. Brill.

———. 1976. "Cultural Models in the Southeast European Enlightenment." *SE* 3(2): 251–6.

Eisner, R. 1991. *Travelers to an Antique Land*. Ann Arbor: University of Michigan Press.

Eisenstein, E. 1979. *The Printing Press as an Agent of Change: Communications and Cultural Transformations in Early Modern Europe*, 2 vols. Cambridge: Cambridge University Press.

Ekmečić, M. 1991. "The Emergence of St. Vitus Day as the Principal National Holiday of the Serbs." In *Kosovo: Legacy of Medieval Battle*, edited by W. S. Vucinich and T. A. Emmert, 331–42. Minneapolis: University of Minnesota Press.

Elsie, R. 1985. *History of Albanian Literature*, 2 vols. Boulder, Colo.: East European Monographs.

———. 1991. "Albanian Literature in Greek Script: The Eighteenth- and Nineteenth-century Orthodox Tradition in Albanian writing." *Byzantine and Modern Greek Studies* 15: 20–34.

Eminov, I. 1997. *Turkish and Other Muslim Minorities in Bulgaria*. New York: Routledge.

Emmert, T. A. 1990. *Serbian Golgotha: Kosovo 1389*. Boulder, Colo.: East European Monographs.

Ergil, D. 1975. "A Reassessment: The Young Turks, their Politics, and Anti-Colonial Struggle." *BS* 16(2): 26–72.

Esman, M. J. 1992. "The Political Fallout of International Migration." *Diaspora* 2(1): 3–42.

Exertzoglou, H. 1989. *Adjustment and Policy of Ottoman Greek Capital. Greek Bankers in Constantinople: The 'Zarifis Zafiropoulos' Company, 1871–1881* Athens: Foundation of Research and Culture, Commercial Bank of Greece (G).

Fadner, F. 1962. *Seventy Years of Pan-Slavism in Russia: Karazin to Danilevski, 1800–1870.* Washington, D.C.: Georgetown University Press.

Falmerayer, J. P. 1830. *Geschite der Halbinsel Morea wahrend des Mittelalters: Ein historischer Versuch.* Stuttgart and Tubingen: Gotta'schen.

Farhi, D. 1971. "The Seriat as a Political Slogan—or the 'Incident of the 31st Mart' " *MES* 7(3):275–300.

Faroghi, S. 1994. "Part II Crisis and Change 1590–1699." In *An Economic and Social History of the Ottoman Empire, 1300–1914,* edited by H. Inalcik with D. Quataert, 411–636. Cambridge: Cambridge University Press.

Featherstone, M., ed. 1990. *Global Culture: Nationalism, Globalization, and Modernity.* London: Sage.

Featherstone, M., Scott Lash, and Roland Robertson, eds. 1995. *Global Modernities.* London: Sage.

Ferguson, A. 1981. "Montenegrin Society, 1800–1830." In *Balkan Society in the Age of Greek Independence,* edited by R. Clogg, 205–28. London: Macmillan.

Filias, V. 1985. *Society and Economy in Greece, 1800–1864.* Athens: Gutenberg (G).

Findley, C. V. 1980. *Bureaucratic Reform in the Ottoman Empire. The Sublime Porte, 1789–1922.* Princeton, N.J.: Princeton University Press.

———. 1982. "The Acid Test of Ottomanism: The Acceptance of Non-Muslims in the Late Ottoman Bureaucracy." In *Christians and Jews in the Ottoman Empire.* Vol. I, *The Central Lands,* edited by B. Braude and B. Lewis, 339–68. New York: Holmes and Meier.

———. 1989. *Ottoman Civil Officialdom: A Social History.* Princeton, N.J.: Princeton University Press.

Fischer, B. J. 1984. *King Zog and the Struggle for Stability in Albania.* Boulder, Colo.: East European Monographs.

———. 1985. "Italian Policy in Albania, 1894–1943." *BS* 26:(1):101–2.

———. 1995. "Albanian Nationalism in the Twentieth Century." In *Eastern European Nationalism in the Twentieth Century,* edited by P. F. Sugar, 21–54. Washington, D.C.: American University Press.

Fischer-Galati, S. 1964. "The Origins of Modern Romanian Nationalism." *Jahrbucher fur Geschichte Osteuropeas* 12: 48–54.

———. 1969. "Romanian Nationalism." In *Nationalism in Eastern Europe,* edited by P. Sugar and I. J. Lederer, 373–95. Seattle: University of Washington Press.

Florescu, R. 1968. "The Fanariot Regime in the Danubian Principalities." *BS* 9(2):303–18.

Forte, M. C. 1998. "Globalization and World-Systems Analysis: Toward New Paradigms of a Geo-Historical Social Anthropology (A Research Review)." *Review* 21(1): 29–99.

Frangos, G. 1973. "The Philiki Etairia: A Premature National Coalition." In *The Struggle for Greek Independence,* edited by R. Clogg, 87–103. London: Macmillan.

———. 1975. "Philiki Eteria." In *History of the Greek Nation,* Vol. 11, 424–32. Athens: Ekdotiki (G).

Frangoudakis, A., and Th. Dragona, eds. 1997. *"What's Our Motherland?" Ethnocentrism in Education.* Athens: Alexandria (G).

Frank, A. 1998. *ReOrient: Global Economy in the Asian Age*. Berkeley: University of California Press.

Frank, A. G., and B. K. Gills. 1992. "World System Cycles, Crises, and Hegemonic Shifts, 1700 B.C. to 1700 A.D." *Review* 15(4, fall): 621–87.

———. 1993. "The 5,000-Year World System: An Interdisciplinary Introduction." In *The World System: Five Hundred Years or Five Thousand?* edited by A. G. Frank and B. K. Gills, 3–58. London and New York: Routledge.

Frazee, C. A. 1979. "The Greek Catholic Islanders and the Revolution of 1821." *EEQ* 13(3): 315–326.

———. 1983. *Catholics and Sultans: The Church and the Ottoman Empire, 1453–1923*. Cambridge: Cambridge University Press.

———. 1987. *Orthodox Church and Greek Independence* [Greek Edition]. Athens: Domos.

Friedman, F. 1996. *The Bosnian Muslims: Denial of a Nation*. Boulder, Colo.: Westview Press.

Friedman, V. A. 1975. "Macedonian Language and Nationalism during the Nineteenth and Early Twentieth Centuries," *Balkanistica* (2): 83–98.

———. 1985. "The Sociolinguistics of literary Macedonian." *International Journal of the Sociology of Language* 52: 31–57.

Gaubard, S. R. ed. 1991. *Eastern Europe . . . Central Europe . . . Europe*. Boulder, Colo.: Westview Press.

Gawrych, G. W. 1986. "The Culture and Politics of Violence in Turkish Society, 1903–1914." *MES* 22(3): 307–30.

Gay, P. 1966. *The Enlightenment: An Interpretation. The Rise of Modern Paganism*. New York: Vintage.

Geanakopoulos, D. J. 1976. "The Diaspora Greeks: The Genesis of the Modern Greek National Consciousness." In *Hellenism and the First Greek War of Liberation (1821–1830): Continuity and Change*, edited by N. P. Diamantouros, J. P. Anton, J. A. Petropulos, and P. Topping, 59–77. Thessaloniki: Institute for Balkan Studies.

Gedeon, M. 1976. *The Spiritual Movements of the Race during the Eighteenth and Nineteenth Centuries*, edited by A. Angelou and P. Iliou. Athens: Ermis (G).

Gellner, E. 1983. *Nations and Nationalism*. Ithaca, N.Y.: Cornell University Press.

Gemerek, B. 1996. *The Idea of Europe*. Cambridge: Polity.

Genchev, N. 1977. *The Bulgarian National Revival Period*. Sofia: Sofia Press.

———. 1981. "The Bulgarian Cultural Revival." *SE* 8(1–2): 97–116.

Georgeoff, P. J. 1973. "Educational and Religious Rivalries in European Turkey before in the Balkan Wars." In *American Contributions to the Seventh International Congress of Slavists*, 143–70. Paris: Mouton.

———. 1982. "The Role of Education in the Bulgarian National Revival." In *Bulgaria, Past and Present: Studies on History, Literature, Economics, Sociology, Folklore, Music and Linguistics*, Proceedings of the Second International Conference on Bulgarian Studies held at Druzhba, Varna, 13–17 June 1978, 138–46. Sofia: Bulgarian Academy of Sciences.

Georgescu, V. 1970. *Memoires et projets de reforme dans les Principautes Roumaines, 1769–1830*. Bucharest: Association Internationale d'Etudes du Sub-Est Européen.

———. 1971. *Political Ideas and the Enlightenment in the Romanian Principalities (1750–1831)*. Boulder, Colo.: East European Quarterly.

———. 1991. *The Romanians: A History*. Columbus: Ohio State University Press.

Georgiev, E. 1978. "Bulgarian Literature in the Context of Slavic and European Literature." In *Bulgaria Past and Present*, edited by T. Bulter, 229–48. Columbus, Ohio: American Association for the Advancement of Slavic Studies.

Gerber, H. 1982. "The Monetary System of the Ottoman Empire." *Journal of the Economic and Social History of the Orient* 25 (p. 3): 308–24.

Geyer, M., and C. Bright 1995. "World History in a Global Age." *American Historical Review* 100(4):1034–60.

Giannaras, C. 1992. *Orthodoxy and the West in Modern Greece*. Athens: Domos (G).

Giannaris, N. V. 1996. *Geopolitical and Economic Changes in the Balkan Countries*. Westport, Conn.: Greenwood.

Giddens, A. 1985. *The Nation-State and Violence*. Berkeley: University of California Press.

Gilb, C. L. 1997. "Whose History? What History?" *Comparative Civilizations Review* 35: 43–62.

Gill, J. S. J. 1980. "The Divine East-Roman Empire." In *Hellenic Perspectives: Essays in the History of Greece*, edited by J. T. A. Koumoulides, 57–80. Lanham, Md.: University Press of America.

Gills, J. R., ed. 1994. *Commemorations: The Politics of National Identity*. Princeton, N.J.: Princeton University Press.

Glenny, M. 1992. *The Fall of Yugoslavia: The Third Balkan War*. New York: Penguin.

Gocek, F. M. 1996. *Rise of the Bourgeoisie, Demise of Empire: Ottoman Westernization and Social Change*. New York: Oxford University Press.

Goffman, D. 1990. *Izmir and the Levantine World, 1550–1650*. Seattle: University of Washington Press.

Goldstone, J. A. 1991. *Revolution and Rebellion in the Early Modern World*. Berkeley: University of California Press.

Gong. G. W. 1984. *The Standard of 'Civilization' in International Society*. Oxford: Clarendon.

Gounaris, V. 1986. "From Macedonia to Goudi: Activities of Macedonian Fighter Officers, 1908–1909." *DIEE* 29:175–227 (G).

Gounaris, V. 1989. "Emigration from Macedonia in the Early Twentieth Century." *JMGS* 7:133–53.

———. 1996. "Social Cleavages and 'National Awakening' in Ottoman Macedonia," *EEQ* 29 (4):409–26

Gounaris, V., and I. Mihailidis. 2000. "The Pen and the Sword: Reviewing the Historiography of the Macedonian Question." In Roudometof (2000b), 99–142.

Gran, P. 1996. *Beyond Eurocentrism: A New View of World History*. Syracuse, N.Y.: Syracuse University Press.

Grancarov, S. 1982. "The Bulgarian Bourgeois Democracy, 1879–1919." *BHR* 10(2):31–4.

Greenfeld, L. 1991. *Nationalism: Five Roads to Modernity*. Cambridge: Harvard University Press.

Grew, R. 1984. "The 19th-century European State." In *Statemaking and Social Movements*, edited by C. Bright and S. Harding, 83–120. Ann Arbor: University of Michigan Press.

Gross, M. 1977. "Social Structure and National Movements among the Yugoslav Peoples on the Eve of the First World War." *Slavic Review* 36(4):628–43.

Gurr, T. R. 1993. *Minorities at Risk: A Global View of Ethnopolitical Conflict.* Washington, D.C.: U.S. Institute of Peace Press.

Hall, J. A. 1993. "Nationalisms: Classified and Explained." *Daedalus* 122(3):1–28.

Hall, Th. D. 1989. *Social Change in the Southwest, 1350–1880.* Lawrence: University Press of Kansas.

Hall, Th. D., and C. Chase-Dunn, eds. 1991. *Core/Periphery Relations in Precapitalist Worlds.* Boulder, Colo.: Westview Press.

Hall, Th. D., and C. Chase-Dunn, eds. 1997. *Rise and Demise: Comparing World-Systems.* Boulder, Colo.: Westview Press.

Hanioglu, S. M. 1989. "Notes on the Young Turks and the Freemasons." *MES* 25(2): 186–97.

———. 1995. *The Young Turks in Opposition.* New York: Oxford University Press.

Harvey, D. 1989. *The Condition of Postmodernity.* Oxford: Basil Blackwell.

———. 1995. "Globalization in Question." *Rethinking Marxism.* 8(4):1–17.

Hayden, R. M. 1992a. *The Beginning of the End of Federal Yugoslavia: The Slovenian Amendment Crisis of 1989.* Pittsburgh, Pa: Carl Beck Series in Russian and East European Studies, Center for Russian and East European Studies, University of Pittsburgh.

Hayden, R. M. 1992b. "Constitutional Nationalism in the Formerly Yugoslav Republics." *Slavic Review* 51(4):654–73.

Hehn, P. N. 1975. "The Origins of Modern Pan-Serbianism—The 1844 Nacertanije of Ilija Garasanin: An Analysis and Translation." *EEQ* 9(2):153–171.

Held, D. 1995. *Democracy and the Global Order: From the Modern State to Cosmopolitan Governance.* Stanford, Calif.: Stanford University Press.

Held, D., A. McGrew, D. Goldblatt, and J. Perraton. 1999. *Global Transformations: Politics, Economics, and Culture.* Stanford, Calif.: Stanford University Press.

Henderson, G. P. 1970. *The Revival of Greek Thought, 1620–1830.* Albany: State University of New York.

Herzfeld, M. 1982. *Ours Once More: Folklore, Ideology, and the Making of Modern Greece.* Austin: University of Texas Press.

Hirschman, A. O. 1970. *Exit, Voice, and Loyalty.* Cambridge: Harvard University Press.

Hobsbawm, E. J. 1959. *Primitive Rebels.* New York: Norton.

———. 1969. *Bandits.* New York: Delacorte.

———. 1990. *Nations and Nationalism since 1780: Programme, Myth, Reality.* Cambridge: Cambridge University Press.

———. 1996. "Ethnicity and Nationalism in Europe Today." In *Mapping the Nation*, edited by G. Balakrishnan, 255–66. London: Verso.

Hobsbawm, E. J., and T. Ranger, eds. 1983. *The Invention of Tradition.* Cambridge: Cambridge University Press.

Hodgson, M. 1993. *Rethinking World History: Essays on Europe, Islam, and World History*, edited and with an introduction and conclusion by Edmund Burke III. New York: Cambridge University Press.

Holton, M., and V. Mihailovich. 1988. *Serbian Poetry from the Beginning to the Present.* New Haven, Conn.: Yale Center for International and Area Studies.

Hopken, W. 1996. "History Education and Yugoslav (Dis-)Integration." In *Oil In Fire? Textbooks, Stereotypes, and Violence in Southeastern Europe*, edited by W. Hopken, 99–124. Hannover, Germany: Verlag Hahnsche Buchhandlung.

———. 1997. "From Religious Identity to Ethnic Mobilization: The Turks of Bulgaria, before, under and since Communism." In *Muslim Identity and the Balkan State*, edited by H. Poulton and S. Taji-Farouki, 54–81. New York: New York University Press.

Hovannisian, Richard G., ed. 1997. *The Armenian People from Ancient to Modern Times*. 2 vols. New York: St. Martin's Press.

Hristov, A. 1971. *The Creation of Macedonian Statehood (1893–1945)*. Skopje: Kultura.

———. 1974. "Paissi of Hilendar: Author of the Slav-Bulgarian History." *EEQ* 8(2): 167–74.

———. 1988. "Foundation and Activity of the Bulgarian Learned Society (1869–1911)." *EEQ* 22(3):333–9.

Huntington, S. P. 1993. "The Clash of Civilizations?" *Foreign Affairs* 72(3): 22–49.

———. 1996. *The Clash of Civilizations and the Remaking of World Order*. New York: Simon and Schuster.

Hupchick, D. P. 1993. *The Bulgarians in the 17th Century: Slavic Orthodox Society and Culture under Ottoman Rule*. Jefferson, N.C.: Mc Farland.

Iancovici, S. 1971a. "Relations Roumano-Albanaises a l'epoque de la Renaissance et de l'emancipation du peuple Albanais I." *RESE* 9(1):5–48.

———. 1971b. "Relations Roumano-Albanaises a l'epoque de la Renaissance et de l'emancipation du peuple Albanais II." *RESE* 9(2):225–48.

Ilchev, Ivan. 2000. "Emigration and the Politics of Identity: The Turkish Minority in Bulgaria." In *The Politics of National Minority in Participation in Post-Communist Europe*, edited by Jonathan P. Stein, 237–68. Armonk, N.Y.: M. E. Sharpe.

Ilchev, I., and D. Perry. 1993. "Bulgarian Ethnic Groups: Politics and Perceptions." *RFE/RL Research Report* 2(12, 19 March): 35–41.

Iliou, P. 1986. *Social Struggles and Enlightenment: The Case of Smyrna 1819*. Athens: E.M.N.E.–Mnimon (G).

———. 1988. *Oh My Lord, Blind Your People: The Pre-Revolutionary Critiques and Nikolaos Pikolos*. Athens: m.p. (G).

———. 1989. *Ideological Uses of Koraism in the Twentieth Century*. Athens: Politis (G).

———. 1993. "School Textbooks and Nationalism: The Approach of Dimitris Glinos." In *Greece of the Balkan Wars, 1910–1914*, 259–78. Athens: ELIA (G).

Inalcik, H. 1972. "The Ottoman Decline and Its Effects upon the Reaya." In *Aspects of the Balkans, Continuity and Change*, edited by H. Birnbaum and S. Vryonis Jr., 338–54. Paris: Mouton.

———. 1977. "Centralization and Decentralization in Ottoman Administration." In *Studies in Eighteenth Century Islamic History*, edited by T. Naff and R. Owen, 27–52. Carbondale: Southern Illinois University Press.

———. 1978a. "Impact of the Annales School on Ottoman Studies and New Findings." *Review* 1(3/4), winter/spring): 69–96.

———. 1978b. *The Ottoman Empire: Conquest, Organization and Economy*. London: Valorium Reprints.

———. 1980. "Military and Fiscal Transformation in the Ottoman Empire, 1600–1700." *Archivum Ottomanicum* 6: 283–337.

———. 1994. "Part I The Ottoman State: Economy and Society, 1300–1600." In *An Economic and Social History of the Ottoman Empire, 1300–1914*, edited by H. Inalcik with D. Quataert, 9–410. Cambridge: Cambridge University Press.

Inalcik, H., with D. Quataert, eds. 1994. *An Economic and Social History of the Ottoman Empire, 1300–1914*. Cambridge: Cambridge University Press.

Ionescu-Niscov, T. 1974. "L'epoque phanariote dans l'historiographie roumaine et etrangere." In *Symposium L'Epoque Phanariote*, 145–58. Thessaloniki: Institute for Balkan Studies.

Iorga, N. 1985. *Byzance apres Byzance* [Greek edition]. Athens: Gutenberg.

Islamoglu, H., and G. Keyder. 1987. "Agenda for Ottoman History." In *The Ottoman Empire and the World-Economy*, edited by H. Islamoglu-Inan, 42–62. Cambridge: Cambridge University Press.

Issawi, C. 1982. "The Transformation of the Economic Position of the Millets in the Nineteenth Century." In *Christians and Jews in the Ottoman Empire*, Vol. 1, edited by B. Braude and B. Lewis, 261–286. New York: Holmes and Meier.

Itzkowitz, N. 1977. "Men and Ideas in the Eighteenth-Century Ottoman Empire." In *Studies in Eighteenth-Century Islamic History*, edited by T. Naff and R. Owen, 15–26. Carbondale: Southern Illinois University Press.

Jacobson, D. 1996. *Rights across Borders: Immigration and the Decline of Citizenship*. Baltimore, Md.: Johns Hopkins University Press.

Jacques, E. E. 1995. *The Albanians*. Jefferson, N.C. and London: McFarland.

Jeffreys, M. 1985. "Adamantios Korais: Language and Revolution." In *Culture and Nationalism in Nineteenth-Century Eastern Europe*, edited by R. Sussex and J. C. Eade, 42–55. Columbus, Ohio: Slavica.

Jekins, R. 1967. "Byzantium and Byzantinism." In *Lectures in Memory of Louis Taft*, 137–78. Princeton, N.J.: Princeton University Press.

Jelavich, B. 1966. "The Philorthodox Conspiracy of 1839: A Report to Metternich." *BS* 7(1):89–102.

———. 1983. *History of the Balkans*, 2 vols. Cambridge: Cambridge University Press.

———. 1991. *Russia's Balkan Entanglements, 1806–1914*. Cambridge: Cambridge University Press.

Jelavich, C. 1962a. "Serbian Nationalism and the Question of Union with Croatia in the Nineteenth Century." *BS* 3(1):29–42.

———. 1962b. *Tsarist Russia and Balkan Nationalism: Russian Influence in the Internal Affairs of Bulgaria and Serbia, 1879–1886*. Berkeley: University of California Press.

———. 1967. "The Croatian Problem in the Habsburg Monarchy in the Nineteenth Century." *Austrian History Yearbook* Vol. 3, Pt. 2:83–115.

———. 1990a. "Serbian Nationalism and the Croats: Vuk Karadzic's Influence on Serbian Textbooks." *CRSN* 17(1–2):31–42.

———. 1990b. *South Slav Nationalisms—Textbooks and Yugoslav Union before 1914*. Columbus: Ohio State University Press.

Jelavich, C., and B. Jelavich. 1977. *The Establishment of the Balkan Nation-States*. Seattle: University of Washington Press.

Jewsbury, G. 1979. "Nationalism in the Danubian Principalities, 1800–25—A Reconsideration." *EEQ* 13(3):287–96.

Johnsen, W. T. 1993. *Deciphering the Balkan Peninsula: Using History to Inform Policy*. Carlisle Barracks, Pa.: Strategic Studies Institute, U.S. Army War College.

Jovanovic-Gorup, R. 1991. "Dositej Obradevic and Serbian Cultural Rebirth." *Serbian Studies* 6(1):35–55.

Judt, T. 1996. *A Grand Illusion? An Essay on Europe*. New York: Hill and Wang.

Jusdanis, G. 1991. *Belated Modernity and Aesthetic Culture: Inventing National Literature*. Minneapolis: University of Minnesota Press.

Kakambouras, D. 1993. *The British Policy, Byron, and the Greeks of '21*. Athens: Istoritis (G).

Kakridis, I. Th. 1989. *The Ancient Greeks in the Modern Greek Tradition*. Athens: Educational Foundation of the National Bank of Greece (G).

Kalliataki Mertikopoulou, K. 1988. *Greek Irredentism and Ottoman Reformation: The Case of Crete, 1868–1877*. Athens: Hestia (G).

Kamperidis, L. 1992. "The Notion of Millet in Mavrocordatos' *Philotheou Parerga* and His Perception of the Enlightened Ottoman Despot." *JHD* 18(1):67–78.

Kaplan, R. 1992. *Balkan Ghosts: A Journey through History*. New York: St. Martin's Press.

Karakasidou, A. 1993a. "Fellow Travelers, Separate Roads: The KKE and the Macedonian Question." *EEQ* 27:453–77.

———. 1993b. "Politicizing Culture: Negating Ethnic Identity in Greek Macedonia." *JMGS* 11:11–28.

———. 1997. *Fields of Wheat, Hills of Blood. Passages to Nationhood in Greek Macedonia, 1870–1990*. Chicago: University of Chicago Press.

———. 2000. "Transforming Identity, Constructing Consciousness: Coercion and Heterogeneity in Northwestern Greece." In Roudometof (2000b), 55–98.

Karal, E. Z. 1982. "Non-Muslim Representatives in the First Constitutional Assembly, 1876–1877." In *Christians and Jews in the Ottoman Empire*. Vol. 1, *The Central Lands*, edited by B. Braude and B. Lewis, 387–400. New York: Holmes and Meier.

Karanovich, Milenko. 1987. "Higher Education in Serbia during the Constitutionalist Regime, 1838–1858." *BS* 28(1):125–50.

———. 1995. *The Development of Education in Serbia and Emergence of its Intelligentsia (1838–1858)*. Boulder, Colo.: East European Monographs.

Karathanasis, A. E. 1991. "Some Observations on the European Cartography with regard to 15th–18th-Century Macedonia." *BS* 32(1):5–17.

Karidis, V. 1981. "A Greek Mercantile Paroikia: Odessa, 1774–1829." In *Balkan Society in the Age of Greek Independence*, edited by R. Clogg, 111–36. London: Macmillan.

Karpat, K. H. 1972. "The Transformation of the Ottoman State, 1789–1908." *IJMES* 3: 243–81.

———. 1973. *An Inquiry into the Social Foundations of Nationalism in the Ottoman Empire: From Social Estates to Classes, from Millets to Nations*. Princeton, N.J.: Center for International Studies, Princeton University.

———. 1975. "The Memoirs of N. Batzaria: The Young Turks and Nationalism." *IJMES* 6:276–99.

———. 1982a. "Millets and Nationality: The Roots of the Incongruity of Nation and State in the Post-Ottoman Era." In *Christians and Jews in the Ottoman Empire*. Vol. 1, edited by B. Braude and B. Lewis, 141–70. New York: Holmes and Meier.

———. 1982b. "The Social and Political Foundations of Nationalism in South East Europe after 1878: A Reinterpretation." In *Der Berliner Kongress von 1878: Die politik der Grossmachte und die probleme der Modernisierung in Sudosteuropa in der zweiten Halftedes 19 Jahrhunderts*, edited by von R. Melville and Hans-Jurgen Schroder, 385–410. Wiesbaden: Steiner.

———. 1986. "Ottoman Views and Policies towards the Orthodox Christian Church." *The Greek Orthodox Theological Review* 31 (spring–summer):131–55.

———. 1989. "Bulgaria's Methods of Nation-Building: The Annihilation of Minorities." *IJTS* 4(2):1–22.

———, ed. 1990. *The Turks of Bulgaria: The History, Culture, and Political Fate of a Minority*. Istanbul: Isis Press.

Kasaba, R. 1988. *The Ottoman Empire and the World Economy: The Nineteenth Century*. Albany: State University of New York Press.

Katardzhiev, I. 1973. "The Internal Macedonian Revolutionary Organization." In *The Epic of Ilinden*, 47–60 Skopje: Macedonian Review.

Katsoulakos, Th., and K. Tsantinis. 1994. *Historiographical Issues in the School Textbooks of the Balkan Countries*. Athens: Ekkremes (G).

Katsoulis, G., M. Nikolinakos, and V. Filias. 1985. *Economic History of Modern Greece*. Vol. I *(1453–1830)*. Athens: Papazisis (G).

Kayali, H. 1995. "Elections and the Electoral Process in the Ottoman Empire, 1876–1919." *IJMES* 27:265–86.

Kedourie, E. 1971. "Introduction." In *Nationalism in Asia and Africa*, edited by E. Kedourie, 1–151. New York: Meridian.

———. 1985. *Nationalism*. London: Hutchinson.

Kellas, J. K. 1991. *The Politics of Nationalism and Ethnicity*. New York: St. Martin's Press.

Kennan, G. F. 1993. "Introduction." In *The Other Balkan Wars: A 1913 Carnegie Endowment Inquiry*. Washington, D.C.: Carnegie Endowment for International Peace.

Keyer, C. 1997. "The Ottoman Empire." In *After Empire: Multiethnic Societies and Nation-Building*, edited by K. Barkey and M. Von Hagen, 30–44. Boulder, Colo.: Westview Press.

Kiel, M. 1985. *Art and Society of Bulgaria in the Turkish Period*. Maastricht, The Netherlands: Van Gorcum.

Kilminster, R. 1997. "Globalization as an Emergent Property." In *The Limits of Globalization: Cases and Arguments*, edited by A. Scott, 257–83. London: Routledge.

Kimball, S. 1969. "The Serbian Matica—Prototype of Austro-Slav Literary Foundations: The First Fifty Years, 1826–1876." *EEQ* 3(3):348–70.

King, R. 1973. *Minorities under Communism: Nationalities as a Source of Tension among Balkan Communist States*. Cambridge: Harvard University Press.

Kitroeff, Λ. 1989. "Continuity and Change in Contemporary Greek Historiography." *European History Quarterly* 19(2):269–98.

Kitromilides, P. M. 1978. *Tradition, Enlightenment, and Revolution: Ideological Change in Eighteenth and Nineteenth-Century Greece*. Ph.D. Dissertation, Department of Political Science, Harvard University.

———. 1979. "The Dialectic of Intolerance: Ideological Dimensions of Ethnic Conflict." *JHD* 6(4):5–30.

———. 1983. "The Enlightenment East and West: A Comparative Perspective on the Ideological Origins of the Balkan Political Traditions." *CRSN* 10(1):51–70.

———. 1985. *Iosipos Moisiodax*. Athens: National Bank of Greece (G).

———. 1990a. *The French Revolution and Southeastern Europe*. Athens: Diatton (G).

———. 1990b. "Greek Irredentism in Asia Minor and Cyprus." *MES* 26(1):3–17.

————. 1996. " 'Balkan Mentality': History, Legend, Imagination." *Nations and Nationalism* 2(2):163–92.

Kitromilides, P. M., and A. Alexandris. 1984/1985. "Ethnic Survival, Nationalism and Forced Migration: The Historical Demography of the Greek Community of Asia Minor at the Close of the Ottoman Era." *DKMS* 5:9–44.

Kitsikis, D. 1973. "Evolution de l'Elite Politique Greque." In *Social Stratification and Development in the Mediterranean Basin*, edited by M. B. Kiray, 218–38. Paris: Mouton.

————. 1982. "Greek Reaction to the Ottoman Imperial Reform Decree of November 3, 1839." *Patristic and Byzantine Review* 1(3):217–24.

————. 1990. *Comparative History of Greece and Turkey in the Twentieth Century* (2nd ed.). Athens: Hestia (G).

Kofos, E. 1964. *Nationalism and Communism in Macedonia*. Thessaloniki: Institute for Balkan Studies.

————. 1980. "Dilemmas and Orientations of Greek Policy in Macedonia, 1878–1886." *BS* 21(1):45–55.

————. 1984. "Attempts at Mending the Greek-Bulgarian Ecclesiastical Schism (1875–1902)." *BS* 25(2):347–75.

————. 1986. "Patriarch Joachim II (1878–1884) and the Irredentist Policy of the Greek State." *JMGS* 4(2):107–20.

————. 1994. *The Vision of the Greater Macedonia*. Thessaloniki: Museum of the Macedonian Struggle (G).

Kohn, H. 1953. *PanSlavism: Its History and Ideology*. New York: Vintage [1960].

————. 1961. *The Idea of Nationalism*. New York: Macmillan.

————. 1962. *The Age of Nationalism: The First Era of Global History*. New York: Harper and Brothers.

Kolev, J. 1991. "The Bulgarian Exarchate as a National Institution and the Position of the Clergy (1878–1912)." *EB* 2:40–54.

Koliopoulos, J. S. 1980. "Regarding 'Social' and Other Bandits in Modern Greece." *DIEE* 23:422–36 (G).

————. 1987. *Brigands with a Cause: Brigandage and Irredentism in Modern Greece, 1821–1912*. Oxford: Clarendon Press.

————. 1994. *Plundered Feelings: The Macedonian Question in Occupied Western Macedonia, 1941–1944*. Thessaloniki: Vanias (G).

Koliopoulos, J., and I. Chasiotis, eds. 1992. *The Modern and Contemporary Macedonia: History, Economy, Society, Culture*. Thessaloniki: Papazisi-Paratiritis (G).

Kondis, B. 1976. "Aspects of the National Movements of Serbia, Greece, and Bulgaria in the Nineteenth Century." *Balkanica* 7:139–51.

Kondis, B., K. Kentrotis, S. Sfetas, and Y. D. Stefanidis, eds. 1993. *Resurgent Irredentism: Documents on Skopje "Macedonian" Nationalist Aspirations (1934–1992)*. Thessaloniki: Institute for Balkan Studies.

Konortas, P. 1998. *Ottoman Views of the Ecumenical Patriarchate*. Athens: Alexandria (G).

Konstadinova, Tatiana. 1995. *Bulgaria 1879–1946: The Challenge of Choice*. Boulder, Colo.: East European Monographs.

Kontogiorgis, G. D. 1977. "The Greek Social and Political Forces in Late Ottoman Rule: The Conditions for the Social and Political Struggle and the Post-liberation Consequences." *Social and Political Forces in Greece*, edited by G. D. Kontogiorgis, 5–38. Athens: Exantas (G).

————. 1982. *Social Dynamics and Political Self-Government: The Greek Communities during Ottoman Rule*. Athens: Livanis (G).

Korais, A. 1971. "Report on the State of Civilization in Modern Greece" (1804). In *Nationalism in Asia and Africa*, edited by E. Kedourie, 153–88. New York: Meridian.

Kordatos, G. 1924/1991. *The Social Significance of the 1821 Greek Revolution*. Athens: Epikerotita (G).

————. 1945/1983. *Rigas Phereos and the Balkan Federation*. Athens: Epikerotita (G).

Korobar P. 1987. *The Macedonian National Culture in the Pirin Part of Macedonia*. Skopje: Macedonian Review Editions.

Kossev D., H. Hristov, and D. Angelov. 1963. *A Short History of Bulgaria*. Sofia: Foreign Languages Press.

Kostelancik, D. J. 1996. "Minorities and Minority Language Education in Interwar Albania." *EEQ* 30(1):74–96.

Koumarianou, C. 1995. *Die Griechische Vorrevolutionare Presse Wien–Paris, 1784–1821*. Athens: Stiftung fur Griechische Kultur.

Koumarianou C., L. Droulia, and E. Layton. 1986. *The Greek Book, 1476–1830*. Athens: National Bank of Greece (G).

Krapsitis, V. 1989. *The True History of Souli* (2nd ed.). Athens: n.p. (G).

Krejci, J., and V. Velimski. 1981. *Ethnic and Political Nations in Europe*. New York: St. Martin's Press.

Kremmydas, V. 1972. *The Commerce of Peloponnesus in the Eighteenth Century*. Athens: n.p. Exautus (G).

————. 1980. *Conjuncture and Commerce in the pre-Revolutionary Peloponnesus, 1793–1821*. Athens: Themelio (G).

————. 1988. *Introduction to the History of Modern Greek Society, 1700–1821* (2nd ed.). Athens: Exantas (G).

Kundera, M. 1984. "The Tragedy of Central Europe." *New York Review of Books*, 26 April.

Kunt, M. I. 1982. "Transformation of *Zimmi* into *Askeri*." In *Christians and Jews in the Ottoman Empire*, Vol. 1, edited by B. Braude and B. Lewis, 55–68. New York: Holmes and Meier.

Kushner, D. 1977. *The Rise of Turkish Nationalism, 1876–1908*. London: Cass.

Kuzmanov, P. 1981. "The 1850 Uprising in Bulgaria through British Eyes." *BHR* 9(4): 61–7.

Ladas, S. P. 1932. *The Exchange of Minorities. Bulgaria, Greece, and Turkey*. New York: Macmillan.

Lampe, J. R. 1979. "Modernization and Social Structure: The Case of the pre-1914 Balkan Capitals." *SE* 5(2):11–32.

Lampe, J. R. 1989. "Imperial Borderlands or Capitalist Periphery? Redefining Balkan Backwardness, 1520–1914." In *The Origins of Backwardness in Eastern Europe*, edited by D. Chirot, 177–209. Berkeley: University of California Press.

Lampe, J. R. 1996. *Yugoslavia as History: Twice There Was a Country*. Cambridge: Cambridge University Press.

Lampe, J. R., and M. R. Jackson. 1982. *Balkan Economic History, 1550–1950: From Imperial Borderlines to Developing Nations*. Bloomington: Indiana University Press.

Lancek, R. L. 1983. "The Enlightenment's Interest in Languages and the National Revival of the South Slavs." *CRSN* 10(1):111–34.

Landau, J. M. 1981. *Pan-Turkism in Turkey: A Study in Irredentism*. London: Hurst.

Lange-Akhund, N. 1998. *The Macedonian Question, 1893–1908: From Western Sources.* Boulder, Colo.: East European Monographs.

Lape, L. 1973. "The Republic of Krusevo." In *The Epic of Ilinden*, 117–52. Skopje: Macedonian Review.

Larrabee, S., ed. 1994. *The Volatile Powder Keg. Balkan Security after the Cold War.* Washington, D.C.: American University Press.

Lash, S., and J. Urry. 1994. *Economies of Signs and Space*. London: Sage.

Lazarescu, D. A. 1975. "Cross-currents in the Intellectual and Political Life of Central and South-Eastern Europe between 1711 and 1821: Enlightenment, Jospehismus, Aufklarung, and 'Megali Idea'." *Nouvelles Etudes d'Histoire*. Bucharest: Etura Academiei Republicii Socialiste Romania.

Lazou, C. D. 1983. *America and Its Role in the 1821 Revolution*, 2 vols. Athens: Papazisi (G).

Lederer, I. J. 1969. "Nationalism and the Yugoslavs." In *Nationalism in Eastern Europe*, edited by P. F. Sugar and I. J. Lederer, 396–438. Seattle: University of Washington Press.

Legg, K. 1969. *Politics in Modern Greece*. Stanford, Calif.: Stanford University Press.

Leon, G. B. 1974. *Greece and the Great Powers, 1914–1917*. Thessaloniki: Institute for Balkan Studies.

Leontaridis, G. 1987. *The Greek Merchant Marine (1453–1850)*. Athens: E.M.N.E.–Mnimon (G).

Leontaridis, G. B. 1990. *Greece and the First World War: From Neutrality to Intervention, 1917–1918*. Boulder, Colo.: East European Quarterly.

Levy, A. 1979. "Ottoman Attitudes to the Rise of Balkan Nationalism." In *War and Society in East Central Europe*. Vol. 1, *Special Topics and Generalizations on the 18th and 19th centuries*, edited by B. K. Kiraly and G. E. Rothenberg, 225–45. New York: Columbia University Press.

Lewis, B. 1965. "The Impact of the French Revolution in Turkey." In *The New Asia*, edited by G. Metraux and F. Crouzet, 31–59. New York: New American Library.

———. 1979. *The Emergence of Modern Turkey*. London: Oxford University Press.

Lew, R. 1971. *Everyday Life in Ottoman Turkey*. London: Batsford and Putnam.

Liakos, A. 1985. *The Italian Unification and the Great Idea*. Athens: Themelio (G).

Lipset, S. M. 1963. *The First New Nation*. New York: Basic.

Lord, A. B. 1963. "Nationalism and the Muses in Balkan Slavic Literature in the Modern Period." In *The Balkans in Transition*, edited by C. and B. Jelavich, 258–96. Berkeley: University of California Press.

Loukas I. 1991. *History of the Greek Freemasonry and Greek History*. Athens: Papazisi (G).

Loukatos, S. D. 1979. "Serbs, Montenegrin, and Bosnians in the fight for Greek Independence 1821–1829." In *Cooperation between Greeks and Serbs during their struggles for Liberation 1804–1830*, 101–51. Thessaloniki: Institute for Balkan Studies (G).

Loukatos, S. D. 1980. "Les relations des revolutionnaires grecs et des Bulgares volontares a la lutte pour l'independance hellenique." In *Greek-Bulgarian Cultural and Political Relations from the mid-15th to the mid-19th Centuries*, 199–209. Thessaloniki: Institute for Balkan Studies (G).

Loukidou-Mavridou, D., and I. Papadrianos. 1980. "Dimitrios Darvaris: Sa contribution a l'evolution litteraire bulgare." In *Greek-Bulgarian Cultural and Political Relations from the mid-15th to the mid-19th Centuries*, 211–26. Thessaloniki: Institute for Balkan Studies (G).

Lukac, D. 1979. "Heterija i Karadjordje." In *Cooperation between Greeks and Serbs during Their Struggles for Liberation, 1804–1830*, 153–9. Thessaloniki: Institute for Balkan Studies.

Lunt, H. G. 1984. "Some Sociolinguistic Aspects of Macedonian and Bulgarian." In *Language and Literary Theory*, edited by B. A. Stolz, I. R. Titunik, and L. Dolezel, 82–132. Ann Arbor: University of Michigan Press.

Lyrintzis, Ch. 1991. *The End of the Tzakia: Society and Politics in 19th-century Achaia*. Athens: Themelio (G).

Mackridge P. 1981. "The Greek Intelligentsia, 1780–1830: A Balkan Perspective." In *Balkan Society in the Age of Greek Independence*, edited by R. Clogg, 40–62. London: Macmillan.

Makridis, V. N. 1988. "Science and the Orthodox Church in 18th and Early 19th Century Greece: Sociological Considerations." *BS* 29(2):265–82.

Malcolm, N. 1994. *Bosnia: A Short History*. New York: New York University Press.

———. 1998. *Kosovo: A Short History*. New York: HarperCollins.

Mamoni, K. 1975. "Les associations pour la propagation de l'instruction Greque a Constantinople (1861–1922)." *BS* 16(1):103–12.

———. 1983. "The Associational Organization of Hellenism in Asia Minor." *DIEE* 26: 63–114 (G).

———. 1988–1990. "Introduction to the History of the Constantinople Associations, 1861–1922." *Mnimosini* 11:211–34 (G).

Mango, C. 1965. "Byzantinism and Romantic Hellenism." *Journal of the Warburg and Courtauld Institutes* 28: 29–43.

———. 1973. "The Phanariots and the Byzantine Tradition." In *The Struggle for Greek Independence*, edited by R. Clogg, 41–66. London: Macmillan.

———. 1980. *Byzantium. The Empire of New Rome*. New York: Scribner.

Mann, M. 1986 and 1993. *The Sources of Social Power*, Vols. 1 and 2. Cambridge: Cambridge University Press.

Mantran, R. 1977. "Transformation du commerce dans l'Empire Ottoman au dix-huitieme siecle." In *Studies in Eighteenth Century Islamic History*, edited by T. Naff and R. Owen, 217–235. Carbondale: Southern Illinois University Press.

Mardin, S. 1962. *The Genesis of Young Ottoman Thought. A Study in the Modernization of Turkish Political Ideas*. Princeton, N.J: Princeton University Press.

Marinescu, F. 1981. "The Trade of Wallachia with the Ottoman Empire between 1791 and 1821." *BS* 22(2): 289–319.

Markova, Z. 1980. "Le Patriarchat de Constantinople et la vie culturelle Bulgare au XVIIIe siecle et durant les premieres decennies du XIXe siecle." In *Greek-Bulgarian Cultural and Political Relations from the mid-15th to the mid-19th Centuries*, 227–37. Thessaloniki: Institute for Balkan Studies (G).

———. 1983. "Russia and the Bulgarian-Greek Church Question in the Seventies of the Nineteenth Century." *EH* 11:159–97.

———. 1985. "The Church Question in the Bulgarian National Revolution." *BHR* 13(3): 38–51.

————. 1988. "Bulgarian Exarchate, 1870–1879." *BHR* 16(4):39–54.

Mavrocordatos, G. Th. 1983a. "The National Schism as a Crisis of National Integration." In *Ellinismos, Ellinikotita*, edited by D. G. Tsaousis, 69–78. Athens: Hestia (G).

————. 1983b. *Stillborn Republic: Social Coalitions and Party Strategies in Greece, 1922–1936*. Berkeley: University of California Press.

————. 1996. *National Schism and Mass Organization. The Reservists of 1916*. Athens: Alexandria (G).

Mavrocordatos, N. 1989 [1718]. *Philotheou Parerga* [French and Greek]. Translated by Jacques Bouchard. Athens: Association pour l'Etude des Lumieres en Grece; Montreal: Presses de l'Universite de Montreal. (Original work published 1800).

Mayall, J. 1990. *Nationalism and International Society*. Cambridge: Cambridge University Press.

Mazarakis-Ainian, I. K. 1986. "From the Young Turk Movement to the Balkan Wars." *DIEE* 29: 157–74 (G).

Mazlish, B., and R. Buultjens, eds. 1993. *Conceptualizing Global History*. Boulder, Colo.: Westview Press.

Mazower, M. 1992. "The Messiah and the Bourgeoisie: Venizelos and Politics in Greece, 1909–1912." *Historical Journal* 35 (4):885–904.

McCarthy, J. 1982. *The Arab World, Turkey, and the Balkans (1878–1914): A Handbook of Historical Statistics*. Boston: G. K. Hall.

————. 1983. *Muslims and Minorities. The Population of Ottoman Anatolia and the End of the Empire*. New York: New York University Press.

McClellan, W. D. 1964. *Svetovar Markovic and the Origins of Balkan Socialism*. Princeton, N.J.: Princeton University Press.

McDermott, M. 1962. *A History of Bulgaria, 1393–1885*. New York: Praeger.

————. 1986. *The Apostle of Freedom: A Portrait of Vasil Levski Against a Background of Nineteenth Century Bulgaria*. Sofia: Sofia Press.

McDonald, T., ed. 1996. *The Historic Turn in the Human Sciences*. Ann Arbor: University of Michigan Press.

McGowan, B. 1981. *Economic Life in the Ottoman Empire: Taxation, Trade, and the Struggle for Land, 1600–1800*. Cambridge: Cambridge University Press.

————. 1994. "Part III The Age of the Ayans, 1699–1812." In *An Economic and Social History of the Ottoman Empire 1300–1914*, edited by H. Inalcik with D. Quataert, 637–758. Cambridge: Cambridge University Press.

McGraw, W. M. 1976. "The Land Issue in the Greek War of Independence." In *Hellenism and the First Greek War of Independence (1821–1830): Continuity and Change*, edited by N. P. Diamandouros, J. P. Anton, J. Petropulos, and P. Tropping, 111–30. Thessaloniki: Institute for Balkan Studies.

McGrew, A., and P. Lewis. 1992. *Global Politics: Globalization and the Nation-State*. Cambridge: Polity Press.

McGrew, W. W. 1985. *Land and Revolution in Modern Greece, 1800–1881: The Transition in the Tenure and Exploitation of Land from Ottoman Rule to Independence*. Kent, Ohio: Kent State University Press.

McKenzie, D. 1967. *The Serbs and Russian PanSlavism, 1875–1878*. Ithaca, N.Y.: Cornell University Press.

————. 1982. "Serbian Nationalist and Military Organizations and the Piedmont Idea, 1844–1914." *EEQ* 16(3):323–43.

————. 1985. *Ilija Garasanin: Balkan Bismarck*. Boulder, Colo.: East European Monographs.

————. 1988. "Ilija Garasanin, Serbia's National Leader, 1843–1867." In *War and Society in East Central Europe* vol. 25, *East Central European War Leaders: Civilian and Military*, edited by B. K. Kiraly and A. A. Nofi, 15–39. Boulder, Colo.: Social Science Monographs, distributed by Columbia University Press.

————. 1989. *Apis, The Congenial Conspirator: The Life of Colonel Dragutin T. Dimitrijevic*. Boulder, Colo.: East European Monographs.

————. 1991. "A Military Coup Which Succeeded: Serbia May 29, 1903." *Serbian Studies* 6(2, fall): 55–76.

————. 1994. "Serbia as Piedmont and the Yugoslav Idea." *EEQ* 28(2, June): 153–82.

————. 1995. *The "Black Hand" on Trial, Salonika, 1917*. Boulder, Colo.: East European Monographs, distributed by Columbia University Press.

McNeely, C. L. 1995. *Constructing the Nation-State*. Westport, Conn.: Greenwood.

McNeill, W. H. 1963. *The Rise of the West*. Chicago: University of Chicago Press.

————. 1985. *Polyethnicity and National Unity in World History*. Toronto: University of Toronto Press.

Meinecke, F. [1909] 1970. *Cosmopolitanism and the National State*. Princeton, N.J.: Princeton University Press.

Meininger, T. A. 1970. *Ignatiev and the Establishment of the Bulgarian Exarchate, 1864–1872: A Study in Personal Diplomacy*. Madison: State Historical Society of Wisconsin, University of Wisconsin.

————. 1974. *The Formation of a Nationalist Bulgarian Intelligentsia*. Ph.D. Dissertation, Department of History, University of Wisconsin.

————. 1976. "The Journalists and Journalism of the Bulgarian Revival." *SE* 3(1):19–31.

————. 1977. "The Response of the Bulgarian People to the April Uprising." *SE* 4(2): 250–61.

————. 1979. "The Social Stratification of the Bulgarian Town in the Third Quarter of the Nineteenth Century." *SE* 5(2):73–104.

Meriage L. P. 1977. "The First Serbian Uprising (1804–1813): National Revival or a Search for Regional Security." *CRSN* 4(2):187–205.

Mestrovic, St., ed. 1996. *Genocide after Emotion: The Postemotional Balkan War*. London: Routledge.

Meyer, J. 1995. "Foreword." In McNeely (1995).

Meyer, J. W., and M. T. Hannan, eds. 1979. *National Development and the World System: Educational, Economic, and Political Change, 1950–1970*. Chicago: University of Chicago Press.

Michalopoulos, D. 1986. "The Moslems of Chameria and the Exchange of Population between Greece and Turkey." *BS* 27(2).

Mihalopoulou, A., P. Tsartas, M. Gainnisopoulou, P. Kafetzis, and E. Manologlou. 1998. *Macedonia and the Balkans: Xenophobia and Development*. Athens: Alexandria (G).

Mihailidis, I. D. 1996. "Minority Rights and Educational Problems in Greek Interwar Macedonia: The Case of the Primer 'Abecedar'." *JMGS* 14(2):329–44.

————. 1998. "The War of Statistics: Traditional Recipes for the Preparation of the Macedonian Salad." *EEQ* 32(1):9–21.

Mihailovich, V. D. 1991. ' "The Tradition of Kosovo in Serbian Literature." In *Kosovo: Legacy of Medieval Battle*, edited by W. S. Vucinich and T. A. Emmert, 141–58. Minneapolis: University of Minnesota.

Mikic, Dj. 1987. "The Albanians and Serbia during the Balkan Wars." In *East Central European Society and the Balkan Wars*, edited by B. K. Kiraly and D. Djordjevic, 165–96. Boulder, Colo.: Social Science Monographs.

Mile, L. 1979. "De l' extension du systeme ciftlig sur les territoires albanais (fin du XVIIIe debut du XIX siecle)." In *The Economic Structure of the Balkan Countries (15th–19th Centuries)*, edited by S. Asdrachas, 185–90. Athens: Melissa (G).

Milios, G. 1997. "The Constitution of the Modern Greek Nation as an Economic and Demographic Process." In *The Minority Issue in Greece: A Contribution from the Social Sciences*, edited by K. Tsikelidis and D. Christopoulos, 281–314. Athens: Kritiki. (G)

Miller, W. 1936. *The Ottoman Empire and Its Successors, 1801–1927, with an appendix 1927–1936*. Cambridge: Cambridge University Press.

Milojkovic-Duric, J. 1994. *PanSlavism and National Identity in Russia and in the Balkans, 1830–1880: Images of the Self and Others*. Boulder, Colo.: East European Monographs.

Minogue, K.R. 1967. *Nationalism*. London: B. T. Batsford.

Mishkova, D. 1994. "Literacy and Nation-Building in Bulgaria, 1878–1912." *EEQ* 28(1): 63–93.

———. 1995. "Modernization and Political Elites in the Balkans before the First World War." *EEPS* 9(1):63–89.

Mitchell, M., and D. Russell. 1996. "Immigration, Citizenship, and the Nation-State in the New Europe." In *Nation and Identity in Contemporary Europe*, edited by B. Jekins and S. A. Sofos, 54–80. London: Routledge.

Mojzes, P. 1994. *Yugoslav Inferno: Ethnoreligious Warfare in the Balkans*. New York: Continuum.

Mojzov, L. 1979. *The Macedonian Historical Themes*. Belgrade: Jugoslovenska Stvatnost.

Momiroski, T. 1993. "Nasite Granici: Macedonian Group Boundaries, 1900–1945." *Journal of Intercultural Studies* 14(2):35–52.

Moore, B. 1966. *The Social Origins of Dictatorship and Democracy*. New York: Beacon.

Moser, C. 1972. *A History of Bulgarian Literature, 865–1944*. The Hague: Mouton.

Moskof, K. 1978. *Thessaloniki: Analysis of the Commercial City*. Thessaloniki: Stochastis (G).

———. 1987. *Introduction to the History of the Working Class Movement: The Constitution of the National and Social Consciousness in Greece* (3rd ed.). Athens: Kastaniotis (G).

Mouzelis, N. 1978. *Modern Greece: Facets of Underdevelopment*. London: Macmillan.

———. 1986. *Politics in the Semiperiphery: Early Parliamentarism and Late Industrialization in the Balkans and Latin America*. New York: St. Martin's Press.

———. 1998. "Ernest Gellner's Theory of Nationalism: Some Definitional and Methodological Issues." In *The State of the Nation: Ernest Gellner and the Theory of Nationalism*, edited by J. A. Hall, 158–65. Cambridge: Cambridge University Press.

Mukerjee, C. 1986. *From Graven Images: Patterns of Modern Materialism*. New York: Columbia University Press.

Musgrave, Th. D. 1997. *Self-Determination and National Minorities*. Oxford: Clarendon Press.

Navari, C. 1975. "The Origins of the Nation-State." In *The Nation-State*, edited by L. Tivey, 13–38. New York: St. Martin's Press.

Nelson, L. 1989. "The Bulgarian Intellectual Emigration in Rumania during the *Vuzrazhdane*." In *Migrations in Balkan History*, edited by R. Samardic and D. Djordjevic, 97–107. Belgrade: Srpka Akademija Nauka I Umetnosti.

Neuremberg, M. 1997. "Bulgaro-Turkish Encounters and the Re-Imagining of the Bulgarian Nation (1878–1995)." *EEQ* 31(1): 1–19.

Nicolaidis, D. 1992. *D'Une Grece a l'autre: Representation des Greces modernes par la France revolutionaire*. Paris: Belles lettres.

Nicoloff. A. 1987. *The Bulgarian Resurgence*. Cleveland, Ohio: n.p.

Nikolaev, R. 1992. "Bulgaria's 1992 Census: Results, Problems, and Implications." *RFE/ RL Research Report*. 2(6). 5 February, 58–62.

Nikolaidis, Th., D. Dialetis, and I. Athanasiadis. 1988. "Natural Sciences and Enlightenment in the Greek Space of the 18th Century." *Istorika* 5(8):123–36 (G).

Nikolopoulos, I. 1988. *Structures and Institutions during the Ottoman Rule: Ambelakia and the Socioeconomic Transformation of the Greek Territory*. Athens: Kavlos (G).

Nikolopoulos, J. 1985. "From Agathangelos to the Megale Idea: Russia and the Emergence of Modern Greek Nationalism," *BS* 26(1):41–56.

Nikolov, S. 2000. "Perceptions of Ethnicity in the Bulgarian Political Culture: Misunderstanding and Distortion." In Roudometof (2000b), 207–36.

Nikolova, V. 1990. "The Problem of Power in the Theory and Practice of the Bourgeois Parties in Bulgaria from the End of the Nineteenth Century to the Year 1912." *EH* 14:75–87.

Norris, H. T. 1993. *Islam in the Balkans: Religion and Society between Europe and the Arab World*. Columbia: University of South Carolina Press.

Oikonomidou, D. B. 1982–1984. "The Romanian Literature on the Movement of Theodor Vladimirescu." *Mnimosini* 9:57–117 (G).

Oldson, W. O. 1983. "The Enlightenment and the Romanian Cultural Revival (Moldavia, Wallachia, Transylvania)." *CRSN* 10(1):29–40.

Orbini, M. 1601. *Il regno degli Slavi*. Pesaro: G. Concordia.

Orhonlu, C. 1977. "Geographical Knowledge amongst the Ottomans and the Balkans in the Eighteenth Century According to Bartili Ibrahim Hambi's Atlas." In *An Historical Geography of the Balkans*, edited by F. W. Carter, 271–92. New York: Academic Press.

Otetea, A., ed. 1970. *History of the Romanian People*. Bucharest: Scientific.

Palairet, M. 1979. "Fiscal Pressure and Peasant Impoverishment in Serbia before World War I." *Journal of Economic History* 39(3; September):719–40.

Palairet, Michael. 1997. *The Balkan Economies c. 1800–1914: Evolution Without Development*. Cambridge: Cambridge University Press.

Palmer, A. W. 1965. *The Gardeners of Salonika*. New York: Simon and Schuster.

Palmer, Alan, 1993. *The Decline and Fall of the Ottoman Empire*. New York: M. Evans & Co.

Palmer, S. E. Jr., and R. E. King. 1971. *Yugoslav Communism and the Macedonian Question*. New York: Archon.

Pamuk, S. 1987. *The Ottoman Empire and European Capitalism, 1820–1913.* Cambridge: Cambridge University Press.

Panayotopoulos, A. J. 1980. "Early Relations between the Greeks and the Young Turks." *BS* 21(1):87–95.

———. 1983. "On the Economic Activities of the Anatolian Greeks." *DKMS* 4:87–128.

Pantazopoulos, N. J. 1988. "Greek Contributions to Maritime Laws and Commercial Customs in the Eastern Mediterranean during the Eighteenth and the Nineteenth Centuries." In *War and Society in East Central Europe.* Vol. 23, *Southeast European Maritime Commerce and Naval Policies from the Mid-Eighteenth Century to 1914,* edited by A. E. Vakalopoulos, C. D. Svolopoulos, and B. K. Kiraly, 311–20. Boulder, Colo.: East European Monographs.

———. 1994. *Studies on Rigas Velenstinlis* Athens (G).

Pantev, A. 1977. "The American Revolution and the Slavs." *BHR* 5:21–33.

Panzac, D. 1992. "International and Domestic Maritime Trade in the Ottoman Empire during the 18th Century." *IJMES* 24:189–206.

Papacosma, V. S. 1977. *The Military in Greek Politics: The 1909 Coup d'Etat.* Kent, Ohio: Kent State University Press.

Papacostea-Danielopolou, C. 1971. "Les Cours de Grec las Ecoles Roumaines apres 1821 (1821–1866)." *RESE* 9(1):71–90.

———. 1986. "Etat Actuel des Recherches sur 'L'epoque Phanariote'." *RESE* 24(3): 227–34.

Papadopoullos, T. H. 1990. *Studies and Documents Relating to the History of the Greek Church and People under Turkish Domination* (2nd ed. with supplementary material). London: Variorum.

Papadopoulos, S. I. 1979. "The 'General Plan' of Philiki Eteria and Their Connection with the Serbs." In *Cooperation between Greeks and Serbs during Their Struggles for Liberation, 1804–1830,* 51–64. Thessaloniki: Institute for Balkan Studies (G).

———. 1980. "Les plans insurrectionnels de la 'Philiki Heteria' et les Bulgares." In *Greek-Bulgarian Cultural and Political Relations from the mid-15th to the mid-19th Centuries,* 105–15. Thessaloniki: Institute for Balkan Studies (G).

Papadopoulos, S., and V. Traikov. 1984. "La societe thraco-bulgare en Grece durant les annees 40 du XIX siecle." *BS* 25(2):573–82.

Papandrianos, I. A. 1993. *The Greek Immigrants in the Yugoslav Countries.* Thessaloniki: Vanias (G).

Papapanagiotou, A. 1992. *The Macedonian Question and the Balkan Communist Movement, 1918–1939.* Athens: Themelio (G).

Pappas, C. P. 1985. *The United States and the Greek War of Independence, 1821–1828.* Boulder, Colo.: East European Monographs.

Paparigopoulos, C. 1865–1874. *History of the Greek Nation.* Athens: Passare (G).

———. 1878. *Histoire de la civilisation hellenique.* Paris: Hachette.

Pasic, N. 1971. "Factors in the Formation of Nations in the Balkans and among the South Slavs." *International Social Science Journal* 23:399–420.

Pavlowich, S. 1981. "Society in Serbia, 1791–1830." In *Balkan Society in the Age of Greek Independence,* edited by R. Clogg, 137–56. London: Macmillan.

Paxton, R. V. 1972. "Nationalism and Revolution: A Re-examination of the Origins of the First Serbian Insurrection, 1804–07." *EEQ* 6(3):337–62.

Pearson, R. 1983. *National Minorities in Eastern Europe, 1848–1945.* New York: St. Martin's Press.

Peerce, J. 1997. "National Minority Rights vs. State Sovereignty in Europe: Changing Norms in International Relations?" *Nations and Nationalism* 3(3):345–64.

Pentzopoulos, D. 1962. *The Balkan Exchange of Minorities and Its Impact upon Greece.* Paris: Mouton.

Perry, D. M. 1988. *The Politics of Terror: The Macedonian Liberation Movements, 1893–1903.* Durham, N.C.: Duke University Press.

———. 1993. *Stefan Stambolov and the Emergence of Modern Bulgaria, 1870–1895.* Durham, N.C.: Duke University Press.

Perselis, E. 1997. *Authority and Religious Education in 19th Century Greece.* Athens: Grigoris (G).

Petkovski, T. 1981. "Macedonian Emigration to the USA." *Macedonian Review* 11(1): 102–10.

Petropulos, J. A. 1968. *Politics and Statecraft in the Kingdom of Greece.* Princeton, N.J.: Princeton University Press.

———. 1976. "Forms of Collaboration with the Enemy during the First Greek War of Independence." In *Hellenism and the First Greek War of Liberation (1821–1830): Continuity and Change,* edited by N. Diamandouros, J. P. Anton, J. Petropulos, and P. Topping, 131–46. Thessaloniki: Institute for Balkan Studies.

Petrovic R. 1992. "The National Composition of Yugoslavia's Population, 1991." *Yugoslav Survey.* 33(1):3–24.

Petrovich, M. B. 1956. *The Emergence of Russian Pan-Slavism, 1856–1870.* New York: Columbia University Press.

———. 1970. "The Emergence of Modern Serbian and Bulgarian Historiography." In *Actes Du Premier Congres International Des Etudes Balkaniques et Sud-Est Europeennes.* Vol. 5, *Histoire,* 297–309. Sofia: Association Internationale des Etudes Balkaniques et Sud-Est Europeennes.

———. 1976. *A History of Modern Serbia, 1804–1918,* 2 vols. New York: Harcourt Brace Jovanovich.

———. 1982. "The Romantic Period of Bulgarian Historiography: From Paisii to Drinov." In *Bulgaria Past and Present,* 128–37. Sofia: Bulgarian Academy of Sciences.

———. 1988. "Karadzic and Nationalism." *Serbian Studies* 4 (spring):41–57.

Pettifer, J., ed. 1999. *The New Macedonian Question.* London: Macmillan.

———. 2000. "The Greek Minority in Albania: Ethnic Politics in a Pre-National State." In *The Politics of National Minority Participation in Post-Communist Europe,* edited by Jonathan P. Stein, 167–88. Armonk, N.Y.: M. E. Sharpe.

Pijakov, Z. 1968. "Quelques Questions de l'Histoire de l'Archeveche-Patriarcat d'Ipek a la Fin du XVIIe s. et l'Autonomie de la Population Non-Musulmane des Pays Balkanqieus aux XVIe et XVIIe siecles." *EH* 4:243–63.

Pinson, M. 1975. "Ottoman Bulgaria in the First Tanzimat Period—The Revolts in Nish (1841) and Vidin (1850)." *MES* 11(2):103–46.

Pippidi, A. 1975. "Phanar, Phanariotes, Phanariotisme." *RESE* 13(2):231–9.

Pitouli-Kitsou, Ch. 1997. *Greek–Albanian Relations and the Northern Epirus Question, 1907–1914.* Athens: Olkos (G).

Plamenatz, J. 1976. "Two Types of Nationalism." In *Nationalism: The Nature and Evolution of an Idea,* edited by E. Kamenka, 23–36. London: Edward Arnold.

Politis, A. 1984. *The Discovery of the Greek Folk Songs.* Athens: Themelio (G).

———. 1993. *Romantic Years: Ideologies and Mentalities in the Greece of 1830–1880.* Athens: EMNE-Mnimon (G).

Pollo, S., and A. Puto 1979. *History of Albania* [Greek edition]. Thessaloniki: Ekdotiki Omada. (1981 English edition)

Poulton, H. 1991. *The Balkans: Minorities and States in Conflict.* London: Minority Rights Group.

———. 1995. *Who Are the Macedonians?* Bloomington: Indiana University Press.

———. 1997a. "Changing Notions of National Identity among Muslims in Thrace and Macedonia: Turks, Pomaks, and Roma." *Muslim Identity and the Balkan State*, edited by H. Poulton and S. Taji-Farouki, 82–102. New York: New York University Press.

———. 1997b. *Top Hat, Grey Wolf, and Crescent. Turkish Nationalism and the Turkish Republic.* New York: New York University Press.

Poulton, H., with the Minnesota Lawyers International Human Rights Committee. 1989. *Minorities in the Balkans.* London: Minority Rights Group. Report no. 82.

Pribic, N. R. 1983. "Dositej Obradevic (1742–1811): Enlightenment, Rationalism, and the Serbian National Tongue." *CRSN* 10:41–9.

Pribichevich, S. 1982. *Macedonia: Its People and History.* University Park: Penn State University Press.

Prodromou, E. H. 1996. "Paradigms, Power, and Identity: Rediscovering Orthodoxy and Regionalizing Europe." *European Journal of Political Research* 30 (September): 125–54.

Protopsaltis, E. G. 1980. "Nicolas Piccolos de Turnavo et son oeuvre politique et litteraire." In *Greek-Bulgarian Cultural and Political Relations from the mid-15th to the mid-19th Centuries*, 55–60. Thessaloniki: Institute for Balkan Studies (G).

Psiroukis, N. 1983. *The Modern Greek Colonial Phenomenon.* Athens: Epikerotita (G).

Pundeff, M. V. 1969. "Bulgarian Nationalism." *Nationalism in Eastern Europe*, edited by P. F. Sugar and I. J. Lederer, 93–165. Seattle: University of Washington Press.

Quataert, D. 1994. "Part IV The Age of Reforms, 1812–1914." In *An Economic and Social History of the Ottoman Empire, 1300–1914*, edited by H. Inalcik with D. Quataert, 759–946. Cambridge: Cambridge University Press.

Rajić, J. 1794–1795. *Istoriia raznykh slavesnmkikh narodon, nipache Bolgar, Khorvatov I Serbon.* Vienna: n.p.

Ramet, P. S. 1992. *Nationalism and Federalism in Yugoslavia, 1962–1991.* Bloomington: Indiana University Press.

———. 1999. *Balkan Babel: The Disintegration of Yugoslavia from the Death of Tito to the War for Kosovo.* Boulder, Colo.: Westview Press.

Ramsaur, E. Jr. 1957. *The Young Turks: Prelude to the Revolution of 1908.* New York: Russell and Russell.

*Review.* 1993. Special issue on Port-Cities of the Eastern Mediterranean, 1800–1914. Vol. 26(4; fall).

Rezun, M. 1995. *Europe and War in the Balkans: Toward a New Yugoslav Identity.* Westport, Conn.: Praeger.

Robertson, R. 1992. *Globalization: Social Theory and Global Culture.* London: Sage.

———. 1995. "Glocalization: Time-Space and Homogeneity-Heterogeneity." In *Global Modernities*, edited by M. Featherstone, S. Lash, and R. Robertson, 24–44. London: Sage.

Robertson, R., and H. H. Khondker 1998. "Discourses of Globalization: Preliminary Considerations." *International Sociology* 13(1):25–40.

Robertson, R., and F. Lechner. 1985. "Globalization, Modernization and the Problem of Culture in World-System Theory." *Theory, Culture, and Society* 2(3):103–18.

Robinson, J. 1943. *Were the Minorities Treaties a Failure?* New York: Institute for Jewish Affairs.

Rokkan, S., and D. Urwin 1983. *Economy, Territory, Identity*. London: Sage.

Rollin, C. 1788. *The Ancient History of the Egyptians, Carthaginians, Assyrians, Babylonians, Medes and Persians, Macedonians, and Grecians* (translated from the French). London: Rivington. (original French edition published in 1730–1738).

Romanides, I. 1975. *Romiosini, Romania, Rumeli*. Thessaloniki: Purnara (G).

Rothschild, J. 1959. *The Communist Party of Bulgaria*. New York: Columbia University Press.

———. 1981. *Ethnopolitics: A Conceptual Framework*. New York: Columbia University Press.

Roudometof, V. 1996a. "The Consolidation of National Minorities in Southeastern Europe." *Journal of Political and Military Sociology* 24(2):187–209.

———. 1996b. "Nationalism and Identity Politics in the Balkans: Greece and the Macedonian Question," *JMGS* 14(2):253–301.

———. 2000a. "From Enlightenment to Romanticism: The Origins of Modern Greek National Identity, 1453–1878." *Thetis: Mannheimer Beiträge zur Klassischen Archäologie und Geschichte Griechenlands und Zyperns*.

———. 2000b. *The Macedonian Question: Culture, Historiography, Politics*. Boulder, Colo.: East European Monographs.

Roudometof, V., and R. Robertson. 1995. "Globalization, World-System Theory, and the Comparative Study of Civilizations: Issues of Theoretical Logic in World-Historical Sociology." In *Civilizations and World-Systems*, edited by S. Sanderson, 273–300. New York: Alta Mira Press.

Runciman, S. 1968. *The Great Church in Captivity: A Study of the Patriarchate of Constantinople from the Eve of the Turkish Conquest to the Greek War of Independence*. Cambridge: Cambridge University Press.

———. 1991. "Rum Mileti: The Orthodox Communities under the Ottoman Sultans." In *The Byzantine Tradition after the Fall of Constantinople*, edited by J. Y. Yiannas, 1–16. Charlottesville and London: University Press of Virginia.

Rusinow D. 1968. *The Macedonian Question Never Dies*. New York: American Universities Field Staff.

———. 1977. *The Yugoslav Experiment, 1948–1974*. London: Hurst.

———. 1982. "Yugoslavia's Muslim Nation." *Field Staff International Report* 8:1–8.

———. 1985. "Nationalities Policy and the 'National Question'." In *Yugoslavia in the 1980s*, edited by P. Ramet, 131–65. Boulder, Colo.: Westview Press.

———, ed. 1988. *Yugoslavia: A Fractured Federalism*. Washington, D.C.: Wilson Center Press.

———. 1995. "The Yugoslav Peoples." In *Eastern European Nationalism in the Twentieth Century*, edited by P. Sugar, 305–412. Washington, D.C.: American University Press.

Rustow, D. A. 1981. "Ataturk as an Institution Builder." In *Ataturk: Founder of a Modern State*, edited by A. Kazancigil and E. Ozbudum. 57–78, London: Hurst.

Sadat, D. R. 1972. "Rumeli *Ayanlari*: The Eighteenth Century." *Journal of Modern History* 44:346–63.

Safrastjan, R. 1989. "Ottomanism in Turkey in the Epoch of Reforms in XIX Century: Ideology and Policy." *EB* 1:34–44.

Said, E. 1978. *Orientalism*. New York: Vintage.

Salamone, S. D. 1989a. "The Dialectics of Turkish National Identity: Ethnic Boundary Maintenance and State Ideology." *EEQ* 23(1):33–61.

Salamone, S. D. 1989b. "The Dialectics of Turkish National Identity (Part II)." *EEQ* 23(2):225–48.

Salecl, R. 1994. "The Crisis of Identity and the Struggle for New Hegemony in the Former Yugoslavia." In *The Making of Political Identities*, edited by E. Laclau, 205–32. London: Verso.

Sanders, I. T. 1979. "Balkan Rural Societies and War." In *War and Society in East Central Europe*. Vol. 1, *Special Topics and Generalizations on the 18th and 19th centuries*, edited by B. K. Kiraly and G. E. Rothenberg. 151–620. New York: Columbia University Press.

———. 1980. "The Social Stratification of the Balkan Town." *EB* 4: 18–26.

Sanderson, S., ed. 1995. *Civilizations and World-Systems*. New York: Alta Mira.

Sarres, N. 1990. *Ottoman Reality*, 2 vols. Athens: Arsenidi (G).

Sassen, S. 1996. *Losing Control? Sovereignty in an Age of Globalization*. New York: Columbia University Press.

Schlesinger, P. 1987. "On National Identity: Some Conceptions and Misconceptions Criticized." *Social Science Information* 26(2):219–64.

Schopflin, G., and N. Wood, eds. 1989. *In Search of Central Europe*. Cambridge: Polity.

Schwartzberg, S. 1988a. "The Lion and the Phoenix—I: British Policy toward the 'Greek Question', 1821–1832." *MES* 24(2):139–77.

———. 1988b. "The Lion and the Phoenix—II." *MES* 24(2):287–311.

Seton-Watson, H. 1977. *Nations and States: An Enquiry into the Origins of Nations and the Politics of Nationalism*. London: Methuen.

Seton-Watson, R. W. 1934. *A History of the Romanians*. Cambridge (England): University Press.

Sewell, W. H. Jr. 1996. "Three Temporalities: Toward an Eventful Sociology." In *The Historic Turn in the Human Sciences*, edited by T. J. McDonald, 245–80. Ann Arbor: University of Michigan Press.

Shashko, P. 1973. "Greece and the Intellectual Bases of the Bulgarian Renaissance." In *American Contributions to the Seventh International Congress of Slavists*. Vol. 3, *History*, 93–121. Paris: Mouton.

———. 1974a. "Bulgarian Literary and Learned Societies during the 1850s–1870s." *SE* 1(1):1–33.

———. 1974b. "Yugoslavism and the Bulgarians in the Nineteenth Century." *SE* 1(2): 136–56.

Shaw, S. J. 1963. "The Ottoman View of the Balkans." In *The Balkans in Transition*, edited by C. Jelavich and B. Jelavich, 56–80. Berkeley: University of California Press.

———. 1971. *Between Old and New: The Ottoman Empire under Sultan Selim III, 1789–1807*. Cambridge: Harvard University Press.

———. 1976. *History of the Ottoman Empire and Modern Turkey*. Vol. 1, *Empire of the Gazis: The Rise and Decline of the Ottoman Empire, 1280–1808.* Cambridge: Cambridge University Press.

———. 1978. "The Ottoman Census System and Population, 1831–1914." *IJMES* 9: 325–38.

Shaw, S. J., and E. K. Shaw. 1977. *History of the Ottoman Empire and Modern Turkey.* Vol. 2, *Reform, Revolution, and the Rise of Modern Turkey, 1808–1975.* Cambridge: Cambridge University Press.

Shoup, P. 1968. *Communism and the Yugoslav National Question.* New York: Columbia University Press.

———, ed. 1990. *Problems of Balkan Security: Southeastern Europe in the 1990s.* Washington, D.C.: Wilson Center Press.

Simsir, B. 1988. *The Turks of Bulgaria (1878–1985).* London: K. Rustem.

Skendi, S. 1967. *The Albanian National Awakening, 1878–1912.* Princeton, N.J.: Princeton University Press.

———. 1980. *Balkan Cultural Studies.* Boulder, Colo.: East European Monographs, Columbia University Press.

Skiotis, D. N. 1975. "Mountain Warriors and the Greek Revolution." In *War, Technology and Society in the Middle East,* edited by V. J. Parry and M. E. Yapp, 308–29. London: Oxford University Press.

———. 1976. "The Greek Revolution: Ali Pasha's Last Gamble." In *Hellenism and the First Greek War of Independence (1821–1830): Continuity and Change,* edited by N. P. Diamandouros, J. P. Anton, J. A. Petropulos, and P. Topping, 97–110. Thessaloniki: Institute for Balkan Studies.

Skocpol, T. 1977. "Wallerstein's World Capitalist System: A Theoretical and Historical Critique." *American Journal of Sociology* 82(5):1075–90.

Skopetea, E. 1988. *The 'Prototype Kingdom' and the Great Idea.* Athens: Politipo (G).

———. 1992. *The Twilight of the East: Images from the Fall of the Ottoman Empire.* Athens: Gnosi (G).

Skrivanic, G. 1982. "The Armed Forces in Karadjordje's Serbia." In *The First Serbian Uprising, 1804–1813,* edited by W. S. Vucinich, 303–40. New York: Columbia University Press.

Slijepcevic, D. 1958. *The Macedonian Question: The Struggle for Southern Serbia.* Chicago: American Institute for Balkan Affairs.

Sluga, G. 1998. "Balkan Boundaries: Writing History and Identity into Territory." In *Europe: Rethinking the Boundaries,* edited by P. Murray and L. Holmes, 105–20. Ashgate: Aldershot.

Smith, A. D. 1984. "Ethnic Persistence and National Transformation," *British Journal of Sociology* 35 (3):452–61.

———. 1986. *The Ethnic Origins of Nations.* Oxford: Basil Blackwell.

———. 1991. *National Identity.* Rhino: University of Nevada Press.

Smith, M. L. 1973. *Ionian Vision: Greece in Asia Minor, 1919–1923.* London: Allen Lane.

Somers, M. 1995. "Narrating and Naturalizing Civil Society and Citizenship Theory: The Place of Political Culture and the Public Sphere." *Sociological Theory* 13(3):229–74.

Sotirelis G. X. 1991. *Constitution and Election in Greece, 1864–1909: The Ideology and Practice of Universal Suffrage.* Athens: Themelio (G).

Souliotis-Nikolaidis, A. 1984. *Organization of Constantinople*. Edited and with an introduction by T. Veremis and K. Boura. Athens: Dodoni (G).

Soysal, Y. N. 1994. *Limits of Citizenship: Migrants and Post-national Membership in
Europe*. Chicago: University of Chicago Press.

Spiridonakis, B. G. 1977. *Essays on the Historical Geography of the Greek World in the
Balkans during the Turkokratia*. Thessaloniki: Institute for Balkan Studies.

Spybey, T. 1996. *Globalization and World Society*. London: Polity Press.

Stahl, H. H. 1980. *Traditional Rumanian Village Communities: The Transition from the
Communal to the Capitalist Mode of Production in the Danube Region*. Cambridge: Cambridge University Press.

Stavrianos, L. S. 1944. *Balkan Federation. A History of the Movement toward Balkan
Unity in Modern Times*. Northampton, Mass.: Department of History, Smith College.

Stavrianos, L. S. 1957. "Antecedents to the Balkan Revolutions of the Nineteenth Century." *Journal of Modern History* 29(4):335–48.

———. 1958. *The Balkans since 1453*. New York: Harper and Row.

St. Clair, W. 1973. *That Greece Might Still Be Free: The Philhellenes in the War of
Independence*. London: Oxford University Press.

Stevenson, F. S. 1971. *A History of Montenegro*. New York: Arno.

Stoianovich, T. 1959. "The Pattern of Serbian Intellectual Evolution, 1830–1880." *CSSH*
1(3):242–72.

———. 1960. "The Conquering Balkan Orthodox Merchant." *Journal of Economic History* 20:234–313.

———. 1974. "Recent Studies in Balkan History." *Southeastern Europe* 1(1):89–97.

———. 1989. "The Segmentary State and *La Grande Nation*." In *Geographic Perspectives in History*, edited by E. D. Genovese and L. Hochberg, 256–280. Oxford:
Basil Blackwell.

———. 1992. *Between East and West: The Balkan and Mediterranean Worlds*. Vol. 1,
*Economies and Societies*. New York: A. D. Karatzas.

———. 1994. *The Balkan Worlds: The First and Last Europe*. New York: M. E. Sharpe.

———. 1995. *Between East and West: The Balkan and Mediterranean Worlds*, Vol. 4.
New York: A. D. Karatzas.

Stojancevic, V. 1979. "Knez Miloseva shratanja srpsko-grcke saradnje protiv osmanskog
carstva." In *Cooperation between Greeks and Serbs during Their Struggles for
Liberation, 1804–1830*, 89–100. Thessaloniki: Institute for Balkan Studies.

———. 1982. "Karadjordje and Serbia in His Time." In *The First Serbian Uprising,
1804–1813*, edited by W. S. Vucinich, 23–40. Boulder, Colo.: Brooklyn College
Press, distributed by Columbia University Press.

Stokes, G. 1973. "The European Sources of Nineteenth Century Thought and the National
Liberation Movement in Serbia." In *American Contributions to the Seventh In-
ternational Congress of Slavists*, Warsaw, 1973, Vol. III, 125–41. The Hague:
Mouton.

———. 1975. *Legitimacy through Liberalism: Vladimir Jovanovic and the Transformation of Serbian Politics*. Seattle: University of Washington Press.

———. 1976. "The Absence of Nationalism in Serbian Politics before 1840." *CRSN*
4(1): 77–90.

———. 1979. "Church and Class in Early Balkan Nationalism." *EEQ* 13 (3): 259–70.

———. 1980a. "Dependency and the Rise of Nationalism in Southeastern Europe." *IJTS* 1: 54–67.

———. 1980b. "The Role of the Yugoslav Committee in the Formation of Yugoslavia." In *The Creation of Yugoslavia, 1914–1918*, edited by D. Djordjevic, 51–72. Oxford: Clio Press.

———. 1987. "The Social Origins of East European Politics." *EEPS* 1(1):30–74.

———. 1990. *Politics as Development: The Emergence of Political Parties in Nineteenth Century Serbia*. Durham, N.C.: Duke University Press.

Stoneman, R. 1987. *Land of Lost Gods. The Search for Classical Greece*. London: Hutchinson.

Stuart, J., and N. Revett 1762–1816. *The Antiquities of Athens*, 4 vols. London: Haberkon.

Subtelny, O. 1986. *Domination in Eastern Europe: Native Nobilities and Foreign Absolutism, 1500–1715*. Kingston: McGill-Queen's University Press.

Sugar, P. 1975. "The Enlightenment in the Balkans: Some Basic Considerations." *EEQ* 9 (4): 449–507.

———. 1977. *Southeastern Europe under Ottoman Rule*. Seattle: University of Washington Press.

Sumner, B. H. 1962. *Russia and the Balkans, 1870–1880*. London: Archon.

Sunar, I. 1987. "State and Economy in the Ottoman Empire." In *The Ottoman Empire and the World-Economy*, edited by H. Islamoglu-Inan, 63–87. Cambridge: Cambridge University Press.

Svolopoulos, C. 1980. "L'initiation de Mourad V a la franc-maconnerie par Cl. Skalieri: Aux origines du mouvement liberal en Turquie." *BS* 21(2): 441–57.

———. 1994. *Constantinople 1856–1908: The Peak of Hellenism*. Athens: Ekdotiki (G).

Svoronos, N. 1981. *Histoire de la Grece Moderne* [Greek edition]. Athens: Themelio.

Tachiaos, A. 1974. *The National Awakening of the Bulgarians and the Appearance of Bulgarian National Movement in Macedonia*. Thessaloniki: Society for Macedonian Studies (G).

Tambaki, A. 1987. "The Transition from Enlightenment to Romanticism in the Greek Nineteenth Century: The Case of Ioannis and Spirydon Zambelios." *DIEE* 30:31–45 (G).

Tappe, E. D. 1973. "The 1821 Revolution in the Rumanian Principalities." In *The Struggle for Greek Independence*, edited by R. Clogg, 135–55. London: Macmillan.

Tashkovski, D. 1976. *The Macedonian Nation*. Skopje: Nasha Kniga.

Taylor, C. 1992. *Multiculturalism and the Politics of Recognition*. Princeton, NJ: Princeton University Press.

Therbon, G. 1995a. *European Modernity and Beyond: The Trajectory of European Societies, 1945–2000*. London: Sage.

———. 1995b. "Routes to/through modernity." In *Global Modernities*, edited by M. Featherstone, S. Lash, and R. Robertson, 124–39. London: Sage.

Thornberry, P. 1991. *International Law and the Rights of Minorities*. Oxford: Clarendon Press.

Todorov, N. 1969. "The Balkan Town in the Second Half of the Nineteenth Century." *EB* 21(8):31–50.

———. 1977. "The Bulgarian National Revolution and the Revolutionary Movements in the Balkans." *EB* 2:35–48.

———. 1982. *The Balkan Dimension of the 1821 revolution. The Bulgarian Case.* Athens: Gutenberg (G).

———. 1985. "Social Structures in the Balkans during the Eighteenth and Nineteenth Centuries." *EB* 4:48–71.

———. 1986. *The Balkan City (15th–19th centuries)*, 2 vols. [Greek edition]. Athens: Themelio.

Todorov, V. 1984. "The Society 'Oriental Confederation' and Its Activities during the 80ties and 90ties of the Nineteenth Century." *BS* 25(2):529–37.

———. 1991. "Nineteenth Century Federalism in Greece: An Attempt at Periodization." *EB* 4:89–106.

———. 1995. *Greek Federalism during the Nineteenth Century (Ideas and Projects).* Boulder, Colo.: East European Monographs.

Todorova, M. 1976. "Composition of the Ruling Elite of the Ottoman Empire in the Period of Reforms (1826–1878)." *EB* 1:103–44.

———. 1990. "Language as Cultural Unifier in a Multilingual Setting: The Bulgarian Case during the Nineteenth Century." *EEPS* 4(3; fall):439–50.

———. 1993. *Balkan Family Structure and the European Pattern. Demographic Developments in Ottoman Bulgaria.* Washington D.C.: American University Press.

———. 1994. "The Balkans: From Discovery to Invention." *Slavic Review* 53(2):453–83.

———. 1995. "The Course and Discourses of Bulgarian Nationalism." In *Eastern European Nationalism in the 20th Century*, edited by P. Sugar 55–102. Washington, D.C.: American University Press.

———. 1996. "The Ottoman Legacy in the Balkans." In *Imperial Legacy: The Ottoman Imprint on the Balkans and the Middle East*, edited by L. C. Brown 45–77. New York: Columbia University Press.

———. 1997. *Imagining the Balkans.* Oxford: Oxford University Press.

Tomasevich, J. 1995. *Peasants, Politics, and Economic Change in Yugoslavia.* Stanford, Calif.: Stanford University Press.

Tomak, J. J. 1985. "Issues and Controversies Concerning the Role and Significance of Education in the Bulgarian National Renaissance (1762–1878)." In *Proceedings of Anglo-Bulgarian Symposium.* Vol. 1, *History*, edited by L. Collins, 29–40. London: School of Slavonic and East European Studies.

Tounta-Fergali, A. 1994. *Minorities in the Balkans: Balkan Conferences, 1930–1934.* Athens: Paratiritis (G).

Tovias, A. 1994. "The Mediterranean Economy." In *Europe and the Mediterranean*, edited by P. Ludlow, 1–46. London: CEPS/Brassey's.

Traikov, V. 1980. "La cooperation bulgaro-greque dans les luttes de liberation nationale." In *Greek-Bulgarian Cultural and Political Relations from the mid-15th to the mid-19th Centuries*, 47–53. Thessaloniki: Institute for Balkan Studies (G).

Trajkov, V. 1984. "The Evolution of G. S. Rakovski's Views on the Establishment of a Balkan Union." *EH* 12:93–110.

Troxel, L. 1992. "Bulgaria's Gypsies: Numerically Strong, Politically Weak." *RFE/RL Research Report*, 6 March, 58–61.

Tsigakou, F. M. 1981. *The Rediscovery of Greece: Travelers and Painters of the Romantic Era.* New York: Karatzas.

Tsikelikis, C., and D. Christopoulos, eds. 1997. *The Minority Issue in Greece. A Contribution of the Social Sciences.* Athens: Kritiki (G).

Tsopotos, D. K. 1983 [1912]. *Land and Peasants of Thessaly during the Ottoman Rule.* Athens: Epikerotita (G).

Tsoukalas, C. 1978. "On the Problem of Political Clientelism in Greece in the Nineteenth Century." *JHD* 5(1; spring):5–15.

———. 1981. *Social Development and the State.* Athens: Themelio (G).

———. 1987. *Dependency and Reproduction. The Social Role of Educational Mechanisms in Greece, 1830–1922.* Athens: Themelio (G).

Turczynski, E. 1972. "Nationalism and Religion in Eastern Europe." *EEQ* 5(4):468–86.

———. 1975. "The Role of the Orthodox Church in Adapting and Transforming the Western Enlightenment in Southeastern Europe." *EEQ* 9(4):415–40.

Tzvetkov, P. S. 1993. *A History of the Balkans: A Regional Overview from a Bulgarian Perspective,* 2 vols. San Francisco: Edwin Mellen Press.

Vakalopoulos, A. 1961. *History of Modern Hellenism,* Vol. 1. Thessaloniki: (G).

———. 1973. *History of Modern Hellenism,* Vol. 4. Thessaloniki: (G).

Vakalopoulos, K. 1986. *Modern History of Macedonia, 1830–1912.* Thessaloniki: Barbounakis (G).

———. 1988. *Young Turks and Macedonia.* Thessaloniki: Kiriakidi (G).

Van Boeshoten, R. 1991a. *From Armatolik to People's Rule: Investigation into the Collective Memory of Modern Greece, 1750–1949.* Amsterdam: A. M. Hakkert.

———. 1991b. "Klephts, Thieves, and Social Banditry." *Mnimon* 13:9–24 (G).

Varda, Ch. 1980–1982. "Military Officers in Politics in Late 19th Century Greece." *Mnimon* 8: (G).

Vasdravellis, J. K. 1975. *Klephts, Armatoles and Pirates in Macedonia during the Rule of the Turks.* Thessaloniki: Society for Macedonian Studies.

Vavouskos, K. 1979. "Ecclesiastical Relations between Serbs and the Ecumenical Patriarchate during the 19th century." In *Cooperation of Greeks and Serbs during their Struggles for Liberation, 1804–1830,* 19–24. Thessaloniki: Institute for Balkan Studies (G).

Velchev, V. 1981. *Paissi of Hilendar: Father of the Bulgarian Enlightenment.* Sofia: Sofia Press.

Velichi, C. 1970. *La contribution de l'emigration bulgare de Valachie a la renaissance politique et culturelle du peuple bulgare, 1762–1850.* Bucharest: Editions de l'Academie R.S.R.

———. 1979. *La Roumanie et le mouvement revolutionnaire bulgare de liberation nationale (1850–1878).* Bucharest: Editions de l'Academie R.S.R.

———. 1982. "The Romanians and the Creation of the Bulgarian National State." *RESE* 20(4):407–14.

Veloudis, G. 1982. *Jacob Phillip Fallmerayer and the Birth of Greek Historicism.* Athens: EMNE-Mnimon (G).

Ventiris, K. 1970. *The Greece of 1910–1920,* 2 vols. Athens: Ikaros (G).

Venturi, F. 1991. *The End of the Old Regime in Europe, 1776–1789,* 2 vols. Princeton, N.J.: Princeton University Press.

Veremis, T. 1980a. "Eleutherios Venizelos and the Officers, 1909–1924." In *Studies on Venizelos and His Time,* edited by O. Dimitrakopoulos and T. Veremis, 563–88. Athens: S. G. Phillippotis (G).

———. 1980b. "Ideological Presuppositions for a Cooperation between Greeks and Turks." *DIEE* 23:405–21 (G).

————. 1982. "Testimonies for the 1909 Coup and its Impact on Greek Political Life."
*DIEE* 25:395–426. (G).
————. 1997. *The Military in Greek Politics*. London: Hurst.
Vergopoulos, K. 1975. *The Peasant Question in Greece*. Athens: Exantas (G).
————. 1994. *State and Economic Policy in the Nineteenth Century*. Athens: Exantas
(G).
Vermulen, H. 1984. "Greek Cultural Dominance among the Orthodox Population of
Macedonia during the Last Period of Ottoman Rule." In *Cultural Dominance in
the Mediterranean Area*, edited by A. Blok and H. Driessen, 225–55. Nijmegen:
Katholieke Universiteit.
Vickers, M. 1995. *The Albanians: A Modern History*. London: Tauris.
————. 1998. *Between Serb and Albanian: A History of Kosovo*. New York: Columbia
University Press.
Voll, J. O. 1994. "Islam as a Special World-System." *Journal of World History* 5(2):
213–26.
Vouri, S. 1992. *Nationalism and Education in the Balkans. The Case of Northwestern
Macedonia, 1870–1914*. Athens: Paraskinio (G).
————. 1993. "The Balkan Wars in the Slavic School Historiography." In *Greece of the
Balkan Wars 1910–1914*, 299–326. Athens: ELIA (G).
————. 1996a. "Greece and the Greeks in Recent Bulgarian History Textbooks." In *Oil
on Fire? Textbooks, Stereotypes, and Violence in Southeastern Europe*, edited by
W. Hopken, 67–78. Hannover, Germany: Verlag Hahnsche Buchhandlung.
————. 1996b. "War and National History—The Case of History Textbooks in the
Former Yugoslav Republic of Macedonia (1991–1993)." In *Oil on Fire? Text-
books, Stereotypes, and Violence in Southeastern Europe*, edited by W. Hopken
179–214. Hannover, Germany: Verlag Hahnsche Buchhandlung.
Vournas, T. 1977. *History of Modern Greece, 1909–1940*. Athens: Tolidi (G).
Voyatzidis, J. C. 1953. "La Grande Idee." *L'Hellenisme Contemporain* 7:280–7.
Vranousis, L. 1957. *Rigas*. Athens: N. Zacharopoulos (G).
————. 1975. "Ideological Molding and Collusions." In *History of the Greek Nation*,
Vol. 11, 433–51. Athens: Ekdotiki (G).
Vucinich, W. S. 1967. "The Serbs in Austria-Hungary." *Austrian History Yearbook*, Vol.
3, 2:3–47.
————. 1968. *Serbia between East and West: The Events of 1903–1908*. New York:
AMS Press.
————. 1979. "Serbian Military Tradition." In *War and Society in East Central Europe*.
Vol. 1, *Special Topics and Generalizations on the 18th and 19th Centuries*, edited
by B. K. Kiraly and G. E. Rothenberg, 284–324. New York: Columbia University
Press.
Wallden, S. 1996. "The Balkans in the International Division of Labor." In *The European
Community and the Balkans*, 79–150. Athens: Sakkoula (G).
Wallerstein, I. 1974. *The Modern World System I*. New York: Academic Press.
————. 1979. *The Capitalist World-Economy: Collected Essays*. Cambridge: Cambridge
University Press.
————. 1989. *The Modern World System III*. San Diego: Academic Press.
————. 1991a. *Geopolitics and Geoculture*. Cambridge: Cambridge University Press.
————. 1991b. *Unthinking Social Science*. London: Polity Press.

———. 1992. "The West, Capitalism, and the Modern World-System." *Review* 15:561–619.

———. 1995. "Hold the Tiller Firm: On Method and the Unit of Analysis." In Sanderson (1995), 239–47.

———. 1998. "The Rise and Future Demise of World-Systems Analysis." *Review* 21(1): 103–12.

Wallerstein, I., H. Decdeli, and R. Kassaba. 1987. "The Incorporation of the Ottoman Empire into the World-Economy." In *The Ottoman Empire and the World-Economy*, edited by H. Islamoglu-Inan, 88–100. Cambridge: Cambridge University Press.

Wallerstein, I., and R. Kasaba. 1983. "Incorporation into the World Economy: Change in the Structure of the Ottoman Empire 1750–1839." In *Economie et societes dans L'Empire Ottoman*, edited by J. L. Bacque-Grammont and P. Dumont, 335–54. Paris: Editions du Centre National de la Recherche Scientifique.

Waters, M. 1995. *Globalization*. London: Routledge.

Weber, E. 1976. *Peasants into Frenchmen: The Modernization of Rural France, 1870–1914*. Stanford, Calif.: Stanford University Press.

West, R. 1941. *Black Lamb and Grey Falcon: A Journey through Yugoslavia*. New York: Vintage.

Wheeler, M. 1996. "Not So Black as It's Painted: The Balkan Political Heritage." *The Changing Shape of the Balkans*, edited by F. W. Carter and H. T. Norris, 1–8. London: University College London.

Wilkinson, H. R. 1951. *Maps and Politics: A Review of the Ethnographic Cartography of Macedonia*. Liverpool: Liverpool University Press.

Wilson, D. 1970. *The Life and Times of Vuk Stefanovic Karadzic, 1787–1864: Literacy, Language, and National Independence in Serbia*. Oxford: Clarendon Press.

Wolf, E. 1982. *Europe and the People without History*. Berkeley: University of California Press.

Wolff, L. 1994. *Inventing Eastern Europe: The Map of Civilization on the Mind of the Enlightenment*. Stanford, Calif.: Stanford University Press.

Woodhouse, C. M. 1969. *The Philhellenes*. Rutherford, N.J.: Fairleigh Dickinson University Press.

———. 1981. "The 'Untoward Event': The Battle of Navarino 20 October 1827." In *Balkan Society in the Age of Greek Independence*, edited by R. Clogg, 1–17. London: Macmillan.

Woodward, S. 1995. *Balkan Tragedy, Chaos and Dissolution after the Cold War*. Washington, D.C.: Brookings Institution.

Xanalatos, D. 1962. "The Greeks and Turks on the Eve of the Balkan Wars· A Frustrated Plan." *BS* 3(2):277–96.

Xydis, S. G. 1969. "Modern Greek Nationalism." In *Nationalism in Eastern Europe*, edited by P. F. Sugar and I. J. Lederer, 207–58. Seattle: University of Washington Press.

Yianoulopoulos, G. 1981. "Greek Society in the Eve of Greek Independence." In *Balkan Society in the Age of Greek Independence*, edited by R. Clogg, 18–39. London: Macmillan.

———. 1999. *'Our Graceful Blindness': Foreign Policy and 'National Issues' from the 1897 Defeat to the Asia Minor Debacle*. Athens: Vivliorama (G).

Yerolympos, A. 1996. *Urban Transformations in the Balkans (1820–1920)*. Thessaloniki: University Studio Press.

Zakynthinos, D. A. 1976. *The Making of Modern Greece: from Byzantium to Independence*. Totowa, N.J.: Rowman and Littlefield.

Zambelios, S. 1852. *Greek Folk Songs, including a Historical Study on Medieval Hellenism*. Kerkyra: Hermes A. Terzake kai Th. Rhomaiou.

Zarev, P. 1977. *History of Bulgarian Literature* [Greek edition]. Athens: Dodoni.

Zlatar, Z. 1979. "Nationalism in Serbia (1804–1918)." *CRSN* 6:100–13.

———. 1990. "Pan-Slavism: A Review of the Literature." *CRSN* 27(1–2):219–33.

———. 1997. "The Building of Yugoslavia: The Yugoslav Idea and the First Common State of the South Slavs." *Nationalities Papers* 25(3):387–406.

Zolberg, A. 1981. "Origins of the Modern World System: A Missing Link." *World Politics* 33(2):253–81.

Zurcher, E. J. 1984. *The Unionist Factor: The Role of the Committee of Union and Progress in the Turkish National Movement, 1905–1926*. Leiden: E. J. Brill.

# Index

Drinov, Marin, 134, 141–42, 154 n.9
Dusan, 234

Eastern Bloc, 204
Eastern Crisis (1875–1878), 87
Eastern Federation, 80
Eastern Orthodox Christian, 190, 209
Eastern Orthodox Church, 52–56; and
Enlightenment, 72 n.10; and Greece,
101, 103; and liberalism, 60–61; and
Ottoman Empire, 53; and secularism,
61; and Serbia, 101, 123. See also Ecumenical Patriarchate; Religion
Eastern Orthodoxy, 1, 106, 109, 131,
147, 148, 151, 152
Eastern Roman Empire, 109
Eastern Romilia, 79, 141
Economy: and Albania, 224; and Balkan
revolutions, 30–31; and Bulgaria, 136;
and Greece, 224; and Greek revolution,
26; and Kosovo, 210; and migration,
36–37; and Muslims vs. Christians,
233; and nationalism, 18 n.5, 237–38;
and Ottoman Empire, 32–37, 81–83,
86; and Ottoman Muslims, 234; and
peasants, 158; and post-World War II
Balkans, 204–6; and Serbia, 23, 170;
and urban sector, 160, 204; urban vs.
rural, 15; and Young Turks, 234; and
Yugoslavia, 215, 216, 224–25. See also
Commerce; Trade
Ecumenical Patriarchate, 53, 54; and Albania, 148; and Bulgaria, 48–49, 132,
133, 137, 138–39, 140, 152; and Bulgarian church, 138; and freemasonry,
61; and Greek Church, 104, 105, 106;
and Kukush, 155 n.17; liberation from,
151; and Midhat pasha, 87; and Ottoman administration, 61; and peshkesi,
153 n.2; and Rum millet, 230; and Velenstinlis, 63. See also Eastern Orthodox Church
Education: and Albania, 147, 148, 149;
and Bucharest, 56–57; and Bulgaria, 49–
50, 69, 112, 134, 136, 140, 142–43,
144–45, 154 n.8, 191, 212, 232; and
CUP, 93; and Danubian principalities,
51; and equality, 85; and ethnocen-

trism, 211–12; and Greece, 106, 108,
110, 111–12, 124, 127 nn.18, 21, 144,
145, 147, 148, 212, 213, 227 n.8; and
Macedonia, 144, 200 n.8, 212; and
Montenegro, 49; and Ottoman Empire,
110; and peasants, 165, 235–36; and
reform, 93; and religion, 49; and Romania, 69; secular, 49; and Serbia, 49,
69, 118, 119, 122, 123, 129 n.35, 144,
145, 167, 211, 212; and Thrace, 186;
and Vojvodina Serbs, 116; and West,
85; Western, 88; and Yugoslavia, 211.
See also Literacy
Egypt, 67, 227 n.7
Eliot, S. G., 87
Enlightenment: and ancient Greece, 60;
Balkan, 70; and boyars, 51; and class,
50; and culture, 47; and France, 58;
and Greece, 127 n.13; and intelligentsia, 57–58; and Orthodox Church, 72
n.10; and Orthodoxy, 109; and
Ottoman Balkan society, 70; and Otto-
man Empire, 61; and politics, 58; and
Rum millet, 68; and secularism, 69;
and Western Europe, 231
Entente, 171, 172, 173
Enver, 90
Enver pasha, 185
Epirus, 40, 189, 223, 224, 237
Equality, 84, 85, 87, 95. See also Ethno-
centrism; Minority
Estate, 20, 21, 22–23, 24. See also Land
Estate (ciftlik) system, 30, 32–33
Ethnic cleansing, 182, 186, 196, 199. See
also Migration; Population, change of
Ethnic group: and intermixing, 14; and
nationhood, 9; as research-defined, 15.
See also specific groups
Ethnicity: and Albania, 156 n.22; and
Bosnia-Herzegovina, 217; and boyars,
51; and Bulgaria, 137; and citizenship,
208; and class, 48; and Croatia, 217;
and federalism, 77; Greek, 53–54; and
labor, 68; and Macedonia, 143; and
merchants, 37; and multiculturalism,
208; and Muslims, 218; and nationalism, 157; and nationhood, 238; and
Rum millet, 53–54, 137; and Serbia,

Volk, 106–7
Voltaire, 58, 61
Voluntarism, 4
Voulgaris, Evyenios, 55, 72 n.9
Vousilmas, Dositheos, 57
Vrachanski, Sofroni, 50

*Wakf*, 22–23
Wallachia, 50–52; and Greece, 41; and
  ideology, 231; and liberation, 19; and
  migration, 36–37; and Napoleon I, 62;
  and Ottoman Empire, 26, 27, 28; and
  population, 36–37; and Romania, 232.
  *See also* Danubian principalities
Wallerstein, I., 5, 6
West: and Albania, 149; and education,
  85; and Greece, 110, 125 n.3
Western Europe: and Balkan nationalism,
  11; and Bulgaria, 135; competition
  with, 204; and education, 57, 88; and
  Hellenism, 231; and homogeneity, 239;
  and ideology, 231; and merchants, 230;
  and nationalism, 239; and Ottoman
  Empire, 33–34, 41, 56, 68, 239; and
  *Rum millet*, 68. *See also* Europe
Westernization, 70, 88, 92, 102, 105,
  106, 217
Western Thrace, 186
Will, popular, 94
William of Wied, 151
Wilson, Woodrow, 180
World-system, 6
World-system analysis, 3, 4, 5, 6
World War I: and Albania, 151, 200 n.9;
  boundaries after, 179–80, 181; and
  Bulgaria, 168–69, 171, 176 nn.7, 8;
  and Greece, 171–73; and Habsburg
  Empire, 81; and Serbia, 171; and
  Serbs, 201 n.20; and Yugoslavia, 194,
  195
World War II, 180, 196–99

Xanthos, Emanuil, 63

Young Bosnians, 171, 193–94
Young Ottomans, 86, 87, 98 n.17
Young Turks: and Albania, 149; composition of, 233–34; and Ferdinand, 168;
  and Kemal, 150; and liberalism, 199
  n.3; and Macedonia, 236; and military,
  95, 98 n.20, 236; and minorities, 185;
  and National Society, 166; and Ottomanism, 88–94, 95; and petit-
  bourgeois, 95; and Turkish nationalism,
  183
Ypsilantis, 29
Yugoslav, as term, 81
Yugoslav Academy of Arts and Sciences,
  81
Yugoslav Committee, 194
Yugoslav Communism, 220
Yugoslavia, 191–96, 213–19; and economy, 205, 206, 207, 224–25; and education, 211; and ethnicity, 224–25;
  inevitability of, 200 n.15; and Macedonia, 220; and minorities, 225; and nationalism, 209; and nationhood, 225–26;
  and population change, 17. *See also*
  Kingdom of Serbs, Slovenes, and
  Croats
Yugoslavism, 80, 94, 97 n.9, 123, 192,
  194, 195, 232, 233. *See also* Federalism
Yugoslav Macedonia, 219
Yugoslav Muslim Organization, 193

Zach, Frantisek, 116
Zambelios, Ioannis, 103
Zambelios, Spiridon, 108, 127 n.14
Zogu, Ahmet, 151
Zora, 121
Zveno, 187

**About the Author**

VICTOR ROUDOMETOF is Visiting Assistant Professor of Sociology at Washington and Lee University in Virginia. He has published widely on globalization, nationalism, and national minorities in the Balkans. He is the editor of *The Macedonian Question: Culture, Historiography, Politics* (2000), *American Culture in Europe: Interdisciplinary Perspectives* (Praeger, 1998), and co-editor of *The New Balkans*.